Fodor's First Edition

W9-BSM-535

Southern Africa

The complete guide, thoroughly up-to-date

Packed with details that will make your trip

The must-see sights, off and on the beaten path

What to see, what to skip

Mix-and-match vacation itineraries

City strolls, countryside adventures

Smart lodging and dining options

Essential local dos and taboos

Transportation tips, distances and directions

Key contacts, savvy travel tips

When to go, what to pack

Clear, accurate, easy-to-use maps

Fodor's Travel Publications • New York, Toronto, London, Sydney, Auckland
www.fodors.com

Fodor's Southern Africa

EDITOR: Melissa Klurman

Editorial Contributors: Andrew Barbour, David Bristow, Bronwyn Howard, Peta Lee, Myrna Robins, Jennifer Stern, Kate Turkington, Tara Turkington, Stephen Wolf

Editorial Production: Stacey Kulig

Maps: David Lindroth, *cartographer*; Rebecca Baer and Robert Blake, *map editors*

Design: Fabrizio La Rocca, *creative director*; Guido Caroti, *art director*; Jolie Novak, *photo editor*

Cover Design: Pentagram

Production/Manufacturing: Mike Costa

Cover Photograph: Peter Guttman

Copyright

First Edition

ISBN 0–679–00409–2

ISSN 1528–4093

Special Sales

Fodor's Travel Publications are available at special discounts for bulk purchases for sales promotions or premiums. Special editions, including personalized covers, excerpts of existing guides, and corporate imprints, can be created in large quantities for special needs. For more information, contact your local bookseller or write to Special Markets, Fodor's Travel Publications, 280 Park Avenue, New York, NY 10017. Inquiries from Canada should be directed to your local Canadian bookseller or sent to Random House of Canada, Ltd., Marketing Department, 2775 Matheson Boulevard East, Mississauga, Ontario L4W 4P7. Inquiries from the United Kingdom should be sent to Fodor's Travel Publications, 20 Vauxhall Bridge Road, London SW1V 2SA, England.

PRINTED IN THE UNITED STATES OF AMERICA

10 9 8 7 6 5 4 3 2 1

Important Tip

Although all prices, opening times, and other details in this book are based on information supplied to us at press time, changes occur all the time in the travel world, and Fodor's cannot accept responsibility for facts that become outdated or for inadvertent errors or omissions. So **always confirm information when it matters,** especially if you're making a detour to visit a specific place.

CONTENTS

Maps

ON THE ROAD WITH FODOR'S

Every Y2K trip is a significant trip. So if there was ever a time you needed excellent travel information, it's now. Acutely aware of that fact, we've pulled out all stops in preparing Fodor's Southern Africa. To guide you in putting together your Southern Africa experience, we've created multiday itineraries and neighborhood walks. And to direct you to the places that are truly worth your time and money in this important year, we've rallied the team of endearingly picky know-it-alls we're pleased to call our writers. Having seen all corners of Southern Africa, they're real experts on the subjects they cover for us. If you knew them, you'd poll them for tips yourself.

About Our Writers

Andrew Bergman was born in Cape Town and lived there for most of his life. He spent nine years as social editor and deputy features editor of the *Cape Times,* where he also wrote a weekly column for the paper's magazine section. He has also hosted a weekly slot on Cape Town's Radio Kfm, featuring wining, dining and leisure in the Western Cape.

David Bristow is an environmental scientist and editor of Africa's largest circulating travel magazine, *Getaway.* He's authored more than a dozen books on Southern Africa and is a passionate mountaineer. He considers his greatest achievement to date to have climbed Africa's four highest peaks (Kilimanjaro and Kenya, and Margheurita and Speke in the Ruwenzori range).

Bronwyn Howard, who wrote our Swaziland chapter and updated Mpumalanga and Durban and KwaZulu-Natal, is a freelance journalist and marketing consultant, writing articles about nearly anything connected with the great outdoors.

Peta Lee is a freelance journalist based in Durban whose passion for adventure has taken her white-water rafting down the Zambezi, abseiling in Lesotho, hot air ballooning in the Magaliesberg, and microlighting in the Eastern Transvaal. She's lived and worked in Namibia and Johannesburg, and has written on everything, from entertainment and health and travel, to fashion, and mining and motoring.

Myrna Robins, who writes for the *Cape Argus* newspaper, is one of South Africa's most popular food writers. Author of several cookbooks, including *Cape Flavour—A Guide to Historic Restaurants of the Cape,* she lives in the shadow of Table Mountain and spends her weekends in the exquisite hamlet of MacGregor, in the Riviersonderend Mountains.

Jennifer Stern, as well as contributing to a number of magazines and newspapers, is the author of *Southern Africa on a Budget* and *Guide to Adventure Travel in Southern Africa.* In the line of duty, she has braved strange wayside pubs, dived pristine reefs, paddled beautiful rivers, walked with wildlife, and ridden mountain bikes, horses, camels and elephants all over the wilder parts of the sub-continent.

Kate Turkington is a South African journalist and broadcaster. She is managing editor of *Marung* and *Flamingo,* the in-flight magazines for Air Botswana and Air Namibia. She has waltzed at dawn in a Beijing square, fallen over an Emperor penguin in Antarctica, stood at the bottom of a rainbow in Ireland, been winched over a raging river 9,000 ft up in the Andes in Peru, and heard the stars sing in the Kalahari Desert.

Tara Turkington is a freelance journalist who lives in Kimberley in the Northern Cape, South Africa's biggest and most sparsely populated province, which she loves for its sense of desolation. She has worked as a writer and photographer for a string of South African newspapers and magazines, on subjects ranging from crime in the Karoo to wine in the Kalahari. She is a regular contributor the *Mail & Guardian,* and to the newly established *Sunday World.*

Don't Forget to Write

Keeping a travel guide fresh and up-to-date is a big job. So we love your feedback—positive and negative—and follow up on all suggestions. Contact the Southern Africa editor at editors@fodors.com or c/o Fodor's, 280 Park Avenue, New York, NY 10017. And have a wonderful trip!

Karen Cure

Karen Cure
Editorial Director

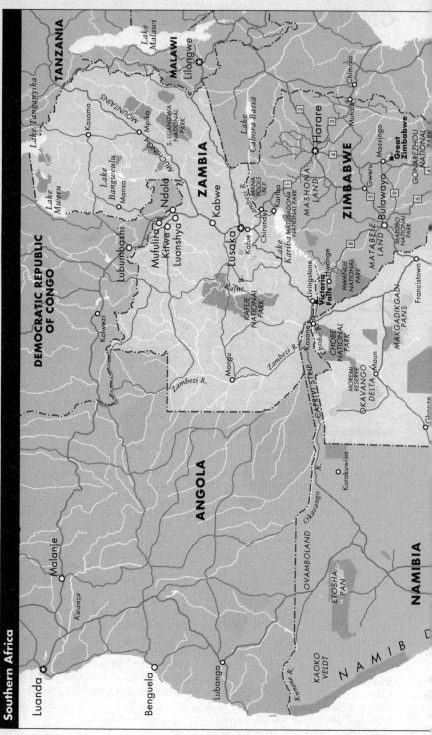

Southern Africa

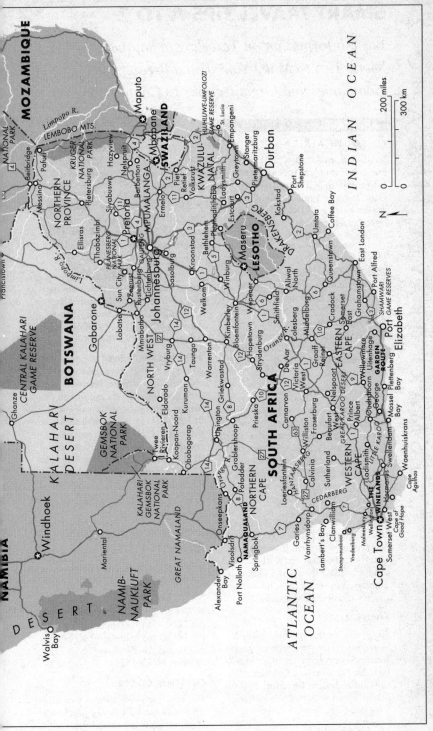

MOZAMBIQUE

NATIONAL PARK

Limpopo R.
LEMBOBO MTS.
Maputo

Beitbridge
Pafuri
Messina

KRUGER
NATIONAL
PARK

NORTHERN
PROVINCE

Ellisras

Mbabane
SWAZILAND
MPUMALANGA

Hazyview
Nelspruit

Siyabuswa
Pietersburg

Thabazimbi
PILANESBERG
NATIONAL
PARK
Sun City

Barberton
Ermelo
Piet
Retief
Volksrust

HLUHLUWE-UMFOLOZI
GAME RESERVE
St. Lucia
Empangeni

KWAZULU-
NATAL

Stanger

Greytown
Pietermaritzburg

Durban

Ladysmith
Estcourt

Port
Shepstone

GAUTENG
Pretoria
Rustenburg
Lichtenburg
Zeerust
Mmabatho

Kroonstad
Bethlehem
Phuthaditjhaba
Maseru
LESOTHO

DRAKENSBERG

Kokstad

Umtata
Coffee Bay

Johannesburg

Gabarone

BOTSWANA

CENTRAL KALAHARI
GAME RESERVE

Ghanze

KALAHARI
DESERT

Lobatse

NORTH WEST

Sasolburg
Winburg
Wepener
Smithfield

Welkom
Kroonstad

Vryburg
Taungo
Warrenton

Kimberley
Bloemfontein

Aliwal
North

Queenstown

East London

Grahamstown

Port Alfred

SHAMWARI
GAME RESERVES

Port
Elizabeth

EASTERN
CAPE

Cradock
Somerset
East

Middelburg

Colesberg
De Aar

Hopetown
Strydenburg

Prieska

Griekwastad
Upington

Kuruman
Koopan-Noord
Eldorado

Groblershoop

Windhoek

NAMIBIA

KALAHARI
DESERT

GEMSBOK
NATIONAL
PARK

KALAHARI
GEMSBOK
NATIONAL
PARK

Twee
Rivieren

Obobogorap

Pofadder

Onseepkans

NORTHERN
CAPE

NAMAQUALAND

Loeriesfontein

Springbok

Port Nolloth

Viooldrift

Alexander
Bay

GREAT NAMALAND

Mariental

NAMIB-
NAUKLUFT
PARK

DESERT

Walvis
Bay

GEMSBOK
NATIONAL
PARK

SOUTH AFRICA

Carnarvon
Victoria
West

Fraserburg

Beaufort
West

Prince
Albert

WESTERN
CAPE

GREAT KAROO DESERT

Graaff
Reinet

Nelspoort

Oudtshoorn
George
Mossel
Bay

Plettenberg
Bay

Willowmore
Uitenhage

GARDEN
ROUTE

Knysna

LITTLE KAROO

Ladismith
Swellendam
Waenhuiskrans

Calvinia
Sutherland

CEDARBERG

Clanwilliam

Vanrhynsdorp

Lambert's Bay

Vredenburg
Stompneusboai

Malmesbury
Wellington
Somerset West

Cape Town

Cape of
Good Hope
Cape
Agulhas

THE
WINELANDS

Hermanus

ATLANTIC
OCEAN

INDIAN OCEAN

N

200 miles
300 km

SMART TRAVEL TIPS A TO Z

*Basic Information on Traveling in Southern Africa,
Savvy Tips to Make Your Trip a Breeze, and
Companies and Organizations to Contact*

AIR TRAVEL

TO SOUTH AFRICA

South African Airways (SAA) flies
nonstop from New York (JFK) to
Johannesburg and from Atlanta to
Cape Town and Johannesburg, sharing the route with Delta. The options
from Europe include SAA and most
European national airlines.

TO ZIMBABWE

To get to Zimbabwe from the United
States, you must connect through
Johannesburg (on South African
Airways or American Airlines) or
through Europe or Australia. Air
Zimbabwe and British Airways fly
direct from London; KLM flies from
Amsterdam. Qantas fly direct from
Perth to Harare.

TO BOTSWANA

To get to Botswana you'll have to
connect through Johannesburg or
Harare. The international gateways to
Botswana are Gaborone (the capital),
Maun (near the Okavango Delta),
and Kasane (near Chobe National
Park).

TO ZAMBIA

There are no direct flights from the
United States to Zambia. Best would
be to connect through Johannesburg
or through London, from where you
can fly British Airways to Lusaka.
There were, at press time, no international flights into Livingstone.

TO NAMIBIA

To get to Namibia from the United
States you'll have to connect through
Johannesburg, Cape Town, or Frankfurt. Air Namibia and Lufthansa fly
to Windhoek from Frankfurt, and Air
Namibia and SAA fly from Johannesburg and Cape Town.

TO SWAZILAND

There are no intercontinental flights
direct to Swaziland, but Royal Swazi

Air connects Mbabane with most
southern African countries, and Swazi
Express Airlines runs scheduled
flights in a light plane from Durban.
Your best bet for a connection is
Johannesburg.

➤ MAJOR AIRLINES: **Air Zimbabwe**
(☎ 212/980–8010). **Alitalia** (☎ 800/
223–5730). **Egypt Air** (☎ 212/315–
0900). **South African Airways** (☎
800/722–9675).

➤ FROM THE U.K.: **Air Zimbabwe**
(☎ 0171/491–3783). **Botswana Air**
(☎ 0181/757–2737). **British Airways**
(☎ 0345/222–111). **South African
Airways** (☎ 0171/312–5000). **Virgin
Atlantic** (☎ 01293/747–747).

➤ WITHIN SOUTH AFRICA: Five major
domestic airlines serve the country's
nine principal airports (numbers are
for Johannesburg offices): **British
Airways** operating as Comair (☎
011/921–0111). **South African Airways** (☎ 011/978–1111) and its
commuter airlines, **SA Airlink** (☎
011/394–2430), **SA Express** (☎ 011/
978–5569), and **Sabena Nationwide**
(☎ 011/390–1660).

➤ WITHIN BOTSWANA: **Air Botswana**
(☎ 35–2812).

➤ WITHIN NAMIBIA: **Air Namibia**
(☎ 061/298–1111).

➤ WITHIN ZAMBIA: **Aero Zambia**
(☎ 01/22–6111, 01/22–6112, or 01/
22–6113).

➤ WITHIN ZIMBABWE: **Air Zimbabwe**
(☎ 14/57–5111), **Zimbabwe Express**
(☎ 14/72–9681 through 14/72–
9689), and **Air Zambezi** (☎ 14/72–
9831 or 14/72–4824).

CUTTING COSTS

The least-expensive airfares to southern Africa must usually be purchased
in advance and are nonrefundable.
It's smart to **call a number of airlines,
and when you are quoted a good**

price, book it on the spot—the same fare may not be available the next day. Always **check different routings** and look into using different airports. Travel agents, especially low-fare specialists (☞ Discounts & Deals, *below*), are helpful.

Consolidators are another good source. They buy tickets for scheduled international flights at reduced rates from the airlines, then sell them at prices that beat the best fare available directly from the airlines, usually without restrictions. Sometimes you can even get your money back if you need to return the ticket. Carefully read the fine print detailing penalties for changes and cancellations, and **confirm your consolidator reservation with the airline.**

➤ CONSOLIDATORS: **Cheap Tickets** (☎ 800/377–1000). **Up & Away Travel** (☎ 212/889–2345). **Discount Airline Ticket Service** (☎ 800/576–1600). **Unitravel** (☎ 800/325–2222). **World Travel Network** (☎ 800/409–6753).

FLYING TIMES

Flying time from Miami to Cape Town is 14 hours; from New York, the flight takes 15 hours. The return from Johannesburg will take 18 hours if it stops at Isla do Sal for refueling. The London–Johannesburg flight lasts about 12 hours.

HOW TO COMPLAIN

If your baggage goes astray or your flight goes awry, complain right away. Most carriers require that you **file a claim immediately.**

➤ AIRLINE COMPLAINTS: U.S. Department of Transportation **Aviation Consumer Protection Division** (✉ C-75, Room 4107, Washington, DC 20590, ☎ 202/366–2220). **Federal Aviation Administration Consumer Hotline** (☎ 800/322–7873).

AIRPORTS

South Africa's major airports are Johannesburg, Cape Town, and, to a lesser extent, Durban.

➤ AIRPORT INFORMATION: For listings of major airline numbers within South Africa, Swaziland, Zimbabwe, Botswana, Namibia, and Zambia *see* the A to Z sections *in* the relevant chapters.

Johannesburg International Airport (☎ 011/975–9963) lies 19 km (12 mi) from the city. Most international flights arrive and depart at this airport. The airport has a tourist information desk, a VAT refund office, and a computerized accommodation service. Several international flights departing from Cape Town are also routed via Johannesburg.

Zimbabwe's **Harare International Airport** (☎ 14/57–5111 or 14/57–5188) is 15 km (9 mi) south of the city center.

Botswana's **Sir Seretse Khama Airport** (☎ 35–1191) is 15 km (9 mi) north of Gaborone.

Zambia's **Lusaka International Airport** (☎ 01/27–1422) is 4 km (2½ mi) northeast of Lusaka.

Namibia's **Hosea Kutako International Airport** (☎ 062/54–0229) is 40 km (25 mi) east of Windhoek.

Swaziland's **Matsapha International Airport** is 8 km (5 mi) west of Manzini and about 40 km (25 mi) southeast of the capital Mbabane.

BUS TRAVEL

Greyhound, Intercape Mainliner, and **Translux Express** operate extensive bus networks that serve all major cities in the region. For travelers with a sense of adventure, a bit of time, and not too much money, the **Baz Bus** runs a daily hop-on, hop-off door-to-door service between backpacker's hostels around South Africa, Swaziland, and Zimbabwe with inexpensive connections to Livingstone in Zambia or Maputo in Mozambique. For more information about local buses in Botswana, Zimbabwe, Zambia, and Namibia *see* the relevant chapters.

FARES & SCHEDULES

Approximate prices for Greyhound, Translux, and Intercape bus service: Cape Town to Pretoria, one-way R350–R380; Cape Town to Springbok, one-way R220–R250; Cape Town to Windhoek, one-way R340–R370; Cape Town to George, one-way R120–R150; Cape Town to Port Elizabeth, one-way R165–R180.

Baz bus fares are higher but include intermediate stops: Cape Town to Durban costs R850, Johannesburg to Victoria Falls R350.

➤ Bus Information: **Greyhound** (Head Office, Pretoria, ☎ 012/315–3492). **Intercape Mainliner** (Cape Town office, ☎ 021/386–4400). **Translux Express** (Johannesburg office, ☎ 011/774–3333). The **Baz Bus** (Head Office in Cape Town, ☎ 021/439–2323).

BUSINESS HOURS

Business hours in the major cities are pretty standard, weekdays from about 9 to 5. Most banks close in mid afternoon, but Bureaux de Change usually stay open longer. In addition, post offices and banks are open on Saturday morning, from about 9 to noon. Many shopping malls are open until 9 or 10 at night, and are open on Sunday. In rural areas and small towns, things are less rigid. Post offices often close for lunch and, in very small towns and some villages, banks may have very abbreviated hours.

CAMERAS & PHOTOGRAPHY

There are camera shops and one-hour photo labs in even the smallest towns in South Africa and in most of the bigger towns in the countries farther north. For properly stored professional film and high-quality processing of transparency film, the best options are **ORMS Professional Photo Warehouse** (✉ Roeland Square, Roeland St., Cape Town, ☎ 021/465–3574), **City Lab** (✉ 369 Umgeni Rd., Durban, ☎ 031/309–2944), and **City Lab** (✉ 150 Pritchard St., Johannesburg, ☎ 011/336–7971).

CAR RENTAL

Rates in South Africa begin at $40 per day and 30¢ per kilometer (about 45¢ per mile) for an economy car. You must rent for a minimum of three to five (depending on the company) days to qualify for a free 200-km (124-mi) daily allowance. Rates for rentals of longer periods range from $40 to $60 a day, including 14% Value Added Tax (VAT) and 200 km (124 mi). For car rental information in Swaziland, Zimbabwe,

Botswana, Namibia, and Zambia *see* relevant chapters.

You can rent four-wheel drives or mobile homes from **Maui Camper Hire** (☎ in South Africa 011/395–4621 Johannesburg, 021/982–5107 Cape Town; in Botswana 31–1912 Gaborone, 66–1286 Maun; in Namibia 061/22–2877 Windhoek; in Zimbabwe 14/88–5550 Harare, 113/3398 Victoria Falls; and in the U.S. 818/981–1270 Los Angeles).

➤ Major Agencies: **Alamo** (☎ 800/522–9696; 020/8759–6200 in the U.K.). **Avis** (☎ 800/331–1084; 800/879–2847 in Canada; 02/9353–9000 in Australia; 09/525–1982 in New Zealand). **Budget** (☎ 800/527–0700; 0144/227–6266 in the U.K.). **Dollar** (☎ 800/800–6000; 020/8897–0811 in the U.K., where it is known as Eurodollar; 02/9223–1444 in Australia). **Hertz** (☎ 800/654–3001; 800/263–0600 in Canada; 0990/90–60–90 in the U.K.; 02/9669–2444 in Australia; 03/358–6777 in New Zealand). **National InterRent** (☎ 800/227–3876; 0345/222525 in the U.K., where it is known as Europcar InterRent).

CUTTING COSTS

To get the best deal **book through a travel agent, who will shop around.** Do **look into wholesalers,** companies that do not own fleets but rent in bulk from those that do and often offer better rates than traditional car-rental operations. Payment must be made before you leave home.

➤ Local Agencies: In South Africa, **Felix Unite Vehicle Rental** (☎ 021/683–6433, 𝖥𝖠𝖷 021/683–6485).

➤ Wholesalers: **Kemwel Holiday Autos** (☎ 914/825–3000 or 800/678–0678, 𝖥𝖠𝖷 914/381–8847).

REQUIREMENTS & RESTRICTIONS

To rent a car, you must be over 25 years old and have a minimum of five years' driving experience. In South Africa your own driver's license is acceptable. An International Driver's Permit is a good idea; it's available from the American or Canadian Automobile Association or, in the United Kingdom, from the Automobile Association or Royal Automobile Club.

SURCHARGES

Before you pick up a car in one city and leave it in another **ask about drop-off charges or one-way service fees,** which can be substantial. Note, too, that some rental agencies charge extra if you return the car before the time specified in your contract. To avoid a hefty refueling fee **fill the tank just before you turn in the car,** but be aware that gas stations near the rental outlet may overcharge.

CAR TRAVEL

South Africa has a superb network of multilane roads and highways, some of which charge a toll. The speed limit on major highways is 120 kph (75 mph), but many drivers far exceed that. In fact, South Africans tend to be aggressive and reckless, thinking nothing of tailgating at high speeds and passing on blind rises. During national holidays, the body count from highway collisions is staggering. The problem is compounded by widespread drunk driving, even though the legal blood-alcohol limit is 0.08. Local minibus taxis pose another threat, swerving in and out of traffic without warning to pick up customers. For obvious reasons, the wearing of seat belts is required by law. It is dangerous to drive at night in rural areas, as roads are not always fenced and domestic or wild animals often stray onto the road. Although the roads are generally good, the distances are significant and fatigue is also a major cause of accidents.

AUTO CLUBS

The **Automobile Association of South Africa** extends privileges to members of the American Automobile Association in the United States and the Automobile Association in Britain. Contact a local office in your home country for more information.

➤ IN AUSTRALIA: **Australian Automobile Association** (☎ 02/6247–7311).

➤ IN CANADA: **Canadian Automobile Association** (CAA, ☎ 613/247–0117).

➤ IN NEW ZEALAND: **New Zealand Automobile Association** (☎ 09/377–4660).

➤ IN SOUTH AFRICA: **Automobile Association of South Africa** (✉ Box 31017, Braamfontein, Johannesburg 2017, ☎ 011/403–2923 in Johannesburg, 021/419–6914 in Cape Town, 031/265–0437 in Durban, 080/001–0101 for 24-hour toll-free emergency).

➤ IN THE U.K.: **Automobile Association** (AA, ☎ 0990/500–600). **Royal Automobile Club** (RAC, ☎ 0990/722–722 for membership; 0345/121–345 for insurance).

➤ IN THE U.S.: **American Automobile Association** (☎ 800/564–6222).

GASOLINE

Huge 24-hour service stations are positioned at regular intervals along all major highways. Self-service stations do not exist, so an attendant will pump the gas, check the oil and water, and wash the windows. In return, tip him or her R2–R3. South Africa now has a choice of unleaded or leaded gasoline, and many vehicles operate on diesel—be sure you get the right fuel. Some South African–manufactured automobiles still need special engine modifications to enable them to run on unleaded fuel—check when booking a hired car as to what fuel to use. Gasoline is measured in liters, and expect to pay the equivalent of US$2–US$2.50 a gallon, about twice what you would pay in the States.

ROAD CONDITIONS

In very remote areas only the main road might be paved, while most secondary roads are of high-quality gravel. Traffic is often light in these areas, so be sure to **carry a spare, a jack, a tire iron, and extra water.**

In Zimbabwe and Botswana, major highways typically have two lanes only. In the remote areas of Zimbabwe, you may still encounter "strip roads," which consist of two paved strips with wide dirt shoulders. When cars approach, drivers move the left side of their cars or trucks onto the dirt, each keeping the right (driver's) side on the pavement. In Namibia, the paved roads are well maintained, as are the many dirt roads, but many are infrequently used, distances are enormous, and the weather is extreme. In some places, you may see only one tiny town (with about 20 buildings) in 500 mi. Always take plenty of drinking water with you when traveling in Namibia. The roads in Zambia are generally pretty terrible.

RULES OF THE ROAD

Southern Africans drive on the left. For pedestrians, that means that you should look right before crossing the street. South African roads have wide shoulders, separated from the main lanes by a yellow line. Slow traffic is expected to pull onto this shoulder to allow faster traffic to pass, but be sure that the shoulder ahead is not obstructed by cyclists, pedestrians, or a stopped vehicle. If a slower vehicle pulls onto the shoulder to allow you past, it's common courtesy to flash your hazard lights a couple of times in thanks. In built-up areas road shoulders are occasionally marked by red lines. This is a strict "no-stopping" zone.

Many cities use mini–traffic circles in lieu of four-way stops. These are extremely dangerous, since many drivers don't bother to stop. Theoretically, the first vehicle to the circle has right-of-way; otherwise, yield to the right. In practice, keep your wits about you at all times.

In South African parlance, traffic lights are known as "robots," and what people refer to as the "pavement" is actually the sidewalk. Paved roads are just called roads. And for Americans and Canadians, don't forget: **Drive left, and look right.**

CHILDREN IN SOUTH AFRICA

If you are renting a car don't forget to **arrange for a car seat** when you reserve.

FLYING

If your children are two or older **ask about children's airfares.** As a general rule, infants under two not occupying a seat fly at greatly reduced fares or even for free. When booking **confirm carry-on allowances** if you're traveling with infants. In general, for babies charged 10% of the adult fare, you are allowed one carry-on bag and a collapsible stroller; if the flight is full the stroller may have to be checked or you may be limited to less.

Experts agree that it's a good idea to use safety seats aloft for children weighing less than 40 pounds. Airlines set their own policies: U.S. carriers usually require that the child be ticketed, even if he or she is young enough to ride free, since the seats must be strapped into regular seats. Do **check your airline's policy about using safety seats during takeoff and landing.** And since safety seats are not allowed just everywhere in the plane, get your seat assignments early.

When reserving, **request children's meals or a freestanding bassinet** if you need them. But note that bulkhead seats, where you must sit to use the bassinet, may lack an overhead bin or storage space on the floor.

LODGING

Many of South Africa's luxury lodges and private game reserves do not accept children under 10 or 12 without prior arrangement, and many other hotels require children to eat dinner at a separate, earlier seating.

➤ BEST CHOICES: **Southern Sun** (☎ 011/482–3500), the giant hotel group that operates Southern Sun and Holiday Inn properties throughout the country, allows children under 18 to stay free if sharing with parents, in select hotels. **Mövenpick** (☎ 011/484–1641) hotels allow children under 16 to stay free when accompanied by a parent, and **Sun International** (☎ 011/780–7800) allows children under 12 to stay free if sharing a room with parents. In every case, meals are charged at a lower rate (usually only for children under 12), and children occupying their own room are charged at the full accommodation rate but less for meals.

SIGHTS & ATTRACTIONS

Places that are especially good for children are indicated by a rubber duckie icon in the margin.

CONSUMER PROTECTION

Whenever shopping or buying travel services in South Africa, **pay with a major credit card** so you can cancel payment or get reimbursed if there's a problem. If you're buying a package or tour, always **consider travel insurance,** which includes default coverage (☞ Insurance, *below*).

➤ LOCAL BBBs: **Council of Better Business Bureaus** (✉ 4200 Wilson Blvd., Suite 800, Arlington, VA 22203, ☎ 703/276–0100, FAX 703/525–8277).

CUSTOMS & DUTIES

When shopping, **keep receipts** for all purchases. Upon reentering the country, **be ready to show customs officials what you've bought.** If you feel a duty is incorrect or object to the way your clearance was handled, note the inspector's badge number and ask to see a supervisor. If the problem isn't resolved, write to the appropriate authorities, beginning with the port director at your point of entry.

IN SOUTH AFRICA

Visitors over 18 years of age may bring in duty-free gifts and souvenirs to the total value of R1250 (about $110), plus 400 cigarettes, 50 cigars, 250 grams of tobacco, 2 liters of wine, 1 liter of other alcoholic beverages, 50 ml of perfume, and 250 ml of toilet water.

IN BOTSWANA, SWAZILAND, ZIMBABWE, NAMIBIA, AND ZAMBIA

Botswana, Swaziland, Zimbabwe, Namibia, and Zambia lie in the Southern Africa Common Customs Union (SACU). Any visitor entering these countries from or through South Africa is not liable for any customs duties. You will, however, need to complete a form listing items imported. If you buy animal products to take home, including skins or legally culled ivory, make sure you get the requisite documentation from the seller. Duty-free allowances (for persons over 16 years of age) are 400 cigarettes, 50 cigars, and 250 grams of tobacco; 2 liters wine and 1 liter spirits; 50 ml perfume and 250 ml toilet water.

IN AUSTRALIA

Australia residents who are 18 or older may bring home $A400 worth of souvenirs and gifts (including jewelry), 250 cigarettes or 250 grams of tobacco, and 1,125 ml of alcohol (including wine, beer, and spirits). Residents under 18 may bring back $A200 worth of goods. Prohibited items include meat products. Seeds, plants, and fruits need to be declared upon arrival.

➤ INFORMATION: **Australian Customs Service** (Regional Director, ✉ Box 8, Sydney, NSW 2001, ☎ 02/9213–2000, FAX 02/9213–4000).

IN CANADA

Canadian residents who have been out of Canada for at least seven days may bring home C$500 worth of goods duty-free. If you've been away less than seven days but more than 48 hours, the duty-free allowance drops to C$200; if your trip lasts 24–48 hours, the allowance is C$50. You may not pool allowances with family members. Goods claimed under the C$500 exemption may follow you by mail; those claimed under the lesser exemptions must accompany you. Alcohol and tobacco products may be included in the seven-day and 48-hour exemptions but not in the 24-hour exemption. If you meet the age requirements of the province or territory through which you reenter Canada, you may bring in, duty-free, 1.14 liters (40 imperial ounces) of wine or liquor *or* 24 12-ounce cans or bottles of beer or ale. If you are 16 or older you may bring in, duty-free, 200 cigarettes and 50 cigars. Check ahead of time with Revenue Canada or the Department of Agriculture for policies regarding meat products, seeds, plants, and fruits.

You may send an unlimited number of gifts worth up to C$60 each duty-free to Canada. Label the package UNSOLICITED GIFT—VALUE UNDER $60. Alcohol and tobacco are excluded.

➤ INFORMATION: **Revenue Canada** (✉ 2265 St. Laurent Blvd. S, Ottawa, Ontario K1G 4K3, ☎ 613/993–0534; 800/461–9999 in Canada).

SMART TRAVEL TIPS A TO Z

IN NEW ZEALAND

Homeward-bound residents 17 or older may bring back $700 worth of souvenirs and gifts. Your duty-free allowance also includes 4.5 liters of wine or beer; one 1,125-ml bottle of spirits; and either 200 cigarettes, 250 grams of tobacco, 50 cigars, or a combination of the three up to 250 grams. Prohibited items include meat products, seeds, plants, and fruits.

➤ INFORMATION: **New Zealand Customs** (Custom House, ✉ 50 Anzac Ave., Box 29, Auckland, New Zealand, ☎ 09/359–6655, FAX 09/359–6732).

IN THE U.K.

From countries outside the EU, including South Africa, you may bring home, duty-free, 200 cigarettes or 50 cigars; 1 liter of spirits or 2 liters of fortified or sparkling wine or liqueurs; 2 liters of still table wine; 60 ml of perfume; 250 ml of toilet water; plus £136 worth of other goods, including gifts and souvenirs. If returning from outside the EU, prohibited items include meat products, seeds, plants, and fruits.

➤ INFORMATION: **HM Customs and Excise** (✉ Dorset House, Stamford St., Bromley Kent BR1 1XX, ☎ 020/7202–4227).

IN THE U.S.

U.S. residents who have been out of the country for at least 48 hours (and who have not used the $400 allowance or any part of it in the past 30 days) may bring home $400 worth of foreign goods duty-free.

U.S. residents 21 and older may bring back 1 liter of alcohol duty-free. In addition, regardless of your age, you are allowed 200 cigarettes and 100 non-Cuban cigars. Antiques, which the U.S. Customs Service defines as objects more than 100 years old, enter duty-free, as do original works of art done entirely by hand, including paintings, drawings, and sculptures.

You may also send packages home duty-free: up to $200 worth of goods for personal use, with a limit of one parcel per addressee per day (and no alcohol or tobacco products or perfume worth more than $5); label the package PERSONAL USE and attach a list of its contents and their retail value. Do not label the package UNSOLICITED GIFT or your duty-free exemption will drop to $100. Mailed items do not affect your duty-free allowance on your return.

➤ INFORMATION: **U.S. Customs Service** (inquiries, ✉ 1300 Pennsylvania Ave. NW, Washington, DC 20229, ☎ 202/927–6724; complaints, ✉ Office of Regulations and Rulings, 1300 Pennsylvania Ave. NW, Washington, DC 20229; registration of equipment, ✉ Registration Information, 1300 Pennsylvania Ave. NW, Washington, DC 20229, ☎ 202/927–0540).

DINING

The restaurants we list are the cream of the crop in each price category. Properties indicated by an ✕⬚ are lodging establishments whose restaurant warrants a special trip. Price categories within South Africa and Swaziland are as follows (Zimbabwe, Zambia, Namibia, and Botswana, price charts appear in the Pleasures and Pastimes sections of the chapters):

CATEGORY	COST*
$$$$	over R80
$$$	R60–R80
$$	R40–R60
$	under R40

Rates are per person, excluding drinks and service.

RESERVATIONS & DRESS

Dress in most restaurants tends to be casual, but draw the line at wearing shorts and a halter top to dinner at any restaurant away from the beach. Very expensive restaurants and old-fashioned hotel restaurants (where colonial traditions die hard) may require a jacket and tie. We mention dress only when men are required to wear a jacket or a jacket and tie.

DISABILITIES & ACCESSIBILITY

South Africa is slowly adding facilities for travelers with disabilities, but standards vary widely from place to place. Many of the large chains now offer one or more rooms in their hotels specially adapted for travelers with disabilities. Zimbabwe, Botswana, Namibia, and Zambia have very few facilities for travelers with disabilities.

LODGING

When discussing accessibility with an operator or reservations agent **ask hard questions.** Are there any stairs, inside *or* out? Are there grab bars next to the toilet *and* in the shower/tub? How wide is the doorway to the room? To the bathroom? For the most extensive facilities meeting the latest legal specifications **opt for newer accommodations.**

TRANSPORTATION

➤ COMPLAINTS: **Disability Rights Section** (⌧ U.S. Department of Justice, Civil Rights Division, Box 66738, Washington, DC 20035-6738, ☎ 202/514–0301; 800/514–0301; 202/514–0301 TTY; 800/514–0301 TTY, FAX 202/307–1198) for general complaints. **Aviation Consumer Protection Division** (☞ Air Travel, *above*) for airline-related problems. **Civil Rights Office** (⌧ U.S. Department of Transportation, Departmental Office of Civil Rights, S-30, 400 7th St. SW, Room 10215, Washington, DC 20590, ☎ 202/366–4648, FAX 202/366–9371) for problems with surface transportation.

TRAVEL AGENCIES

In the United States, although the Americans with Disabilities Act requires that travel firms serve the needs of all travelers, some agencies specialize in working with people with disabilities.

➤ TRAVELERS WITH MOBILITY PROBLEMS: **Access Adventures** (⌧ 206 Chestnut Ridge Rd., Rochester, NY 14624, ☎ 716/889–9096), run by a former physical-rehabilitation counselor. **Accessible Journeys** (⌧ 35 W. Sellers Ave., Ridley Park, PA 19078, ☎ 610/521–0339 or 800/846–4537, FAX 610/521–6959). **Flying Wheels Travel** (⌧ 143 W. Bridge St., Box 382, Owatonna, MN 55060, ☎ 507/451–5005 or 800/535–6790, FAX 507/451–1685). **Hinsdale Travel Service** (⌧ 201 E. Ogden Ave., Suite 100, Hinsdale, IL 60521, ☎ 630/325–1335, FAX 630/325–1342).

DISCOUNTS & DEALS

Be a smart shopper and **compare all your options** before making decisions. A plane ticket bought with a promo-tional coupon from travel clubs, coupon books, and direct-mail offers may not be cheaper than the least expensive fare from a discount ticket agency. And always keep in mind that what you get is just as important as what you save.

DISCOUNT RESERVATIONS

To save money **look into discount-reservations services** with toll-free numbers, which use their buying power to get a better price on hotels, airline tickets, even car rentals. When booking a room, always **call the hotel's local toll-free number** (if one is available) rather than the central reservations number—you'll often get a better price. Always ask about special packages or corporate rates.

When shopping for the best deal on hotels and car rentals **look for guaranteed exchange rates,** which protect you against a falling dollar. With your rate locked in, you won't pay more, even if the price goes up in the local currency.

➤ AIRLINE TICKETS: ☎ **800/FLY–4–LESS.**

➤ HOTEL ROOMS: **Steigenberger Reservation Service** (☎ 800/223–5652).

PACKAGE DEALS

Don't confuse packages and guided tours. When you buy a package, you travel on your own, just as though you had planned the trip yourself. Fly-drive packages, which combine airfare and car rental, are often a good deal.

ECOTOURISM

Water is a precious resource and should be used sparingly. Take short showers and always turn taps off when not in use, especially when shaving and brushing teeth. When outdoors, don't litter or pick flowers. When hiking, don't take short cuts on mountain slopes; this exacerbates erosion, already a major problem in many parts of the region. If you're camping, don't wash with soap or shampoo in streams, springs, or lakes. Also, avoid feeding wild animals; at best it can make them sick, at worst it may cause them to expect food from future visitors who may be attacked and killed when they don't provide the expected food.

ELECTRICITY

To use your U.S.-purchased electric-powered equipment, **bring a converter and adapter.** The electrical current in 220 volts, 50 cycles alternating current (AC); wall outlets in most of the region take 15-amp plugs with three round prongs (the old British system) but some take the straight-edged, three-pronged plugs, also 15 amp.

If your appliances are dual-voltage, you'll need only an adapter. Don't use 110-volt outlets, marked FOR SHAVERS ONLY, for high-wattage appliances such as blow-dryers. Most laptops operate equally well on 110 and 220 volts and so require only an adapter.

EMERGENCIES

South Africa's national emergency number for the police is 10111; for an ambulance it is 10177. Consult the front page of the local telephone directories for other emergency numbers. You can call Medical Rescue International (MRI, ☎ 011/242–0112, 0800/111–9990 toll-free).

In **Zimbabwe,** dial 994 (ambulance), 993 (fire), and 995 (police); also call Medical Air Rescue Services (MARS, ☎ 04/73–4513).

In **Botswana,** dial 997 (ambulance), 998 (fire), and 999 (police) or, if you are in a remote area, contact MRI in Johannesburg (☞ *above*) for emergency evacuation.

In **Namibia,** dial 10111 (police) or 061/23–0505 for MRI (Medical Rescue International) or Aeromed (ambulance). Other numbers are specific to cities, so check local directories.

In **Zambia,** dial 999 for fire and ambulance, 991 for police, or contact Speciality Emergency Services in Lusaka (☎ 01/27–3303 or 01/27–3304) or MRI in Johannesburg or MARS in Harare (☞ *above* for both).

In **Swaziland,** dial 5–2221 for general emergency, or contact MRI for medical emergency.

GAY & LESBIAN TRAVEL

The major cities of South Africa are very gay-friendly, particularly Cape Town, which has a very large gay population. The other countries in the region are somewhat more conservative and gay people should act with circumspection, especially in Zimbabwe, which has a very homophobic president and where homosexuality is, technically, illegal.

➤ GAY- AND LESBIAN-FRIENDLY TRAVEL AGENCIES: **Different Roads Travel** (✉ 8383 Wilshire Blvd., Suite 902, Beverly Hills, CA 90211, ☎ 323/651–5557 or 800/429–8747, FAX 323/651–3678). **Kennedy Travel** (✉ 314 Jericho Turnpike, Floral Park, NY 11001, ☎ 516/352–4888 or 800/237–7433, FAX 516/354–8849). **Now Voyager** (✉ 4406 18th St., San Francisco, CA 94114, ☎ 415/626–1169 or 800/255–6951, FAX 415/626–8626). **Skylink Travel and Tour** (✉ 1006 Mendocino Ave., Santa Rosa, CA 95401, ☎ 707/546–9888 or 800/225–5759, FAX 707/546–9891), serving lesbian travelers.

HEALTH

The most serious health problem facing travelers is malaria, which occurs in the prime game-viewing areas of Mpumalanga and the Northern Province, and in northern Kwa-Zulu-Natal, in South Africa. The high-lying areas of Zimbabwe, Swaziland, and Zambia are malaria-free, but the low-lying river valleys are high-risk areas. Most of Namibia and Botswana are malaria-free; the exceptions are the Caprivi Strip of Namibia and the Okavango Delta of Botswana. All travelers heading into malaria-endemic regions should consult a knowledgeable health-care professional **at least one month before departure** for advice. Unfortunately, the malarial agent, *Plasmodium sp*, seems to be able to develop a hardy resistance to new prophylactic drugs pretty quickly so, even if you are taking the newest miracle drug, **take great care to avoid being bitten.** After sunset, wear light-color, loose, long-sleeve shirts; long pants; and shoes and socks; and apply mosquito repellant. Always sleep in a mosquito-proof room or tent and, if possible, keep a fan going in your room. **If you are pregnant, or trying to conceive, avoid malaria areas if at all possible.**

Many lakes and streams, particularly east of the watershed, i.e., in rivers flowing toward the Indian Ocean, are infected with bilharzia (schistosomiasis), a parasite carried by a small freshwater snail. The fluke enters through the skin of swimmers or waders, attaches itself to the intestines or bladder, and lays eggs. Avoid wading in still waters or in areas close to reeds. If you have been wading or swimming in doubtful water, dry yourself off vigorously with a towel immediately on exiting the water, as this will help to dislodge any flukes before they can burrow into the skin. Fast-moving water is considered safe.

During summer, ticks may be found all over the region, even in open areas close to cities. If you intend to walk or hike anywhere, use a suitable insect repellent. After your walk, examine your body and clothes for ticks, looking carefully for pepper ticks, which are tiny but just as virulent as their parents and can cause tick-bite fever. If you find a tick has bitten you, **do not pull it off.** If you do, you may pull the body off and the head will remain embedded in your skin, causing an infection. Rather, smother the area with petroleum jelly and the tick will eventually let go, as it will be unable to breathe; you can then scrape it off with a fingernail. If you are bitten, keep an eye on the bite. If the tick was infected, the bite will swell, itch, and develop a black necrotic center—this is a sure sign that you will develop tick-bite fever, which usually hits after about 8 to 12 days. Symptoms may be mild or severe, depending on the patient. This is not usually life-threatening in healthy adults, but it is horribly unpleasant.

The low-lying areas of Zimbabwe, Botswana, and Zambia harbor tsetse flies, so wear light-color clothing and insect repellent in these areas. (Tsetse flies are attracted to dark colors, especially black, dark brown, and bright blue.) Don't spend ages agonizing over whether you've been bitten by a tsetse fly or not. You'll know, as it is very painful. The risk of contracting sleeping sickness is not great, but the disease can be fatal, and it can move very fast, so be aware.

Southern Africa has no national health system, so check your existing health plan to see whether you're covered while abroad and supplement it if necessary. South African doctors are generally excellent. The equipment and training in private clinics rival the best in the world, but public hospitals in all the countries covered tend to suffer from overcrowding and underfunding.

Upon returning home, if you experience any unusual symptoms, including fever, painful eyes, backache, diarrhea and severe headache, general lassitude, blood in urine or stools, be sure to tell your doctor where you have been. These symptoms may indicate malaria, tick-bite fever, bilharzia, sleeping sickness (although the latter is unlikely), or possibly even some other tropical malady.

FOOD & DRINK

Unless signs indicate otherwise, you can drink the tap water and eat all fresh produce in South Africa, Zimbabwe, Botswana, and most of Namibia. Tap water in Zambia may be suspect, especially in the rainy season, when water sources may easily become contaminated. Diseases that can be carried in contaminated water, food, or utensils include cholera and hepatitis A.

➤ HEALTH WARNINGS: **National Centers for Disease Control** (✉ CDC, National Center for Infectious Diseases, Division of Quarantine, Traveler's Health Section, 1600 Clifton Rd., M/S E-03, Atlanta, GA 30333, ☎ 404/332–4559, ℻ 404/332–4565).

MEDICAL PLANS

No one plans to get sick while traveling, but it happens, so **consider signing up with a medical-assistance company.** Members get doctor referrals, emergency evacuation or repatriation, hot lines for medical consultation, cash for emergencies, and other assistance.

SMART TRAVEL TIPS A TO Z

➤ MEDICAL-ASSISTANCE COMPANIES: **AEA International SOS** (✉ 8 Neshaminy Interplex, Suite 207, Trevose, PA 19053, ☎ 215/245–4707 or 800/523–6586, FAX 215/244–9617; ✉ 12 Chemin Riantbosson, 1217 Meyrin 1, Geneva, Switzerland, ☎ 4122/785–6464, FAX 4122/785–6424; ✉ 331 N. Bridge Rd., 17-00, Odeon Towers, Singapore 188720, ☎ 65/338–7800, FAX 65/338–7611).

SHOTS AND MEDICATIONS

Aside from needing malaria tablets, travelers entering South Africa within six days of leaving a country infected with yellow fever require a yellow-fever vaccination certificate. The South African travel clinics are now also recommending that you be vaccinated against hepatitis A and B, particularly if you intend to travel to more-isolated areas. Cholera vaccinations are widely regarded to be useless, so don't let anyone talk you into having one.

INSURANCE

The most useful travel insurance plan is a comprehensive policy that includes coverage for trip cancellation and interruption, default, trip delay, and medical expenses (with a waiver for preexisting conditions).

Without insurance you will lose all or most of your money if you cancel your trip, regardless of the reason. Default insurance covers you if your tour operator, airline, or cruise line goes out of business. Trip-delay covers expenses that arise because of bad weather or mechanical delays. Study the fine print when comparing policies.

If you're traveling internationally, a key component of travel insurance is coverage for medical bills incurred if you get sick on the road. Such expenses are not generally covered by Medicare or private policies.

Always **buy travel policies directly from the insurance company**; if you buy it from a cruise line, airline, or tour operator that goes out of business you probably will not be covered for the agency or operator's default, a major risk. Before you make any purchase **review your existing health**

and home-owner's policies to find what they cover away from home.

➤ TRAVEL INSURERS: In the U.S. **Access America** (✉ 6600 W. Broad St., Richmond, VA 23230, ☎ 804/285–3300 or 800/284–8300), **Travel Guard International** (✉ 1145 Clark St., Stevens Point, WI 54481, ☎ 715/345–0505 or 800/826–1300). In Canada **Voyager Insurance** (✉ 44 Peel Center Dr., Brampton, Ontario L6T 4M8, ☎ 905/791–8700; 800/668–4342 in Canada).

➤ INSURANCE INFORMATION: In the U.K. the **Association of British Insurers** (✉ 51–55 Gresham St., London EC2V 7HQ, ☎ 020/7600–3333, FAX 020/7696–8999). In Australia the **Insurance Council of Australia** (☎ 03/9614–1077, FAX 03/9614–7924).

LANGUAGE

South Africa has a mind-numbing 11 official languages: English, Afrikaans, Ndebele, North Sotho, South Sotho, Swati, Tsonga, Tswana, Venda, Xhosa, and Zulu. Happily for visitors, English is the widely spoken, unofficial lingua franca, although road signs and other important markers often alternate between English and Afrikaans (South-African Dutch). Be warned that street names often alternate between the English and Afrikaans names, so, for example "Wale Street" and "Waal Street" are the same road.

South African English is heavily influenced by Afrikaans and, to a lesser extent, by some of the African languages. First-time visitors may have trouble understanding some regional South African accents. Listed below are some of the words that you should know. For a list of culinary terms, *see* Dining in Pleasures and Pastimes *in* Chapter 1.

Bakkie: pickup truck

Bonnet: hood (of a car)

Boot: trunk (of a car)

Bottle store: liquor store

Bra/bru/My Bra: Brother, term of affection or familiarity

Dagga/Zol: marijuana

Jol: a party or night on the town

Howzit?: literally, "How are you?," but a general greeting

Izit?: Really?

Just now: recently or any time in the near or distant future

Lekker: nice

Pavement: sidewalk

Petrol: gasoline

Robot: traffic light

Shame: "How cute" or "What a pity"

Shebeen: township bar

Sis: gross, disgusting

Sisi, or Usisi: Sister, term of affection or respect

Skollie/Skebenga/Tsotsi: thug, ruffian

Takkie: sneaker

Toyi-toyi: to dance in protest

Veld: open countryside

Yebo: yes or hello

Zimbabwe's official languages are Shona, Ndebele, and very widely spoken English. **Botswana**'s official languages are Setswana and English, which is widely spoken. The minority languages—Hambakushu, Kalanga, and the many San (Bushman) dialects, collectively referred to as *BaSarwa*—are not given much recognition. **Zambia** has more than 70 different dialects, but there are four main languages, Lozi, Bemba, Nyanja, and Tonga. English is widely spoken. **Namibia**'s official language is English, which is not that widely spoken, except in the cities, and then often as a second language. Afrikaans is spoken by many residents of various races, and there is a large population of German-speaking people. The most widely spoken indigenous languages are Kwanyama (a dialect of Owambo), Herero, and a number of Nama (San) dialects, which are spoken by almost no one other than native speakers.

LODGING

The South African Tourism Board (Satour) operates a grading system rating the quality of a hotel. A one-star rating suggests the bare essentials, while a hotel with a five-star rating (the highest) can be assumed to meet high international standards. Bear in mind, though, that stars relate to the level of facilities provided (e.g., TV, heated towel rack, room service, etc.), not the quality of the hotel, and many one-star establishments offer great service and good value for the money. In a second, more subjective rating system, Satour awards silver plaques to those few hotels and guest houses that offer an extraordinary level of service.

Most hotel rooms come with en suite bathrooms, and you can usually choose between rooms with twin or double beds. A full English breakfast is often included in the rate, particularly in more traditional hotels. In most luxury lodges, the rate usually covers the cost of dinner, bed, and breakfast, while in game lodges the rate includes everything but alcohol.

Be warned, though, that in southern Africa words do not necessarily mean what you think they do. The term "lodge" is a particularly tricky one. A guest lodge or a game lodge is almost always an upmarket, full-service facility with loads of extra attractions. But the term "lodge" when applied to city hotels often indicates a minimum-service hotel. These are usually very well appointed and comfortable but have no bar, restaurant, or room service and thus offer very good-value bed-and-breakfast accommodation. Examples are the Protea Lodges (as opposed to Protea Hotels), City and Town Lodges, and Holiday Inn Garden Courts.

The lodgings we list are the cream of the crop in each price category. We always list the facilities that are available—but we don't specify whether they cost extra: When pricing accommodations, always ask what's included and what costs extra. Properties indicated by an ✕🏨 are lodging establishments whose restaurant warrants a special trip. Mailing addresses, if different from the street address, are given in parentheses in the service information at the end of the review.

Price categories within South Africa and Swaziland are as follows (in Zimbabwe, Botswana, Namibia, and Zambia, price charts appear in the Pleasures and Pastimes sections of the chapters):

CATEGORY	COST CHAPTERS 2, 4, 5, 6 & 8*	COST CHAPTERS 3 & 7*
$$$$	over R600	over R750
$$$	R400–R600	R500–R750
$$	R250–R400	R250–R500
$	under R250	under R250

Rates are for a double room, including VAT. The cost may also include breakfast and dinner.

Assume that hotels operate on the European Plan (EP, with no meals) unless we specify that they use the Continental Plan (CP, with a Continental breakfast daily), Breakfast Plan (BP, with a full breakfast daily), Modified American Plan (MAP, with breakfast and dinner daily), or Full American Plan (FAP, including all meals and most activities). Most game lodges use the FAP plan.

B&BS

There are thousands of B&B's scattered all over the region. As in most other parts of the world, many are very small and personalized, giving the visitor an insight into the lives of locals. For more info contact **BABASA (Bed and Breakfast Association of South Africa)** (✉ 2005, Groenkloof, 0027, ☎ FAX 012/46–2761).

FARM STAYS

Jacana Country Homes and Trails (✉ Box 95212, Waterkloof 0145, ☎ 012/346–3550–2, FAX 012/346–2499) offers a range of farms, coastal and country cottages, as well as privately operated hiking, biking, and horse trails in country areas.

Farm and Country Holiday (✉ Box 247, Durbanville 7551, ☎ 021/96–8621, FAX 021/96–9790).

GAME LODGES

Safariplan/Wild African Ventures (✉ 673 E. California Blvd., Pasadena, CA 91106, ☎ 800/358–8530) and **Classic Safari Camps of Africa** (✉ Box 2441, Northriding 2162, South Africa, ☎ 011/465–6427, FAX 011/465–9309) represent a number of the best and most exclusive game lodges in southern and east Africa. *See* Portfolio of Places and Where in Zimbabwe *below* for a wider choice.

HOSTELS

No matter what your age you can **save on lodging costs by staying at hostels.** In some 5,000 locations in more than 70 countries around the world, Hostelling International (HI), the umbrella group for a number of national youth-hostel associations, offers single-sex, dorm-style beds and, at many hostels, couples rooms and family accommodations. Membership in any HI national hostel association, open to travelers of all ages, allows you to stay in HI-affiliated hostels at member rates (one-year membership is about $25 for adults; hostels run about $10–$25 per night). Members also have priority if the hostel is full; they're eligible for discounts around the world, even on rail and bus travel in some countries.

➤ ORGANIZATIONS: **Backpacker Tourism South Africa–BTSA** (✉ c/o Cloudreak, 219 UpperBuitenkant St., Cape Town, 8001, ☎ 021/465–1688, FAX 021/461–1458). **Australian Youth Hostel Association** (✉ 10 Mallett St., Camperdown, NSW 2050, ☎ 02/9565–1699, FAX 02/9565–1325). **Hostelling International—American Youth Hostels** (✉ 733 15th St. NW, Suite 840, Washington, DC 20005, ☎ 202/783–6161, FAX 202/783–6171). **Hostelling International—Canada** (✉ 400–205 Catherine St., Ottawa, Ontario K2P 1C3, ☎ 613/237–7884, FAX 613/237–7868). **Hostelling International South Africa** (✉ 73 St. George's Mall, Box 4402, Cape Town 8000, ☎ 021/424–2511, FAX 021/424–4119). **Youth Hostel Association of England and Wales** (✉ Trevelyan House, 8 St. Stephen's Hill, St. Albans, Hertfordshire AL1 2DY, ☎ 01727/855215 or 01727/845047, FAX 01727/844126). **Youth Hostels Association of New Zealand** (✉ Box 436, Christchurch, New Zealand, ☎ 03/379–9970, FAX 03/365–4476). Membership in the U.S. $25, in Canada C$26.75, in the U.K.

£9.30, in Australia $44, in New Zealand $24.

HOTELS

International hotel groups, such as **Hyatt International** (☎ 800/228–9000) and **Sheraton** (☎ 800/325–3535), are moderately well represented around the region, and **Mövenpick** (☎ 011/484–1641 central reservations) has recently taken over the locally owned Karos group. Major South African conglomerates include **Protea** (☎ 021/419–8800 central reservations, 0800/11–9000 toll-free) and the **Southern Sun Group** (☎ 011/482–3500 central reservations), which runs Southern Sun Hotels and Holiday Inn Hotels, and manages the budget French hotel chain, **Formule 1** (☎ 011/807–0750) and the South African **Inter-Continental Hotels** (☎ 011/802–6876). **Cresta** (☎ 011/341–4440) is the biggest chain in Botswana and Zimbabwe.

Portfolio of Places (☎ 011/880–3414 in Johannesburg, FAX 011/788–4802) publishes *The Country Places Collection,* a widely respected list of South Africa's best small country hotels and lodges, as well as select city hotels. Portfolio also publishes a similar guide to bed-and-breakfasts.

Where Publishing (✉ Box 158, Triangle, Zimbabwe, ☎ 133/5200, FAX 133/6714 or 133/6568) publishes *Where in Zimbabwe,* a descriptive list of some of the best small country hotels and lodges, as well as select city hotels in Zimbabwe.

All hotels listed have private bath unless otherwise noted.

➤ TOLL-FREE NUMBERS: **Adam's Mark** (☎ 800/444/2326). **Baymont Inns** (☎ 800/428–3438). **Best Western** (☎ 800/528–1234). **Choice** (☎ 800/221–2222). **Clarion** (☎ 800/252–7466). **Colony** (☎ 800/777–1700). **Comfort** (☎ 800/228–5150). **Days Inn** (☎ 800/325–2525). **Doubletree and Red Lion Hotels** (☎ 800/222–8733). **Embassy Suites** (☎ 800/362–2779). **Fairfield Inn** (☎ 800/228–2800). **Forte** (☎ 800/225–5843). **Four Seasons** (☎ 800/332–3442). **Hilton** (☎ 800/445–8667). **Holiday Inn** (☎ 800/465–4329). **Howard Johnson** (☎ 800/654–4656). **Hyatt Hotels &** **Resorts** (☎ 800/233–1234). **Inter-Continental** (☎ 800/327–0200). **La Quinta** (☎ 800/531–5900). **Marriott** (☎ 800/228–9290). **Le Meridien** (☎ 800/543–4300). **Nikko Hotels International** (☎ 800/645–5687). **Omni** (☎ 800/843–6664). **Quality Inn** (☎ 800/228–5151). **Radisson** (☎ 800/333–3333). **Ramada** (☎ 800/228–2828). **Renaissance Hotels & Resorts** (☎ 800/468–3571). **Ritz-Carlton** (☎ 800/241–3333). **Sheraton** (☎ 800/325–3535). **Sleep Inn** (☎ 800/753–3746). **Westin Hotels & Resorts** (☎ 800/228–3000). **Wyndham Hotels & Resorts** (☎ 800/822–4200).

MAIL & SHIPPING

The mail service in southern Africa is not spectacularly reliable. Mail can take weeks to arrive, and money and other valuables are frequently stolen from letters and packages. You can buy stamps only at post offices, open weekdays 8:30–4:30 and Saturdays 8–noon. In South Africa, stamps for local use marked STANDARDISED POST may be purchased from newsagents in booklets of 10 stamps. Federal Express and several other express-mail companies offer more reliable service, as do the new Fast Mail and Speed Courier services.

Except in South Africa, postal codes are not used, because of the relatively small populations of southern African countries.

RECEIVING MAIL

The central post office in each city has a poste restante desk that will hold mail for you. Be sure the post office's mail code and your name are prominently displayed on all letters. Most hotels also accept faxes and express-mail deliveries addressed to their guests. A better place to receive mail is American Express offices; for a list of offices worldwide, write for the Traveler's Companion from **American Express** (✉ Box 678, Canal St. Station, New York, NY 10013).

MONEY MATTERS

Because of inflation and currency fluctuations it's difficult to give exact prices. It's safe to say, though, that the region is an extremely cheap destination for foreign visitors. With the weakness of southern African currencies against major foreign currencies, visitors will find the cost of meals, hotels, and entertainment considerably lower than at home. Botswana, with its stable economy and currency, is probably the most expensive destination in the region.

A fabulous bottle of South African wine costs about $10 (double or triple in a restaurant), and a meal at a prestigious restaurant won't set you back more than $40 per person. Double rooms in the country's finest hotels may cost $500 a night, but $100 is more than enough to secure high-quality lodging in most cities. Hotel rates are at their highest during peak season, November through March, when you can expect to pay anywhere from 50% to 90% more than in the off-season.

Not everything in South Africa is cheap. Expect to pay international rates and more to stay in one of the exclusive private game lodges in Mpumalanga, the Northern Province, or KwaZulu-Natal. Mala Mala, one of the the most glamorous lodges in the country, charges about $1,000 per couple per night. Flights to South Africa and within the country itself are also extremely expensive.

The following were sample costs in **South Africa** in US$ at press time: cup of coffee $1; bottle of beer in a bar $1; ¼ roasted chicken with salad and drink at a fast-food restaurant $3–$4; room-service sandwich in a hotel $4–$7; a 2-km (1-mi) taxi ride $6.

The following were sample costs in **Zimbabwe** in US$ at press time: cup of coffee $1; bottle of beer in a bar 75¢; average cost of lunch in cities $3.50; room-service sandwich in a hotel $5; a 2-km (1-mi) taxi ride $1.

The following were sample costs in **Botswana** in US$ at press time: cup of coffee $1.50; bottle of beer in a bar $1.50; average cost of lunch in cities $8–10; room-service sandwich in a hotel $8; a 2-km (1-mi) taxi ride $5.50.

The following were sample costs in **Namibia** in US$ at press time: cup of coffee 75¢–$1.50; bottle of beer in a bar $1; average cost of lunch in cities $3–$5; room-service sandwich in a hotel $4–$7; a 2-km (1-mi) taxi ride $4–$5.

The following were sample costs in **Zambia** in US$ at press time: cup of coffee $1; bottle of beer in a bar 75¢; average cost of lunch in cities $3.50; room-service sandwich in a hotel $5; a 2-km (1-mi) taxi ride US$1.

The following were sample costs in **Swaziland** at press time: cup of coffee 75¢–$1; bottle of beer in a bar 80¢–$1.50; average cost of lunch in cities $3–$6; room-service sandwich in a hotel $3.50; a 2-km (1-mi) taxi ride $4–$6.

Prices quoted throughout the book are in local currency where possible. Most operators in Zambia will only accept foreign currency, as the local money is rather volatile and even some operators in Zimbabwe, Botswana, and Namibia quote in US$ or Deutchmark. Prices throughout this guide are given for adults. Substantially reduced fees are almost always available for children, students, and senior citizens. For information on taxes, *see* Taxes, *below*.

ATMS

Before leaving home, **make sure that your credit cards have been programmed for ATM use in South Africa** (most South African ATMs take four-digit PIN numbers). Note that Discover is accepted mostly in the United States. Local bank cards often do not work overseas or may access only your checking account; **ask your bank about a MasterCard/Cirrus or Visa debit card,** which works like a bank card but can be used at any ATM displaying a MasterCard/Cirrus or Visa logo. These cards, too, may tap only your checking account; check with your bank about their policy.

CREDIT CARDS

Throughout this guide, the following abbreviations are used: **AE,** American Express; **DC,** Diners Club; **MC,** MasterCard; and **V,** Visa.

In both Namibia and Zambia, MasterCard and Visa are preferred by business owners to American Express because of substantial charges levied by Amex to proprietors. Even with MasterCard and Visa, business owners in Zambia often prefer cash (or traveler's checks) to credit cards, and some smaller hotels levy a fee up to 10% to use credit.

➤ REPORTING LOST CARDS: **Amex** (☎ 011/358–5000 or toll free 080/953–4300), **Diners Club** (☎ 021/686–1990, or 011/482–2203), **MasterCard** (☎ toll free 080/099–0418), **Visa** (☎ toll free 080/099–0475).

CURRENCY

The unit of currency in **South Africa** is the rand (R), with 100 cents (¢) equaling R1. Bills come in R10, R20, R50, R100, and R200 denominations, which are differentiated by color. Coins are minted in R5, R2, R1, 50¢, 20¢, 10¢, 5¢, 2¢, and 1¢ denominations.

Namibia's currency is the Namibian dollar, which is linked to the South African rand, as is **Swaziland**'s lilangeni (plural emalangeni). In both these countries, you can use rand quite freely, but their currency is not usable in South Africa, except unofficially at border towns.

Zimbabwe's currency is the dollar. There are $2, $5, $10, $20, and $50 bills; coins come in 1¢, 5¢, 10¢, 20¢, 50¢, and $1 denominations.

Botswana's Pula is the most stable currency is southern Africa and is broken down into 100 thebe. There are P1, P2, P5, P10, P20, and P50 bills, and 1t, 2t, 5t, 10t, 25, 50t, and P1 coins.

Zambia's currency is the Zambian kwacha, which comes in denominations of 5, 10, 50, 100, 500, 1,000, 5,000, and 10,000 bills, necessitating the carrying of huge wads of notes. The kwacha is theoretically divided into 100 ngwee, but, as you can buy nothing for one kwacha, a ngwee is as useless as it is difficult to pronounce.

CURRENCY EXCHANGE

At press time, **conversion rates** (to the US$) for southern Africa were as follows: **South Africa** R6.10 (Namibian dollar and Swaziland lilangeni the same); **Zimbabwe** Z$37.50;

Botswana P4.53; and **Zambia** ZK2,388.

For the most favorable rates, **change money through banks.** Although ATM transaction fees may be higher abroad than at home, ATM rates are excellent because they are based on wholesale rates offered only by major banks. You won't do as well at exchange booths in airports or rail and bus stations, in hotels, in restaurants, or in stores. To avoid lines at airport exchange booths **get a bit of local currency before you leave home.**

In Zambia or Zimbabwe you may be invited to do a little informal foreign exchange by persuasive street financiers, who will offer you excellent rates. Resist the temptation—it's not worth the risk of being ripped off or caught and arrested.

To avoid administrative hassles, keep all foreign-exchange receipts until you leave southern Africa, as you may need them as proof when changing any unspent local currency back into your own currency. You may not take more than R5,000 in cash out of South Africa. For more information, you can contact the **South African Reserve Bank** (✉ Box 427, Pretoria 0001, ☎ 012/313–3911).

➤ EXCHANGE SERVICES: **International Currency Express** (☎ 888/842–0880 on East Coast; 888/278–6628 on West Coast). **Thomas Cook Currency Services** (☎ 800/287–7362 for telephone orders and retail locations).

TRAVELER'S CHECKS

Do you need traveler's checks? It depends on where you're headed. If you're going to rural areas and small towns, go with cash; traveler's checks are best used in cities. Lost or stolen checks can usually be replaced within 24 hours. To ensure a speedy refund, buy your own traveler's checks—don't let someone else pay for them: Irregularities like this can cause delays. The person who bought the checks should make the call to request a refund.

PACKING

In southern Africa, it's possible to experience muggy heat, bone-chilling cold, torrential thunderstorms, and scorching African sun all within a couple of days. The secret is to pack lightweight clothes that you can wear layers, and at least one sweater. Take along a warm jacket, too, especially if you're going to a private game lodge. It can get mighty cold sitting in an open Land Rover at night.

South Africans tend to dress casually, donning shorts and T-shirts as soon as the weather turns pleasant. Businessmen still wear suits all over the region, but, especially in South Africa, dress standards have become less rigid and more interesting since ex-president Nelson Mandela redefined the concept of sartorial elegance with his "Madiba Shirts." You can go almost anywhere in neat, clean, casual clothes, but you can still get dolled up to go to the theater or opera, if you wish. Dinner on the Blue Train and in some of the smarter hotels is formal. An interesting development since 1994 is that invitations to social and official events prescribe dress code as "formal or traditional," so it really is quite acceptable for men to appear at the opera or the Opening of Parliament in skirts made of monkey tails. (But don't try it as a foreigner, although you may wear a kilt or Native American feathered headdress if it is culturally appropriate for you.) No kidding!

In summer, lightweight cottons are ideal, but highveld (the high interior plateau of South Africa, Zimbabwe and Zambia) evenings can be decidedly cool and the desert nights in Botswana and Namibia are downright freezing. Despite the chilly nights and mornings, daytime temperatures in these regions can get pretty high—easily over 21°C (70°F) in winter and over 37°C (100°F) in summer. In the low-lying areas of the northern part of the region, the summer temperatures often go over 100°F with an accompanying high humidity.

It's easy to get fried in the strong African sun, especially in mile-high Johannesburg, where the temperature can be deceptively cool. Pack plenty of sunscreen, sunglasses, and a hat. An umbrella comes in handy during those late-afternoon thunderstorms.

If you're heading into the bush, consider packing binoculars, a strong insect repellent like 100% DEET, and sturdy pants (preferably cotton) that can stand up to the wicked thorns that protect much of the foliage. Avoid black, white, or garish clothing that will make you more visible to animals (and insects, which tend to mistake you for a buffalo if you wear black); medium tones will make you blend in most, but you don't have to look like an extra on the set of *Out of Africa,* so don't rush out and buy a suitcase of designer khaki—you'll just look like a tourist. And leave behind perfumes, which mask the smell of the bush and also attract insects. Lightweight hiking boots are a good idea if you plan to set out on any of South Africa's great trails; otherwise, a sturdy pair of walking shoes should suffice.

Make copies of all your important documents and leave them with someone at home who can courier them to you if you should be unlucky enough to lose them all.

CHECKING LUGGAGE

How many carry-on bags you can bring with you is up to the airline. Most allow two, but not always, so make sure that everything you carry aboard will fit under your seat, and get to the gate early. Note that if you have a seat at the back of the plane, you'll probably board first, while the overhead bins are still empty.

If you are flying internationally, note that baggage allowances may be determined not by piece but by weight—generally 88 pounds (40 kilograms) in first class, 66 pounds (30 kilograms) in business class, and 44 pounds (20 kilograms) in economy.

If you are visiting one of the lodges in the Okavango Delta, you will be arriving by light plane and they really do restrict you to 10 kilograms (22 pounds) of luggage in a soft bag. Excess luggage can be stored in Maun. You may find similar restrictions on some flights into game reserves or to the Bazaruto Archipelago (but they'll always make space for dive gear, less weights and cylinder).

Airline liability for baggage is limited to $1,250 per person on flights within the United States. On international flights it amounts to $9.07 per pound or $20 per kilogram for checked baggage (roughly $640 per 70-pound bag) and $400 per passenger for unchecked baggage. You can buy additional coverage at check-in for about $10 per $1,000 of coverage, but it excludes a rather extensive list of items, shown on your airline ticket.

PASSPORTS & VISAS

When traveling internationally **carry a passport even if you don't need one** (it's always the best form of ID), and **make two photocopies of the data page** (one for someone at home and another for you, carried separately from your passport). If you lose your passport promptly call the nearest embassy or consulate and the local police.

U.S. CITIZENS

All U.S. citizens, even infants, need only a valid passport to enter South Africa, Swaziland, Botswana, Zimbabwe, Zambia, or Namibia for holidays of up to 90 days. Business visitors to Namibia need visas. Visitors to Zimbabwe must buy a visa at the border at a cost of between US$25 and US$40. Visitors to Zambia will be issued a multiple-entry visa valid for three years at a cost of US$40. Mozambican visas must be obtained prior to entry and cost between R45 (about US$8) and R225 (about US$40) for a single-entry visa and between R140 (about US$24) and R850 (about US$145) for a multiple-entry visa. The price difference is due to the urgency with which the application is processed, so it pays to think ahead.

➤ INFORMATION: **Office of Passport Services** (☎ 202/647–0518).

CANADIANS

You need only a valid passport to enter South Africa, Swaziland, Namibia, Zimbabwe, Zambia for stays of up to 90 days. Mozambican visas must be obtained prior to entry and cost between R45 (about US$8) and R225 (about US$40) for a single-entry visa and between R140 (about US$24) and R850 (about US$145)

for a multiple-entry visa. The price difference is due to the urgency with which the application is processed, so it pays to think ahead.

➤ INFORMATION: **Passport Office** (☎ 819/994–3500 or 800/567–6868).

U.K. CITIZENS

Citizens of the United Kingdom need only a valid passport to enter South Africa, Swaziland, Namibia, and Zimbabwe for stays of up to 90 days. Zambian visas cost US$33 for a single-entry or US$45 for a multiple-entry visa. Mozambican visas must be obtained prior to entry and cost between R45 (about US$8) and R225 (about US$40) for a single-entry visa and between R140 (about US$24) and R850 (about US$145) for a multiple-entry visa. The price difference is due to the urgency with which the application is processed, so it pays you to think ahead.

➤ INFORMATION: **London Passport Office** (☎ 0990/21010) for fees and documentation requirements and to request an emergency passport.

PASSPORT OFFICES

The best time to apply for a passport or to renew is during the fall and winter. Before any trip, check your passport's expiration date, and, if necessary, renew it as soon as possible.

➤ AUSTRALIAN CITIZENS: **Australian Passport Office** (☎ 131–232).

➤ CANADIAN CITIZENS: **Passport Office** (☎ 819/994–3500 or 800/567–6868).

➤ NEW ZEALAND CITIZENS: **New Zealand Passport Office** (☎ 04/494–0700 for information on how to apply; 04/474–8000 or 0800/225–050 in New Zealand for information on applications already submitted).

➤ U.K. CITIZENS: **London Passport Office** (☎ 0990/210–410) for fees and documentation requirements and to request an emergency passport.

➤ U.S. CITIZENS: **National Passport Information Center** (☎ 900/225–5674; calls are 35¢ per minute for automated service, $1.05 per minute for operator service).

SAFETY

Crime is a major problem in the whole region, particularly in large cities, and all visitors should take precautions to protect themselves. Do not walk alone at night, and exercise caution even during the day. Avoid wearing flashy jewelry (even costume jewelry), and don't invite attention by wearing an expensive camera around your neck. If you are toting a handbag, wear the strap across your body; even better, wear a money belt, preferably hidden from view, under your clothing. When sitting at airports or at restaurants, especially outdoor cafés, loop your leg through the handle of your bag, or clip it around your chair—otherwise it may just quietly "walk off" when you're not looking.

Carjacking is another problem, with armed bandits often forcing drivers out of their vehicles at traffic lights, in driveways, or during a fake accident. Keep your car doors locked at all times, and leave enough space between you and the vehicle in front so you can pull into another lane if necessary. If you are confronted by an armed assailant, do not resist. Due to the number of sophisticated antihijacking and vehicle tracking devices being used, carjackers may try to force you off the road, so as to steal the car with the engine running. Alternatively, you may be forced to accompany them for some time, showing them where the hidden emergency switches are. If this happens, don't panic, scream, or otherwise draw attention to yourself. Follow their instructions very carefully, do not attempt to try to remove your valuables or other items from the car, and you've a far better chance of emerging from the experience unscathed.

Make sure that you know exactly where you're going. Purchase a good map and obtain comprehensive directions. Taking the wrong exit off a highway into a township could lead you straight to disaster. Many cities are ringed by "no-go" areas. Establish from your hotel or the locals which areas to avoid.

Never, ever visit a township or squatter camp on your own. Unemployment is rife, and obviously affluent foreigners are easy pickings. If you wish to see a township, there are reputable companies that run excellent tours and know which areas to avoid. Book yourself on one of these instead.

The countryside is less intense and crime is not as common, but always remain alert and don't let a false sense of security lead you into behaving foolishly. Avoid wandering alone in deserted areas, unless you know where you are. Most hiking trails and tourist areas are reasonably safe, but crime can and does happen anywhere.

Before your trip, check with the U.S. State Department (☎ 202/647–5225, travel.state.gov) to see if there are any current advisories about the country you are planning to visit.

SENIOR-CITIZEN TRAVEL

Senior citizens in South Africa often receive substantial discounts on admission prices and tickets, if they can show a valid pensioner's card that proves they are on a fixed income, as age itself is no indication of financial status. It doesn't hurt to ask for a discount, though.

To qualify for age-related discounts **mention your senior-citizen status up front** when booking hotel reservations (not when checking out) and before you're seated in restaurants (not when paying the bill). When renting a car ask about promotional car-rental discounts, which can be cheaper than senior-citizen rates.

➤ EDUCATIONAL PROGRAMS: **Elderhostel** (✉ 75 Federal St., 3rd floor, Boston, MA 02110, ☎ 877/426–8056, 𝔽𝔸𝕏 877/426–2166).

SHOPPING

Southern Africa is not the sort of place to shop for high-tech consumer goods, as they are quite expensive and import duties are so high that you will almost certainly get a better deal on any nonlocal goods at home.

By and large, you'll find that South Africa has more Pan-African crafts and artifacts than you will find in

Zimbabwe or Botswana. If you see a hand-painted Ghanese barbershop sign that you like in Cape Town or Johannesburg, for example, don't expect to find any others in Harare or Gaborone.

If you look around, you can find some excellent clothing buys, ranging from traditional "African chic" outfits to haute couture and including, of course, some very well made and reasonably priced outdoor goods.

SMART SOUVENIRS

Traditional arts and crafts—whether they're made in South Africa or other African countries—are better buys. Keep an eye out for Zulu baskets, Ndebele beaded aprons, Zimbabwean printed fabrics, Kuba cloth from Zaire, fetishes and masks from West Africa, and Mali mud cloth and wedding blankets.

WATCH OUT

Be wary of cheap imitations: "Ebony" carvings often achieve their black luster through the use of shoe polish. Real ebony is heavy, and you can't scratch the black off—although think hard before buying it, anyway, as wood carving is contributing to the deforestation of Africa. Be aware that ivory is freely sold in southern Africa but only to local residents, so don't be tempted to buy any, as you won't be able to get it home. You will also find (especially in Vic Falls) many small carvings from hippo tooth; if you buy these, you may need to do some smart talking to get them across borders, as it is almost indistinguishable from ivory.

WINE

Many wineries will mail your wine purchases to your home. Wine dispatched to the United States and Canada is usually sent as an "unsolicited gift" at the buyer's risk. It's not strictly legal, and if customs stops the shipment they will either make you pay customs duties or confiscate it outright. Some wine shippers in South Africa report no problems mailing wines to the United States and Canada; others report a high failure rate.

➤ SHIPPERS: **Steven Rom** (✉ Checkers Galleria Centre, 76 Regent Rd., Sea Point, South Africa, ☎ 021/439–6043, FAX 021/434–0401).

Vaughan Johnson's Wine Shop (✉ Pier Head, Dock Rd., Box 50012, Waterfront, 8002 South Africa, ☎ 021/419–2121, FAX 021/419–0040).

➤ IMPORTERS: If you don't want to take the risk, contact one of the companies in the United States and Canada that import a wide range of Cape wines: **Cape Venture Co.** (☎ 203/329–6663), **South African Wine Club** (☎ 800/504–9463), or **Maisons Marques & Domaines U.S.A.** (☎ 510/286–2010); and in Canada, **Remy Canada Inc.** (☎ 416/485–3633) or **Peter Mielzynski Agencies Ltd.** (☎ 905/820–8180).

STUDENTS IN SOUTH AFRICA

To save money, **look into deals available through student-oriented travel agencies.** To qualify you'll need a bona fide student ID card. Members of international student groups are also eligible.

➤ STUDENT IDs & SERVICES: **Council on International Educational Exchange** (CIEE, ✉ 205 E. 42nd St., 14th floor, New York, NY 10017, ☎ 212/822–2600 or 888/268–6245, FAX 212/822–2699) for mail orders only, in the U.S. **Travel Cuts** (✉ 187 College St., Toronto, Ontario M5T 1P7, ☎ 416/979–2406 or 800/667–2887) in Canada.

STA Travel (✉ 31 Riebeeck St., Cape Town, 8001, ☎ 021/418–6570, FAX 021/418–4689) specializes in youth and student travel.

➤ GREAT OPTION: One of the best ways of getting around is on the **Baz Bus** (✉ 8 Rosedene Rd., Sea Point, Cape Town 8005, ☎ 021/439–2323, FAX 021/439–2343), a budget, door-to-door bus catering especially to the needs of backpackers and going around the whole of South Africa and Swaziland, as well as to Victoria Falls and Bulawayo. You don't have to be young, but a cool attitude helps.

SMART TRAVEL TIPS A TO Z

TAXES

HOTEL

South African hotels that participate in Satour's grading system add a Tourism Promotion Levy of R1.70–R5.70 per room to the bill, depending on the establishment's star rating.

VALUE-ADDED TAX (VAT)

In South Africa, the VAT, currently a whopping 14%, is included in the price of most goods and services, including hotel accommodations and food. To get a VAT refund, foreign visitors must present their receipts (minimum of R250) at the airport and be carrying any purchased items with them or in their luggage. You must fill out Form VAT 255, available at the airport VAT refund office. Whatever you buy, **make sure that your receipt is an original tax invoice, containing the vendor's name and address, VAT registration number, and the words "tax invoice."** Refunds are given in the form of a check, which can be cashed immediately at an airport bank. If you have packed your purchases in luggage that you intend to check, be sure you visit the VAT refund desk before you go through check-in procedures. For items in your carry-on baggage, visit the refund desk in the departures hall.

TELEPHONES

The phone system in the region is pretty good, with Botswana's probably being the most reliable, but there are problems. A major one is the high cost of scrap copper, so it's not unknown for a couple of miles of telephone cable to go missing overnight, leaving large areas incommunicado—even in Johannesburg. Mobile phones, locally called cellphones, are ubiquitous and, especially in South Africa, have quite extensive coverage. Cellphones can be rented by the day, week, or longer from the airport on your arrival; contact **GSM** (☏ 021/934–4951, 011/394–8834, 031/469–2796, or 041/507–7370).

COUNTRY & AREA CODES

The country code for South Africa is 27; for Swaziland, 268; for Zimbabwe, 263; for Botswana, 267; for Namibia, 264; and for Zambia, 260.

When dialing from abroad, drop the initial 0 from local South African, Namibian, Zambian, Mozambican, and Zimbabwean area codes. Swaziland and Botswana have no area codes. When dialing a South African number from abroad, drop the initial 0 from the local area code. The country code is 1 for the United States and Canada, 61 for Australia, 64 for New Zealand, and 44 for the United Kingdom.

DIRECTORY & OPERATOR INFORMATION

In South Africa, for directory assistance dial 1023 (local) or 1025 (national).

LOCAL CALLS

In South Africa a three-minute local call costs 41¢. Calls are significantly cheaper between 7 PM and 7 AM (weekdays) and over weekends and public holidays.

Phone numbers are not standardized, so don't be surprised to find some telephone numbers with fewer digits than others in the same country. Some remote farms and lodges still use a manual exchange, which means you will have to ask the operator for the number. And many operators in remote areas speak English as a second or third language—just keep your sense of humor and you'll eventually get through. This is slowly changing; some of the numbers in this book may already be out of date, in which case call directory assistance at 1023 (local) or 1025 (national) in South Africa. You do not need to dial the area code when making a local call, unless from a mobile phone.

LONG-DISTANCE SERVICES

AT&T, MCI, and Sprint access codes make calling long distance relatively convenient, but you may find the local access number blocked in many hotel rooms. First ask the hotel operator to connect you. If the hotel operator balks ask for an international operator, or dial the international operator yourself. One way to improve your odds of getting connected to your long-distance carrier is to travel with more than one company's calling card (a hotel may block Sprint, for example, but not MCI). If all else fails call from a pay phone. **In Botswana and Swaziland, there are no access agreements to allow you to use U.S. long distance services.** Thus you will not be able to make calls using your U.S. calling card from Botswana or Swaziland.

➤ ACCESS CODES: **AT&T USA Direct** (☎ 0800/99–0123 from South Africa, 0800/110–899 from Zimbabwe). **MCI Call USA** (☎ 0800/990–011 from South Africa). **Sprint Express** (☎ 0800/990–001 from South Africa; 0800/180–280 from Botswana).

PHONE CARDS

Available in R10, R20, R50, and R100 denominations, South African phone cards are incredibly useful, saving you the hassle of juggling handfuls of coins. In addition, a digital readout tells you how much credit remains while you're talking. Telephone cards are available at newsagents, convenience stores, and Telkom (the national telephone company) offices.

PUBLIC PHONES

South Africa has two types of pay phones: coin-operated phones that accept a variety of coins and card-operated phones.

TIME

The whole of southern Africa operates on CAST (Central African Standard Time), which is two hours ahead of Greenwich Mean Time. That makes it seven hours ahead of North American eastern standard time (six hours ahead of eastern daylight time). The only exception is Namibia, which operates on Winter Time (one hour behind CAST) from 2 AM on the first Sunday of April till 2 AM on the first Sunday of September.

TIPPING

Tipping is an integral part of South African life, and tips are expected for services that you might take for granted at home. Most notable among these is when you fill up with gas; there are no self-service stations, and you should tip the attendant R2–R3 if he or she offers to clean your windshield, check your oil and water, and is generally helpful. In restaurants, the size of the tip should depend on the quality of service, but 10% is standard, unless, of course, a service charge has already been added to the bill. Give the same percentage to bartenders, taxi drivers, and tour guides. Hotel porters should receive R1.50–R2 per bag. Informal parking attendants operate in the major cities in South Africa and even in some tourist areas. Although they often look a bit seedy, they do provide a good service, so tip them a couple of rand if your car is still in one piece when you return to it.

Tipping is less common in Botswana, Swaziland, Zimbabwe, and Namibia, but it is always appreciated. Loose change or 10% is appropriate. *See* Big-Game Adventures *in* Chapter 14 for advice on tipping guides, game rangers, and trackers throughout southern Africa.

Please note that **tipping is illegal in Zambia.** If you have had really good service, you may tip the person responsible only through the manager of the hotel or lodge.

TOURS & PACKAGES

On a prepackaged tour or independent vacation everything is prearranged so you'll spend less time planning—and often get it all at a good price.

BOOKING WITH AN AGENT

Travel agents are excellent resources. But it's a good idea to collect brochures from several agencies, because some agents' suggestions may be influenced by relationships with tour and package firms that reward them for volume sales. If you have a special interest **find an agent with expertise in that area;** ASTA (☞ Travel Agencies, *below*) has a database of specialists worldwide.

Make sure your travel agent knows the accommodations and other services of the place being recommended. Ask about the hotel's location, room size, beds, and the availability of a pool, room service, or programs for children, if you care about these. Has your agent been there in person or sent others whom you can contact?

SMART TRAVEL TIPS A TO Z

Do some homework on your own, too: Local tourism boards can provide information about lesser-known and small-niche operators, some of which may sell only direct.

BUYER BEWARE

Each year consumers are stranded or lose their money when tour operators—even large ones with excellent reputations—go out of business. So **check out the operator.** Ask several travel agents about its reputation, and try to **book with a company that has a consumer-protection program.** (Look for information in the company's brochure.) In the United States, members of the National Tour Association and United States Tour Operators Association are required to set aside funds to cover your payments and travel arrangements in case the company defaults. It's also a good idea to choose a company that participates in the American Society of Travel Agent's Tour Operator Program (TOP); ASTA will act as mediator in any disputes between you and your tour operator.

Remember that the more your package or tour includes the better you can predict the ultimate cost of your vacation. Make sure you know exactly what is covered, and **beware of hidden costs.** Are taxes, tips, and transfers included? Entertainment and excursions? These can add up.

➤ TOUR-OPERATOR RECOMMENDATIONS: **American Society of Travel Agents** (☞ Travel Agencies, *below*). **National Tour Association** (NTA, ✉ 546 E. Main St., Lexington, KY 40508, ☎ 606/226–4444 or 800/682–8886). **United States Tour Operators Association** (USTOA, ✉ 342 Madison Ave., Suite 1522, New York, NY 10173, ☎ 212/599–6599 or 800/468–7862, ℻ 212/599–6744).

TRAIN TRAVEL

A trip aboard the famous **Blue Train** (✉ Box 2671, Joubert Park 2044, ☎ 011/773–7631, ℻ 011/773–7643) has long been one of the highlights of any trip to South Africa. Since the train's inception in 1923, its 24-hour passage between Cape Town and Johannesburg through the Karoo Desert has served as a standard for luxury and shameless pampering. The Blue Train has been revamped and standards have improved after dropping slightly in recent years. Rooms are now air-conditioned and have button-operated blinds and curtains, radios, and a personal mobile phone for contacting your butler/valet or making outgoing calls. The comfortably furnished lounge car offers refreshments and drinks throughout the day and is a good place to meet fellow travelers. There are two trains, the classic and the African theme, which, while maintaining the same very high standard, is decorated with African touches such as faux animal-skin furniture and somewhat more exotic uniforms for the staff. Food in the well-appointed dining car, where you can now expect silver cutlery and the crispest of linen, has also improved. Men are required to wear a jacket and tie to dinner. On the Pretoria–Cape Town route, guests are treated to champagne when the train stops in Kimberley and taken by coach on a tour of the historic diamond-mining town.

In addition to its regular run between Cape Town and Pretoria, the Blue Train does monthly trips between Pretoria and Hoedspruit in the Northern Province, where you can spend some time viewing game, and Victoria Falls in Zimbabwe and also between Cape Town and Port Elizabeth via the Garden Route. All meals and alcohol are included in the ticket price, which ranges from R3,200 for a single luxury low season between Hoedspruit and Pretoria to R12,600 for a deluxe double high season between Vic Falls and Pretoria, both one-way.

A new competitor that is earning rave reviews at the expense of the Blue Train is romantic **Rovos Rail** (✉ Box 2837, Pretoria 0001, ☎ 012/323–6052, ℻ 012/323–0843). Sixty beautifully restored Edwardian-era carriages make up three trains drawn by a steam engine on certain sections. This luxury train carries a maximum of 72 passengers, attended by up to 21 staff members, including two gourmet chefs. Regular weekly trips are run between Pretoria and Cape Town and Pretoria and Victoria Falls (both two nights). Fortnightly overnight trips are run between Cape Town and George and Pretoria to Komatipoort on the Mozambique Border, through Mpumalanga and the Northern Province, in season. Every May, a 7-day trip from Cape Town to Swakopmund (and back) is run, and in July, there is a 13-day epic from Cape Town to Dar es Salaam (and, of course, back again). Prices per person sharing range from R3,295 for a deluxe suite on the Pretoria–Komatipoort run to R16,925 for the Royal Suite on the Cape Town–Swakopmund trip, with a single occupancy supplement of 50%. The Cape Town–Dar es Salaam trip ranges from R43,900 to R53,680 with a single supplement of R12,200. The ticket covers everything, including alcohol, meals, and scheduled excursions.

Mainline Passenger Services (⊠ Box 2671, Joubert Park 2044, ☎ 011/773–2944), part of the South African rail network known as Spoornet, operates an extensive system of passenger trains connecting most major cities. Departures are usually limited to one per day, although trains covering minor routes leave less frequently. Distances are vast, so many journeys require overnight travel. The service is good and the trains safe and well maintained, but this is far from a luxury option. Traveling first class doesn't cost much more than second class but also doesn't offer much more. Basically, you'll be sharing your compartment with a maximum of three others; in second, there is a maximum of five. In practice, the second-class compartments are rarely full (except in peak season); in either case, you will be using a communal toilet and shower (if you dare). The compartments have a washbasin. Bedding can be rented. The dining car serves pretty ordinary food, but it's reasonably well cooked and inexpensive. Third class is an adventure! Spoornet has recently started a new service with much better food and slightly better service, but you still have to deal with that communal bathroom. You must reserve tickets in advance for first- and second-class accommodation, whereas third-class tickets require no advance booking. You can book up to three months in advance with travel agents, reservations offices in major cities, and at railway stations.

Namibian train travel is much the same standard as South African. Train travel in Zimbabwe is cheap and, much like Spoornet, not bad, although the communal toilets seem to get into a worse state by the end of the trip. Train travel in Botswana is also not bad, but the distances don't warrant overnight travel. **Zambian railways are best avoided,** especially between Livingstone and Lusaka, as track maintenance is somewhat erratic. Swaziland is so tiny there's not much point in catching a train. All the above options are in the budget range.

TRAVEL AGENCIES

A good travel agent puts your needs first. Look for an agency that has been in business at least five years, emphasizes customer service, and has someone on staff who specializes in your destination. In addition **make sure the agency belongs to a professional trade organization.** The American Society of Travel Agents (ASTA), with 27,000 agents in some 170 countries, is the largest and most influential in the field. Operating under the motto "Integrity in Travel," it maintains and enforces a strict code of ethics and will step in to help mediate any agent-client disputes if necessary. ASTA also maintains a Web site that includes a directory of agents. Note that if a travel agency is also acting as your tour operator, *see* Buyer Beware *in* Tours & Packages, *above.*

➤ LOCAL AGENT REFERRALS: American Society of Travel Agents (ASTA, ☎ 800/965–2782 24-hr hot line, 𝔽𝔸𝕏 703/684–8319, www.astanet. com). Association of British Travel Agents (⊠ 68–271 Newman St., London W1P 4AH, ☎ 020/7637–2444, 𝔽𝔸𝕏 020/7637–0713). Association of Canadian Travel Agents (⊠ 1729 Bank St., Suite 201, Ottawa, Ontario K1V 7Z5, ☎ 613/521–0474, 𝔽𝔸𝕏 613/521–0805). Australian Federation of Travel Agents (⊠ Level 3, 309 Pitt St., Sydney 2000, ☎ 02/

SMART TRAVEL TIPS A TO Z

9264–3299, FAX 02/9264–1085).
**Travel Agents' Association of New
Zealand** (⊠ Box 1888, Wellington
10033, ☎ 04/499–0104, FAX 04/499–
0786).

VISITOR INFORMATION

SOUTH AFRICA

For information about traveling to
and within South Africa before you
go, contact the nearest office of the
South African Tourism Board
(Satour).

➤ SOUTH AFRICAN GOVERNMENT
TOURIST OFFICES: **U.S.** (⊠ 500 5th
Ave., Suite 2040, New York, NY
10110, ☎ 800/822–5368, FAX 212/
764–1980; ⊠ 9841 Airport Blvd.,
Suite 1524, Los Angeles, CA 90045,
☎ 800/782–9772, FAX 310/641–
5812). **Canada** (⊠ 4117 Lawrence
Ave. E, Suite 2, Scarborough, Ontario, M1E 2S2, ☎ 416/283–0563,
FAX 416/283–5465). **South Africa**
(⊠ Private Bag X164, Pretoria, 0001,
☎ 012/347–0600, FAX 012/347–
6199). **U.K.** (⊠ 5–6 Alt Grove, Wim-
bledon SW19 4DZ, ☎ 0181/944–
8080, FAX 0181/944–6705).

ZIMBABWE

➤ ZIMBABWE TOURIST OFFICE: **U.S.**
(⊠ 1270 Ave. of the Americas, Suite
2315, New York, NY 10020, ☎ 212/
332–1090). **Canada** (⊠ Zimbabwe
High Commission, 332 Somerset St.,
West Ottawa, Ontario K2P 0J9, ☎
613/237–4388). **U.K.** (⊠ Zimbabwe
Tourism Office, 429 Strand, London
WC2R 05A, ☎ 171/240–6169, FAX
171/379–1167). **Zimbabwe** (⊠ Zimbabwe Tourist Authority, Box CY286
Harare, ☎ 04/75–8730 through 04/
75–8734, FAX 04/75–8712 through 04/
75–8714).

BOTSWANA

➤ DEPARTMENT OF TOURISM, MIN-
ISTRY OF COMMERCE AND INDUSTRY:
Botswana (⊠ Private Bag 0047,
Gaborone, ☎ 35–3024 or 31–3314,
FAX 30–8675). **U.S. and Canada** (⊠
3400 International Dr. NW, Suite 7M,
Washington, DC 20008, ☎ 202/244–
4990). **U.K.** (⊠ 6 Stratford Pl., Lon-
don W1N 9AE, ☎ 171/499–0031).

NAMIBIA

➤ NAMIBIAN EMBASSY: **U.S. and
Canada** (⊠ 1605 New Hampshire
Ave. NW, Washington, DC 20009,
☎ 202/986–0540, FAX 202/986–
0443). **U.K.** (⊠ 6 Chandos St., London W1MOLQ, ☎ 171/636–6244,
FAX 171/636–7594). **Namibia** (Min-
istry of Environment and Tourism,
⊠ Private Bag 13346, Windhoek,
☎ 061/284–2366, FAX 061/22–1930).

ZAMBIA

➤ ZAMBIAN NATIONAL TOURIST
BOARD: **U.S. and Canada** (⊠ 237 E.
52nd St., New York, NY 10022,
☎ 212/308–2155), FAX 212–758–
1319). **U.K.** (⊠ 2 Palace Gate, Kens-
ington, London W85NG, ☎ 171/
589–6343, FAX 171/581–1353).

SWAZILAND

➤ SWAZILAND HIGH COMMISSION: **U.S.
and Canada** (⊠ 3400 International
Dr. NW, Suite 3M, Washington, DC
20008, ☎ 202/362–6683).

All the countries listed above are
members of **RETOSA** (Regional
Tourism Organization of Southern
Africa), based in Johannesburg
(⊠ Box 7381, Halfway House, 1685,
☎ 011/315–2420, FAX 011/315–2422).

➤ U.S. GOVERNMENT ADVISORIES: **U.S.
Department of State** (⊠ Overseas
Citizens Services Office, Room 4811
N.S., 2201 C St. NW, Washington,
DC 20520, ☎ 202/647–5225 for
interactive hot line, 301/946–4400
for computer bulletin board, FAX 202/
647–3000 for interactive hot line);
enclose a self-addressed, stamped,
business-size envelope.

WEB SITES

Do **check out the World Wide Web**
when you're planning. You'll find
everything from up-to-date weather
forecasts to virtual tours of famous
cities. Fodor's Web site, www.fodors.
com, is a great place to start your on-
line travels. For more information
specifically on South Africa, visit:
www.satour.org; on Botswana,
www.gov.bw; on Swaziland, www.
mintour.gov.sz; on Namibia,
www.iwwn.com.na/namtour/

namtour.html; on Zambia, www.africa-insites.com/zambia; on Zimbabwe, www.mediazw.com.

WHEN TO GO

As southern Africa is in the southern hemisphere, its seasons are opposite to those in the northern hemisphere—it's summer there during the North American and European winter.

Peak tourist season is from November through March, when hotel prices rise dramatically and making a reservation can be difficult. The situation is exacerbated during major school holidays—especially December 1–January 15, the South African summer vacation—when South African families take to the roads in droves. Schools also have two weeks' vacation around Easter and a month in July, when the warmer parts of the region, especially Kariba, Vic Falls, Mozambique, and KwaZulu-Natal, are particularly popular. Zimbabwean winter holidays are in August.

The most popular time to visit Cape Town is from November through January, although February and March offer the best weather. Keep in mind, however, that the shoulder months of October and April can be fabulous and uncrowded. Cape winters (May–August) are notorious for cold, windy, rainy weather, but, in reality, these are miserable days interspersed with glorious sunny days that rival the best summer days in Britain. This season is known as the "secret season," during which really good deals can be had. As long as you stay for a week or more, you're bound to have at least a few days of gorgeous weather.

Much of the rest of the region receives its rain in the hot summer months, which is the worst time for watching game, as the abundant standing water enables the animals to spread out over a large area and the luxuriant new growth makes it difficult to see anything. The rains usually end in about March or April, from which point the standing water starts to dry up and the vegetation to be eaten, so game-viewing improves throughout the dry season. By October, there is usually very little standing water and vegetation cover, making game viewing excellent, although the hot, humid conditions may be a bit uncomfortable. Once the rains start, usually in November, game viewing takes a second place to bird-watching as the summer migrants arrive.

Johannesburg and the highveld enjoy glorious summers, with hot, sunny days broken by afternoon thunderstorms. Winter nights are frosty; days are generally mild and sunny but can be decidedly chilly, with rain, sleet, and even a little snow. The high-lying areas of South Africa can get snow at any time of year, although it is pretty rare.

The coastal areas of KwaZulu-Natal are warm year-round, but summers are steamy and hot, and August sees high winds buffet the coastline. The water along the KwaZulu-Natal coast is warmest in February, but it seldom dips below 17°C (65°F) at any time of year. The Drakensberg Mountains can be bitterly cold in winter, often with snow, and are dry and brown. In summer, the mountains are a bright green with new grass, and it is warm, but spectacular thunderstorms pose a real threat to hikers in that high altitude.

Southern Africa, like the rest of the world, has been experiencing erratic climate recently, and whether it's from global warming, El Niño, La Niña, or just bad luck is moot point. The bottom line is to pack good rain gear wherever you go; remember to bring layers for the colder days; and always bring shorts, T-shirts, sandals, a sun hat, and a swimsuit.

CLIMATE

The following are average daily maximum and minimum temperatures for some major cities in South Africa. For information on seasonal temperatures in the other countries covered, *see* the When to Tour sections at the beginning of the relevant chapters.

➤ FORECASTS: **Weather Channel Connection** (☎ 900/932–8437), 95¢ per minute from a Touch-Tone phone.

SMART TRAVEL TIPS A TO Z

CAPE TOWN

Jan.	79F	26C	May	68F	20C	Sept.	66F	19C
	61	16		48	9		48	9
Feb.	81F	27C	June	64F	18C	Oct.	70F	21C
	61	16		46	8		52	11
Mar.	77F	25C	July	64F	18C	Nov.	75F	24C
	57	14		45	7		55	13
Apr.	73F	23C	Aug.	64F	18C	Dec.	77F	25C
	54	12		46	8		59	15

DURBAN

Jan.	82F	28C	May	77F	25C	Sept.	73F	23C
	70	21		57	14		59	15
Feb.	82F	28C	June	73F	23C	Oct.	75F	24C
	70	21		52	11		63	17
Mar.	82F	28C	July	73F	23C	Nov.	77F	25C
	68	20		52	11		64	18
Apr.	79F	26C	Aug.	73F	23C	Dec.	81F	27C
	63	17		55	13		68	20

JOHANNESBURG

Jan.	79F	26C	May	66F	19C	Sept.	73F	23C
	59	15		45	7		50	10
Feb.	77F	25C	June	61	16C	Oct.	75F	24C
	57	14		39	4		52	11
Mar.	75F	24C	July	63F	17C	Nov.	75F	24C
	55	13		39	4		55	13
Apr.	70F	21C	Aug.	66F	19C	Dec.	77F	25C
	50	10		43	6		57	14

SKUKUZA (KRUGER NATIONAL PARK)

Jan.	91F	33C	May	82F	28C	Sept.	84F	29C
	70	21		50	10		55	13
Feb.	90F	32C	June	79F	26C	Oct.	86F	30C
	68	20		43	6		61	16
Mar.	88F	31C	July	79F	26C	Nov.	88F	31C
	66	19		43	6		64	18
Apr.	84F	29C	Aug.	81F	27C	Dec.	90F	32C
	59	15		48	9		68	20

1 DESTINATION: SOUTHERN AFRICA

THE RAINBOW NATION

MY FAMILY first came to South Africa from England three decades ago. Earlier, Nigeria had been home for seven years. And as clichéd as it might sound, once Africa gets into your blood, it's hard to deny her pull. Now it was South Africa's sunshine and opportunities that beckoned.

We were immigrants, equipped only with an old car, lots of enthusiasm, and three young children—"Not enough," the white Afrikaner Immigration official growled after we landed at Cape Town in those now seemingly long-ago apartheid days. "We need more white children." Undaunted, we set off north through the Karoo Desert for Egoli—Johannesburg, City of Gold—blissfully ignorant about the complex, stunningly beautiful country that we would settle in.

Today, in spite of South Africa's ongoing problem with crime and violence, we still wouldn't choose to live anywhere else. There's no room or time for Old World boredom or complacency when you can live in a country where people debate in 11 different official languages—Archbishop Desmond Tutu christened us "the Rainbow Nation" for our racial and cultural diversity and the name has stuck—and that has the world's newest and most liberal constitution. It's difficult to imagine a country more vibrant and alive than this.

The whole world knows of our infamous past. Our ground-breaking Truth and Reconciliation Commission continues to ensure that we don't forget it. Although so much heartbreak, trauma, truth, and lies have been revealed at the public hearings, most of us firmly believe that to know the past is part of the process of understanding it, coming to terms with it, and moving on. Amazingly, there's little bitterness or racial conflict—a lead set by our first democratically elected president, Nelson Mandela, arguably one of the 20th century's most respected leaders.

His successor, seasoned diplomat Thabo Mbeki, although lacking Mandela's charisma, is well respected at home and abroad and seems intent on keeping South Africa afloat economically, politically, and morally. He has taken a strong stand against corruption, aiming for "discipline, hard work and effectiveness, not popularity." The public comforts itself with the knowledge that when yet another corruption scandal erupts, at least these days the corruption—although not dealt with as firmly and swiftly as it would like—is "transparent." Transparency is one of the buzz words of the new government—it is determined not to copy the cloak-and-dagger "dirty tricks" tactics of the former Nationalist governments.

So what's the mood in today's country? South Africans who think positively know that the honeymoon is over and there's a long road ahead but that good things will come to those who wait. Unfortunately, thousands of white professionals have emigrated, because of perceived fears of South Africa's becoming yet another stereotypical African country spiraling into a potential one-party state, and fears for their children's educational prospects in government schools bursting at the seams.

Those of us who have stayed take comfort in the burgeoning economy and remind ourselves that we live in the newest, most liberal democracy in the world—and the one with the best weather in the world.

Blacks and whites mix freely in public places, and the only apartheid now is that between the haves and the have-nots—as with anywhere else in the world. We're a noisy, vociferous lot who argue our opinions wherever and whenever anybody will listen—opinions not hidden or submerged by hypocrisy or warm, fuzzy euphemisms but discussed openly and up-front in the media, in schools and universities, in the home, and wherever people are gathered together. Change is still the keynote of the new South Africa. And energy, buzz, vibrations (both good and bad) permeate the air. Friends of mine, back from two years in Canada, are delighted to be home. In South Africa, they claim, you'll never be bored, there's no chance here of the bland leading the bland.

As a foreigner in South Africa, you'll meet with tremendous hospitality. A friend from Boston, visiting the Kimberley Mine Museum, ended up spending a few days in this historic and fascinating city with a local schoolmaster and his family. Talk, talk, talk to everyone you can—South Africans love to talk about their country. Other than Ireland, I can't think of a place where people are so keen and ready to discuss their country, warts and all, with such honesty and heady enthusiasm. Sure, we know we have problems, but we are the Rainbow Nation and proud of it.

So welcome, then, to one of the most beautiful and diverse countries on earth, where sea, mountains, rolling plains, mighty rivers, deep gorges and the bush, with its big game, more than 800 birds, and amazing biodiversity will hook you from day one. Your first visit certainly won't be your last.

— By Kate Turkington

WHAT'S WHERE

Johannesburg

A mile high, South Africa's largest city sprawls across the highveld plateau, its soaring skyscrapers giving way to endless suburbs. Johannesburg was built—literally and figuratively—on gold, and the relentless pursuit of wealth has imbued it with a pulsing energy. Much of the anti-apartheid struggle was played out in the dusty black townships ringing the city, and a tour of Soweto and the city center will give you a feel for the new South Africa. Johannesburg itself is an unlovely city, with few attractions to hold you long. Arrange a trip down a gold mine, and then take yourself north to Pretoria, the genteel capital of South Africa, or to Sun City, a glittering fantasyland of casinos, golf, water rides, and big-game adventure.

Mpumalanga and Kruger National Park

Classic Africa—the Africa of heat, thorn trees, and big game—unfolds before you in the Mpumalanga, a wild and beautiful province abutting Mozambique. The great allure here is game watching, either in famed Kruger National Park or in an exclusive private reserve. But the province has much more to offer than animals. The Drakensberg ("Dragon Mountains" in Afrikaans) divides the subtropical lowveld from the high interior plateau. Tucked away in these mountains of mists, forests, waterfalls, and panoramic views lie some of South Africa's most luxurious hotels and lodges, as well as beautiful hikes and historic gold-rush towns.

Cape Town and the Peninsula

Capetonians tend to look with pity upon those who don't have the good fortune to live in their Eden. Their attitude is understandable—Cape Town is indeed one of the world's fairest cities. Backed by Table Mountain, the city presides over a coastline of unsurpassed beauty: of mountains cascading into the sea, miles of beaches, and 17th-century wineries snoozing under giant oaks. Modern South Africa was born here, and the city is filled with historic reminders of its three centuries as the sea link between Europe and the East.

The Western Cape

This diverse region serves as the weekend playground for Capetonians. The jewel of the province is the Winelands, a stunning collection of jagged mountains, vine-covered slopes, and centuries-old Cape Dutch estates that produce some of the world's finest wine. Farther afield, the Overberg is a quiet region of farms and beach resorts that ends at Cape Agulhas, the southernmost tip of Africa. The long, lonely coastline is a marvel of nature—rocky mountains dropping sheer to the sea, pristine beaches, and towering dunes. The west coast and Namaqualand is a desolate landscape dotted with tiny fishing villages and isolated diamond mines. Every spring the semi-desert region's wildflower explosion is a nonpareil sight. Inland, the pretty towns of the Cedarberg (Cedar Mountains) and Hantam Plateau make great bases for long hikes and drives.

The Northern Cape

A rugged, lonely land, much of it with vistas of desert and semi-desert, the Northern Cape reaches across a third of South Africa and incorporates some of the country's most unforgettable travel destinations. Along the country's north-western seaboard lies Namaqualand, which each year produces a springtime paradise of wildflowers famous the world over. In the central north is the Kalahari, a harsh landscape of dunes and scrub that is home to a host of species specially adapted to desert conditions. On the province's eastern border and in the country's geographical center, lies the historic city of Kimberley, where diamonds have been mined for 130 years.

The Garden Route and Little Karoo

The Garden Route is a beautiful 208-km (130-mi) stretch of coast that takes its name from the region's year-round riot of vegetation. Here, you'll find some of South Africa's most inspiring scenery: forest-cloaked mountains, myriad rivers and streams, and golden beaches backed by thick, indigenous bush. You'll also find Plettenberg Bay, South Africa's glitziest beach resort, and Knysna, a charming town built around an oyster-rich lagoon. The Little Karoo, separated from the coast by a range of mountains, is a semi-arid region famous for its ostrich farms, turn-of-the-century "feather palaces," and the Cango Caves, one of the world's most impressive networks of underground caverns.

Durban and KwaZulu-Natal

Steamy heat, the heady aroma of spices, and a polyglot of English, Indian, and Zulu give the bustling port city of Durban a tropical feel. Some of the country's most popular bathing beaches extend north and south of the city; inland you can tour the battlefields where Boer, Briton, and Zulu struggled for control of the country. The Drakensberg are a breathtaking sanctuary of soaring beauty, crisp air, and some of the country's best hiking. In the far north, Hluhluwe-Umfolozi and several private reserves have wildlife rivaling that of Mpumalanga.

Swaziland

From the rolling hills in the northwest to the purple Lubombo Mountains in the east, Swaziland has the look of an African paradise, where you can explore crafts markets, ride horses through Ezulwini Valley, and raft the mighty Usutu River.

Zimbabwe

If you arrive in Zimbabwe from South Africa, with its mix of peoples and races, you'll notice straight away that this is black Africa. In Zimbabwe's cities life moves slowly. And of course there are the country's landscapes and wildlife: from hippos snorting in the Zambezi River to elfin klipspringer antelope bounding around the granite hills of Matobo National Park. In between are the ancient stone ruins of Great Zimbabwe, more national parks, and the world's best white-water rafting.

Botswana

Botswana itself is a natural wonder. Its variety of terrains, from vast salt pans to the waterways of the Okavango Delta to the Kalahari Desert, have diversity seldom found in such a small area. And with so little industry, you may have never seen stars as bright as this. The Kalahari Bushmen say that you can hear the stars sing—listen.

Namibia

Although all of the countries in southern African are beautiful, perhaps there's none quite as spectacularly unique as Namibia. Huge canyons, eerie desertscapes, dramatic coastlines, and Etosha National Park all vie for your attention. Hand-in-hand with some of Africa's most awesome wilderness goes a first-world infrastructure and German efficiency—the legacy of more than 100 years of colonial rule. You'll also encounter a strong sense of quiet here, as Namibia has fewer people per square mile than almost anywhere else in Africa.

Zambia

Crossing the Victoria Falls bridge from Zimbabwe to Zambia takes you a step deeper into "darkest" Africa. The roads deteriorate by the mile, and the towns and even cities are decidedly shabby. But that's the price you pay for the unending wilderness that awaits you. Here there are no fences, indeed the line between village and game park if so blurred as to be indistinct to an outsider. However, the country has a vibrant, if young, safari industry promising small camps and on the whole excellent guiding in the wild. Most camps are basic by South African standards, but creature comforts are never neglected.

PLEASURES AND PASTIMES

Beaches

South Africa has some of the finest beaches on earth—hundreds of miles of golden sands, often without a soul on them. The surf is big, and dangerous undertows and side washes are common. Beaches in major cities have lifeguards, and helicopters periodically patrol the coastline. Cape Town and the entire Western Cape have glorious beaches, but the water is extremely cold year-round, and wind can be a problem. The water is warmer along the Garden Route, with the best swimming at Plettenberg Bay. Around Durban and the resorts of KwaZulu-Natal, the water is ideal for swimming, but keep an eye out for the stinging Portuguese man-of-war (bluebottle), particularly when the wind is coming from the east. All major resort beaches in KwaZulu-Natal are protected by shark nets. For truly deserted beaches and warm water, head to Rocktail Bay Lodge in the far north of KwaZulu-Natal. For great snorkeling and diving, follow the lead of locals in Johannesburg and hop a quick flight to the deserted island beaches of Mozambique's Bazaruto Archipelago.

Big Game Adventures

Southern Africa may not have the vast herds of East Africa, but it has far more species of animals. In fact, nowhere else on the continent do wild animals enjoy better protection than in southern Africa, and nowhere do you have a better chance of seeing Africa's big game—elephant, black and white rhino, lion, buffalo, cheetah, leopard, and hippopotamus. The antelopes and smaller animals—giraffe, zebra, kudu, sable, springbok, waterbuck, impala, warthog, and predators like hyena, wild dog, bat-eared fox, and jackal—are no less fascinating than the larger animals. The experience of tracking game in a Land Rover or of walking in the wild with an armed ranger will fill you with awe for the elemental magic of the African bush. Binoculars are a must, and bring a zoom-lens for your camera if you have one.

Bird-Watching

South Africa itself ranks as one of the finest bird-watching destinations on the planet. Kruger National Park alone has recorded more than 500 different bird species, many of breathtaking beauty. Birds in Zimbabwe, Botswana, and Namibia are spectacular as well. Look for sacred ibis, a variety of eagles and falcons and vultures, red-and-yellow billed hornbills, numerous egrets and storks, and the favorite lilac-breasted roller, to name a few. The best time for bird-watching is October–April, when migrants are in residence.

Canoeing and White-Water Rafting

The world's most incredible white-water rafting is on the Zambezi River, through the gorges below Victoria Falls and Mosi-oa-Tunya. It's an adventure you won't soon forget, and no prior experience is necessary. A great canoe trek, from three to seven days long, is on the Zambezi below Lake Kariba, where the water meanders between Zimbabwe and Zambia, afloat with hippos and crocs under the distant Zambezi Escarpment.

Cricket

White South Africans are crazy about cricket—during international matches, you'll often find crowds gathered in front of the windows of electronics stores watching the action. These international competitions, known as test matches, are played against teams from England and former colonies like India, the West Indies, and Australia. A one-day test match is as riveting as anything baseball can produce. The longer five-day test matches involve subtle nuances of strategy that will confound—and probably bore—anyone not born to the game. South Africa's provinces also compete against each other in the annual Castle Cup. A major push is under way to introduce cricket into black communities, but it remains an essentially white sport.

Dining

South Africa won't unseat France anytime soon from its culinary throne. But there are three bright spots that you should keep in mind. The first is the abundance of fresh seafood, from plump Knysna oysters to enormous Mozambiquean prawns to the Cape's magnificent clawless lobsters, known as crayfish. The second is the country's love affair with Indian cuisine, first brought to South Africa by Indian laborers in the 19th century. Samosas and curries appear on almost every menu, and

Durban's bunny chow is a fast-food curry-filled loaf of bread. Third, Cape Malay represents South Africa's own cuisine, a centuries-old blend of recipes brought by early Dutch settlers and slaves transported from the Dutch East Indies. Most evident in the Cape, the cuisine is characterized by mild, slightly sweet curries and the use of aromatic spices.

A brief glossary of cooking terms:

Biltong. An integral part of South African life, biltong is air-dried meat, made of everything from beef to kudu. Unlike jerky, it's not smoked. Strips of meat are dipped in vinegar, rolled in salt and spices, and hung up to dry. You can buy it in strips or ready-cut into bite-size chunks.

Bobotie. A classic Cape Malay dish consisting of delicately spiced ground beef or lamb topped with a savory custard.

Boerewors. Afrikaans for farmer's sausage (pronounced "*boor*-ah-vorse"), this coarse, flavorful sausage has a distinctive spiciness. It's a standard feature at *braais*.

Braai. Short for *braaivleis* (grill meat), a braai is the South African equivalent of a barbecue—and a way of life. South Africans consume enormous amounts of meat, and a braai invariably consists of more than a hamburger thrown on the grill. Expect lamb chops, boerewors (☞ *above*), chicken, steak, and beer, beer, beer.

Bredie. Bredie is a slow-cooked stew, made with everything from meat to water lilies.

Line fish. This is the generic restaurant term for fish caught with a pole, as opposed to a net, and the assumption is that quality is better as a result. Kingklip is one very common and tasty linefish.

Pap. Also known as *putu*, pap (pronounced "puhp") is a maize-meal porridge that is a staple for many black South Africans. At braais, you may find it served as an accompaniment to boerewors, topped with stewed tomato and onion.

Peri-Peri. Based on the searing hot piri-piri chile, peri-peri sauce was introduced by Portuguese immigrants from neighboring Mozambique. There are as many recipes as there are uses for this tasty condiment and marinade. Some recipes are tomato-based while others use garlic, olive oil, and brandy.

Potjiekos. This is another type of stew (pronounced "*poy*-key-koss"), simmered in a three-legged wrought-iron cooking pot. Visitors to private game lodges are likely to sample impala potjiekos at least once during their stay.

Sadza. In Zimbabwe, this is the staple corn mash served with stew and vegetables.

Sosaties. In this South African version of a kebab, chunks of meat are marinated in Cape Malay spices and grilled.

Fishing

South Africans are among the most avid anglers in the world. During peak holidays, the long coastline is lined with surf-casters trying for everything from cob to stumpnose, rock cod, shad, blacktail, and moonfish. Trout-fishing in the Natal Midlands and Mpumalanga Drakensberg is also a major draw. In the Okavango Delta and all along the Zambezi River in Zimbabwe you can experience the thrill of a lifetime—tiger fishing. Aptly named, the tiger fish is an incredibly strong fighter, with jaws like a bear trap. They make bass look like blue-gills.

Flora

South Africa's floral wealth is astounding. Many small parks in South Africa support more plant species than the entire British Isles. Nowhere is this blessing of nature more evident than in the Cape, home to the smallest and richest of the world's six floral kingdoms. More than 8,500 species of plants grow in the province, of which 5,000 are endemic. Much of the Cape vegetation consists of *fynbos* (pronounced "*feign*-boss"), hardy, thin-leaved plants ideally suited to the Cape environment. Proteas, including the magnificent king protea, are examples of fynbos.

Golf

The success of local heroes like Gary Player, David Frost, and Ernie Els confirms that golf in South Africa has a fervid following. The country has dozens of championship-quality courses, many designed by Gary Player himself. The stretch of coastline extending south from Durban has gone as far as to christen itself "the Golf Coast." You can play on almost any course in the country, and greens fees are low compared with those in the United States. Don't expect golf carts—a caddy carries your clubs—and the pace of play tends to be faster than it is stateside.

Hiking

Hiking is a major activity in South Africa, and you'll find trails almost everywhere you go. Perhaps the most exciting hikes are the wilderness trails conducted by rangers in Kruger National Park and Hluhluwe-Umfolozi, where hikers sleep out in the bush and spend the day tracking animals, learning about the ecology, and becoming familiar with the ways of the wild. The country's most famous route is the Otter Trail, a five-day hike that runs through pristine wilderness along the coast of the Garden Route. More traditional hikes, ranging in length from a couple of hours to a week, wend through the scenic splendors of the Drakensberg, the Cedarberg in the Cape, or Blyde River Canyon in Mpumalanga.

Hiking is less an opportunity in Zimbabwe and Botswana—unless you have an armed guide with you—because the national parks are filled with predators and dangerous animals like buffalo, rhinoceros, hippopotamus, and elephant. One exception to this is Matobo National Park, where you can climb around on the rocks at leisure while the animals are in a separate reserve bordering the park.

Rugby

Although long associated with white Afrikaners, rugby became a unifying force in South Africa during the 1995 Rugby World Cup, when South Africa's "Springboks" beat the New Zealand "All Blacks" in the final, sparking a nationwide celebration among all races. Except for standouts like Chester Williams, rugby is still a largely white sport and inspires a devotion bordering on religion. In addition to a series of international matches staged each year, the rugby calendar is notable for the Currie Cup, played to decide the best provincial team in the country.

Surfing

In the cult movie *Endless Summer,* globetrotting surfers discovered the perfect wave at Cape St. Francis, near Port Elizabeth. South Africa *is* one of the major surfing countries in the world, with South Africans figuring prominently on the professional circuit. Durban is probably the center of wave mania, hosting a series of international competitions each year; other great surfing spots include Port Elizabeth and Plettenberg Bay. The beaches around Cape Town and up the West Coast (Elands Bay, particularly) are famous, too, although you need a wet suit to survive the cold water.

Wine

Forgotten during the years of international sanctions, South African wines are only now getting the recognition they deserve. Visitors to South Africa will be delighted by the quality and range of wines available, including Pinotage, a uniquely South African blend of pinot noir and cinsault grapes (cinsault is known in South Africa as hermitage). Equally appealing are the low, low prices: Expect to pay no more than $10 for a superior bottle of wine. Generally speaking, South African reds tend to be a shade less refined than the whites, although some winemakers are recognizing this and making softer cabernets that drink better when young. Among the whites, sauvignon blanc and riesling are very well made. Some of the best results are in the country's ports.

FODOR'S CHOICE

Special Moments

South Africa

★ **A sunset picnic atop Table Mountain, Cape Town.** Pack a bottle of chilled Cape wine, and good bread and cheese, and take the cable car to the summit, where views stretch forever and sunset never quits. Warning: This is *extremely* romantic.

★ **Walking in wildflowers in spring, Namaqualand.** "The Garden of the Gods" is an apt epithet for the annual wildflower spectacular, when the drab desert hillsides explode in a rainbow of colors.

★ **Watching whales at Hermanus.** From July to November, whales make their annual procession up the coast of South Africa. From the cliff-top walkways of Hermanus, you look straight down on these graceful behemoths.

★ **Hiking at Cathedral Peak, Drakensberg.** The awe-inspiring beauty of the mountains around Cathedral Peak makes it a hiker's dream, with dozens of walks and trails that tackle the surrounding peaks or disappear into hidden gorges and valleys. Take a cooling dip in a mountain stream, search for ancient Bushman paintings, or just drink in the unbelievable views.

⭐ **A game drive in Sabi Sand Game Reserve.** Few things in life are more thrilling than trailing a pride of lions through the bush in an open Land Rover. And nowhere are you more likely to see this spectacle than in Sabi Sands, the country's foremost private game reserve.

Zimbabwe

⭐ **Great Zimbabwe National Monument.** The stone ruins of this once-great citadel bring to mind the pre-European might of Africa, a continent of powerful kingdoms and trade routes that stretched across this vast continent.

⭐ **Twilight on the Zambezi River, Mana Pools.** If the quiet water lazing past and the Zambian mountains across the river weren't enough, you might have a band of elephants lope by your camp to get to the river for an evening drink.

⭐ **White-water rafting on the Zambezi River, below Victoria Falls.** A white-water trip down one of Africa's great rivers is a nonstop roller-coaster ride of thrills and spills, with the added grandeur and drama of the surrounding landscape.

Botswana

⭐ **Messing about in a mokoro.** Glide silently with your solitary, skillful poler through the crystal-clear waters of the Okavango Delta. It will be a moment of peace that will return to you long after you've left the Delta and Africa behind.

⭐ **Sunset on the Chobe river.** Take to the water—in a canoe, a motorboat, or open-sided cruise boat—to view the great elephant and buffalo herds silhouetted against flaming pink, red, and orange skies as they come down to drink. Sunsets are spectacular on this broad, beautiful, quintessentially African river.

Namibia

⭐ **Etosha National Park.** Choose a waterhole to call your own at this vast, dry park and then wait for a close-up view as herds of animals come to drink right in front of you.

⭐ **Sossusvlei.** Watch the sun rise or begin to set over the highest and possibly most beautiful sand dunes in the world. To watch the colors change from pale honey to amber, rose, russet and deep pink is a memorable—and spiritual—experience.

⭐ **The Skeleton Coast.** Experience the rugged, untamed beauty of this dangerous coast, with its shipwrecks, rolling fogs, and array of unique flora and fauna, one of the last true wilderness areas of the world.

Zambia

⭐ **Bungee Jumping, Livingstone.** Take your life in your hands and throw your body off the Victoria Falls bridge. It's 100 meters down the Batoka Gorge: some say it's the ultimate kick, some say it's madness, but you'll never know till you try it.

⭐ **Walking safari in South Luangwa National Park.** Deep into the bush, far from any semblance of civilization, these walking trails are considered by many to be the ultimate wildlife experience.

Dining

South Africa

⭐ **Bosman's, Paarl.** Superb Continental cuisine and peerless service make dinner at this elegant Winelands restaurant in the famous Grand Roche Hotel an affair to remember. *$$$$*

⭐ **Buitenverwachting, Cape Town.** A gorgeous, historic winery provides the backdrop for the best food in the Cape, a mouthwatering blend of Continental savoir faire and the freshest Cape ingredients. Simply not to be missed. *$$$$*

⭐ **Cybele Forest Lodge, Kiepersol.** Traditional five-course dinners, prepared with flair and skill, make a trip to this cozy sanctuary in the hills well worthwhile. *$$$$*

⭐ **Linger Longer, Johannesburg.** When goose-liver pâté sets you on cloud nine before you even reach main courses of crisped duckling or boned loin of lamb with garlic and mustard, this is, without a doubt, Johannesburg's finest. *$$$$*

⭐ **Royal Grill, Durban.** This lovely restaurant is a standard-bearer of culture in Durban, a reminder of a grander, more gracious age. Delicate Continental cuisine complements its turn-of-the-century elegance. *$$$$*

⭐ **Artists' Café, Sabie.** Eccentric, uneven, but ever delightful, this Italian spot hides in an old railway station in the mountain mists of Mpumalanga. $$

⭐ **Muisbosskerm, Lambert's Bay.** Traditional Afrikaner food and alfresco dining on the beach are the draws of this West Coast favorite, where you watch seafood being cooked on open fires and in huge black pots. It's rustic, beautiful, and a lot of fun. $$

Lodging

South Africa

⭐ **Mount Nelson, Cape Town.** The grande old dame of Cape Town, this historic hotel has been the place to see and be seen in Cape Town for nearly a century. $$$$

⭐ **Palace of the Lost City, Sun City.** For sheer, unadulterated extravagance, you can't beat this fantastic and fantastical hotel, built to resemble an ancient African palace. No expense has been spared, and the results are breathtaking. $$$$

⭐ **Arniston Hotel, Waenhuiskrans.** In a remote Cape Malay fishing village on a coastline of towering dunes and crystal water, this is one of South Africa's great beach retreats. $$$

⭐ **Simunye Pioneer Settlement, Melmoth.** Nowhere do you come closer to traditional Zulu culture than at this remote luxury lodge. Horses carry you in, and there's no electricity, but it's an unforgettable, magical experience—a rare opportunity to meet South African blacks one-on-one. $$$

Private Game Lodges

South Africa

⭐ **Londolozi Tree Camp, Sabi Sands.** This small lodge does almost everything right, from rooms of unmatched elegance to superb cuisine and game viewing. A class act all the way. $$$$

⭐ **Phinda Forest Lodge, Zululand.** Hidden in the green world of a sand forest, this elegant lodge uses glass instead of walls to make you feel like you're living outside. The effect is startling and magnificent, as are the animal watching and range of activities. $$

⭐ **Tanda Tula, Timbavati.** You sleep under canvas, but luxury is the name of the game at this super bush camp. Enjoy en-suite bathrooms, comfy beds, and tasteful furnishings while listening to lions roar outside your tent. $$

⭐ **Nottens Bush Camp, Sabi Sands.** Hurricane lanterns, rustic cabins, and down-home hospitality give you a real taste of life in the bush. Don't come for the game, but the sheer thrill of being in Africa. $

⭐ **Rocktail Bay Lodge, Maputaland.** With miles of empty beaches, giant turtles, dune forests—nothing but nature as far as the eye can see—this tiny lodge is one of the most special places in the country. $

Zimbabwe

⭐ **Matetsi Game Lodges, near Victoria Falls.** The last word on safari style in Zimbabwe, the near-perfection of Matetsi's two lodges—one on a dry river bed, the other on the banks of the Zambezi—are matched by service both in the bush and in camp. $$$$

⭐ **Ruckomechi Camp, Mana Pools.** The Zambezi River coursing by on one side, fertile terraces reaching back to thick woodlands, and the country's finest wildlife make time spent at Ruckomechi an African idyll. $$$$

Botswana

⭐ **Camp Okavango, Okavango Delta.** In the heart of one of the world's most beautiful and pristine wilderness areas, this tented camp is the epitome of charm, elegance, and grace. $$$$

⭐ **Jack's Camp, Makgadikgadi Pans.** At the only desert camp in the harshly mesmerizing Kalahari, venture into the impenetrable Makgadikgadi salt pans on four-wheel-drive quad bikes, search for Stone Age implements where no one may have set foot for eons, and sleep out under the desert stars. $$$$

⭐ **Kwando Camp, Chobe area.** The Kwando wildlife experience captures the essence of Botswana—ancient, immense, and unspoiled. With only two camps of six tents apiece, you are guaranteed exclusivity and privacy as you watch wall-to-wall big game in a half-million acres of uncharted wilderness. $$$$

Namibia

⭐ **Wilderness Damaraland Camp, Damaraland.** From your comfortable walk-in tent look out over a landscape of awesome craggy beauty formed by millions of years of unending geological movement. *$$$$*

⭐ **Ongava Lodge, Etosha National Park.** Set on the southern boundary of Etosha, this luxurious and beautifully sited lodge has its own surrounding game reserve as well as its own entrance into Etosha. *$$$$*

Zambia

⭐ **Tongabezi, Livingstone area.** Colonial finesse meets arcadian Africa here on the bank of the mighty Zambezi River. Choose the Tree House, Bird House, or Honeymoon suite for the most romantic and breathtaking bush accommodation in Africa. Then enjoy a game of lawn tennis followed by gin and tonics and champagne. *$$$$*

FESTIVALS AND SEASONAL EVENTS

South Africa's top seasonal events are listed below. Contact the South African Tourism Board (Satour) or provincial tourist organizations for exact dates and further information.

SUMMER

EARLY JAN.➤ The 17-day **Cape Coon Carnival** celebrates the New Year in grand style, as thousands of coloreds (the South African term for people of mixed Malay, black, and/or European descent) dressed in bright costumes take to the streets of Cape Town to sing and dance.

AUTUMN

APR.➤ The **Two Oceans Marathon** draws 8,000 runners for perhaps the most scenic race in the world, a grueling 56-km (35-mi) course that circumnavigates part of the Cape Peninsula, including the dizzying heights of Chapman's Peak Drive.

WINTER

JUNE➤ The **Comrades Marathon** is an agonizing, 80-km (50-mi) double marathon and South Africa's most famous sporting event. The race, run between Pietermaritzburg and Durban, wends through the glorious scenery of the Valley of a Thousand Hills.

JUNE–JULY➤ The **sardine run** occurs every year, when huge shoals of these small fish migrate up the south coast of KwaZulu-Natal. Men, women, and children race into the water, using whatever's at hand—buckets, nets, even clothing—to capture the slippery fish.

JULY➤ The **Durban July** is the country's biggest horse race and fashion love-fest, where women race-goers compete to wear the most outrageous, glamorous attire.

JULY➤ The **Durban Tattoo,** a 17-year tradition, is a military pageant filled with music, color, pomp, and ceremony.

JULY➤ The **Gunston 500 Surfing Championships** in Durban draw the world's best to compete in the South African leg of the international surfing circuit.

JULY➤ The **National Arts Festival** in Grahamstown is the country's most famous celebration of the arts, a wild and wacky 10-day extravaganza showcasing the best of South African theater, film, dance, music, and art.

SPRING

AUG.–SEPT.➤ The **wildflowers of Namaqualand and the West Coast** are one of nature's great spectacles, with bright spring blooms emerging in their millions from the seemingly barren semidesert. Several of the region's towns hold major flower festivals.

AUG.–NOV.➤ The annual **whale migration** along the Western Cape coast of the Overberg brings southern right whales, humpback whales, and Bryde's whales close to shore, giving even landlubbers a great view of these graceful leviathans.

OCT.➤ Purple **jacaranda blossoms** blanket the pleasant capital city of Pretoria, whose quiet streets are lined with these elegant trees.

2 JOHANNESBURG

Vast in size and in human ambition, Johannesburg is built on gold, and the relentless pursuit of wealth has imbued it with a pulsing energy. Much of the country's anti-apartheid struggle was played out in the dusty black townships ringing the city, and a tour of Soweto and the city center will give you a feel for the new South Africa. Arrange a trip down a gold mine, and then take yourself north to Pretoria, the genteel capital of South Africa, or to Sun City, a glittering fantasyland of casinos, golf, water rides, and big-game adventure.

By Andrew
Barbour

Updated by
David Bristow

JOHANNESBURG IS THE LARGEST CITY in sub-Saharan Africa—a modern, bustling metropolis that powers the country's economy. It is the center of a vast urban-industrial complex that covers most of the province of Gauteng ("*cowteng*"—the "place of gold" in Xhosa language). Home to more than 6 million people, it sprawls across the featureless plains of the mile-high highveld, spawning endless suburbs that threaten even Pretoria, more than 50 km (30 mi) distant. It feels like Los Angeles in the veld, and most visitors leave almost as quickly as they arrive.

Jo'burg, as it is known, owes its existence to vast underground riches. Although substantial deposits were recorded as early as 1881, gold was officially discovered here in 1886 by an Australian, George Harrison, who stumbled upon a surface deposit while prospecting on the Witwatersrand (White Water Ridge). Unknown to him, he was standing atop the world's richest gold reef, and his discovery sparked a gold rush unrivaled in history. Gold remains the lifeblood of Johannesburg, and the mines that ring the city now delve more than 3 km (2 mi) into the earth to extract the precious yellow metal.

It's difficult to overstate the impact of these goldfields on the development of Johannesburg and modern South Africa. In 1899, Britain engineered a war with the Boer republics just to get its hands on them, and the entire cultural and political fabric of black South Africa has been colored by gold. During the course of the last century, British and Irish fortune hunters, many of whom became wealthy mining magnates and settled in today's Parktown suburb, together with millions of blacks from South Africa, Mozambique, Zimbabwe, and Botswana, made the long journey to eGoli (a Zulu name meaning "the place of gold") to work in the mines. Forced to live in all-male hostels far from their families, the black mine workers developed a distinct mine culture that they took with them when they returned to their villages. Go to a wedding in a remote corner of Zululand, and you'll notice that traditional dancers keep their arms and legs close to their bodies, a dance style that developed from necessity in mining hostels' narrow, overcrowded corridors. Today, this has evolved into the stamping, rhythmic "gumboot dancing."

More than anything else, gold has brought about the urbanization—and politicization—of the black population. People follow money, and Johannesburg became a magnet for hundreds of thousands of unemployed rural blacks. By the start of World War II, huge squatter camps—the precursors of townships like Soweto (an abbreviation for "southwestern townships")—had sprouted on the periphery of the city. By the 1960s, township poverty and overcrowding had become the kindling onto which South Africa's hated apartheid legislation poured gasoline. In June 1976, police fired on Soweto students protesting the use of Afrikaans in schools, and the townships burst into flame. More than 1,000 people lost their lives in the year of rioting that followed. Ten years later the townships were ungovernable, and the country began its slow movement toward civil war.

Now, under South Africa's first democratic government, the word is out throughout Africa about job opportunities, and blacks continue to pour into the city. And like the first miners who rushed to stake their claims here, they have gold fever. Everyone, it seems, is out to make a buck. The sad truth, however, is that there's not enough to go around as the masses continue to flood in, with overcrowding and so-called squatter camps being the unfortunate result. Nevertheless, the city thrives on an invisible energy, an explosive combination of need, greed, and ambition. It's no surprise that Johannesburg moves faster than any other city on the continent.

Very little of the city's past—white or black—has survived this single-minded pursuit of money. Johannesburg builds constantly, paving over the unsightly cracks of history. Even the old mine tailings, the very symbols of the city's raison d'être, are rapidly disappearing. New methods for extracting gold have made it profitable to reprocess these familiar yellow mountains. From a traditional traveler's perspective, Johannesburg is a bust, which is why most visitors spend a night here after their flight and then head straight to more scenic locales.

It would be a mistake to pass through Johannesburg, though, and not tour Soweto or see different aspects of the city, for they provide glimpses of the country's future. Downtown, amid the concrete canyons of the country's financial heart, a new South Africa is emerging, one previously hidden in the townships: The sidewalks are suddenly alive with vendors hawking vegetables, young women ladling out *pap* (maize meal) and sauce, and herbalists dispensing *muthi* (traditional medicine). At the same time, the high-rise bastions of the city's "old money" are being vacated and boarded up one by one, or being left to fall into disrepair.

Most businesses have now relocated to the affluent northern suburbs, most notably Sandton; it's difficult to find even a decent coffee stand in downtown Johannesburg these days. The trend bears an uncanny resemblance to the collapse of America's inner cities. The major rap against the city center is violent crime, and there *is* a good chance of being mugged, or worse. Do what you have to—travel in a group, hire a bodyguard, or just don't carry any valuables—but at least take a look downtown. If you restrict yourself to the affluent northern suburbs, you might as well have booked a flight to New Jersey.

Less than an hour north of Johannesburg lies Pretoria, the country's pleasant capital. Though it was once a bastion of hard-line Afrikanerdom, the town now has a refreshing cosmopolitan breeze blowing through the streets. In addition to several historic buildings, Pretoria is most famous for its jacaranda trees, whose purple blossoms blanket the city in September and October. Like Johannesburg, Pretoria lies in the tiny province of Gauteng, a conurbation on the highveld, 6,000 ft above sea level. You have to travel 90 minutes beyond the borders of Gauteng to reach Sun City, an entertainment and gambling resort set amid the arid beauty of North West province. You'll find Las Vegas–style hotels, championship golf courses, and water rides, as well as Pilanesberg, a pocket-size national park covering an ancient, collapsed volcanic caldera.

If you travel northwest of Johannesburg and Pretoria, you'll reach the wonderful outdoor playground of the Magaliesberg hills, where the countryside is bisected by spectacular, deep gorges. The area is home to baboons, monkeys, small antelope, and a wide variety of birds. For the wild at heart who want to get away from city limits, the Magaliesberg is definitely the place to go. You can take a hike or explore the area's numerous *kloofs* (gorges) and rock faces, visit delightful roadside stalls, admire the scenic vistas across Hartebeesport Dam, and explore country pubs or tea gardens.

Caution: For information on personal safety, *see* Safety *in* Smart Travel Tips A to Z.

Pleasures and Pastimes

Arts and Crafts

Partly as a result of a recession, Johannesburg has spawned several delightful arts-and-crafts markets. Most are open on weekends, and you can pick up some good bargains. Try the Rooftop Market at Rosebank Mall on Sundays, when crowds meander past bright pottery, leather goods, bonsai, and clothing alongside tables of homemade breads, cheeses, cakes, and *biltong* (jerky). The sidewalks outside are chock-a-block with merchandise from all over the continent, the best of which are the authentic curios from West Africa. The largest flea market in Johannesburg is held Sunday on Bruma Lake, just east of the city center. Or head into the countryside on Johannesburg's northwestern side on the first weekend of every month, when the region's creative talent hosts the wonderful Crocodile River Ramble. Drive down farm roads to visit the galleries and studios of artists, sculptors, potters, woodworkers, and others.

Dining

Unlike Cape Town, Johannesburg has no cuisine of its own. What it does have is an array of first-class restaurants serving cuisine from all over the world, including some of the country's finest French and Italian eateries. Some restaurants prepare South African favorites. Surprisingly, seafood in Jo'burg restaurants is often better than what you find down at the coast. Most restaurants lie in the northern suburbs and are accessible only by car. For less expensive food, the area has its share of pizzerias, steak houses, and fast-food chains. The wonderful weather allows ample opportunities to enjoy sidewalk cafés in Rosebank, Melville, and Sandton Square. For a description of South African culinary terms, *see* Pleasures & Pastimes *in* Chapter 1. For price ranges, *see* Dining *in* Smart Travel Tips A to Z.

Hiking

Out of town, the Melville Koppies, near the suburb of Northcliff, has good places to walk—which are enhanced by the company of a member of the botanical society on the third weekend of every month. Hikers and climbers revel in the Magaliesberg region, a magnificent geologic fault that runs northwest of Johannesburg between Rustenburg and Pretoria. Most resorts here have a network of walking trails; you can also explore several exquisite kloofs with the local hiking and mountain clubs. The Rustenburg Nature Reserve, at the western extreme of the Magaliesberg Range, has an overnight backpacking trail with wild, though not dangerous, game and splendid vegetation and scenery.

Lodging

When you are choosing a hotel in Johannesburg, your most important consideration should be location. Almost all of the main hotels in the CBD have closed down and been replaced by new ones in the northern suburbs. These tend to be a great deal safer, with easy access to shopping malls, movie houses, and restaurants. Rosebank and Sandton are rapidly developing into major commercial centers. For price ranges, *see* Lodging *in* Smart Travel Tips A to Z.

EXPLORING JOHANNESBURG

The city is extremely spread out, and although the major centers tend to be laid out on an easy gridwork of streets, suburban areas often consist of roads running at odd angles. Get yourself a good street map if you want to become fully acquainted with as many areas of Johannesburg as possible.

Downtown Johannesburg's high crime rate deters inner-city investment. Many of the finer shops and restaurants have closed, their owners migrating northward. A brief tour will nevertheless help you get acquainted with the city—and the country's odd First World–Third World mix in the city center, where the two often exist cheek-by-jowl. You'll find more evidence of this juxtaposition when you head west to Newtown and the Oriental Plaza, an eclectic mélange of history and people, in which race matters little in the struggle to adapt to a rapidly changing South Africa. Or you can head northeast to the Afro-Bohemian enclave of Yeoville and the once trendy, but now sleazy, Rockey Street. Northwest of the city center is Melville, the currently trendy area.

In the northern suburbs, you'll find fantastic chrome-and-glass shopping malls encompassing luxury goods and pleasant restaurants in underground courts. You can go to movies and shop long after dark here—and your car will probably still be in the parking lot when you're ready to leave. In chic districts like Rosebank and Melville, the mood alternates between sleepy suburbia and trendy vitality.

Though Johannesburg is rarely associated with the great outdoors, it has its share of pleasant parks and nature reserves hugging the outskirts of the city. In the outer areas it's possible to envision how the inland plateau must have appeared to the first settlers in the region. Beyond this, encircled by cities, platinum mines, and the old Bophuthatswana homeland, lies the Magaliesberg region. Still largely unspoiled, it is a haven from the busy city for many—a place where it's still possible to see wildlife up close.

Pretoria, the Jacaranda City, is generally warmer and more wholesome than its up-country cousin. Leafy avenues crisscross peaceful suburbs, and much of its cultural heritage remains intact, preserved in museums and national monuments. It's altogether quieter, gentler, and more gracious than Johannesburg.

Great Itineraries

You won't need a great deal of time to explore the area. If you don't intend to go beyond city limits, two days is probably sufficient. If you want to look at areas beyond Johannesburg, such as Pretoria, the Magaliesberg, or Sun City, allow yourself at least five days.

Johannesburg sprawls, and sights can be some distance from one another. Buses are not reliable, and many places you'll be visiting don't have taxi stands, so it's a good idea to rent a car. Try to arm yourself with a detailed map of the city beforehand. Automobile Association maps and those published by Map Studio are generally excellent. They are available at most bookstores.

The three tours that follow these itineraries combine driving and walking. You may want to create your own tour by choosing a few sights from all three.

Numbers in the text correspond to numbers in the margin and on the Johannesburg map.

IF YOU HAVE 2 DAYS

If you are adventurous and are comfortable in urban areas, you may enjoy exploring downtown Johannesburg on foot, taking in sights such as the City Hall and Johannesburg Library. (The city center can be dangerous—keep your wits about you at all times and avoid carrying cameras and looking like a tourist.) Continue northwest into Braamfontein and see the **Gold Mining Statue** ⑧ at the top end of Rissik Street. It's a longish but relatively pleasant walk through Braam-

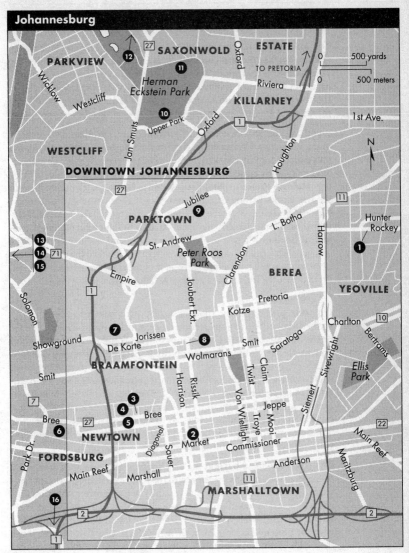

Johannesburg

City Hall, **2**

Gertrude Posel
Gallery, **7**

Gold Mining
Statue, **8**

Gold Reef City, **16**

Johannesburg
Botanical Gardens
and Emmarentia
Dam, **15**

Johannesburg
Zoo, **10**

Market Theatre
Complex, **3**

Melville, **13**

Melville Koppies, **14**

Museum Afrika, **4**

Oriental Plaza, **6**

Parktown, **9**

Rockey Street, **1**

Rosebank, **12**

SA Centenary Centre
Breweries Museum, **5**

South African
National Museum of
Military History, **11**

fontein to the University of the Witwatersrand's **Senate House.** Hidden inside is the **Gertrude Posel Gallery** ⑦.

You may also wish to head south to visit the fabulous **Museum Afrika** ④ and the **Market Theatre Complex** ③, both of which will probably keep you busy for a few hours. If you've built up an appetite after sightseeing you can stop for a bite at one of the pubs or small restaurants in the complex. Farther down Bree Street, toward Fordsburg, you'll find the **Oriental Plaza** ⑥ Johannesburg's 1970s-style version of little India.

If you feel you've seen enough of Johannesburg, spend your second day in the leafy city of **Pretoria.** Start off at the **Voortrekker Monument and Museum** on the city outskirts. It's fairly easy to reach inner-city sights, as they're a lot closer together. Depending on your schedule, visit either **Melrose House** or **Paul Kruger House Museum.** If you are keen to see the works of one of the country's greatest painters, head to the **Pierneef Museum,** or if wildlife sounds better, take in the **Transvaal Museum.** Also consider driving northward to the splendid **National Zoological Gardens.** You'll probably want to spend what remains of the day here. Or head toward Arcadia to see the beautiful **Union Buildings,** from which you'll have a bird's-eye view of the city. If you missed Pierneef, drive down the hill to the **Pretoria Art Museum.**

IF YOU HAVE 4 DAYS

On your first day, visit the sights of downtown Johannesburg described above. Spend your second day exploring the northern suburbs or the northwest section of Johannesburg. (You'll need a car.) A good way to see the colonial houses on the **Parktown** ⑨ Westcliff Ridge is to reserve a tour. Allow two to three hours for the tour. Afterward, travel north via Jan Smuts Avenue to the **Johannesburg Zoo** ⑩ and **National Museum of Military History** ⑪. Then head to trendy **Melville** to explore interesting shops and enjoy a cup of coffee or an outdoor meal on 7th Street. As an alternative, go to the suburbs of **Rosebank** ⑫ or **Sandton** and spend time shopping at the Rosebank Mall or Sandton City, where you'll also find good eateries.

If you want to head beyond the city limits, make your way northwest to the **Kromdraai Conservancy** with its many excellent restaurants (including theme eateries Greensleeves and the Carnivore), and guest and game lodges. Explore the archaeological wonders of Sterkfontein Caves or the moderately pretty but somewhat overrated Wonder Cave, view game at Lion and Rhino Park, or fish at Rainbow Trout Farm. If it's the first weekend of the month, you can visit a few art galleries or pottery studios on the **Crocodile River Arts & Crafts Ramble.**

Here you have a choice: to spend the third and fourth days in the **Magaliesberg** and **Pretoria** or to go to the glitzy **Sun City** and **Pilanesberg Game Reserve** (for the latter option, skip to the seven-day itinerary, *below*).

It's a 90-minute drive from the northern suburbs to the sleepy town of **Magaliesberg.** Nearby is the Mount Grace Country House Hotel, where you can spend the night away from the city and get a jump on exploring the Magaliesberg the next day. Smaller and even more enjoyable is De Hoek Country House, a stone and timber manor in tranquil rural surrounding. From there travel down the R24 until you reach the junction onto the R560 to **Hekpoort.** You'll drive through undulating countryside filled with fruit and flower farms. The spectacular cliffs of the **Magaliesberg range** will be on your left. After a hike, continue on to the **Hartebeesport Dam,** the resort town of **Hartebeesport,** and the **Hartebeesport Cable Way,** from which you'll have a marvelous view of the surrounding area. Take the R511 back to Johannesburg.

Spend the fourth day exploring Pretoria—this will probably take the whole day, if you follow the itinerary for the second day described *in* If You Have 2 Days, *above*. Allow an hour each way for the drive between Johannesburg and Pretoria. Avoid traveling during rush hour (7 AM–8:30 AM and 4 PM–5:30 PM).

IF YOU HAVE 7 DAYS

For the first four days, follow the itinerary outlined *above*. On the fifth day, get off to an early start on the way to the **Rustenburg Nature Reserve.** Spend a few hours here, enjoying either the self-guided walk or the automobile trail. Alternatively, take two full days to do the backpacking trail through the reserve.

Then head to fantasyland: **Sun City.** Spend the rest of the day exploring the complex—don't forget to take in the fabulous Lost City. Play the slots or, if you prefer the outdoors, enjoy the water rides and manmade beach at the Waterworld playground. You can attend a rock concert, enjoy a round of golf, and stay overnight in one of Sun City's impressive hotels.

On your last two days, take the short drive from Sun City east (toward Rustenburg) to the **Pilanesberg Game Reserve.** You should probably plan to spend a day or two exploring the park, which is situated within an ancient volcanic crater. The hides (blinds for observing wildlife) are well worth going to; bird-watching is generally excellent. In addition, look out for the Big Five—lions, elephants, rhinos, buffalos, and leopards. The park also has ranger-led night drives.

Return to Johannesburg or continue on to other destinations in South Africa on the afternoon of day seven.

Central Johannesburg

Sights to See

❷ **City Hall.** This Edwardian survivor is lovely to look at both outside and in; at its heart is a domed concert hall. Statues and wood-framed windows overlook the park in Harrison Street. The main entrance is on Pritchard Street. Inside, you'll find high, pressed-tin ceilings and old-fashioned theater boxes. Look in the pages of the *Star* newspaper to find out if anything is scheduled here. Phone ahead first to arrange to see the interior, as the hall is closed to casual visitors when in use for certain functions. Ask the caretaker or supervisor to show you around. ⊠ *Harrison and President Sts. Entrance opposite Loveday St.,* ☎ *011/ 836–4671.* ☞ *Free.* ☉ *Daily 7 AM–midnight.*

❸ **Market Theatre Complex.** For two decades this theater complex (the city's original fruit market) has kept the flag of quality and experimental theater alive on the highveld. You'll also find an interesting collection of alternative shops, galleries, bars, and coffeehouses here. ⊠ *Bree and Wolhuter Sts., Newtown.*

❹ **Museum Afrika.** This is the first major museum to attempt to give credit to the blacks' contributions to the development of the city. An excellent exhibit traces the impact of gold on the lives of the black population, from the miners forced to live in male-only hostels to the residents of the burgeoning townships with their squatter camps, *shebeens* (bars), and vibrant jazz. Another exhibit covers the fight for democracy and the events leading to the elections that gave Nelson Mandela the presidency. The museum also has first-rate displays of ancient San (Bushmen) rock art, Ghandi's sojourn in Johannesburg, and the Boer pioneer history. Upstairs, the Bensusan Museum examines the art and technology of cameras with fun hands-on exhibits. ⊠ *121 Bree St., Newtown,* ☎ *011/833–5624.* ☞ *R5.* ☉ *Tues.–Sun. 9–5.*

❻ **Oriental Plaza.** With its heady smell of spices and incense, this enormous mall (really a series of undercover and open-air bazaars, which in the early 1970s replaced the shanty stalls of Ferreirasdorp) will take you straight to India. Mingle with multiracial crowds as you explore small shops and colorful stalls selling everything from Indian spices and foods to fabric and curtains. It's a great place to pick up bargains, particularly on fabric, but watch out for flaws, as the Plaza specializes in "seconds." ✉ *Bree and High Sts., Fordsburg.* ☉ *Mon.–Sat. 9–5.*

❶ **Rockey Street.** The street is a slice of New York's East Village in Africa. However, it is fast degenerating into a slum. Hard-rock clubs and ethnic eateries rub shoulders with tattoo parlors, secondhand bookshops, lingerie and leather stores, and boutiques selling African beads. Out on the street, white youths with pink mohawks and nose rings hang out with blacks dressed in the latest fashions. Say what you will, but it's one of the few places where black and white mix easily in the city.

❺ **SA Centenary Centre Breweries Museum.** This unique museum is dedicated to a great South African favorite—beer! (And South African Breweries is the country's—and now Africa's—largest brewery.) You'll find out all about the history of beer brewing in South Africa and the process of beer making. Afterward, enjoy a complimentary beer in a delightful country-style pub. ✉ *President and Bezuidenhout Sts. (entrance on Becker St.), Newtown,* ☎ *011/836–4900.* 🎟 *R10.* ☉ *Tues.–Sat. 10–6.*

Northern Suburbs

A Good Tour

We recommend you start this tour in the south and head northward. Take the M1 south to Braamfontein, leaving the highway at Jan Smuts Avenue. Cross Empire Road and drive up the hill. The main sight here is the **Gertrude Posel Gallery** ⑦, situated in Senate House, Wits University. Because of the one-way streets, getting there is not very straightforward. It's best if you drive under an ornate pedestrian bridge (Wits University is on your right) at Stiemens Street and turn right at the second intersection thereafter, onto De Korte Street, going west. After three blocks, turn right on Eendracht Street. After one block, turn right onto Jorissen Street, a one-way street going east. Senate House is about halfway down the block. It is clearly marked. Ample street parking is available in the vicinity. Inside, the gallery is not well marked and is difficult to locate. Ask the person on duty at the information desk for directions.

Afterward, continue driving down Jorissen Street and turn right onto Biccard Street after four blocks. After three more blocks, turn left onto Smit Street. Travel two blocks and take the slipway left onto Rissik Street. Keep to the center of Rissik Street, which is a one-way street going north. As Rissik becomes Loveday Street, you will see the **Gold Mining Statue** ⑧ on your right. Traffic coming up from the city center can be fast and furious. Park nearby and walk back to the statue to take a closer look if you wish. Parking is available at the Civic Centre across the road on the left (as you come up Rissik/Loveday Street).

Those interested in historic buildings will want to walk through **Parktown** ⑨; contact the Parktown-Westcliff Heritage Trust (☞ Sights to See, *below*) for full details and addresses of historic houses, churches, and schools and information about building tours. To get to Parktown, keep to the second lane from the left on Loveday Street to get onto Hoofd Street. As Hoofd curves to the left, it becomes Joubert Street Extension. Follow the road down the hill and reach the traffic lights at Empire Road. Cross Empire Road and continue up the hill. The road is now called Victoria Street. Continue along Victoria Street and cross three sets of traffic lights. At the third set, continue straight on and cross the bridge over the highway. The road will curve sharply left. Take the first turn to the right, onto Rockridge Road, and park on Rockridge Road, which is close to all of Parktown's historic houses. Of greatest interest are those designed by South Africa's modern architectural prophet Sir Herbert Baker. Trained in the English Arts and Crafts movement, Baker championed (and almost single-handedly saved) the Cape Dutch heritage style and often blended it with Queen Anne and medieval monastic features. Stone House on Rockridge Road is one of his finest—but unfortunately you won't get to see the breathtaking view because the private house is only open to the public a few times a year for specially arranged tours.

Afterward, relax at **Johannesburg Zoo** ⑩ or Zoo Lake. The **South African National Museum of Military History** ⑪ is nearby. To reach the zoo, drive north along Jan Smuts Avenue from central Johannesburg. (If you're going from Parktown, travel west along Rockridge Road. This becomes Eton Road. In turn, this intersects with Jan Smuts Avenue. Turn right onto Jan Smuts Avenue.) Continue north for some distance. As you reach Forest Town, turn right onto Upper Park Drive and follow signs to zoo parking. Parking for the South African Museum of Military History is farther on Upper Park Drive, after the road has become Erlswold Way. Look for signs to the museum; parking is available near the War Memorial. Afterward, you might consider relaxing at tranquil Zoo Lake. To get there from the War Memorial, turn left as you leave the parking area onto Erlswold Way. Continue on Erlswold Way, and take the next road right onto Westwold Drive. Then take the first left (after a short distance) onto Prince of Wales Terrace. Off-street parking is available on the left-hand side of the road.

If you're interested in shopping or outdoor dining, head for **Rosebank** ⑫; the easiest way to get there is along Jan Smuts Avenue either from the zoo or the center of town. If you're going after your visit to Zoo Lake, continue on Prince of Wales Terrace until you reach Avonwold Road. Turn right onto Avonwold Road and continue for three blocks until you reach Jan Smuts Avenue. Turn left onto Jan Smuts Avenue and head north. After seven blocks, you will reach the 7th Avenue–Tyrwhitt Road intersection; turn right onto Tyrwhitt Road. After three blocks, turn right onto Bath Street (a one-way street going south). Toward the end of the first block is Rosebank Mall on your left-hand side, where you can park safely under cover.

TIMING

This is a very long tour, so we suggest you decide in advance what interests you in particular and stay with that. Braamfontein and the Gertrude Posel Gallery should take no more than 30 minutes to see. However, if you plan to visit Parktown, you should allow at least a morning. If you're doing a guided walk, ask how long this is likely to take. Alternatively, tell the guide how much time you want to spend beforehand. It will take about four hours to see all of the sights around the zoo. As for Rosebank, remember that shops generally close at 5, although some stay open a little later. Cafés and restaurants remain open fairly late.

Sights to See

❼ **Gertrude Posel Gallery.** Don't let the mediocre exhibitions of contemporary art upstairs put you off—go downstairs to see the first-rate Standard Bank Collection of African Art. Much of the work, particularly the beadwork, comes from southern Africa. There are also masks, headrests, pots, drums, and initiation statues from West Africa, as well as Kuba cloth from Zaire. ⊠ *Campus level, Senate House, University of Witwatersrand, Jorissen St.,* ☎ *011/716–3780.* ▧ *Free.* ⊙ *Tues.– Fri. 10–4.*

⑧ Gold Mining Statue. One of the most famous symbols of the city, the 1960 statue depicts three men—two black and one white—drilling a rock face. It's a beautifully balanced sculpture that captures the physical effort of mining for gold deep underground. The bronze statue, by sculptor David McGregor, was a gift from the Transvaal and Orange Free State Chambers of Mines. ⊠ *Rissik and De Korte Sts., Braamfontein.*

⑩ Johannesburg Zoo. This park is a pleasant but unremarkable place that can be swamped with schoolchildren during the week. If you're in Johannesburg on the first Sunday of the month, you might like to see— or even participate in—the monthly Walk for Wildlife, a fund-raising walk around the zoo. ⊠ *Upper Park Rd., Forest Town,* ☎ *011/646– 2000.* ▧ *R15.* ⊙ *Daily 8:30–5:30.*

⑨ Parktown. A superb way to introduce yourself to the colonial history of early Johannesburg is to stroll through this suburb perched on the Braamfontein Ridge. The city's early mining magnates, such as the Oppenheimers and the Cullinans, settled here and commissioned renowned architects—most notably, Sir Herbert Baker—to build their magnificent houses, many of which are national monuments. In many cases, interiors have been converted to modern uses but exteriors remain authentic. The Parktown-Westcliff Heritage Trust fought to preserve these old mansions, many of which were almost demolished to make way for the ubiquitous office blocks that cover much of southern Parktown.

Perhaps the cream of the suburb's architectural treasures is **Northwards** on Rockdale Avenue, designed by Sir Herbert Baker, one of South Africa's premier architects during the late 1800s and early 1900s. For many years, it was the home of socialite Jose Dale Lace, whose ghost is still said to grace Northwards's Mistral's Gallery. What is now Wits Business School on St. David's Place is the mansion **Outeniqua,** built in 1906 for the managing director of Ohlssons Breweries. Across the road is a house known as **Eikenlaan,** built in 1903 for James Goch, a professional photographer and the first to use flash photography in South Africa. In June 1985, the home was turned into a rather garish Mike's Kitchen franchise steak house.

Contact the **Parktown-Westcliff Heritage Trust** (☎ 011/445–8100, mornings only) to arrange a guided tour of the area. If you're going to be in town on a Thursday morning, book one of the weekly tours of Northwards. During May, the trust hosts a Heritage Weekend offering "topless bus" and walking tours, accompanied by informative guides. The trust also has guided weekly bus tours, costing R60 and lasting about 3½ hours; book through any Computicket outlet (☎ 011/445–8000).

⑫ Rosebank. This suburb linking Parktown and Sandton is attractive, but it lacks the old-world charm of places such as Melville. Street vendors clutter the sidewalks selling curios including large wooden African animals, malachite jewelry, and colorful printed fabrics. The large shopping malls here have lots of chrome and glass; shops are interspersed with several restaurants. Rosebank Mall (☞ Shopping, *below*) is home to a large cinema complex specializing in art-house movies from around the world. You can, however, find quiet squares away from the constant hive of activity. On sunny highveld days (of which there are many), you can dine alfresco at one of Rosebank's numerous sidewalk cafés.

⑪ **South African National Museum of Military History.** Set in a park, the two exhibition halls and rambling outdoor display here focus on South Africa's role in the major wars of the 20th century, with an emphasis on World War II. The Anglo-Boer War memorial is the most striking landmark of the northern suburbs. On display are Spitfire and Messerschmidt fighters (including what is claimed to be the only remaining ME110 jet night fighter), various tanks of English and American manufacture, and a wide array of artillery. Among the most interesting exhibits are the modern armaments South Africa used in its war against the Cuban-backed Angolan army during the 1980s, including highly advanced artillery, French-built Mirage fighters, and Russian tanks stolen by the South Africans from a ship en route to Angola. More recent exhibits include the national military art collection, memorabilia from the Anti-Conscription Campaign, and an exhibit on the history of Umkhonto-we-Sizwe "spear of the nation" or MK (the African National Congress's military arm), from inception until their incorporation into the South African National Defence Force. ✉ *20 Erlswold Way,* ☎ *011/646–5513.* ⊡ *R5.* ☉ *Daily 9–4:30.*

Northwestern Johannesburg

A Good Drive

Consider driving to **Melville** ⑬ if you want to browse through quaint shops and dine outdoors. The easiest way to reach this area from the northern suburbs is to take the N1 highway south. Take the DF Malan Drive exit and turn left onto DF Malan Drive. Pass through the suburbs of Northcliff, Franklin Roosevelt Park, and Montgomery Park. DF Malan Drive becomes Main Street as it reaches Melville. Three blocks after this, turn left onto 9th Avenue and, after two blocks, right on 4th Street, where you'll find stores, coffee shops, and outdoor cafés.

Continue on to the **Melville Koppies** ⑭ (assuming you're there when it's open). Backtrack on DF Malan Drive and turn right on Judith Road. The entrance to the koppies is on the right. Most people park on the sidewalk in the vicinity.

Next, to proceed to the **Johannesburg Botanical Gardens and Emmarentia Dam** ⑮, head back to DF Malan Drive and turn right. Take the next right turn onto Thomas Bowler Avenue. Continue down Thomas Bowler Avenue for four blocks. Turn right on Olifants Road. The entrance is about halfway down the block on your right. If you cross the dam wall, you've gone too far. There is ample free parking near the entrance to the gardens.

TIMING

Allow at least a morning to see both Melville and the Johannesburg Botanical Gardens and Emmarentia Dam. If you have more time, you might want to spend a morning in Melville and the afternoon at Emmarentia Dam. Remember to allow sufficient time for driving (Melville is about 30 minutes from Sandton and Rosebank and 20 minutes from central Johannesburg). Allow yourself at least three to four hours to see Melville Koppies.

Sights to See

⑮ **Johannesburg Botanical Gardens and Emmarentia Dam.** This gigantic parkland is a wonderful haven amid the bustle of a big city and a fine place to walk. You may relax on benches beneath weeping willows surrounding the dammed pond or wander across to the rose and herb gardens, filled with arbors, statues, fountains, and ponds. If you're here on a Saturday or Sunday, expect to bump into several bridal parties. ✉ *Olifants Rd., Emmarentia,* ☎ *011/782–7064.* 🎫 *Free.* ☉ *Daily sunrise–sunset.*

⑬ Melville. The trendy suburb essentially grew around the South African Broadcasting Company (SABC) in nearby Auckland Park. It was once an average middle-class enclave until several well-known South African television and radio personalities migrated to the area, turning it into one of the hippest places in the northern suburbs. Seventh Street has a number of pleasant shops and coffeehouses with sidewalk seating. Although you may not find anything uniquely African here, you'll see how suburban white South Africa entertains itself, particularly over weekends when coffeehouses are filled and shop and boutique owners do a brisk trade. If you're here on the second Saturday of the month, take in the atmosphere of the Melville Mardi Gras, when the streets are closed to traffic and buskers entertain the crowds.

⑭ Melville Koppies. This small nature reserve is across Judith Road on the southern side of the Johannesburg Botanical Gardens. You can enjoy guided ecology walks with volunteer guides, many of whom are members of the local botanical society; they will introduce you to the rich diversity of highveld flora found here. There is also an archaeological site dating back to the Iron Age. Bird-watching is excellent here; expect to see many varieties of grassland and highveld birds as well as species found in the area's suburban gardens. ✉ *Judith Rd. and DF Malan Dr., Melville,* ☎ *011/788–7571.* 🎫 *Free.* ☉ *Sept.–May, 1st and 3rd Sun. of each month 3–6; 2nd Sun. of each month 9–noon.*

SOUTH OF TOWN

⑯ Gold Reef City. Fifteen kilometers (9 miles) south of downtown is the most popular tourist attraction in the city. Go figure. The place is a rinky-dink theme park that transforms a bona fide part of Johannesburg's gold-mining history into banal kiddie rides and trite entertainments. Tucked away amid all the dross are some original 19th-century mining cottages and a couple of interesting museums, but it's all difficult to take seriously. The only redeeming aspects of a visit are going down an old gold mine (additional fee), seeing molten gold being poured, and watching a gumboot dance, a riveting hostel dance developed by black miners. ✉ *Northern Pkwy., off N1, Ormonde,* ☎ *011/496–1600.* 🎫 *R28.* ☉ *Tues.–Sun. 10–4:40. Dancing at 11:30 and 3; mine tours every 30 mins 10–5.*

Around Johannesburg

Crocodile River Arts & Crafts Ramble. Local artists, potters, sculptors, and other craftspeople host this event. Their studios and galleries, in a delightful country setting northwest of Johannesburg, are open to the public on the first weekend of every month. You may purchase crafts, clothing, and knitted garments; enjoy light meals or picnic outdoors; and watch an artist at work. Maps are obtainable along the route or from Johannesburg Publicity Association. ✉ *Follow DF Malan Dr. in a westerly direction, toward Swartkops, Muldersdrift, and Kromdraai. Signboards, painted white and bearing a green crocodile, will direct you to the studios,* ☎ *011/784–1354.*

Cullinan Diamond Mine. Forty-eight kilometers (30 miles) east of Pretoria is this fully operational mine three times the size of the famous hole at Kimberley. The 3,106-carat Cullinan diamond was unearthed here in 1905, a giant crystal that was later cut into several smaller stones including the Star of Africa. Machinery extracts 12 tons of kimberlite and 6,000 carats of diamonds each day. About 80% of these are for industrial use, but the rest are high-grade gems. On the mine's one daily tour you'll see the big hole, watch a 12-minute video, pass through a typical mine security check, view replicas of the most famous diamonds, and travel through a mock-up of an underground tunnel. You can buy diamonds and custom-made pieces from the resident jeweler. You must reserve in advance for tours; no children under 10 are permitted. The delightful old Victorian mine manager's house is now Oak House guest house, which costs R200 a person a night (☎ 012/305–2364). ✉ *Premier Diamond Tours, 95 Oak Ave., Cullinan,* ☎ *012/734–0260.* ✆ *R22.* ☉ *Tours weekdays at 10 and 2:30, weekends at 10.*

Kromdraai Conservancy. This wonderful, and apparently little-known, area is just a 45-minute drive from the northwestern suburb of North-cliff. Begin at the archaeological treasure of **Sterkfontein Cave** (☎ 011/355–1900), where in 1936 Dr. Raymond Dart discovered his now famous "Mrs. Ples," or Australopithecus africanus, the first identified "missing link" providing evolutionary evidence of the connection between humans and apes. Guided tours take about one hour. Unfortunately the limestone formations were almost totally stripped by early miners. However, you can head on to the smaller but more intact **Wonder Cave** (☎ 011/957–0106), where the profusion of stalactites and stalagmites rivals the famous Cango Caves in the Cape. Go on to try your hand at fly-fishing in stocked ponds at **Rainbow Trout Farm** (☎ 011/957–0008), where you can buy the fish you've caught (or others, if you haven't). Rods and tackle may be rented for an additional fee. You can spot most of the Big Five at nearby **Rhino and Lion Park** (☎ 011/957–0109), where ostriches peck at your windows in the vain hope of being fed, herds of wildebeest and antelope dot the plains, and rhinos slumber in thorn tree thickets. Don't miss the lion, wild dog, and cheetah enclosures, and the vulture hide and "restaurant" (feeding area), but be warned—the animals tend to be very frisky. Feeding times vary between species and age groups, so phone to check. If you're there on the first weekend of the month (Crocodile River Ramble weekend), pop in at **Iris Ridge Farm** (✉ Off the R47 to Tarlton, ☎ 011/957–0205) to enjoy tea and scones. At other times, phone the farm beforehand to arrange to see an 1875 gold mine, one of the earliest on the reef. The proprietor will probably regale you with details of its history, making this a very interesting visit.

Lippizaner Centre. Midway between Johannesburg and Pretoria, this complex is home to white Lippizaner stallions, a distinguished breed of horses with a centuries-old lineage. The horses are trained in the classic Spanish riding style and during their weekly shows perform a complex ballet of exercises to the strains of Verdi, Mozart, and Handel. ✉ *Dahlia Rd., Kyalami,* ☎ *011/702–2103.* ✆ *R50.* ☉ *Performances Sun. at 11. Closed mid-Oct.–mid-Nov.*

Witwatersrand Botanical Gardens. In the relatively open countryside on the extreme western edge of Johannesburg, you'll find these gardens, which comprise vast expanses of lawn fringed with trees. You can cross the Hennops River as it meanders through the grounds and admire indigenous cycads and aloes. You will also observe resident black eagles soaring, sometimes above a waterfall; you may walk above the waterfall for a bird's-eye view of the eagles' nesting sites. If you're hungry, take a light meal at the kiosk or enjoy a more formal lunch or dinner at the Garden Restaurant. If you're here on a Sunday afternoon, arrange to take a picnic lunch and enjoy the bimonthly evening concerts (May–August), hosted by the National Symphony Orchestra, the Welsh Men's Choir, and South Africa's top classical music talent. ✉ *Malcolm Rd., Poortview, Roodepoort,* ☎ *011/958–1750.* ✆ *R7.*

DINING

Downtown

$$$ ✕ **Gramadoelas at the Market Theatre.** A cosmopolitan clientele of diplo-
★   mats, playwrights, and actors frequents this attractive restaurant,
      which has recently moved from traditional South African cuisine to
      offer a Pan-African cuisine, or "from Cape to Cairo" as the propri-
      etors explain. The decor is a fascinating jumble of Africana, including
      huge Cape Dutch canvases and rustic oil lamps. On the menu are
      Afro-Sharizi recipes from Zanzibar, Moroccan *tagines* (stews) served
      with couscous, and Ethiopian *dharawat* (chicken with paprika and peri-
      peri). For dessert, order a Moroccan *kneffa,* layers of almond cream,
      or delicious Cape *malva,* pudding made with apricot jam and vinegar
      topped with cream and sugar. ✉ *Market Theatre, Wolhuter St., New-
      town,* ☎ *011/838–6960. AE, DC, MC, V. Closed Sun. No lunch Mon.*

$ ✕ **Chon Hing.** Tucked away in a side street and looking a little world-
      weary, this Chinese restaurant is still one of the best-kept secrets of
      the cognoscenti. No cloths mask the Formica tabletops, and the chairs are
      upholstered in red plastic, but in a place like this it's the food that keeps
      people coming back. You can order one of the set menus, but you're
      better off selecting dishes from the two pages at the back of the menu.
      Good choices are beef flank served with noodles or rice, prawns stuffed
      with minced chicken, and calamari in black bean sauce. For a real treat,
      order steamed rock cod. ✉ *26 Alexander St., at John Vorster Sq., Fer-
      reirastown,* ☎ *011/834–3206. AE, DC, MC, V. BYOB.*

Northern Suburbs

$$$$ ✕ **Daruma.** Long regarded as *the* Japanese restaurant in town, Daruma
      has recently moved from Melrose to the Sandton Sun Hotel, and con-
      tinues to draw crowds despite its high prices. You can sit at the sushi
      bar or opt for the small Shogun-Noma room, divided into private din-
      ing areas by wood-and-paper screens. The menu covers the full range
      of Japanese cuisine, from sashimi to *soba* (buckwheat) noodles. You
      can also order various set menus. The ingredients are absolutely fresh
      and the presentation superb. ✉ *5th and Alice Sts.,* ☎ *011/780–5000.
      Reservations required. AE, DC, MC, V. Closed Mon. No lunch Sun.*

$$$$ ✕ **Linger Longer.** Ever since the annual "Top Ten" restaurant awards
      ★   were initiated by *Wine* magazine a decade ago, this restaurant has stood
      among the top three. Set in the spacious grounds of a former home in
      Wierda Valley, it has an air of gracious elegance. Some rooms have a
      Wedgwood-like quality—deep green walls with pale trim and striped
      curtains—whereas others glow in salmon pink. A goose-liver pâté ap-
      petizer is one of the dishes that made Linger Longer famous. Excellent
      main courses include crisp duckling in ginger sauce and boned loin of
      lamb with garlic, parsley, and coarse-grain mustard. Among the imag-
      inative desserts, crepes filled with warm cream cheese, vanilla, and
      brandied raisins are particularly good. ✉ *58 Wierda Rd., Wierda Val-
      ley,* ☎ *011/884–0465. AE, DC, MC, V. Closed Sun. No lunch Sat.*

$$$$ ✕ **Ma Cuisine.** Alas, well-loved chef-patron Jorn Pless is no more, but
      widow Inger continues the tradition of shaping a table d'hôte around
      what she buys fresh at the market each day. There is a small menu,
      which changes daily, offering only three choices each of starter, main
      courses, and dessert. If that smacks of culinary roulette, rest assured
      that almost everyone comes out a winner. Most diners find that they
      haven't tasted anything as exquisite as these well-balanced meals in
      years—among them Queen Elizabeth II. Lunch is a three-course affair,
      dinner a full-blown five courses, including a starter, fish, sorbet, main

Downtown Johannesburg Dining and Lodging

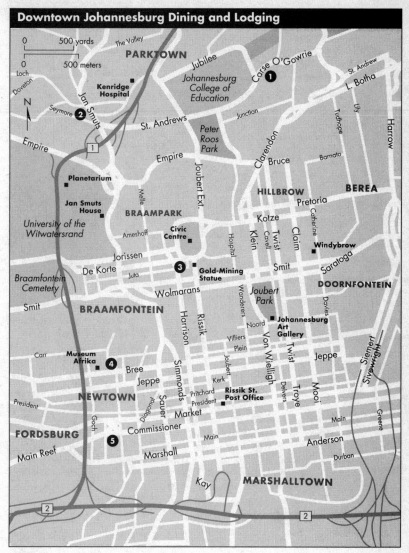

Dining
Chon Hing, **5**
Gramadoelas at the
Market Theatre, **4**

Lodging
Protea Parktonian, **3**
Holiday Inn
Sunnyside Park
Hotel, **1**
The Westcliff, **2**

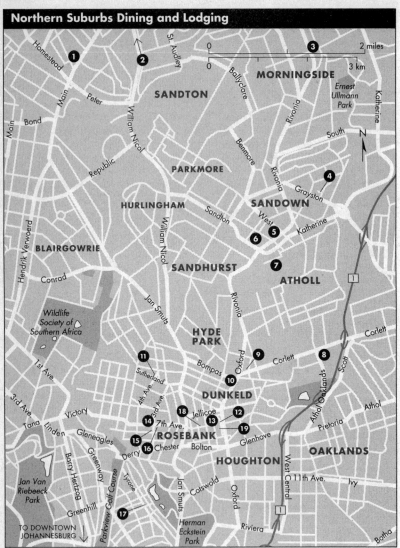

Dining

Daruma, **8**

Franco's Pizzeria &
Trattoria, **17**

Giovann's, **14**

Ile de France, **1**

Leipoldt's, **3**

Linger Longer, **7**

Ma Cuisine, **16**

Osteria Tre
Nonni, **11**

Paros Taverna, **12**

Pescador
Restaurant, **4**

Plaka Taverna, **9**

Red Chamber
Mandarin
Restaurant, **19**

The Ritz, **15**

Lodging

The Michelangelo, **5**

Mövenpick Indaba, **2**

Park Hyatt Hotel, **13**

Rosebank Hotel, **18**

Sandton Sun &
Towers Inter-
Continental, **6**

Ten Bompas, **10**

course, and dessert. You can watch the chefs at work in the glassed-in kitchen. ⊠ *40 7th Ave., Parktown North,* ☎ *011/880–1946. Reservations required. AE, DC, MC, V. Closed Sun. and Mon.*

$$$$ ✗ **Pescador Restaurant.** Tucked away in a suburban shopping center, this Portuguese restaurant serves some of the best seafood in Gauteng. Diners come from far and wide for butterflied grilled queen prawns marinated in a beer, garlic, and chili sauce. The combination platter of succulent, tender calamari and juicy prawns is another favorite. Don't forget to ask about the line fish specials, especially if it's the season for musselcracker or "74," two of South Africa's tastiest fish. The atmosphere is relaxed and friendly, and the decor has a distinctly Portuguese flavor, with murals of villages and fishing bric-a-brac on the walls and old sails on the ceiling. ⊠ *Grayston Centre, Grayston Dr., Sandown,* ☎ *011/884–4429. AE, DC, MC, V. No lunch Sat.*

$$$ ✗ **Ile de France.** Chef-owner Marc Guebert is the only member in Africa
★ of the Maîtres Cuisiniers de France, that illustrious group of chefs that includes the likes of Roger Vergé, Pierre Troisgros, and Paul Bocuse. Each member specializes in a particular culinary realm, and Guebert champions soufflés. In fact, to visit his restaurant and not eat his soufflé Grand Marnier is considered something of a gastronomic gaffe. For starters, try grilled goose liver served with a Madeira sauce, or fried calves' brains in black butter and capers. His quenelles, flavored with smoked salmon and coated with chardonnay sauce, are light as clouds. More down to earth is a superb rack of lamb. For a gastronomic treat, try the menu dégustation, a six-course tasting menu that costs about R135. ⊠ *26 Cramerview Centre, 227 Main Rd., Bryanston,* ☎ *011/706–2837. AE, DC, MC, V. Closed Mon. No lunch Sat.*

$$$ ✗ **Osteria Tre Nonni.** Paintings and yellowed photographs of aged grandfathers peer down from the whitewashed walls of this northern Italian restaurant in Craighall. Prices are highish, but the place is always abuzz with Italian families tucking into authentic dishes from Umbria and Tuscany. Although the menu changes regularly, prawns and other seafood are specialties—try the sole baked in foil with porcini and truffles or, for meat eaters, the delicious *filetto al pepe verde* (beef fillet with whiskey, cream, and green Madagascar peppercorns). Carpaccio is a magnificent starter. ⊠ *9 Grafton Ave., Craighall,* ☎ *011/327–0095. Reservations required. DC, MC, V. Closed Sun. and Mon.*

$$$ ✗ **The Ritz.** A quaint old house in Parktown North where you can sit inside under the lovely pressed-tin ceiling or opt for the adjoining conservatory, with hanging plants and a large skylight. For starters try the delectable duck livers sautéed in chili and mango and served with a light coconut-coriander sauce and nan bread. Stay with the duck for your main course, glazed with a fresh fruit compote and served with gooseberry and orange sauce. Try the chocolate mousse gateau—layers of light and dark chocolate mousse, on a chocolate sponge, floated on a chocolate coulis—for a decadent ending to your meal. ⊠ *17 3rd St., Parktown North,* ☎ *011/880–2470. AE, DC, MC, V. Closed Sun. No lunch Sat.*

$$ ✗ **Giovann's.** Tables spill out onto the sidewalk at this trendy restaurant in Parktown North where Mama Lucia serves a small but tasty menu of Mediterranean fare. Choose a starter portion or full-size homemade pasta dish—*vongole* (clams) or *scampi* (prawns) in a tomato base, or salmon in a light cream sauce. For rice, try seafood or black mushroom and vegetable risotto. There are also seven pizza options, the best topped with tangy Italian sausage. ⊠ *3rd and 7th Aves., Parktown North,* ☎ *011/447–5462. AE, DC, MC, V. Closed Sun.*

$$ ✗ **Leipoldt's.** Named after the writer who first celebrated the national cuisine, this restaurant focuses on traditional South African fare, much of which traces its origins to the Cape Malay community. More than

60 dishes are served buffet-style, and you can try as many as you'd like. Typical offerings are tomato *bredie* (lamb casserole in a tomato sauce), *sosaties* (grilled kebabs made with meat, dried apricots, green peppers, mushrooms, and onions), *bobotie* (casserole with minced meat, raisins, apricots, onions, and curry powder served with rice and chutney), and *boerewors* (coarse farmer's sausages). For dessert, try syrupy *koeksisters* (very sweet doughnuts). Faded historic photographs and animal heads on the walls provide South African ambience. ⊠ *Pavilion Shopping Centre, Rivonia Rd. and Kelvin Dr., Morningside,* ☏ *011/804–4321. AE, DC, MC, V. Closed Sun. No lunch Sat.*

$$ ✕ **Paros Taverna.** This Greek restaurant is hidden at the top of a flight of stairs in the Rosebank's Mutual Gardens, where, on warm summer nights, you can sit outside on the sheltered terrace and sip a bottle of retsina while dipping into bowls of *tzadziki* (yogurt and garlic), *taramousalata* (fish-roe dip), and *baba ganoush* (pureed eggplant). By far the best dish on the menu is *kalamarakia,* incredibly tender squid grilled in olive oil, garlic, and lemon. A couple of orders of kalamarakia and a mixed platter of nine *mezede* (appetizers or side dishes) can easily feed four. For dessert don't miss homemade halvah ice cream. ⊠ *Mutual Gardens, Oxford Rd., Rosebank,* ☏ *011/788–6211. AE, DC, MC, V. No dinner Sun.*

$ ✕ **Franco's Pizzeria & Trattoria.** Dark wood paneling, red-check tablecloths, and soft Italian music give this spot a welcoming appeal. Chef-owner Franco Forleo comes from Brindisi and specializes in southern Italian cuisine. The menu includes 14 pizzas and a range of pasta dishes, but habitués usually choose one of the specials, such as *capellini al salmone e caviale* (angel-hair pasta with smoked salmon and caviar), or seasonal *frutti di mare* like butterfish, yellowtail, or kabeljou. Remember that you need to bring your own wine—and that this is one of the few restaurants open for lunch on Saturday. ⊠ *Parkview Centre, 54 Tyrone Ave.,* ☏ *011/646–5449. AE, DC, MC, V. Closed Mon.*

$ ✕ **Plaka Taverna.** Greek music floats above the buzz of conversation, a gyro spit turns slowly near the door, and a refrigerated case displays an array of mezede. Most people sit on the roofed terrace or at the few street-side tables. Start with a couple of ouzos and share a platter of gyro meat, feta, olives, cucumber, and tomato. Follow that with a platter of meze, a Greek salad, and a carafe of wine, and your bill will still be less than R40 per person. If you're really hungry, choose the spit-roasted lamb or grilled marinated chicken. ⊠ *3A Corlett Dr., Illovo,* ☏ *011/788–8777. AE, DC, MC, V. Closed Mon.*

$ ✕ **Red Chamber Mandarin Restaurant.** This is where the Chinese community gathers on Sunday morning for its traditional dim sum or *yum char* (tea and snacks). During the rest of the week, chefs from Taiwan, Hong Kong, Beijing, and Guangzhou turn out some of the best Chinese food in the city, drawing a loyal following of wealthy Chinese locals. There are more than 100 dishes on the menu, but feel free to make special requests; some of the best dishes aren't listed. Highlights include cubes of eggplant and chili cooked and served in a sizzling wok, and steamed shrimp dumplings. ⊠ *Shop 168, Hyde Park Shopping Centre, Jan Smuts Ave.,* ☏ *011/788–5536. AE, DC, MC, V.*

LODGING

Downtown

$$$ 🏨 **Holiday Inn Sunnyside Park Hotel.** Just minutes by car from the city center, this Parktown hotel is one of the few in the city with a history. Built in 1895 as a mansion for a mining engineer, it later served as the residence of Lord Milner, eventual governor of the Transvaal. New sections have been added to the original mansion, but wood paneling and old prints help recapture something of the hotel's illustrious past. Rooms are pleasant, done in autumnal tones with bird prints and wicker furniture. Request a front-facing room overlooking the gardens. Service is not one of the hotel's strong points: rooms may not be ready by mid-afternoon and the front-desk staff could be more helpful. The surrounding area is generally safe during the day, but it's not advisable to wander at night. ⊠ *2 York Rd., Parktown (mailing address: Box 31256, Braamfontein 2017),* ☎ *011/643–7226,* ⅢX *011/642–0019. 96 rooms. Restaurant, 2 bars, room service, pool. AE, DC, MC, V.*

$$$ 🖭 **Protea Parktonian.** Close to the Rotunda transport center, the major theaters, and just a three-minute drive from the central business district, this Braamfontein property offers the best value in the city—even if its neighborhood isn't safe to walk in at night. The guest rooms are all suites, by far the largest of any city hotel. All have a separate living room and bedroom, minibar, cable TV, and veranda. You can enter the hotel directly from a secure parking garage. ⊠ *120 De Korte St., Braamfontein (mailing address: Box 32278, Braamfontein 2017),* ☎ *011/403–5740,* ⅢX *011/403–2401. 294 rooms. 2 restaurants, bar, room service, pool, health club. AE, DC, MC, V.*

$$$ 🖭 **The Westcliff.** Since the closure of the once standard-setting Carl-
★ ton, the Westcliff has assumed the mantle of top city hotel, first for its pedigree in the *Orient Express* stable and second for its setting and breathtaking views of the wooded northern suburbs, best appreciated from the secluded swimming pool terrace. Bedrooms are located in multistoried villas, each with its own balcony as well as fax and modem: some face twisting lanes and others the highveld beyond. The feel is cozy Mediterranean, with soft pink structures blending with the sandstone foundations. The cuisine, service, and facilities are all world class. ⊠ *67 Jan Smuts Ave.,* ☎ *011/646–2400,* ⅢX *011/646–3500. 106 rooms, 14 suites. 2 restaurants, 2 bars, room service, pool, beauty salon, tennis court, exercise room, business center. AE, DC, MC, V.*

Northern Suburbs

$$ ✕🖭 **Ten Bompas.** There are a number of small boutique hotels and guest houses in the northern suburbs, but none quite match the elan of this eclectic hotel-cum-restaurant and art gallery. Each of the suites has been individually created by a different interior designer, and decor ranges from art deco–African to muted romantic. The restaurant matches the hotel's fashionable decor, and the service and food are some of the best in the city. ⊠ *10 Bompas Rd., Dunkeld West (mailing address: Box 786064, Sandton 2146),* ☎ *011/325–2442,* ⅢX *011/341–0281. 10 suites. Restaurant, bar. BP. AE, DC, MC, V.*

$$$$ 🖭 **Park Hyatt Hotel.** If you like lots of black, gold, and glass decor, this one's for you. Enormous picture windows have stunning views over the northern suburbs. The black-and-gold theme extends to the rooms, which are the last word in luxury with televisions, minibars, wardrobe safes, 24-hour room and laundry service, complimentary magazines, a choice of smoking and no-smoking accommodations, and twin, queen, or king-size beds. Should you book one of the Regency Club suites, you'll have complimentary cocktails and even more glorious views. Local art lines the walls in discreetly lit passageways, and there's an ultramodern restaurant and wine bar, a luxurious health club, and a solar-heated pool on the roof. The hotel has an airport greeting service and makes arrangements for baby-sitting and car rental. ⊠ *Oxford Rd. and Bierman Ave., Rosebank (mailing address: Box 1536, Saxonwold 2132),* ☎ *011/280–1234,* ⅢX *011/280–1238. 244 rooms. 2 restaurants, bar, room service, pool, health club, laundry service. AE, DC, MC, V.*

$$$$ **Sandton Sun & Towers Inter-Continental.** This highly regarded hotel adjoins one of the largest and most exclusive malls in the country. The Sun and Sun Towers are two nominally separate hotels, linked by a walkway and sharing facilities. Both occupy high-rises with commanding views of the northern suburbs and the highveld. The focal point of each hotel is a central atrium soaring the height of the building. Guest rooms are small but superbly laid out, with understated lighting and elegant decorative touches. There is little to recommend one hotel over the other, although the Towers is smaller and farther removed from the bustle of Sandton Mall. The Towers also has two full floors of executive suites, with their own bar, breakfast room, and full-time staff. ✉ *5th and Alice Sts., Sandton,* ☎ *011/780–5000,* FAX *011/780–5002. 525 rooms, 39 suites. 4 restaurants, bar, coffee shop, room service, beauty salon, sauna, health club, concierge floor, business services. AE, DC, MC, V.*

$$$ 🏨 **The Michelangelo.** As though taken from a street in Florence, this hotel forms the northern facade of much-touted, piazza-inspired Sandton Square. But whereas the hotel is unusually tasteful, even grand, the square—to quote a local architect—is to an Italian piazza what Donald Duck is to Swan Lake. A member of the Leading Hotels of the World group, it has all the class, comforts, and facilities you'd expect from a top establishment. The atrium-style pool area is a feature to note, and the hotel caters to physically handicapped guests. For serious pampering (including your own chef and butler), try one of two Presidential Suites at around R5,000 a night. ✉ *West St., Sandton Square (mailing address: Box 784682, Sandton 2146),* ☎ *011/282–7000,* FAX *011/282–7171. 242 rooms. Restaurant, 2 bars, room service, pool, sauna, health club. AE, DC, MC, V.*

$$$ 🏨 **Mövenpick Indaba.** "Indaba" is an African word for meeting place, and an apt name for one of the major conference venues in Johannesburg, capable of hosting several major functions simultaneously in a wide variety of boardrooms, auditoriums, and ballrooms. The property is huge, covering more than 30 acres on the outskirts of Johannesburg, about 30 minutes by car from both the airport and the city center. The hotel itself is very attractive, with a thatched roof lending rustic African charm to an otherwise business-oriented establishment. Rooms in the older thatched section are comfortable but a bit dark. Newer rooms are lighter, done in attractive greens and rusts, and have their own verandas and minibars, as well as separate bath and shower. Sunday brunch under the jacarandas on the hotel's terrace is a local favorite. ✉ *Hartebeespoort Dam Rd., Witkoppen (mailing address: Box 67129, Bryanston 2021),* ☎ *011/467–0656 central reservations,* FAX *011/465–1423 hotel. 210 rooms. Restaurant, bar, pool, tennis court, health club. AE, DC, MC, V.*

$$$ 🏨 **Rosebank Hotel.** Ideally situated 15 minutes by car from the city center and minutes on foot from the shops, cinemas, and restaurants of Rosebank's malls, the hotel is another favorite among businesspeople who appreciate low-key atmosphere and efficient service. Rooms are attractively decorated with prints and dark wood furniture and paneling. There is airport shuttle service (by request). For walkers, this is a much better choice than the Sunnyside or the Parktonian: the streets of Rosebank are among the safest and most interesting in Johannesburg. ✉ *Tyrwhitt and Sturdee Aves., Rosebank (mailing address: Box 52025, Saxonwold 2132),* ☎ *011/447–2700,* FAX *011/447–3276. 318 rooms. 3 restaurants, 2 bars, room service, pool, beauty salon, exercise room, parking (fee). AE, DC, MC, V.*

NIGHTLIFE AND THE ARTS

The best place to find out what's going on in Johannesburg is in the "Tonight" section of the the *Star,* Johannesburg's major daily. Another great source of information is the weekly *Mail & Guardian.* Make your bookings through **Computicket** (☎ 011/445–8445 for information, 011/445–8000 for credit card purchases), which has outlets throughout the city, including most major malls.

The Arts

Classical Music
The **National Symphony Orchestra** (☎ 011/714–4501 information, 011/445–8000 Computicket) stages concerts in **Linder Auditorium** (⊠ Johannesburg College of Education, St. Andrew's Rd., Parktown) and occasionally at **City Hall** (⊠ President and Simmonds Sts., Johannesburg Central). Concerts generally start at 8 PM, and you can attend pre-concert talks at 7:15 PM. Other events include musical fireworks concerts, picnic concerts at Johannesburg Zoo, a Christmas Concert, and Songs of Praise, a festival of Easter music and hymns. If you're visiting the city in September, consider making a reservation for the incredibly popular Johannesburg Pops concerts, held in one of the city's enormous parks. Concerts showcase contemporary music, played in classical style. Picnic baskets are sold (order when making a reservation) and each evening ends with a fireworks display.

Theater
The beautiful **Alhambra Theatre** complex (⊠ Sivewright Ave. and Beit St., Doornfontein, ☎ 011/402–6174 information, 011/445–8000 Computicket) is made up of three theaters: the Alhambra, the Rex Garner, and the Richard Haines. The complex presents primarily mainstream productions, like West End and Broadway material.

The **Civic Theatre** (⊠ Loveday St., Braamfontein, ☎ 011/403–3408 information, 011/445–8000 Computicket) is Johannesburg's principal cultural venue. Housed in a slick, modern complex, the Civic has one enormous theater and three smaller stages. Many productions have a South African focus—works by such famous local talents as Pieter-Dirk Uys and Paul Slabolepszy.

The **Market Theatre** (⊠ Bree and Wolhuter Sts., ☎ 011/832–1641, 011/445–8000 Computicket) occupies an old produce market that dates back to the early 1900s. Now completely refurbished, the three-theater complex has a wealth of character and includes a great bar and restaurant and an art gallery with changing exhibits. Theater productions encompass everything from plays by Athol Fugard to imported West End comedies. The theater occasionally features ethnic African music. Experimental plays get the litmus test of audience approval at the Market Theatre Laboratory, across Bree Street.

Nightlife

Multiracial Hillbrow used to be the city's nightlife center, but the neighborhood has become a crime-ridden, no-go zone full of hookers, massage parlors, and porno houses. In its place, **Rosebank** has emerged as the hot new spot, and you'll find clubs, bars, and coffee shops scattered through the neighborhood, particularly along Oxford Road. **Rockey Street** in Yeoville also has a happening nightlife scene, with clubs and bars offering everything from jazz to grunge. Unfortunately, the street is also a popular hangout for drug dealers and addicts. Many white residents of the northern suburbs, concerned about personal safety, head to the modern **Randburg Waterfront** (⊠ Republic Rd., Randburg), a gimmicky, mall-like development of almost a hundred restaurants, bars, and clubs clustered around an artificial lake.

Bars and Pubs

The **Guildhall Executive Bar and Restaurant** (⊠ Meischkes Bldg., Market St., ☎ 011/836–5560), in the city center, is the oldest bar in Johannesburg. Walk through swinging doors into a paneled room rich with wood and smoke. **Kofifi** (⊠ Market Theatre complex, Bree St., Newtown, ☎ 011/832–1450), an active bar, is also a restaurant, true to the flavor of the new Africa, serving dishes like coconut chicken or, for the brave, tripe and dumplings, until late.

Live Music and Nightclubs

Kippies (⊠ Market Theatre complex, off Bree St., Newtown, ☎ 011/833–3316) is the city's premier jazz venue, featuring traditional and township South African jazz. It also serves light meals from Kofifi's kitchen (☞ *above*). **Picasso Bistro** (⊠ Old Mutual Sq., 169 Oxford Rd., Rosebank, ☎ 011/788–1213) is a sophisticated wine bar and coffeehouse. Open late, it's the place to see and be seen.

Radium Beer Hall (⊠ 282 Louis Botha Ave., Orange Grove, ☎ 011/728–3866), opened in 1929, is the oldest pub still operating in the city. The 18-piece jazz band Fat Sound blasts off at around midnight Wednesday, Friday, and Saturday and on the first Sunday of every month. Known for its hearty Portuguese food (prego rolls, peri-peri chicken), it is casual verging on the rough. Don't go here at night except in a group or with locals.

The **Bass Line** (⊠ 7 7th St., Melville, ☎ 011/482–6915) is the trendiest, young hangout in town, featuring mostly jazz and world music—an origin-sensitive combination of rock and roll, rap, and Afro-rock.

OUTDOOR ACTIVITIES AND SPORTS

Participant Sports

Golf

Johannesburg's finest golf courses are open to foreign visitors, although weekend play tends to be restricted to members only. Expect to pay R70–R100 for a round. The century-old **Royal Johannesburg Golf Club** (⊠ Fairway Ave., Linksfield North, ☎ 011/640–3022) has two courses: The East Course is the more famous of the two and has hosted the South African Open seven times. The **Wanderers Golf Club** (⊠ Rudd Rd., Illovo, ☎ 011/447–3311), permanent host of the South African PGA Championship, is a tough course, well bunkered and with plenty of water on the early holes; it demands exacting iron shots to its small greens. **Glendower Club** (⊠ Marais Rd., Bedfordview, ☎ 011/453–1013) lies in a nature reserve. The addition of more water hazards and extra length makes this one of the most challenging courses in the country. You can rent clubs at Royal Johannesburg and at **Roger Manning Golf Shop** (⊠ Huddle Park Golf Course, adjoining Royal Johannesburg, Linksfield North, ☎ 011/640–3065).

Spectator Sports

Cricket

The **Wanderers' Club** (⊠ 21 North St., Illovo, ☎ 011/788–5010) is the country's premier cricket ground and the site of many of the international contests between South Africa and touring sides from England and its former colonies.

Rugby

South Africa's showcase rugby stadium is **Ellis Park** (⊠ Staib St., Doornfontein, ☎ 011/402–8644), where the Springboks beat New Zealand's All Blacks to win the 1995 World Cup. It's a magnificent stadium, capable of seating nearly 65,000 people. It's home to the Transvaal rugby team, which competes against other provincial sides in the annual Bankfin Currie Cup competition.

SHOPPING

Johannesburg is the best place in the country to buy quality African art, whether it's tribal fetishes from Central Africa or oil paintings by early white settlers. Dozens of galleries and curio shops are scattered throughout the city, often selling the same goods at widely different prices. Newtown Market Africa, which you should consider seeing before making purchases elsewhere, has the best prices (☞ Markets, *below*).

And if you thought America had a thing for malls, wait until you see Jo'burg's northern suburbs. Blink and another mall has gone up. Even more astonishing is how exclusive they are, lined with chichi shops selling the latest from Italy, France, and the States—at twice the price you would pay at home. Most malls also have department stores like Edgars and Woolworth's, as well as cinemas and restaurants.

Malls

The major mall in Johannesburg is **Sandton City** (⊠ Sandton Dr. and Rivonia Rd.), with hundreds of stores and a confusing layout that guarantees you'll get lost for days. The wing of shops leading from the mall to the Sandton Sun Hotel has some worthwhile African art galleries. Adjoining Sandton City is **Sandton Square** (⊠ 5th St.), built to resemble an Italian piazza (but a bland facsimile), complete with expensive Italian shops (including an ice cream parlor), bakeries, and restaurants. Closer to the city, **Hyde Park Corner** (⊠ Jan Smuts Ave., Hyde Park, ☎ 011/325–4340) is the city's most upscale shopping center, where fashion victims come to sip cappuccino and browse in Exclusive Books, a branch of the country's best chain of bookstores. Rosebank is a happening suburb focused on a conglomeration of **five shopping centers** (⊠ Cradock St., between Biermann Ave. and Baker St.). The great plus about **Rosebank Mall** (⊠ Between Bath and Cradock Aves.) and the surrounding area is that you can actually walk and sit outside—something of a novelty in security-conscious Johannesburg. This is the place to come for casual alfresco lunches at one of the area's many cafés and restaurants. More recently, however, the area has seen the introduction of extensive hawking along the pavements—here you can shop for curios including artifacts fashioned from coat-hanger wire, clay pots decorated Ndebele style, ubiquitous guinea fowls, soapstone carvings, and malachite jewelry. Downtown, adjoining the Carlton Hotel, the **Carlton Centre** (⊠ Commissioner and von Weilligh Sts.) is home to 200 stores, and the sidewalks thereabouts are packed with sellers of fruit, shoes, clothes, trinkets, and snacks.

Markets

Newtown Market Africa, a flea market held every Saturday in front of the Market Theatre (☞ Sights to See, *above*), is the best place in town for African art and curios at low, low prices. Vendors from Cameroon, Nigeria, and Zaire come here to sell masks, fetishes, traditional wood pillows, Kuba raffia cloth, and Mali blankets. Bargain hard and you should be able to get vendors to knock a third off the price. ⊠ *Wolhuter St., between Bree and Jeppe Sts.* ☉ *Sat. 9–4.*

Rosebank's Rooftop Fleamarket features a lot of locally made crafts, kitsch, bread, cheese, biltong, and mass-produced African curios, like the dark-wood Malawian wood carvings. Frequently, African musicians, dancers, and buskers entertain the roving Sunday crowds. Flea markets both here and in Cape Town have become the best place on the continent to source genuine, and often very valuable, curios from far and wide, particularly the Congo and West Africa—snap up any Benin bronzes you come across, for they are the bargain of the millennium. ⊠ *Rosebank Mall, 50 Bath Ave., Rosebank,* ☎ *011/442–4488.* ☉ *Sun. 9:30–5.*

Specialty Stores

AFRICAN ART

Everard Read Gallery is one of the largest privately owned galleries in the world. It acts as agent for several important South African artists, as well as a number of international contemporary artists. The gallery specializes in wildlife paintings and sculpture. ⊠ *6 Jellicoe Ave., Rose-bank,* ☎ *011/788–4805.* ☉ *Mon.–Sat. 9–6.*

Kim Sacks Gallery, in a lovely old home, has one of the finest collections of authentic African art in Johannesburg. Displayed throughout its sunny rooms are Zairian raffia cloth, Mali mud cloth, Zulu telephone-wire baskets, and an excellent collection of original masks and carvings from across the continent. Prices are high. ⊠ *153 Jan Smuts Ave., Park-wood,* ☎ *011/447–5804.* ☉ *Weekdays 9–5, Sat. 10–5, Sun. 10–3.*

Rural Craft has a good collection of Xhosa and Ndebele beadwork, in-cluding wedding aprons and jewelry. The shop also sells fabrics made by rural Ndebele, Xhosa, and Zulu women. ⊠ *Shop 42E, Mutual Gar-dens, 31 Tyrwhitt Ave., Rosebank,* ☎ *011/880–9651.* ☉ *Weekdays 8:30–4:30, Sat. 9–2:30.*

Soweto Art Gallery, tucked away in three small rooms in a shabby down-town office block, is a no-nonsense shop where the paintings are mostly unframed or stacked against the wall. Elegant it's not, but the gallery features the works of some very talented African artists from townships all over the Johannesburg area. The subject matter is pure Africa, culled from the ghettos of the townships and brought to life in vibrant canvases. ⊠ *34 Harrison St., Suite 34, 2nd floor, Johannes-burg,* ☎ *011/836–0252.* ☉ *Weekdays 8–6, Sat. 8–1.*

Totem Gallery specializes in artifacts from West and Central Africa, in-cluding Kuba cloth from Zaire, Dogon doors from Mali, glass beads, masks from Burkina Faso, and hand-painted barbershop signs. Some pieces come with detailed descriptions of their history. Prices are high. ⊠ *Sandton City,* ☎ *011/884–6300.* ☉ *Weekdays 9–6, Sat. 9–5.* ⊠ *The Firs, Rosebank,* ☎ *011/447–1409.* ☉ *Weekdays 9–5, Sat. 9–4.*

BOOKS

Exclusive Books is the best chain of bookstores in the country, with a great selection of African literature, history, travel, and culture. ⊠ *Sand-ton City,* ☎ *011/883–1010;* ⊠ *Hyde Park Corner,* ☎ *011/325–4298.*

Facts & Fiction allows you to browse not only through the bookshelves but also the Internet at the Internet Café. The store has a good vari-ety of CD-ROMs, as well as a coffee bar where you can enjoy tasty cakes while you flip through magazines and newspapers. ⊠ *Rosebank Mall,* ☎ *011/447–3028;* ⊠ *Sandton Square,* ☎ *011/784–5419.*

GOLD AND DIAMONDS

Krugerrands, with images of President Kruger and a springbok on ei-ther side, are among the most famous gold coins minted today. They lost some of their luster during the apartheid years, when they were banned internationally. Krugerrands are sold individually or in sets containing coins of 1 ounce, ½ ounce, ¼ ounce, and ¹⁄₁₀ ounce of pure gold. You can buy Krugerrands through most city banks, but several branches of First National Bank sell them over the counter. The most convenient branches are in Sandton City, Carlton Centre, and Rosebank.

Schwartz Jewellers (✉ Sandton City, ☎ 011/883–5015) is a diamond wholesaler and manufacturing jeweler offering a large range of classical and ethnic African pieces.

SIDE TRIPS FROM JOHANNESBURG

Soweto

A strange place indeed, this South Western Township, as it was dubbed by Johannesburg's white counselors who established it between the two world wars as a dormitory enclave to serve the city's growing industrial needs. At the time of writing it still had no tourist accommodation, no restaurant or nightclub to compare with any other "real" city—other than the colorful and usually rowdy *shebeens* (essentially drinking houses serving basic food such as stews) . . . not even any building exceeding three stories. And yet this city within a city is home to between 2 and 3 million people—all black.

But what it lacks in material substance it more than makes up for in soul; the still largely working-class population here knows how to live for the day, which accounts for the high energy level of this place, which seethes with music, jive, and humor. Everywhere you turn it seems a party is breaking out. And what other place on earth can boast of having had two Nobel laureates living within a block of each other: For most of his adult life, Anglican archbishop Desmond Tutu lived on Vilakazi Street in Orlando West, otherwise known as Phefeni. And for most of that time his close neighbor would have been an attorney named Nelson Rorihlala Mandela, except that the latter spent most of *his* adult life incarcerated on Robben Island. (South Africa has two other Nobel Peace Prize winners—the first was ANC founder Albert Luthuli, and the fourth was ex-president F. W. De Klerk.)

A Good Tour

Soweto is a chaotic, virtually homogenous sprawl that, even if you found your way in, you'd probably struggle to find your way out of again—let alone around. Your only opportunity to see the place, therefore, is to take a guided tour. There are bus tours offered by various companies, but it is preferable to commission one of the specialist freelance guides who work through Gold Reef City or one of the few reputable private operators in Soweto.

A logical place to start your tour is in the raggedy neighborhood of **Kliptown,** which was born from hope at a time earlier this century, before black people were disallowed from owning their own property. It is here that you'll find **Freedom Square,** which holds a place more dear to most South Africans than any other. For it was on an open piece of ground here that South Africa's first genuinely democratic forum was formed, under the banner of the ANC, on June 25, 1955. During this three-day meeting, the Freedom Charter was drawn and adopted as the blueprint of the liberation struggle. In South African history it has the significance of the drawing up of the U.S. Declaration of Independence and the Bill of Rights.

As you enter Soweto proper from this side, the first site that greets you is not the community's prettiest face: **Mandela Squatter Camp,** a post-1994 phenomenon encouraged by the great man himself as an act of freedom of expression and the overthrowing of oppressive land legislation. However, the flourishing of this "commune" is the cause of some anxiety among Soweto's established society, which itself has only recently been given the right to own houses they have occupied in some cases for two or even three generations. Residents openly criticize the former president for encouraging a "free for all" mentality here without the attendant responsibilities of those who fought long for their freedoms and comforts.

Thereafter, you enter Orlando West, one of the original "suburbs" when Soweto was founded, and the area of greatest interest in Soweto: it is here that you'll see not only the **Tutu and Mandela houses,** but two famous churches as well the first of which is **Holy Cross Church,** the home parish of Bishop Tutu. But even more central to the liberation struggle was the Catholic **Regina Mundi Church,** which throughout the harshest years of repression, from 1976 to 1990, was a refuge of peace, sanity, and steadfast moral focus for the people of Soweto.

On a previously open plot opposite Holy Cross, a stone's throw (in those days literally) from the Tutu and Mandela homes, is the **Hector Peterson Memorial,** not much to look at perhaps but a crucial landmark for the city. This young man was the first victim of police fire on fateful June 16, 1976, when the schoolchildren rose up virtually as one to protest their second-rate "Bantu" education system. The police and government were aghast that such a happening could occur right under their jackboot of control and possibly overreacted. But that picture of young Hector Peterson lying dead in the arms of his crying comrade flashed across the world, and things were never the same. From this incident can be traced the events that eventually brought the white Nationalist domination if not to its knees then at least to the negotiating table.

On a small hill overlooking Orlando West is the empty fortress-home of **Winnie Mandela,** an arrogant symbol of both her relationship with former husband Nelson and her wielding of power gone wrong. And beyond that is old-town **Diepkloof** side by side with new **Diepkloof Extension,** dating back to the mid-1970s when bank loans first became available to black property owners. The difference in the two is quite startling: dreary prefabricated "box" houses of Diepkloof next to what looks like a lower-middle-class suburb anywhere.

From here you proceed deeper into the heart of the city, through **Orlando** proper (named after the Johannesburg counselor Edwin Orlando), who persuaded his council to build simple but sturdy homes for the squatters here back in 1932) with its famous soccer stadium, home ground to the fantastically popular Orlando Pirates team; and **Dube,** named after the ANC founding father and where many of the better shebeens are found.

Compared to what came later, these were acceptable homes each on a decent piece of ground. How different things might have been if the Nationalists who came to power in 1948 had not curtailed home building and had forbidden the citizens here to own property (let alone deprived them of citizenship!). It was to Dube that the evicted residents of **Sophiatown**—a melting pot of music, bohemianism, crime, and multiracialism that insulted Afrikaner Calvinism and Nationalism—were resettled in 1959. At the time, they brought an exciting vibe to the dreary, homogenous dormitory town, and this can still be seen in the relative variety of houses here.

Finally you enter the city center itself, **Jabulani** (be happy). The houses are much the same as elsewhere, but you notice subtle signs of central place—the city's only fire station; a huge, rambling police headquarters; and a low-rise shopping area. In reality, it is a sad and crass excuse for a CBD that serves the country's greatest urban concentration. Back in the 1960s, then chairman of the Anglo American Corporation Harry Oppenheimer donated £60 million to the city, which was used to build around 10,000 homes. In remembrance of this is **Oppenheimer Park,** the only official green space in Soweto (as opposed to stream courses and wetlands) and a favorite venue for wedding photos but alas little else.

Soweto A to Z

GUIDED TOURS

Gold Reef City (☎ 011/496–1400 or 011/496–1401, or call Stan direct at 011/984–5972 or 083/263–9505) has Satour-registered guides such as ex-Agfa PRo Stan Mbense of Rockville who work through Gold Reef City and offer standard or customized tours of the area. **Lizwe Tours** (☎ 011/988–6046 or 082/662–1129) Isaac Sithole is based in Dobsonville and offers tours of Soweto and farther afield. **Jimmy's Face to Face Tours** (☎ 011/331–6209) does more than just the standard tour; they will take you *jolling* (partying) in Soweto, night or day, and to other places such as Rockey Street in Yoeville to give you the real lowdown on Jo'burg's happening areas.

4-H Tourist Information. Contact the **Office of Art and Culture** in Soweto (☎ 011/857–1510).

The Magaliesberg

The Magaliesberg is a range of hills stretching 120 km (74 mi) between Pretoria and the town of Rustenburg, about a 90-minute drive northwest of Johannesburg. The Boer War once raged here, and the remains of British blockhouses can still be seen. However, the region is most remarkable for its natural beauty. Grassy slopes cleft by ocher buttresses, streams adorned with ferns, waterfalls plunging into pools, and superb rock formations contribute to the Magaliesberg's unique beauty. You can get surprisingly close to wildlife on foot: you can view mountain reedbuck, klipspringers, baboon troops, or vervet monkeys. Or search the skies for large raptors such as Cape griffons; black eagles are common even so close to the region's industrial heartland. Activities in the area focus on the outdoors—you can go hiking, backpacking, and mountain biking; swim in crystal streams; take a picnic lunch to one of the natural hideaways; or go on a dawn balloon flight over the area followed by champagne breakfast.

The Magaliesberg is very popular with locals, and the main areas and attractions get extremely crowded on weekends. Advance booking for weekends is advisable—many places limit numbers of visitors, while others (especially hiking and rock-climbing venues) are accessible only through clubs.

Hiking in the Magaliesberg can be extremely hot and dry and in midsummer can get much hotter than Johannesburg. However, this is also when nature—as well as swimming in mountain streams—is at its best. Use a daypack or small rucksack, carry an ample water supply, and use adequate sun protection. Remember to take your own lunch and wear sturdy footwear. A raincoat, swimsuit, and small towel may come in handy in summer.

Much of the Magaliesburg is privately owned, although a protected nature area near the summit remains undeveloped by law. Don't go wandering around unless you're in a resort—you may be trespassing. (Many landowners here are descendents of the Voortrekkers, who consider shooting at trespassers to be their natural right.)

Exploring

For driving directions to the Magaliesberg, *see* Arriving and Departing, *below.* From the R560 and R27, the Magaliesberg's northern aspect is magnificent. Small farms have pink peach blossoms in spring and yellow sunflowers in autumn. **Olifantsnek** is a rock formation that bears an uncanny likeness to an elephant, for which it is named. Slightly beyond is Olifantsnek Dam.

Hartebeesport Dam is beautifully situated on R560 at the foot of the Magaliesberg's impressive southern scarp; the area is popular with fishing and water-sports enthusiasts, as well as with the "breakfast" motorcycle run from the city. The **Cableway** (☎ 014/577–1733), open weekdays 9–3:30 and weekends 9–5, with a fee of R20 round-trip, on the eastern side of the dam is the best way to view the surrounding countryside from on high—and local paragliders floating alongside the cliffs. The dam site was a location for the film version of *Tigers Don't Cry* by popular South African author Wilbur Smith.

If you walk or drive across the **Dam Wall,** you get a bird's-eye view of the whole thing—particularly spectacular after heavy rains when the sluice gates are open.

The resort town of **Hartebeesport** is a tropical oasis where bougainvillea cascades everywhere in summer. Explore the crafts shops and dine alfresco as you watch the world go by.

As you continue westward, you'll find numerous delightful **tea gardens**—and a country pub or two. Many are run by Afrikaaners who've escaped the rat race. The food is generally satisfying; however, expect service to be laid back. A few establishments have small curio shops selling basketware, African masks, *kieries* (walking sticks), and semi-precious stones.

Tranquil **Rustenburg Nature Reserve** lies at the western edge of the range. At the visitor center, you may find out about the area's geology, fauna, and flora. Be sure to take a walk on Peglerae Interpretive Trail, a 5-km (3-mi) walk-by-numbers with rare plants (particularly *Aloe peglerae*) and unusual rocks. Afterward, enjoy a picnic lunch at a picnic site. A self-guided auto trail is also available, but the best way to soak up the natural splendor of this range and its many hidden secrets is on the two-day backpacking trail. ⊠ *Box 511, Rustenburg, 0300.* ☎ *014/ 533–2050.* 🖾 *R10.*

Dining and Lodging

$$ ✕🏨 **De Hoek Country House.** In France this would be called an *auberge,* or country inn, and it wouldn't be out of place in Provence with its dressed stone and heavy timber-beam construction. De Hoek is very exclusive and set in semi-indigenous gardens in the exquisite Magalies River valley. In 2000, the seven deluxe suites inside the manor will be converted into common areas and will be replaced by 20 stone cabins set along the wooded river. Service here is on a very personal and discreet level, which is appealing to guests who are used to pampering or those who like to swim au natural. Food is too mundane a word for what Swiss owner-chef Michael Holenstein conjures up, and his five-course dinners alone are worth the price of your stay. ⊠ *Signposted off the R24 just north of Magaliesburg town (mailing address: Box 117 Magaliesburg, 2805),* ☎ *011/577–1198,* 🖾 *011/577–3787. 7 rooms. Pool, archery, croquet, hiking, fishing, library. AE, DC, MC, V.*

$$$ 🏨 **Mount Grace Country House Hotel.** This peaceful country hotel near the town of Magaliesberg has accommodations in delightful thatched buildings of differing heights, which have glorious views of the mountain. The Mountain Village is the most luxurious lodging, with sunken baths, heated towel rails, a minibar, and endless views of the area. If you're looking for more privacy, you might prefer to stay at Grace Village, which is a little more secluded and farther down the mountain. The most reasonable lodging is the Thatchstone Village. Country-style decor—thatch, wood, and wicker—creates a delightful ambience in the hotel, and the food is wholesome country fare. ⊠ *On the R24 to Hekpoort, near the town of Magaliesburg (mailing address: Box 251 Magaliesburg 2805),* ☎ *014/577–1350,* FAX *014/577–1202. 65 rooms. Restaurant, bar, pool, tennis court, bowling, croquet, hiking, fishing, billiards, library. AE, DC, MC, V.*

Magaliesberg A to Z

ARRIVING AND DEPARTING

From Sandton, take the N1 south toward Roodepoort and get off at the 4th Avenue/Fairlands exit. At the bottom of the exit, turn right onto 4th Avenue toward the suburb of Constantia Kloof. Proceed under the highway bridge and turn right at the second set of traffic lights, onto the M47/R47 to Tarlton. After crossing the R28 from Krugersdorp, the R47 becomes the N17. Continue to the T-junction and turn right, toward Hekpoort. You are now on the R563. Keep to the right-hand lane as the left-hand lane peels off soon afterward. The road will wind a little, and you'll have beautiful views of the Magaliesberg. After you have passed a Boer War blockhouse high on a hill on the right-hand side, look for the "Bekker Schools" sign at the bottom of the hill, and turn left onto this road. At another T-junction, turn right toward Rustenburg, onto the R560. Shortly after passing Hartebeesport Dam on your right, you will reach another T-junction. Turn left onto the R27, again going toward Rustenburg.

Another route is the R24, which approaches the Magaliesberg from Krugersdorp, passes the town of Magaliesberg, and joins the R560. The Johannesburg branch of the Automobile Association has an excellent map of the Magaliesberg showing major routes and resorts.

HIKING

The **Johannesburg Hiking Club** (☎ 011/465–9888) hikes the Magaliesberg and surrounding areas every Sunday; it's open weekdays 8:30–noon.

The **Mountain Club of South Africa (Southern Transvaal Section)** has regular hiking and climbing meets. For events in the area, call the club's main office in Cape Town (☎ 021/45–3412).

HOT-AIR BALLOONING

For a special experience, sail high above the Magaliesberg in a hot-air balloon, sipping sparkling wine with **Bill Harrop's Original Balloon Safaris** (☎ 011/705–3201, FAX 011/705–3203) and enjoying a sumptuous breakfast afterward.

VISITOR INFORMATION

The **tourist information office** (⊠ On R24, ☎ 014/577–1733) for the area is on the main road through Magaliesberg town (on the southern side of town if you're driving from Krugersdorp).

Pretoria

Pretoria is overshadowed by Johannesburg, 48 km (30 mi) to the south, and few people outside South Africa know it as the country's capital. It's a pleasant city, with historic buildings and a city center that is easily explored on foot. Pretoria is famous for its jacaranda trees, and the best time to visit is in spring (September–October), when the city is blanketed with their purple blossoms. Founded in 1855, the city was named after Andries Pretorius, the hero of the Battle of Blood River

(☞ *below and* Chapter 7), and it has remained a bastion of Afrikaner culture. With the triumph of the Nationalist Party in 1948, it also became the seat of Afrikaner power, and the city developed a reputation for hard-line Afrikaner insularity. Much of that has changed in recent years, and President Thabo Mbeki now occupies the lovely Union Buildings overlooking the city. International acceptance of the new South Africa has also seen an influx of foreign embassies and personnel, bringing a refreshing cosmopolitanism to Pretoria. As a result, many of the country's finest restaurants are here.

A Good Tour
Numbers in the text correspond to numbers in the margin and on the Pretoria map.

If you're coming from Johannesburg, your first stop should be the **Voortrekker Monument and Museum** ⑱. To get there, take the Fountains/Voortrekkerhoogte exit from the R28. At the traffic lights at the bottom of the exit, turn left toward Voortrekkerhoogte. Turn right at the next set of traffic lights. The entrance gates to the monument are on the right-hand side of the road, shortly after the traffic lights. Brown information signs will in any event direct you to the monument from the highway. Return to the highway (R28) and drive north into the city. The R28 becomes Potgieter Street going into Pretoria central. (This is a one-way street going north.) Turn right on Kerk Street. The **Kruger House Museum** ⑲ is on your left. Street parking is available. Walk four blocks east down Kerk to **Church Square** ⑳. Walk one block north from Church Square on Paul Kruger Street and turn right onto Vermeulen Street to reach the **Pierneef Museum** ㉑.

Head back to Kerk Street and collect your car. Drive one block east to Schubart Street (a one-way street going south) and turn right onto Schubart Street. Drive four blocks south until you reach Visagie Street. Turn left on Visagie Street and drive two blocks. You will now be on the north side of the **Transvaal Museum** ㉒, the best natural science museum in the country. Across Paul Kruger Street from the museum stands **City Hall** ㉓. Walk south down Paul Kruger Street for two blocks and turn left on Jacob Maré Street to reach the High Victorian landmark and national monument **Melrose House** ㉔. Cross the street to view the beautiful **Burgers Park** ㉕.

Continue down Jacob Maré Street and turn left on Van der Walt Street at the corner. Walk three blocks to Skinner Street. At the corner of Skinner Street, you'll pass the brick **Staats Model School** ㉖, the first school in this pioneer town. Continue north along Van der Walt Street for two blocks until you reach Pretorius Street and the vulgar, monumental **J. G. Strijdom Square** ㉗, named for one of South Africa's prime ministers. To the right of the square is the awe-inspiring State Theatre and Opera House. Walk west on Pretorius Street for two blocks to reach Paul Kruger Street once more. Walk south down Paul Kruger Street for three blocks to reach the Transvaal Museum, where you will have parked your car.

Drive south on Paul Kruger Street to Jacob Maré Street; turn left and pass Burgers Park on your left. Take the next road right, turning north on the one-way Van der Walt Street. Continue for 12 blocks until you reach the one-way DR Savage Drive and turn left. Drive three blocks and turn right on Bosman Street, and after a block, turn left on Boom Street. Another 1½ blocks will take you to the entrance to the **National Zoological Gardens** ㉘ on your left. To continue on to the **Union Buildings** ㉙, keep driving west on Boom Street and turn left onto Hamilton Street. At Edmond Street turn left, and the Union Buildings will be on

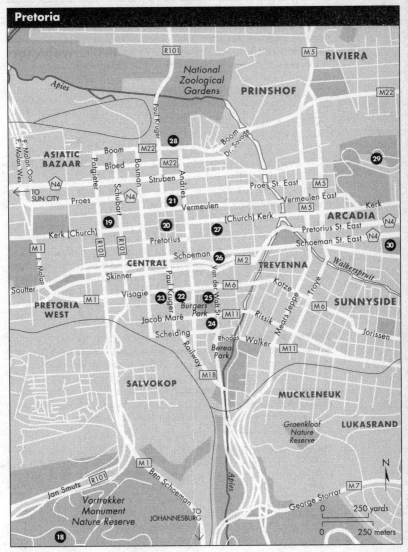

Pretoria

Burgers Park, **25**

Church Square, **20**

City Hall, **23**

J.G. Strijdom
Square, **27**

Kruger House
Museum, **19**

Melrose House, **24**

National Zoological
Gardens, **28**

Pierneef Museum, **21**

Pretoria Art
Museum, **30**

Staats Model
School, **26**

Transvaal
Museum, **22**

Union Buildings, **29**

Voortrekker
Monument and
Museum, **18**

the left. This road becomes a wide throughway with ample parking. In
the valley directly below the Union Buildings lies the **Pretoria Art Museum** ㉚. To reach this, drive south down Hamilton Street once you've
had your fill of the Union Buildings. Drive five blocks to reach the one-
way Schoeman Street and turn left. Drive two long blocks to reach Wessels Street. The Pretoria Art Museum is on the corner.

To get back to the R28 and the N1S to Johannesburg, head south down
Wessels Street for one block to reach Park Street, turn right, drive for
one block, and then turn left on Leyds Street. After three blocks, turn
left onto Church Street. Continue for seven blocks, and then turn left
on Andries Street. After four blocks, turn left onto Visagie Street,
going west. After three blocks, turn left on Schubart Street and follow
the signs back to Johannesburg. Going back to Johannesburg, the R28
becomes the N1S. Follow the signs to the N1S if you don't want to
end up in Krugersdorp.

TIMING
It will take about 30 minutes to travel from Johannesburg to Pretoria
on the N1. As you near Pretoria, the N1 branches. Take the R28 to
enter the city center. If you want to see everything, we suggest you schedule an entire day in Pretoria. The walk alone will probably take a morning. You might want to drive to Kruger House and then continue
north to see the Union Buildings. Arrange to take a picnic lunch, as
the gardens are a lovely place for a picnic.

Sights to See

㉕ **Burgers Park.** This lovely parkland lies across the road from Melrose
House. Note the gates, which are all that remain of yet another Victorian mansion that lost out to the developers. Heady scents will lead
you to fragrant rose gardens and flower beds filled with indigenous
plants. At the center of the park, a converted Victorian house now contains a delightful restaurant. ⊠ *Jacob Maré St., between Van der Walt
and Andries Sts.* ☒ *Free.*

⑳ **Church Square.** A statue of President Kruger by Anton van Wouw dominates the pleasant square, which is flanked by some of Pretoria's most
historic buildings: the Old Raadsaal (Town Hall), built in early Italian Renaissance style; the Palace of Justice, which was used as a military hospital during the Boer War; and the modern Provincial
Administration Building. President Kruger arranged for the construction of many of these buildings. ⊠ *Bordered by Paul Kruger St. and
Church St.*

㉓ **City Hall.** An imposing structure that borrows freely from classical architecture, the building has a tympanum on the front by Coert Steyn-
berg, one of South Africa's most famous sculptors—it symbolizes the
growth and development of Pretoria. Statues of Andries Pretorius, the
hero of the Battle of Blood River, and his son Marthinus, the city's
founder, stand in the square fronting City Hall. ⊠ *Paul Kruger St. (opposite Transvaal Museum, at the end of the gardens),* ☎ *012/326–5012.*
☉ *Weekdays 8–3.*

㉗ **J. G. Strijdom Square.** The square is dominated by a huge bust of former prime minister Strijdom. Despite the fervid anticommunist stance
of the old Nationalist government, the square's monumental architecture
bears a striking resemblance to that of former Soviet states; J. G. Strijdom's head could just as easily be Lenin's. ⊠ *Church and Van der Walt
Sts., next to the State Theatre.*

⑲ **Kruger House Museum.** This was once the residence of Paul Kruger,
president of the South African Republic between 1883 and 1902 and

one of the most revered figures in South African history. The home, still fully furnished, is humble and somber, befitting this deeply religious leader who loved to sit on the front *stoep* (veranda) and watch the world go by. Exhibits in the adjoining museum trace Kruger's career, culminating in his exile by the British and eventual death in Switzerland in 1904. Of particular interest are the expressions of support that Kruger received from all over the world, including the United States, when Britain instigated the Boer War (1899–1902). Across the road is the Dutch Reformed Church (now a national monument) where Mrs. Kruger was buried. ⊠ *Kerk St. at Potgieter St.,* ☎ *012/326–9172.* ☞ *R7.* ☉ *Weekdays 8:30–4, weekends 9–4.*

㉔ Melrose House. Built in 1886, this opulent structure is one of the most beautiful Victorian homes in the country, with marble columns, mosaic floors, and lovely stained-glass windows. The house is furnished in period style. Its dining room is where the 1902 Treaty of Vereeniging was signed, ending the Boer War. ⊠ *275 Jacob Maré St.,* ☎ *012/322–2805.* ☞ *R3.* ☉ *Tues.–Sun. 10–5.*

㉘ National Zoological Gardens. Pretoria's zoo is considered one of the world's best, with an enormous collection of animals from almost every continent. The animal enclosures here are much larger than those of most zoos, but a cage is still a cage. However, like any modern zoo worth its name, this is just the public facade for a much larger organization that specializes in the research and breeding of endangered species. A cable car (R6.50) transports visitors high above the zoo to a hilltop lookout. ⊠ *Boom St.,* ☎ *012/328–3265.* ☞ *R17.* ☉ *Daily 8–5:30.*

㉑ Pierneef Museum. In a turn-of-the-century house, the museum displays works by Jacob Pierneef (1886–1957), one of South Africa's finest painters. Remarkable for his great range of styles, he is most famous for his unique, almost abstract renderings of South African landscapes. ⊠ *Vermeulen St., between Andries and Paul Kruger Sts.,* ☎ *012/323–1419.* ☞ *Free.* ☉ *Weekdays 8:30–4.*

㉚ Pretoria Art Museum. This unimpressive gallery space houses a very impressive collection of South African art. Much of the collection consists of works by famous white artists, including Pierneef, van Wouw, Irma Stern, and Hugo Naudé, but more and more black artists are now receiving recognition—look for works by Ephraim Ngatane (1938–71), an early exponent of township art. The museum also stages changing exhibitions. ⊠ *Schoeman and Wessels Sts.,* ☎ *012/344–1807 or 012/344–1808.* ☞ *R3.* ☉ *Tues.–Sat. 10–5, Wed. 10–8, Sun. noon–5.*

㉖ Staats Model School. The building is a fine example of a late-19th-century Transvaal Republic school. During the Boer War it served as a prison for British officers. It was from here that Winston Churchill made his famous escape after Boers captured him near Ladysmith. Appropriately, the school now houses an education department. It is not open to the public. ⊠ *Skinner and Van der Walt Sts.*

☞ **㉒ Transvaal Museum.** The extensive collection of land and marine animals from around the world, with an emphasis on African wildlife, is worth a visit. The museum also contains the Austin Roberts Bird Collection, the most comprehensive display of African birds in southern Africa. Much of the museum is laid out with students in mind, and exhibit descriptions are exceptionally informative. Of particular interest are the Genesis exhibits, tracing the evolution of life on earth, and the geology section, with displays of weird and wonderful rocks and minerals. This is a great place to bring kids. Note: The museum is currently being extended—you may find certain halls and exhibits closed due to renovations. ⊠ *Paul Kruger St., across from City Hall,* ☎ *012/322–7632.* ◪ *R6.* ⊙ *Mon.–Sat. 9–5, Sun. 11–5.*

㉙ **Union Buildings.** Designed by Sir Herbert Baker, this impressive cream sandstone complex is his masterpiece and home to the administrative branch of government, which now serves as the headquarters of President Thabo Mbeki. The complex incorporates a hodgepodge of styles—an Italian-tile roof, wood shutters inspired by Cape Dutch architecture, and Renaissance columns—that somehow works beautifully. Formal gardens step down the hillside in terraces, dotted with war memorials and statues of former prime ministers. The view of the city from the large, rambling gardens here is superb. ⊠ *Access off Kerk or Edmond St.*

⑱ **Voortrekker Monument and Museum.** This unabashed tribute to the ideals at the heart of apartheid doesn't have a place in the new South Africa, but for the moment it remains, as much a part of Pretoria's landmarks as the sprawling edifice of UNISA (the University of South Africa, a correspondence school) as you enter the city from the south. Completed in 1949, the monument honors the Voortrekkers, Boer families who rejected British rule in the Cape and in 1835–38 trekked into the hinterland to found their own nation. The Hall of Heroes traces in its frieze the momentous events of their Great Trek, culminating in the Battle of Blood River (December 16, 1838), when a small force of Boers defeated the Zulu army without losing a single life (☞ Chapter 7). The Voortrekkers considered this victory a confirmation of their special relationship with God. An adjoining museum displays scenes and artifacts of daily Voortrekker life, as well as the Voortrekker Tapestries, 15 pictorial weavings that trace the historical high points of the Great Trek. Even if you don't appreciate all the symbolism, the sheer grandeur of the monolith is worth seeing. ⊠ *Off M7 (follow brown signs off R28),* ☎ *012/323–0682.* ◪ *Monument R10, museum R5.* ⊙ *Daily 9–4:45 (last entry at 4:30).*

Dining

$$$$ **✕ Chagalls at Toulouse.** At the end of their meal, a contingent of visiting French chefs gave this restaurant a standing ovation. The food is *that* good. Chef Eric Springer has worked in the kitchens of some of Paris's most famous restaurants, and his haute cuisine *française* is considered the finest in South Africa. The menu changes twice a year and invariably creates a stir. Start with such appetizers as creamed cauliflower with crumbed Irish salmon, or lobster and potato charlotte in caviar and salmon-egg butter. Main courses may include lightly roasted breast of wild duck served with warm potato salad and confit of duck leg, and marinated fillet of kudu antelope dressed with apple and nuts. The restaurant's setting, in a country lodge on the outskirts of Pretoria, is lovely. ⊠ *Fountains Valley, Pretoria,* ☎ *012/342–1200. Reservations required. Jacket and tie. AE, DC, MC, V. Closed Sun. No lunch Sat.*

$$$ **✕ La Madeleine.** Noted for its classic and creative French cuisine, this
★ restaurant ranks among the country's top 10. The wine list, too, has won a slew of awards. The menu changes daily, depending on what's available at the market. For starters expect calamari tubes stuffed with ratatouille or oysters and mussels in a cream-curry sauce. For a main dish try to select among rack of lamb with fresh vegetables and olives, line fish in champagne sauce, ostrich fillet with cranberry sauce, or veal in Muscat sauce. Desserts include such heavenly treats as honey ice cream with chocolate mousse cake and crème brûlée. ⊠ *258 Esselen St., Sunnyside, Pretoria,* ☎ *012/44–6076. Reservations required. AE, DC, MC, V. Closed Sun. and Mon. No lunch Sat.*

$$$ ✕ **La Perla.** This grand Continental restaurant is a favorite haunt of ambassadors and ministers. The interior, with wood-paneled walls and tables separated by etched-glass panels, is ideal for private power lunches. Specials are all seasonal, but the menu could include dishes like panfried quail with fresh herbs or saddle of game. Starters include baked snails or prawns on a skewer. Meticulous preparation and service make up for any lack of innovation in the menu. The wine list is also outstanding. ✉ *211 Skinner St., Pretoria,* ☎ *012/322–2759. Reservations required. AE, DC, MC, V. Closed Sun. No lunch Sat.*

$$ ✕ **Brasserie de Paris.** This delightful French oasis occupies an unassuming building in suburban Hatfield. In typical Parisian style, café tables adorn the outside veranda. Appetizers include frogs' legs Provençal and delicious pâté en croute. For a main course, choose between ox tongue in white wine sauce with gherkins and mustard, and duck leg cooked slowly with veal stock and red wine, served with a shallot sauce. Fish is also on the menu, including skate wings. ✉ *525 Duncan St., Hatfield,* ☎ *012/342–5057. AE, DC, MC, V. Closed Sun. No lunch Sat.*

Lodging

$$$$ 🏨 **Heia Safari Ranch.** Why put up with the anonymity of a large town
★ hotel when you can stay on this game ranch? Accommodation is in thatched *rondawels* (huts), each with two bedrooms and a large bathroom, set on a wooded estate. Don't be surprised to see zebras grazing on the lawns or giraffes browsing the acacia trees around the swimming pool (remember they can be dangerous). The main complex is all under thatch and has a spacious lounge, large restaurant, and bar with game trophies. Very popular are the Sunday barbecues followed by a two-hour program of traditional African dance at the authentic Phumanena Zulu village at the far end of the estate (where you can also spend the night). Between Heia and the village is the game ranch, which has 22 species of animal. ✉ *Off the M5 (D. F. Malan Dr./Swartkops Rd.), turnoff 5½ km (3½ mi) north after crossing the M28 (Pretoria–Krugersdorp) highway (mailing address: Box 1387, Honeydew 2040),* ☎ *011/659–0605,* 🅵🅰🆇 *011/659–0709. 45 rondawels. Restaurant, bar, pool, tennis court. AE, DC, MC, V.*

$$$$ 🏨 **Sheraton Pretoria.** This luxury hotel actually works on two levels. The first five floors consist of standard or classic rooms, decorated in shades of cream with Italian marble tiles. The top two floors, only accessible with a special pass, comprise "The Towers": 43 suites, each with a personal computer, decorated in subtle African theme with shades of green, brown, and ocher. The Royal Suite has, of all things, bullet-proof glass. Ask for a room overlooking the Union Building Gardens. The jazz bar has live performances nightly. ✉ *643 Church St, at Wessels,* ☎ *012/ 429–9999,* 🅵🅰🆇 *012/429–9300. 132 rooms, 43 suites. 2 restaurants, 2 bars, pool, massage, sauna, health club. AE, DC, MC, V.*

$$$ 🏨 **Illyria House.** Although there are more grand hotels in town, sheikhs and presidents have been known to request to be moved to this small but very special suburban guest house on Muckleneuk Hill overlooking the city bowl. The house takes its name from the mythical place where Shakespeare set his romantic *Twelfth Night* comedy, and the house and gardens feel as though they're part of an elaborate stage set for the play. Presiding over the array of French antiques and over-the-top Venetian light fittings is vivacious owner and host Marietjie van der Walt. There is a dining room but no set menu—the butler and chef will discuss options with you each day and then shop just for you. Nothing is too much, which explains something of the lodge's appeal. Previously, reservations were by referral only, but Marietjie will now accept private inquiries. If it's available, ask for the Katarina suite, with its view of the Union Buildings. Or you can hire the whole house at

R10,000 a day. ✉ *327 Bourke St., Muckleneuk, Pretoria,* ☎ *012/344–5193.* FAX *012/344–3978. 7 suites. BP. AE, DC, MC, V.*

$$ 🏨 **Irene Country Lodge.** This tranquil village and adjacent meadows
★ is where soldier, philosopher, and statesman Jan Christiaan Smuts
chose to make his home when he craved nature during his political ca-
reer—a sort of Walden Pond. Majestic old oak trees add to the sense
of country, but it's just a stone's throw from Pretoria and close to both
Johannesburg and its airport. Rooms are spacious and decorated in a
variety of themes ranging from light florals to a dark blue wild duck
motif. The Oak Tree restaurant is justification for not having to ven-
ture further for your needs. ✉ *Irene Village, Nellmapius Dr., Irene,*
☎ *012/667–6464,* FAX *012/667–6476. Restaurant, bar, coffee shop, room
service, pool. 46 rooms, 4 suites. BP. AE, DC, MC, V.*

The Arts

CLASSICAL MUSIC

The **New Arts Philharmonic Orchestra, Pretoria (NAPOP)** plays in the
State Theatre (✉ Church St., ☎ 012/322–1665).

THEATER

The **State Theatre Pretoria** (✉ Church St., ☎ 012/322–1665) is home
to the Performing Arts Council Transvaal (PACT), a state-funded
group that supports a wide range of theater, as well as ballet and opera
companies. To fully appreciate this grand theater, book a guided tour,
which includes the backstage areas. (You can make a tour reservation
one week in advance.)

Spectator Sports

The place to see rugby (in winter) in Pretoria is at the gigantic **Loftus
Versveld Stadium** (✉ Kirkness St., Sunnyside, Pretoria, ☎ 012/344–
4045), shrine to the white population's national obsession. When you
go to a rugby match here, it's almost more interesting to watch the spec-
tators—the local team, Northern Province, are known as the Blue
Bulls and spectators arrive wearing blue hats adorned with mock blue
horns. The heckling from the stands is an education in itself. If you
want to take a more serious interest in the game, take along a pair of
binoculars.

Pretoria A to Z

ARRIVING AND DEPARTING

By Bus. Translux (☎ 012/334–8000) and **Greyhound** (☎ 012/323–1154)
buses run regularly between **Pretoria** (✉ Pretoria Station, at Paul
Kruger and Scheiding Sts.) and Johannesburg's Rotunda on their way
to destinations around the country.

By Car. The quickest way to reach Pretoria from Johannesburg is via
the **N1 highway,** which turns into the R28 as it nears the city. Outside
rush hour, the 50-km (30-mi) drive takes no more than half an hour.

EMBASSIES AND CONSULATES

Australian High Commission. ✉ *292 Orient St., Arcadia, Pretoria,* ☎
012/342–3740.

British High Commission. ✉ *255 Hill St., Arcadia, Pretoria,* ☎ *012/
483–1200.*

Canadian High Commission. ✉ *1103 Arcadia St., Hatfield, Pretoria,*
☎ *012/342–6923.*

U.S. Embassy. ✉ *877 Pretorius St., Arcadia, Pretoria,* ☎ *012/342–1048.*

VISITOR INFORMATION

Pretoria Tourist Information Centre. ✉ *Sammy Marks Center, Ver-
meulen St.,* ☎ *012/308–8909.*

The **National Parks Board** handles accommodation reservations for all national parks and can furnish information. ✉ *643 Leyds St., Muckleneuk (mailing address: Box 787, Pretoria 0001),* ☎ *012/343–1991,* FAX *012/343–0905.*

Pilanesberg National Park

Abutting Sun City, the 150,000-acre Pilanesberg National Park rises from the arid parchment of the North West Province. Like Tanzania's Ngorongoro Conservation Area, Pilanesberg is centered on the caldera of an extinct volcano dating back some 100 million years. It lacks the drama and mind-numbing scale of Ngorongoro, but it's lovely nevertheless—rings of concentric mountains converge on a central lake filled with crocodiles and hippos. Open grassland, rocky crags, and densely forested gorges provide ideal habitats for a wide range of plains and woodland game, including rare brown hyenas, sable, and gemsbok.

With the introduction of lions in 1993, Pilanesberg National Park can boast the Big Five. Since 1979, more than 6,000 animals have been relocated to the park, including some elephants that spent most of their lives in the United States. Today, it's hard to believe that the park, reclaimed from farmland, was ever anything but wild. The lion and elephant populations are still low for an area this size, but the park should reach its full carrying capacity within a few years. The park is a bird-watcher's paradise, with a vast range of grassland species, water birds, and birds of prey.

Most tourists combine a trip to the Pilanesberg with a visit to Sun City next door. Safari companies based in Sun City can show you the park on game drives, but many people opt to drive themselves. As beautiful as the park is, however, it's no substitute for a trip to the Mpumalanga and Kruger National Park. Its major pluses are its proximity to Sun City and Johannesburg, just 90 minutes away—and the fact that it's malaria-free.

Lodging

$$$$ ▦ **Bakubung.** Abutting the national park, this lodge sits at the head of a long valley with terrific views of a hippo pool that forms the lodge's central attraction—it's not unusual to have hippos grazing 100 ft from the terrace restaurant. Despite this, the lodge never really succeeds in creating a bush feel, perhaps because it's such a big convention and family destination. Its brick buildings also feel vaguely institutional. Nevertheless, the guest rooms, particularly the executive studios, are very pleasant, thanks to light pine furniture, colorful African bedspreads, and super views of the valley. Ask for an upstairs room if you want a thatched ceiling. The lodge conducts game drives (fee) in openair vehicles, and ranger guided walks. A shuttle bus (R20 return) runs to Sun City, 10 km (6 mi) away. ✉ *Pilanesberg National Park (mailing address: Box 294, Sun City 0316),* ☎ *01455/2–1861, 011/780–7444 reservations,* FAX *01455/2–1621. 76 rooms, 50 chalets. Restaurant, bar, café, pool, tennis. MAP. AE, DC, MC, V.*

$$$$ ▦ **Kwa Maritane.** You won't hear too many complaints about this lodge's setting, in a bowl of rocky hills on the edge of the national park. Unfortunately, the hotel fails to take advantage of its greatest asset: many of the hotel buildings look inward onto swimming pools and lawns. And, as at Bakubung, the bustle of convention goers and children tends to drown out the mesmerizing sound of the bush. The big exception is the resort's terrific blind, overlooking a water hole and connected to the lodge via a tunnel. Guest rooms, with high thatched ceilings and large glass doors that open onto a veranda, are comfortable, if

generic. Guests can pay to go on day or night game drives in open-air vehicles, or on guided walks with an armed ranger. A free shuttle runs to Sun City; the return trip costs around R4. ⊠ *Pilanesberg National Park (mailing address: Box 39, Sun City, 0316),* ☎ *01455/2–1820, 011/ 780–7444 reservations,* FAX *01455/2–1147. 155 rooms. Restaurant, bar, 2 pools, sauna, tennis court, miniature golf. MAP. AE, DC, MC, V.*

$ 🏨 **Manyane.** The cheapest lodging in the Sun City area, the park's main rest camp lies in thinly wooded savanna east of the Pilanesberg's volcanic ridges. Modeled after Kruger's modern rest camps, Manyane is short on charm but long on functional efficiency and cleanliness. Thatched roofing helps soften the harsh lines of bare tile floors and ugly brick. Guests can choose either a two-, four-, or six-bed chalet, all with fully equipped kitchens and bathrooms. Among the camp's greatest attractions are the enormous walk-in aviaries, housing many of the region's more spectacular bird species. Short, self-guided nature trails from the chalets are available. You won't see anything large, however, but a short interpretative trail gives interesting background to the geology and flora of the park and leads to a small water hole. ⊠ *Pilanesberg National Park,* ☎ *01455/55–0351, 018/382–2663 Golden Leopard Resorts. 60 chalets. Restaurant, bar, pool, miniature golf, playground. AE, DC, MC, V.*

GAME LODGE

$$$$ 🏨 **Tshukudu Game Lodge.** Few private lodges can match the beauty
  ★   of this tiny luxury lodge inside Pilanesberg. Built into the side of a steep, rocky hill, Tshukudu overlooks open grassland and a large water hole where elephants come to bathe. If you watch long enough, you'll probably see most of the Big Five from your veranda. Winding stone stairways lead up the hill to lovely, thoughtfully set thatched chalets with private balconies, wicker furniture, bold African materials, and blackslate floors. Fireplaces, minibars, and mosquito nets are standard, and sunken bathtubs command spectacular views of the water hole. It's a long, 132-step climb to the main lodge on the summit, making this an impractical choice for the elderly or those with disabilities. At night, you can use a spotlight to illuminate game at the water hole below.

Game Experience: Tshukudu lies in the middle of the 135,850-acre Pilanesberg National Park and as a result must share the park roads with other visitors. The biggest drawback is a park regulation banning off-road driving, which means rangers can't follow animals into the bush. Under these circumstances, you're unlikely to see a hunt or a kill. Your chances of seeing the Big Five will be virtually guaranteed, however, if the proposed plan to put radio collars on animals is adopted. By just following the signal, rangers will be able to track down any animal they choose. You'd get to see all the game, but gone would be the adventure and suspense of tracking—and you might as well go to a zoo. Instead, learn the names of Pilanesberg trees and grasses or follow the spoor of wild animals on walks with knowledgeable field guides. ⊠ *Box 6805, Rustenburg, 0300,* ☎ FAX *01455/21–620, 011/ 780–7444 central reservations. 6 cottages, 2 cabins. Bar, pool. No children under 12. No private vehicles allowed. AE, DC, MC, V.*

Pilanesberg A to Z

ARRIVING AND DEPARTING
For information about getting to and from the park, *see* Sun City, *below.*

GUIDED TOURS
Pilanesberg Safaris (☎ 01455/5–6135) conducts 2½-hour game drives in open-air vehicles. Game drives leave early in the morning, in the afternoon, and at night, when rangers illuminate nocturnal animals with a powerful spotlight. Rangers are in radio contact with other vehicles

in the field, allowing them to coordinate the search for game. The company also offers 3½-hour bush walks, led by an armed ranger who focuses on the small details of the bush, ranging from the medicinal uses of various trees to the identification of animal spoor. If you prefer to see the big picture, go up in a **hot-air balloon** (☎ 01455/2–1561); a one-hour flight costs R1,550 per person, which includes game drives, sparkling wine, and full breakfast at Bakubang or Kwa-Maritane.

RESERVATIONS AND FEES
Entry to the park costs R20 a person and R15 a vehicle. The park gates are open daily September–March 5:30 AM–7 PM and April–August 6 AM–6:30 PM. Direct all inquiries to **Pilanesberg National Park** (✉ Box 6651, Rustenburg 0300, ☎ 01455/5–5351).

Sun City

Sun City is a huge entertainment and resort complex in the middle of dry bushveld, 177 km (110 mi) northwest of Johannesburg. It's the dream child of Sol Kerzner, the South African entrepreneur who first saw the possibilities of a casino in the rocky wilds of the Pilanesberg mountains (which, being in Bophuthatswana, were exempt from South Africa's then strict antigambling laws). Now, nearly two decades later, Sun City comprises four hotels, two casinos, major amphitheaters, and a host of outdoor attractions. The complex is split into two parts: the original Sun City and the Lost City, a new project anchored by the magnificent Palace Hotel.

Comparisons with Las Vegas are inappropriate. Sun City is a resort, not a city, although it does rely on the same entertainments: gambling, slot machines, topless revues, and big-time extravaganzas. Sun City stages enormous rock concerts, major boxing bouts, the annual Sun City Golf Challenge, and the occasional Miss World Pageant. It also displays that familiar Vegas sense (or lack) of taste—the Palace being a notable exception—doling out the kind of ersatz glitter and glare that appeals to a shiny polyester crowd. Whatever your feelings about the complex, you have to admire Kerzner's creativity when you see the Lost City, where painted wild animals march across the ceilings, imitation star-spangled skies glitter even by day, lush jungles decorate the halls, and stone lions and elephants keep watch over it all.

The resort burst onto the international scene in the apartheid era, when a few American and British music stars broke the cultural boycott to play Sun City. Back then, it was part of Bophuthatswana, one of the nominally independent homelands designed to give blacks a semblance of self-government. Today, Bophuthatswana has been reabsorbed into South Africa as part of the new North West Province.

Sun City's genuine appeal lies not in the slots but in the remarkable Palace Hotel and the nearby Pilanesberg National Park (☞ *above*). You can either drive yourself through the park or join guided tours in open-air Land Rovers; all of the safari companies will pick you up at your hotel.

Sun City also has a full round of outdoor sports and activities, including two Gary Player–designed golf courses and a man-made lake where visitors can water-ski, parasail, and sailboard. The latest addition is Valley of the Waves, a giant pool that creates perfect waves for body-surfing onto a man-made beach. For the adventurous, there's the heart-stopping Temple of Courage, a water chute designed to hurtle you down a 300-ft rock face at speeds of up to 35 kph (21 mph).

Lodging

Accommodations in Sun City are very expensive, and only the Palace can justify its rates. You may opt to stay instead in the nearby rest camps and private lodges of the Pilanesberg National Park (☞ *above*).

CATEGORY	COST*
$$$$	over R900
$$$	R700–R900
$$	R500–R700
$	under R500

All prices are for a standard double room, including VAT.

$$$$ ⊞ **Palace of the Lost City.** Even if you never go near the rest of Sun
★   City, consider staying at this soaring, magnificent complex. It's the most spectacular hotel in the country and has become an attraction in its own right. Given the tackiness of Sun City, you would think any hotel based on the concept of a lost African palace would suffer from theme-park syndrome. Nothing could be further from the truth—although trade-union problems in recent years have led to complaints of erratic service standards. Sculpted cranes and leaping kudu appear to take flight from the hotel towers, elephants guard triumphal stairways and bridges, and graceful reminders of Africa strike you at every turn. No expense has been spared—the hotel cost R800 million—and the attention to detail is mind-boggling. All rooms have hand-carved doors and furnishings; the jungle paintings on the ceiling of the lobby's rotunda took 5,000 hours to complete; and the hand-laid mosaic floor is made up of 300,000 separate tiles. Guest rooms, done in rich earth tones, blend African motifs with delicate Eastern touches. Carved wooden screens open into an elegant bathroom with separate bath and shower, and a huge wood armoire hides a safe, TV, and minibar. If you really want to splurge, choose one of the grand suites (at more than R11,000 per night). The hotel's two restaurants serve some of the finest cuisine in the country. ⊠ *Box 308, Sun City 0316,* ☎ *01455/7–3000, 011/780–7800 central reservations,* FAX *01455/7–1131. 338 rooms. 2 restaurants, 2 bars, room service, pool. AE, DC, MC, V.*

$$$ ⊞ **The Cascades.** The lavish use of mirrors, brass, and black marble in the lobby sets the tone for this sophisticated high-rise hotel, only yards from the Lost City's massive entertainment center. Rooms have an understated African elegance, decorated in soothing rust colors highlighted with bold blues and yellows. All overlook the Gary Player golf course, the gardens, and an artificial waterfall. For the best views, request a room on an upper floor. ⊠ *Box 7, Sun City,* ☎ *01455/7–1000, 011/780–7800 central reservations,* FAX *01455/7–3447. 243 rooms. 2 restaurants, 2 bars, room service, pool. AE, DC, MC, V.*

$$$ ⊞ **Sun City Hotel.** This is the original Sun City property, and it still houses the gaming casino, banks of slot machines, and a topless extravaganza. If gambling and nonstop action are your scene, this will appeal to you, but most people find its tackiness overwhelming. The main room is decked out like a Tarzan jungle, with palms and man-made waterfalls, rope walkways, and rain forest and bamboo murals. The sound of rushing water drowns out the jangle of the slots somewhat, but nothing can conceal the glitter of this lurid spectacle. Thankfully, the rooms are a big improvement. Cream-and-white decor predominates, and the furniture is inspired by elegant, old Cape designs. ⊠ *Box 2, Sun City,* ☎ *01455/2–1000, 011/780–7800 central reservations,* FAX *01455/7–4210. 340 rooms. 4 restaurants, 2 bars, room service, pool, casino. AE, DC, MC, V.*

$$ ⊞ **The Cabanas.** After the bells and whistles of the Sun City Hotel (☞ *above*), this budget option comes as a peaceful surprise. Paths thread through pleasant gardens to the rooms, in small apartment blocks overlooking a man-made lake. They are clean and cheerful, with tile floors, bright bedspreads, and sliding glass doors that open onto the lawns. All have TV, tea/coffeemakers, and air-conditioning. The hotel's proximity to Waterworld, a playground, and a petting zoo makes it popular with families. ✉ *Box 3, Sun City,* ☎ *01455/7–1000, 011/780-7800 central reservations,* FAX *01455/7–4227. 380 rooms. 2 restaurants, 2 bars, pool. AE, DC, MC, V.*

Sun City A to Z

ARRIVING AND DEPARTING

By Bus. Impala Rand Tours (☎ 011/445–8000 Computicket) operates a daily bus service to Sun City from Johannesburg's Rotunda (✉ Leyds and Loveday Sts., Braamfontein). The bus leaves Braamfontein at 9 and leaves Sun City at 6 during the week. A same-day return ticket costs R90, and a one-way fare costs R60. The bus also has stops at the airport and the Sandton Sun Hotel. Additional buses depart from the airport and Rotunda on Friday and Saturday afternoons. The Friday and Saturday buses depart from Sun City at 8 and midnight. Discount vouchers for the area are included if you take the bus.

By Car. Plan about 1½–2 hours to drive the 177 km (110 mi) to Sun City from Johannesburg. The best route is up the N1 to Pretoria, then west by way of the N4. Entry costs R40 for day visitors.

Bazaruto Archipelago–Mozambique

Lying offshore from the old Portuguese colonial town of Vilanculos, and leading north from the Cabo San Sebastian peninsula, is a string of coral islands that form the Bazaruto Archipelago, a popular weekend getaway spot from Johannesburg. Vilanculos is a small town on the mainland, lying far north of the capital Maputo—or any other place of note. However, because of the popularity of the island lodges, it is served by several regional airlines. The islands are popular with South Africans because of their convenient location and natural beauty: picture palm trees swaying and pristine beaches where you can walk for miles and see only birds instead of people. The official language is Portuguese, so brush up on your *obrigados* (thank yous) and *faz favors* (pleases), although staff at all the beach lodges speak English. This is prime game-fishing country, including surf fly-fishing for the real aficionados of line and lure. The common culinary currency here is seafood, especially shellfish: the queen prawns are famous throughout Southern Africa. The islands lie about 25 km (15 mi) off the mainland. Bazaruto Island is 35 km (22 mi) long while Bengeula is 11 km (6 mi) long and 5 km (3 mi) wide. There are a few smaller ones, as well as numerous sand spits; they generally lie between 1 km (½ mi) to 2 km (1 mi) apart.

Two Mile Reef is considered the best dive site of the archipelago: you'll see eagle rays, green or leatherback turtles, great clouds of fusiliers, and other denizens of the deep.

The best time to visit these paradisiacal islands is from May to October—be it for fishing, sun worshiping (a favored cult), or scuba diving—while December to March is cyclone season. It is a malarial area, so be sure to take the necessary precautions. The atmosphere is decidedly casual, and all you really need to take is a swim suit, sun hat, suntan lotion, sandals, and something warm for evenings.

A final word on paradise: the shells may look beautiful, but don't succumb to buying them, as the animals are taken live and this depletes the sensitive and endangered coral reefs.

Dining and Lodging

Note: Most establishments prefer U.S dollars but will accept S.A. rand as well.

$$$–$$$$ ✕🏠 **Benguerra Lodge.** This is romance with an aquamarine lining. Secluded, stilted chalets with wood floors, reed walls, and thatched roofs are built in an indigenous forest just 20 yards from the coral beach. Generous balconies offer fantastic sea views. It's a desirable honeymoon hideaway with long, coral beaches tickled by palms; there's great food, cozy couches for curling up in, picnics, and seafood barbecues. Curried crab, grilled prawns, peri-peri cashew nuts, coconuts . . . it seems so perfect you expect Robinson Crusoe and Man Friday to stroll across the gardens to meet you. But the castaways here are far more affluent; many wealthy Southern Africans use Benguela as their desert-island getaway. ✉ *Box 87416, Houghton 2041, Johannesburg,* ☎ *27–11/483–2734 or 27–11/483–2735,* 🗷 *2711/728–3767. 13 rooms. Restaurant, bar. AE, MC, V.*

$$ ✕🏠 **Bazaruto Lodge.** Most visitors here come to fish; rods lie around like pick-up-sticks, and pictures of fishermen posing with their prizes at the weighing gantry decorate the walls. The lodge was built in the days of the Portuguese colony and lacks the romance of the newer hotels. Still, despite the no-frills experience, you'll be more than compensated by the Portuguese food and the friendly people. The A-frame huts are built of timber and reeds and are small and appointed very ordinarily—in fact they're even a tad dingy. But remember, you came here for the sea, the beach, and the seafood. And what seafood it is: the dining tables groan with crayfish (lobsters), giant queen prawns, and gamefish steaks. The way to eat them all is with fiery Santa Anna peri-peri (chili) sauce. ✉ *Box 1214, Saxonwold 2132, Johannesburg,* ☎ *27–11/447–3528,* 🗷 *27–11/788–6499. 16 rooms. AE, DC, MC, V.*

Mozambique A to Z

ARRIVING AND DEPARTING

Visas are required by all visitors and must be bought in advance at a Mozambican embassy through the National Tourist Company in Johannesburg for around US$50. Also, the date of expiration on your passport must be at least six months after the end of your intended trip. In the United States contact the **Mozambique Embassy** (✉ 1990 M St. NW, No. 570, Washington, DC, 20036-3404, ☎ 202/293–7146 through 202/293–7148), 🗷 202/835–0245).

➤ BY AIR: Each of the islands has its own airstrip but, when flying in, you must clear customs at Vilanculos International Airport on the mainland. **SA Airlink** (☎ 394–2430 in Johannesburg) flies from Durban or Johannesburg via Nelspruit (where you clear South Africa immigration) on Tuesday and Friday. Round-trip airfare from Durban or Johannesburg to Vilankulos is R2500, and one-way from Nelspruit to Vilankulos is R840.

South African Airways and **LAM,** Mozambique Airlines (✉ Box 2060, Maputo, ☎ 46–5810), regularly fly to Maputo International Airport (☎ 46–5133). LAM also flies from Maputo to Vilankulos.

EMBASSIES AND CONSULATES

Canadian Consulate (✉ 22 Joacquim Lapa, 4th floor, Room 4, Maputo, ☎ 01/43–0217); **United Kingdom** (Caixa Postal 55, Maputo, ☎ 01/42–0111); **United States** (Caixa Postal 783, Maputo, ☎ 01/49–1215).

EMERGENCIES

Medical service in Mozambique is completely sub-par. In case of emergency contact **Medical Air Rescue Service (Mars)** (☎ 09263–4/73–4513 Harare, 🗷 09263–4/73–4517).

TOUR OPERATORS
Mozambique Connection. ✉ *Box 2861, Rivonia 2128, Johannesburg,* ☎ *011/803–4185 or 803–4908 in Johannesburg, 23/2–9021 in Mozambique,* FAX *011/803–3861 in Johannesburg.*

VISITOR INFORMATION
Mozambican Tourism Directorate. ✉ *Av. 25 de Setembro 1502 3, CP 614 Maputo, Mozambique,* ☎ *42-6888,* FAX *42-1166 or, in Johannesburg* ✉ *Box 2042, Rivonia 2128,* ☎ *27–11/234–0599,* FAX *27–11/803–2382.*

JOHANNESBURG A TO Z

Arriving and Departing

By Bus

All **inter-city buses** depart from the Rotunda (✉ Leyds and Loveday Sts., Braamfontein), the city's principal transport hub. **Greyhound** (☎ 011/830–1301) and **Translux** (☎ 011/774–3333) operate extensive routes around the country. **Intercape Mainliner** (☎ 012/654–4114) runs to Cape Town.

By Car

Major rental agencies with offices in either the city or in Sandton include **Avis** (✉ 167A Rivonia Rd., Sandton, ☎ 011/884–2221), **Budget** (✉ Holiday Inn Crowne Plaza, at Rivonia Rd. and Grayston Dr., Sandton, ☎ 011/784–2321), **Europcar** (✉ Box 4613, Kempton Park 1620, ☎ 011/396–1309), **Hertz** (✉ Box 4785, Kempton Park 1620, ☎ 011/454–1503), and **Imperial** (✉ Sandton Sun Hotel, at 5th and Alice Sts., Sandhurst, ☎ 011/883–4352).

By Plane

Johannesburg International Airport (☎ 011/975–9963), formerly known as Jan Smuts, lies 19 km (12 mi) from the city. Most international flights depart from this airport. Major airlines serving Johannesburg include **Air Namibia** (☎ 011/442–4461), **Air Zimbabwe** (☎ 011/331–1541), **Alitalia** (☎ 011/880–9254), **British Airways** (☎ 011/441–8600), **KLM Royal Dutch Airlines** (☎ 011/881–9696), **Lufthansa** (☎ 011/484–4711), **Qantas** (☎ 011/884–5300), **Singapore Airlines** (☎ 011/880–8566), **South African Airways** (☎ 011/395–3333), **Swissair** (☎ 011/484–1980), and **Virgin Atlantic Airlines** (☎ 011/340–3400).

In addition to South African Airways, the major domestic carriers serving Johannesburg are British Airways, operating as **Comair** (☎ 011/921–0222), and **S.A. Airlink** (☎ 011/394–2430).

The airport has a tourist information desk, a VAT refund office, and a computerized accommodation service.

BETWEEN THE AIRPORT AND JOHANNESBURG
Impala Rand Tours (☎ 011/974–6561, 011/445–8000 Computicket) runs buses between the airport and the Rotunda (✉ Leyds and Loveday Sts., Braamfontein), near the city center. Buses make the 30-minute trip every half hour and charge R30. **Magic Bus** (☎ 011/328–8092) operates a minibus airport service every half hour that calls at the Holiday Inn Crowne Plaza (Sandton), the Balalaika, and the Sandton Sun & Towers. The trip costs R40 and takes 35–50 minutes. Magic Bus also offers door-to-door pickup anywhere in the city for R120; two or more passengers pay R65 each.

Rental-car companies with offices at the airport include **Avis** (☎ 011/394–5433), **Budget Rent-a-Car** (☎ 011/394–2905), **Europcar Car Hire**

(☎ 011/394–8832), **Hertz** (☎ 011/390–2066), **Imperial** (☎ 011/394–4020), and **Tempest Car Hire** (☎ 011/394–8626).

Taxis are available from the ranks outside the terminals. Licensed taxis must have a working meter. Expect to pay about R80–R120 for a trip to the city center or to Sandton.

By Train

Johannesburg's **train station** is opposite the Rotunda (⊠ Leyds and Loveday Sts.) in Braamfontein. The famous, luxurious *Blue Train,* which makes regular runs to Cape Town as well as the lowveld and Victoria Falls (☞ Rail Travel *in* Smart Travel Tips A to Z), departs from here, as do **Mainline Passenger Services** (☎ 011/773–2944) trains to cities around the country. Trains to other major cities include the TransKaroo to Cape Town, the Komati to Nelspruit in Mpumalanga, and the TransNatal to Durban. Many of these national services have overnight trips and are acceptable but not terribly comfortable, offering good value for the money. You should probably skip the dining car because the food is not very appetizing—rather, opt for the light meals and snacks.

Getting Around

Most visitors need concern themselves only with the city center and the northern suburbs. The city center is laid out in a grid, making it easy to get around, but it's not advisable to tour the area on foot except in groups or with a local guide. Jan Smuts Avenue runs north from the city center right through the major suburbs of Parktown, Rosebank, Dunkeld, Hyde Park, Craighall, and Randburg. The William Nicol Highway splits off this avenue and runs toward Sandton, the emerging new city center. An easier way to get from the city center to Sandton is up the M1, which splits to become the N1 South, leading toward Roodepoort and the southern suburbs, or the N1 North, leading toward Pretoria and Pietersburg.

By Taxi

Don't expect to rush out into the street and hail a taxi. There are taxi ranks at the airport, the train station, and the Rotunda, but as a rule you must phone for a cab. Taxis should be licensed and have a working meter. Three of the most reliable companies are **City Taxi** (☎ 011/336–5213), **Maxi Taxi** (☎ 011/648–1212), and **Rose Taxis** (☎ 011/403–9625). Ask the taxi company how long it will take the taxi to get to you—many taxis are radioed while on call and the time to get to your area may vary considerably, depending on whether there is a taxi in the vicinity already. The meter starts at R2 and clicks over at a rate of R3.20 per kilometer. Expect to pay about R120 to the airport from town and about R60 to the city center from Sandton. Charge for waiting time is about R36 per hour.

Contacts and Resources

Embassies and Consulates

Pretoria is the capital of South Africa, and most embassies are located there (☞ Pretoria A to Z, *above*). Some countries also maintain consulates in Johannesburg.

U.K. Consulate. ⊠ *275 Jan Smuts Ave., Dunkeld West,* ☎ *011/327–0015.*

Emergencies

Ambulance (☎ 999). **Police** (☎ 10111).

In the event of a **medical emergency,** you're advised to seek help at one of the city's private hospitals. Among the most reputable are **Mil-**

park Hospital (✉ Guild Rd., Parktown, ☎ 011/480–5600) and **Sandton Medi-Clinic** (✉ Main St. and Peter Pl., Lyme Park, ☎ 011/709–2000).

Guided Tours

DIAMOND TOURS

Mynhardts conducts 45-minute tours of its diamond-cutting operation. You can also purchase diamonds if you wish. (For information on a tour of a working diamond mine, *see* Cullinan, *above*.) ✉ *240 Commissioner St., Johannesburg Central,* ☎ *011/334–8897.* ⊞ *Free.* ⊙ *Weekdays 8:30–4:30, by appointment only.*

Schwartz Jewellers has tours of its workshops in Sandton, where you can see stone grading and gold pouring and, of course, buy the finished product. Tours are by appointment only and include a delicious tea. ☎ 011/783–1717. ⊞ R30.

GENERAL-INTEREST TOURS

For city tours, call **Springbok Atlas** (☎ 011/396–1053) or **Jimmy's Face to Face Tours** (☎ 011/331–6209). They both have two- to three-hour tours of the city that may include visits to the Johannesburg Stock Exchange, the diamond-cutting works, and some of the city's more interesting parks and suburbs. Other tours explore Pretoria; Cullinan, a working diamond mine; Sun City; and the Pilanesberg National Park.

TOWNSHIP TOURS

Jimmy's Face to Face Tours (☎ 011/331–6209) has the most flexible tours of the townships. The three-hour Soweto tour takes you in minibuses through the largest black city in Africa. The tour looks past the headlines to show visitors how urban blacks live from day to day. Jimmy's Johannesburg Night Tour features an authentic local meal, a theater production, and some township jazz. There are also the guides working through **Gold Reef City** ☎ (011/496–1400 or 011/496–1401) who are all SATOUR-registered.

Travel Agencies

American Express Travel Service. ✉ *Braampark, 33 Hoofd St., Braamfontein, Johannesburg,* ☎ *011/359–0111;* ✉ *Upper Mall, Hyde Park Square,* ☎ *011/325–4424.* ⊙ *Weekdays 8:30–5, Sat. 9–12:30.*

Rennies Travel is the representative of Thomas Cook in South Africa and has its own tours through southern Africa, known as Options, which enable you to tailor-make your itinerary. ✉ *Shop L14, Sandton City Shopping Centre, Rivonia Rd., Sandton,* ☎ *011/884–4035,* FAX *011/ 883–7022;* ✉ *Surrey House, 35 Rissik St., Johannesburg,* ☎ *011/ 492–1990.* ⊙ *Weekdays 8:30–4.*

Visitor Information

Gauteng Tourism Centre sells lots of useful guides and distributes free brochures. ✉ *Rosebank Mall,* ☎ *011/327–2000.*

3 MPUMALANGA AND KRUGER NATIONAL PARK

Archetypal Africa—open country full of big game and primal wilderness—unfolds before you in Mpumalanga. Its most obvious allure is game-watching in and around Kruger National Park. But don't miss out on the majestic Drakensberg—mountains of mists, forests, waterfalls, and panoramic views around which you'll find some of South Africa's most luxurious hotels and lodges, as well as historic gold-rush towns and fantastic hiking and fishing.

MPUMALANGA SPREADS EAST from Gauteng to the border of Mozambique. In many ways it's South Africa's wildest and most exciting province. The 1,120-km (700-mi) Drakensberg Range—which originates in KwaZulu-Natal—divides the high, interior plateau from a low-lying subtropical belt that stretches to Mozambique and the Indian Ocean. The Lowveld—where Kruger National Park alone covers a 320-km (200-mi) swathe of wilderness—is classic Africa, with as much heat, dust, untamed bush, and big game as you can take in.

Updated by
Bronwyn
Howard

Larger than Israel and approximately the same size as Wales, Kruger National Park encompasses diverse terrain ranging from rivers filled with crocodiles and hippos to rocky outcrops and thick thornscrub. Roaming this classic slice of Africa are animals in numbers large enough to make a conservationist squeal with delight: 1,500 lions, 7,500 elephants, 1,300 white rhinos, and 30,000 buffalo—although you'll usually see them in far smaller herds of several dozen at a time. With credentials like these, it's not a surprise that Kruger and the private game reserves abutting its western borders provide the country's best and most fulfilling game experience; in fact, it's highly likely that you will see all of the Big Five in an average two- to three-day stay at one of the private game reserves.

The Drakensberg Escarpment rises to the west of Kruger and provides a marked contrast to the Lowveld: it's a mountainous area of trout streams and waterfalls, endless views, and giant plantations of pine and eucalyptus. Lower down, the forests give way to banana, mango, and papaya groves. People come to the escarpment to hike, unwind, soak up its beauty, and get away from the heat of the Lowveld. Touring the area by car is easy and rewarding and you can reach many of the best lookouts without stepping far from your car.

Some of South Africa's most interesting historical events took place here. In the settlement's early days, there were frequent conflicts between the local Pedi people and European settlers. This subsequently gave way to eruptions between Boer and Brit, both seeking control of what was turning out to be a rich land. Then there was the Pilgrim's Rest gold strike of 1873, creating the very substance of bush lore and adding to Mpumalanga's appeal.

The gold rush here was every bit as raucous and wild as those in California and the Klondike, and legend has it that you can still find a few old-time prospectors panning for gold in the area. Fortune-seekers from all over the world descended on these mountains to try their luck in the many rivers and streams. Although the safest route to the goldfields was the 800-km (500-mi) road from Port Natal (now Durban), many opted for a 270-km (170-mi) shortcut from Lourenço Marques (now Maputo), in Mozambique—through the wilds of the Lowveld, where malaria, yellow fever, lions, and crocodiles exacted a dreadful toll. Part of that route still survives (albeit in a more refined version) in the form of Robber's Pass, a scenic route winding down from Lydenburg to Pilgrim's Rest.

Those early gold-mining days have been immortalized in *Jock of the Bushveld*, a classic of South African literature. Jock was a Staffordshire terrier whose master, Sir Percy Fitzpatrick, worked as a transport rider during the gold rush. After a stint at the Barberton *Herald* (now Nelspruit's *Louvelder*) as a staff reporter, Sir Percy entertained his children with tales of Jock's exploits as they logged their miles in Mpumalanga, braving leopards, baboons, and all manner of dangers. Rudyard Kipling, who wandered this wilderness as a reporter covering the First Anglo-

Boer War in the early 1880s, encouraged Fitzpatrick to write down the stories. One hundred years later Jock is still a household name in South Africa. You'll see dozens of Jock-of-the-Bushveld markers all over Mpumalanga, seemingly wherever he cocked a leg.

Although some of the "*bundu*-bashing" (bushwhacking) and gold-rush atmosphere still exists here, depending on where you go, the rough-and-ready days of the pioneering Lowveld are almost gone. If you dig deep, you can still find traces of the last of the big-game hunters and pioneers of the Lowveld—which can make for entertaining conversation at the tap. More and more, however, luxury guest lodges prove to be the modern-day gold rush. People from around the globe come to indulge in the lodges' elegant dinners and huge English breakfasts in a variety of stunning locales.

Warning: The Lowveld area, which stretches from Malelane (East of Nelspruit) to Komatipoort on the Mozambique border and up throughout Kruger National Park, is a malarial zone, in which you are advised to take antimalarial drugs.

Pleasures and Pastimes

Big-Game Adventures
There is nothing quite like tracking rhinos on foot—with an armed ranger leading the way, of course—or having an elephant mock-charge to within yards of your Land Rover. The slow-motion gallop of a giraffe, the cocky trot of a hyena, and the interactions of the smaller creatures of the bush—such as the banded mongoose or the Cape pangolin—are all Mpumalanga musts. If you don't stay in one of the area's private game lodges, be sure to go out with a park ranger on one of the wilderness trails to get your feet on the ground in the wilds of South Africa.

Dining
As Mpumalanga continues to get more tourist traffic, the region's culinary scene keeps getting better—both in higher-end restaurants and attractive cafés. A number of private game lodges on the fringe of Kruger National Park serve fairly sophisticated fare, which can add romance to a couple of nights in the bush.

For a description of South African culinary terms, *see* Pleasures and Pastimes *in* Chapter 1. For price ranges, *see* Dining *in* Smart Travel Tips A to Z.

Lodging
The quality of service and accommodation in Mpumalanga and Kruger is very high by South African standards. Even when you're paying premium rates, though, don't be surprised to see dogs, cats, pet monkeys, and birds breaking into the dining room. Almost every escarpment lodge has its contingent of free-roaming pets, so if you're allergic or dislike animals, do some research before you reserve. At the same time, some lodges display an almost monastic respect for peace and quiet, even eliminating TVs and radios from the rooms. So if you find yourself whispering in the bar, just order another round of martinis.

Luxury lodges are not for everyone, and you can choose from several other options, including regular hotels. If you're watching your pennies, consider staying at a self-catering cottage and driving to one of the lodges for dinner—usually a good value.

At most guest lodges on the escarpment, prices include a dinner consisting of three to five courses and a full English breakfast. Vegetarians should call ahead to make special arrangements. Some lodges and hotels have special rates, particularly midweek or during the winter low season. Many do not accommodate children under 12 or 14—inquire when you make reservations if you have children. For price ranges, *see* Lodging *in* Smart Travel Tips A to Z.

In the Kruger National Park region, the decision is whether to stay in a national-park rest camp or a private game lodge, a choice that might have everything to do with your budget: rest camps cost about R350 per night for a couple (lodging only), and private lodges cost between R750 and R4,000 per person, per night (room, board, and activities included). That said, for the price, the intimacy and expertise of private lodges and their staff often make for the experience of a lifetime. Prices for private game reserves and lodges are located in a separate price chart at the end of this chapter.

Exploring Mpumalanga and Kruger National Park

Great Itineraries

Mpumalanga has a wealth of activities, from poking around cultural villages to hiking on mountain trails, looking into local history, taking in panoramic views, and driving and tramping around game reserves. If you have only a couple of days in the area, split them between the mountain scenery of the escarpment and wildlife viewing in the Lowveld. If you have more time, you could complete a tour of the Drakensberg Escarpment area in two days, but you're better off budgeting three or more if you plan to linger anywhere. To take in parts of Kruger National Park or one of the private game lodges—which is simply a must—add another three days or more. The best way to get around Mpumalanga is by car, either from Johannesburg or after flying into Nelspruit. Don't forget that Swaziland (☞ Chapter 9) is less than two hours southeast of Nelspruit. If you plan to go to Swaziland, the town of Barberton makes a pleasant stopover on the way south.

Numbers in the text correspond to numbers in the margin and on the Mpumalanga map.

IF YOU HAVE 3 DAYS

Fly into the regional capital of Nelspruit; then rent a car and drive to ⛺ **Pilgrim's Rest** ⑦ or ⛺ **Graskop** ⑨ for lunch, followed by an afternoon of taking in views of the escarpment's edge at the **Pinnacle** ⑩, **God's Window** ⑪, and one of the spectacular local waterfalls. If you feel like going on a longer-range afternoon drive, head up to spectacular **Blyde River Canyon Nature Reserve** for a look at the **Three Rondawels** ⑮ rock formations. Stay overnight in Graskop, Pilgrim's Rest, or Sabie. The next morning make your way down to the Lowveld to Kruger National Park or one of the private lodges listed at the end of this chapter. Whether you opt for the national park or a private reserve, be sure to get in a day or night bush drive *and* a bush walk with an armed ranger. These complementary activities will give you the broadest experience of wildlife. If animals are actually your prime reason to come to Mpumalanga, you could decide to spend all three days in the park or at a private reserve. If you plan to spend the rest of your vacation in civilization, a minimum of three days in the bush is advisable.

IF YOU HAVE 5 DAYS

With five days, the biggest decision will be how much time to spend wildlife-watching and how much to explore the escarpment and its historic towns. If you are planning to see game in Zimbabwe or Botswana, take three days around the mountains and two in and around Kruger National Park. Start off on a drive from Johannesburg to ⛺ **Dullstroom** ①, which is known for its restaurants and lodges, and for superb trout fish-

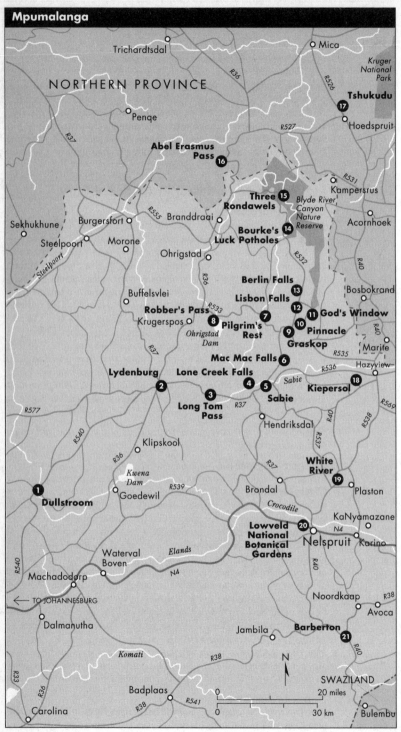

Mpumalanga

Trichardtsdal

NORTHERN PROVINCE

Mica

Kruger National Park

R36

R526

Tshukudu

17

Hoedspruit

Penqe

R527

R37

Abel Erasmus Pass

16

R531

Kampersrus

Sekhukhune

Burgersfort

R555

Branddraai

Three Rondawels

15

Blyde River Canyon Nature Reserve

14

Bourke's Luck Potholes

Acornhoek

Steelpoort

Morone

Ohrigstad

R532

R40

Steelpoort

Buffelsvlei

R36

Berlin Falls

13

Bosbokrand

Robber's Pass

8

R533

Lisbon Falls

7

12

11

God's Window

Krugerspos

Pilgrim's Rest

9

10

Pinnacle

Ohrigstad Dam

Graskop

R40

R535

Marife

R37

Mac Mac Falls

6

Hazyview

Lydenburg

2

Lone Creek Falls

4

5

Sabie

R536

Kiepersol

18

3

Sabie

R569

Long Tom Pass

R37

R577

R540

Hendriksdal

R538

R537

Klipskool

R40

White River

19

R36

Kwena Dam

Goedewil

R539

Brondal

Plaston

1

Dullstroom

Crocodile

KaNyamazane

Lowveld National Botanical Gardens

20

Nelspruit

Karino

Waterval Boven

Elands

N4

R40

Machadodorp

TO JOHANNESBURG

Noordkaap

R38

Avoca

R540

Dalmanutha

Jambila

Barberton

21

R40

Komati

R38

N

SWAZILAND

R33

R36

Badplaas

R541

20 miles

0

Carolina

R38

30 km

Bulembu

ing. If you don't spend the night, have lunch and continue through **Ly-denburg** ②. Beautiful **Long Tom Pass** ③ will take you toward ☒ **Sabie** ④, which is a good town in which to overnight. The next day, head to ☒ **Pilgrim's Rest** ⑦ to take in a little local history at the town's museums or through **Graskop** ⑨ to see some of the escarpment's most scenic vistas. If you are going to spend three days in the bush, head down to Kruger or a private lodge to make it there in time for dinner and a night game drive. Otherwise, spend the night in Pilgrim's Rest or Graskop and start out early the next morning for **Blyde River Canyon Nature Reserve** with its hiking trails and escarpment scenery.

An alternative route out of Johannesburg would take you straight to the **Lowveld National Botanical Gardens** ⑳ outside of Nelspruit. From there, continue to ☒ **White River** ⑲, taking a day trip, perhaps, to **Barberton** ㉑, an early gold-rush town with interesting period houses and nearby outdoor activities. You could then approach Kruger National Park from the south.

IF YOU HAVE 7 TO 10 DAYS

The best way to structure a longer stay in Mpumalanga is to set aside four or more days in the bush—half at Kruger and half in a private lodge, perhaps. Then split the rest of your time between the escarpment and the Lowveld. If you're planning to continue to Swaziland, note that it's an extremely rough dirt road to Swaziland from Barberton, although the town is a mere 35 km (21 mi) to the border post at Josefsdal-Bulembu. It's a much better option to travel to Malelane on the N4 and then take the road to the border at Matsamo–Jeppe's Reef. That road is paved all the way and affords spectacular views as it winds through the hills.

When to Tour Mpumalanga and Kruger National Park

Where you stay on the escarpment may well dictate the kind of weather you get. High up, around Pilgrim's Rest, Graskop, and Sabie, the weather can be chilly, even in summer. At these elevations fog and mist can also be a hazard, especially while driving. On the other hand, summer in the Lowveld is downright sultry.

Kruger National Park is hellishly hot in midsummer (December–March), with afternoon rain a good possibility. The bush is green, the animals sleek and glossy, and the bird life prolific, but you won't see as many animals. Dense foliage makes finding them harder, and they don't need watering holes and rivers, which make them easy to spot as they come to drink. Winter is great for game viewing, on the other hand, as trees are bare and animals congregate around the few available water sources. With cooler weather, you might even see lions and leopards hunting by day. Lodges drop their rates as much as 30%–40% off of peak season highs. The drawbacks are cold weather, bare trees and bush, and animals that can look thin and out of condition.

Shoulder seasons are a happy compromise. October and November weather is pleasant, trees are blossoming, and migrant birds are arriving. Even better, antelope herds begin to drop their young. April temperatures are also fine, many migrant birds are still around, and the annual rutting season has begun, when males compete for the right to mate with females and are much more active and visible.

There are various annual festivals worth seeing as well. Komatipoort hosts an agricultural and prawn festival in April in which you can take part in a *bok-drol-spoeg*—in Afrikaans, literally "buck-dropping-spit"—competition, in which local lads see who can spit gazelle pellets the farthest. Sabie has its annual Forest Festival in April, where you can see lumberjacks cutting up logs in a matter of seconds. In Northern Province, Hoedspruit hosts an annual Wild Festival on a mid-April weekend, when you can taste all kinds of game meat and *biltong* (much-loved local jerky).

Nelspruit hosts the Lowveld Agricultural Show in August, if you're interested in a look at South African farm life. In September there is a fly-fishing competition in whichever town hosts it for the year, such as Dullstroom, Lydenburg, or Machadodorp. Dates for these festivals vary from year to year; SATOUR (☞ Mpumalanga A to Z *below*) and local publicity associations will have specific dates.

MPUMALANGA

Next to Cape Town and the Winelands, Mpumalanga should be high on your South African itinerary. Nowhere else in the country can you spend one day seeing spectacular wildlife, the next climbing or gazing over the escarpment, and a third poking around some of the country's most historic towns—spending a minimum amount of time in the car getting from place to place.

Dullstroom

❶ *2½ hrs east of Johannesburg on the N4, turn off for Belfast and follow the R540 out of town for 35 km (21 mi).*

The tiny hamlet of Dullstroom sits amid rolling, grass-covered mountains and sparkling streams. At 6,600 ft, it's one of the coldest towns in South Africa, and sweaters and roaring fires are common comforts even in midsummer. Dullstroom is the trout-fishing capital of Mpumalanga. The fish were introduced into the streams of the Mpumalanga Drakensberg at the turn of the century, and trout-fishing is now the third-largest moneymaker in the region, after timber and tourism. There is very good dining and lodging in town.

Situated just off the R540, approximately 9 km (6 mi) from Dullstroom as you drive toward Lydenburg, the **Dullstroom Bird of Prey Center** houses several species of South African birds of prey that have been injured and rehabilitated and are now semi-tame. Birds can be viewed in aviaries, but time your visit to arrive at 10:30 AM or 2:30 PM, when the staff flies the birds and gives talks on their hunting and survival techniques. Enjoy the antics of the lesser spotted owl, see lanner falcons hunting a lure, and watch the falconer "call in" booted or tawny eagles. The session takes about an hour and is well worth the stop. ⊠ *R540,* ☎ *013/254–0777.* ☒ *R15.*

While you're visiting the center, stop in at the **Owl and Oak Trading Post,** a three-shop complex that sells a variety of country and home-decor gifts complete with a small restaurant where you can have a cup of tea or a full meal. ⊠ *R540.*

Dining and Lodging

$$ ✕ **Die Tonteldoos Bistro and Deli.** This small bistro is a popular stop for breakfast, lunch, or dinner (until 8:30 PM) on your way to or from the Lowveld. Owner Brian Whitehorn's menu is heavily influenced by French cuisine, with many sauces based on rich reductions. Highly recommended are the steak fillet topped with Camembert and red wine sauce as well as any of the game pies. For something lighter, try *spanikopita* (spinach and feta cheese wrapped in phyllo dough) or a silky trout terrine accompanied by sage and olive bread. Garden salads and open sandwiches on chunky whole-wheat bread are popular snacks. ⊠ *On*

R540, Dullstroom, ☎ *01325/4–0115. Reservations essential weekends.* ◷ *Weekdays 7–5, weekends 7–8:30. AE, DC, MC, V.*

$$$$ ✕🏨 **Walkersons.** Set on a 1,500-acre farm of grass-covered hills laced with trout streams, the main lodge, built of stone and thatch, overlooks a small dam and is decorated with a wealth of antiques and works of arts including Persian rugs, French tapestries, and 19th-century English oils. All rooms face the lake and have sponge-painted walls, mosquito nets, and fireplaces. Two-thirds of the farm has been made into a nature reserve populated with wildlife like wildebeest, springbok, blesbok, and zebra. There are several walking trails to follow through the reserve, or you can take a two-hour game drive in an open Land Rover. The lodge's five-course dinner is flawlessly presented. A meal might begin with Roquefort mousse with figs or smoked trout in phyllo baskets. Following a soup of brandied butternut squash and nutmeg, expect a main course such as beef fillet with green pepper sauce and rosemary potatoes. ✉ *Off R540, 13 km (8 mi) north of Dullstroom (mailing address: Box 185, Dullstroom 1110),* ☎ *01325/4–0246,* 𝔽𝔸𝕏 *01325/4–0260. 18 rooms, 2 suites. Restaurant, bar, pool, hot tub, fishing, hiking, horseback riding. MAP. AE, DC, MC, V.*

$$$ ✕🏨 **Critchley Hackle Lodge.** Foreign travelers often use this country lodge midway between Johannesburg and Kruger Park as a one-night stopover on their way to the Lowveld, but for South Africans it's more of a weekend getaway, with its lovely antiques and crackling fireplaces. Not surprisingly, the atmosphere is very relaxed and the staff quite friendly. Rooms in stone and brick cottages arranged around a trout dam all have their own fireplaces. Wooden chests, floral curtains, and rough brick walls contribute to the atmosphere of warm rusticity. The lodge boasts a large, informal dining room overlooking the dam— a perfect location to savor the delicious four-course dinners. The breakfast buffet and à la carte lunch are served on the patio. ✉ *On R540 (mailing address: Box 141, Dullstroom 1110),* ☎ *01325/4–0145,* 𝔽𝔸𝕏 *01325/4–0262. 23 rooms. Restaurant, bar, pool, tennis, fishing. MAP. AE, DC, MC, V.*

$$ ✕🏨 **Dullstroom Inn.** In an old trading store that dates from 1910— which is still famous for its pub—the inn has rooms that are small but attractively done in colonial style, with floral patterns and old-fashioned iron bedsteads. No rooms have a phone or TV. If you're not staying at the inn, it's still worth stopping at the wood-paneled pub, with its roaring fire and excellent selection of draft lagers and bitters. The extensive menu has such staples as steak-and-kidney pie, ploughman's lunch, and oxtail. Try the trout specialties and sticky toffee pudding. ✉ *Teding van Berkhout and Oranje Nassau Sts. (mailing address: Box 44, Dullstroom 1110),* ☎ *01325/4–0071,* 𝔽𝔸𝕏 *01325/4–0278. 11 rooms with bath. Restaurant, pub. CP. AE, DC, MC, V.*

Lydenburg

❷ *58 km (36 mi) northeast of Dullstroom on the R540.*

In an open plain between the Drakensberg and Steenkampsberg mountains, Lydenburg was founded in 1849 after the early Boer settlers (Voortrekkers) were forced to abandon their original homestead at Andries-Ohrigstad, where many of them died from malaria. Shaken by those years of death and misery, the survivors gave the new town the name Lydenburg, which means "town of suffering." Ironically, Lydenburg prospered so well that in 1857 its citizens seceded from the Transvaal during the incessant bickering that marked relations among Voortrekker factions. "De Republiek Lydenburg en Zuid-Afrika," as the new country was known, remained independent for three years before rejoining the Transvaal.

❸ Spectacular as **Long Tom Pass** is, this mountain pass is more famous for its historical associations than its scenic beauty. For it was here, from September 8 to 11, 1900, that one of the last pitched battles of the Second Anglo-Boer War (1899–1902) was fought. Lydenburg had fallen easily to the British on September 7, but the retreating Boers reformed on the heights above town and began shelling the British with their two remaining Creusot siege guns. Known as Long Toms because of their long barrels and range, these guns could hurl a 90-pound shell a distance of nearly 9½ km (6 mi). The guns were a tremendous headache for the British, who could not match their range. The Boers, struggling to get these monsters up the pass, can hardly have felt any more kindly toward them—at least 16 oxen were required to pull each gun. It took the British two days to push the Boers out of their positions on the pass and drive them over the steep wall of the escarpment. Even then, the Boers managed to set up a gun position on the other side of the valley to shell the British as they maneuvered down the Staircase, a series of switchbacks zigzagging down the pass. You can still see shell holes in the Staircase. From town, follow the R37 toward Sabie as it begins its winding ascent to the pass.

If you're bypassing Sabie and want to go straight to Pilgrim's Rest from Lydenburg, try **Robber's Pass,** another spectacular mountain drive. The pass was originally the road linking Lydenburg with Pilgrim's Rest and Delgoa Bay (now Maputo) and was called the Berg Road. During the gold rush, the region attracted its share of thieves and desperate men, and "highway robberies" became common; in fact, so many stage coaches were held up by highwaymen that the Berg Road was dubbed "Robber's Pass"—a name it bears to this day. The scenic pass affords panoramic vistas of high, rolling hills and deep, green valleys. Small farms abound and eucalyptus and wattle plantations alternate with open grassland. A number of view sites enable you to take your fill of the picturesque scenery. Shortly after entering the pass, you'll see the turnoff to **Origstad Dam** on your right. The dam is a favorite with birdwatchers, with a wide variety of grassland and mountain species being recorded. To reach Robber's Pass, take the R36 from Lydenburg toward Origstad; approximately 29 km (18 mi) from town, turn right toward Pilgrim's Rest on the R533. The road winds some 27 km (17 mi) down to its final destination.

Sabie

❺ *30 km (19 mi) east of Lydenburg.*

As you descend Long Tom Pass, the town of Sabie comes into view far below, in a bowl formed by the surrounding mountains. It is by far the most pleasant and enjoyable town in the region, with plenty of restaurants, shops, and bars. It makes a great base for exploring.

Gold was first discovered in appreciable amounts in Mpumalanga around present-day Sabie. On November 6, 1872, a prospector named Tom McLachlan located deposits of gold in a creek on the farm known as Hendriksdal, now a small hamlet about 16 km (10 mi) from Sabie. Sabie itself owes its origins to an altogether luckier strike. In 1895, Henry Glynn, a local farmer, hosted a picnic at the Klein Sabie Falls. Loosened up by a few drinks, his guests started taking potshots at empty bottles arrayed on a rock ledge. The flying bullets chipped shards of rock off the cliff face, revealing traces of gold beneath. Fifty-five years later, when mining operations closed down, more than 1 million ounces of gold had been taken from the Klein Sabie Falls.

Today, timber has replaced gold as the community's livelihood. The town sits in the heart of the world's largest man-made forest: more than

1,154,000 acres of exotic pine and eucalyptus. The first forests were planted in 1876 to provide the area's mines with posts and supports. Today, much of the timber is still used to prop up shafts in the Gauteng gold mines.

As its name suggests, the town's **Market Square** was the commercial hub of Sabie in its early days. On the square, pleasant gardens surround **St. Peter's Anglican Church.** The solid stone building was designed by famed architect Sir Herbert Baker and built by Italians in 1913. Just outside the First National Bank you can still see the old **hitching rail** (1911), where travelers would tether their horses. Also in the square is a **Jock of the Bushveld marker,** said to commemorate Jock and Sir Percy Fitzpatrick's arrival in Sabie in 1885.

❹ **Lone Creek Falls** is the prettiest and most peaceful of three local waterfalls. An easy, paved walkway leads to the falls, which plunge 225 ft from the center of a high, broad rock face framed by vines and creepers. The path crosses the river on a wooden bridge and loops through the forest back to the parking lot. If you're feeling energetic, follow the steep steps leading up to the top of the falls. Leave town on Main Road and turn left onto Old Lydenburg Road. This 6½-km (4-mi) dead-end road leads to three of the region's principal waterfalls—Bridal Veil Falls, Horseshoe Falls, and, the last stop along the road, Lone Creek Falls, which is the most accessible of the three to the elderly and those with disabilities.

❻ Another local waterfall, **Mac Mac Falls,** is arguably the most famous of all in Mpumalanga. Set in an amphitheater of towering cliffs, the water plunges 215 ft into a pool, and rainbows play in the billowing spray. The falls owe their interesting name to President Thomas Burger, who, while visiting the nearby gold diggings at Geelhoutboom in 1873, noticed that many of the miners' names began with "Mac," revealing their Scottish background. He promptly dubbed the area Mac Mac.

Unfortunately, you can view the falls only from an observation point surrounded by thick wire fencing, which destroys much of the atmosphere. On top of that, the fence is in poor condition, and the litter lying around it is dismaying. But if you are passing here on the way from Sabie to Graskop or Pilgrim's Rest, you might want to stop nonetheless. There are also a number of curio peddlers here; they are among the cheapest in the area.

Dining and Lodging

$$$ ✕ **Loggerhead Restaurant.** An attractive eatery centrally situated on the Old Lydenburg Road in Sabie, the Loggerhead, as you might expect from the name, is dominated by heavy wooden furniture; however, colorful napkins and sparkling glass and tableware brighten the room. Lounge furniture arranged around the fireplace and a small bar make pleasant nooks to gather for a predinner drink. As with many establishments on the escarpment, trout features on the menu, along with a wide range of standard dishes such as grilled steaks, schnitzels, fresh line fish, and desserts like ice cream with chocolate sauce and apple pie. ⊠ *Old Lydenburg Rd. and Main St. 1260 (mailing address: Box 334, Sabie 1260),* ☎ *013/764–3341,* 𝔽𝔸𝕏 *013/764–3089. AE, DC, MC, V. Closed Mon. No dinner Sun.*

$$$ ✕ **The Zeederberg Coachhouse.** The restaurant is a showcase for local art; the pictures line the walls and complement the art deco–like architecture and dark wood interior. It's a warm, pleasant place to while away an evening—and very convenient if you're staying at Percy's Place next door (☞ *below*). Specialties include trout stuffed with nuts, black mushrooms, bacon, and cream cheese served on a bed of savory rice

as well as grilled ostrich medallions with a brown onion sauce and green peppercorns. On the vegetarian menu the mushrooms au gratin topped with cream cheese, spinach, feta, and mozzarella is a standout choice. ⊠ *Ford St., Sabie,* ☎ *013/764–2630. AE, DC, MC, V.*

$$ 🍴 **Sabie Town House.** A beautifully appointed bed-and-breakfast with sweeping views of the hill country around Sabie, the main house features local Sabie River stone and lush gardens: on entering the driveway, you could be forgiven for thinking you had wandered into an atrium. The spacious rooms are individually decorated and four have their own entrances, so you can come and go as you please. Public areas are light and airy and include a large swimming pool area where breakfast is sometimes served. ⊠ *1 Power St., Sabie 1260 (mailing address: Box 134, Sabie 1260),* ☎ *013/764–2292,* ℻ *013/764–1988. 4 rooms, 2 suites. Lounge, minibars, pool. BP. AE, DC, MC, V.*

$ 🍴 **Percy's Place.** This tiny establishment in the center of Sabie is the best value in the entire Mpumalanga. Rooms are decorated in a bright country style and have tea- and coffeemakers and overhead fans. Breakfast is not included, but several cafés are within easy walking distance. Guests check in next door at the Zeederberg Coachhouse. ⊠ *Ford and 10th Sts., Sabie 1260,* ☎ *013/764–2630. 5 rooms with bath. MC, V.*

Pilgrim's Rest

❼ *16 km (10 mi) north of Sabie on R533.*

Pilgrim's Rest is a delightful, albeit touristy, reminder of gold-rush days. It was the first proper gold-mining town in South Africa, centered on the richest gold strike in Mpumalanga. Alec "Wheelbarrow" Patterson, a taciturn Scot who had struck out on his own to escape the hordes of new miners at Mac Mac, discovered gold here in September 1873. Mining operations ceased only in 1972, and since then the entire town has been declared a national monument. Many of the old corrugated-iron houses have been beautifully restored and now serve as museums, hotels, gift shops, and restaurants. It's definitely worth a visit, even for just a few hours.

Those corrugated-iron houses that you see today date from the more staid years after 1900 when Pilgrim's Rest had become a company town. During the mad years of 1873–75, when most of the alluvial gold was panned by individual prospectors, Pilgrim's Rest consisted of nothing more than a collection of tents and mud huts. Rumors about the richness of the strike quickly carried around the world, and miners drifted in from California, Australia, and Europe. By January 1874, more than 1,500 diggers were working Pilgrim's Creek. Only a few struck it rich; the rest spent their earnings in local canteens until their claims played out and they drifted off.

Your first stop should be the **Information Center** in the middle of town, where you can buy tickets to the various museums. ⊠ *Main St.,* ☎ *013/768–1060,* ℻ *013/768–1113.* ⊘ *Daily 9–12:45 and 1:15–4:30 (will stay open until later if you phone ahead).*

Start your walking tour at the top end of town at **St. Mary's Anglican Church.** Built in 1884, the iron-roof stone building replaced the original makeshift wattle-and-daub structure. It really must have been an uphill battle for the early ministers to lure miners from the town's 18 canteens. After a backbreaking week spent on the sluices, Holy Communion just didn't pack the punch of a belt of Cape brandy or Squareface gin. ⊠ *Main St.*

The tiny **Pilgrim's and Sabie News Printing Museum** is full of displays of antique printing presses and old photos. The building, constructed in the late 19th century as a residence, later served as the offices of the weekly *Pilgrim's and Sabie News*. The first newspaper in Pilgrim's Rest was the *Gold News*, published in 1874 and notable for its libelous gossip. The editor, an Irishman by the name of Phelan, felt obliged to keep a pair of loaded pistols on his desk. The printing museum is up Main Street from St. Mary's church. ✉ *Main St., Uptown,* ☎ *no phone.* 💳 *R5 combined ticket good also for the Dredzen Shop and House Museum and the House Museum. Tickets available from Information Center (☞ above).* ⊙ *Daily 9–1 and 1:30–4.*

NEED A BREAK?	If you do nothing else in Pilgrim's Rest, stop for a drink at the **Royal Hotel bar** (✉ Main St., Uptown, ☎ 013/768–1100). The building first served as a chapel at a girls' school in Cape Town. It was dismantled in 1870, shipped to Lourenço Marques (now Maputo), then carried by ox wagon to Pilgrim's Rest, where it ministered a different kind of spirit to thirsty miners. The bar retains much of its gold-rush atmosphere, with wood-panel walls, an antique cash register, and a wonderful old bar counter. If you're hungry, you can order fish-and-chips or steak and eggs.

The **House Museum,** across and up the street from the Royal Hotel, re-creates the way of life of a middle-class family in the early part of this century. The house was built in 1913 of corrugated iron and wood and is typical of buildings erected at the time throughout the area. ✉ *Main St., Uptown,* ☎ *no phone.* 💳 *R5 combined ticket good also for the Pilgrim's and Sabie News Printing Museum and the Dredzen Shop and House Museum. Tickets available at Information Center (☞ above).* ⊙ *Daily 9–12:45 and 1:15–4:30.*

The **Pilgrim's Rest Cemetery** sits high on the hill above Main Street. The fascinating inscriptions on the tombstones evoke the dangers and hardship of life in Mpumalanga a century ago. That of Fred Sanders, for example, tells how he was "shot in a skirmish on the 27th August, 1878, aged 24." Tellingly, most of the dead were in their 20s and 30s, and hailed from Wales, Scotland, and England. The cemetery owes its improbable setting to the Robber's Grave, the only grave that lies in a north–south direction. It contains the body of a thief who was banished from Pilgrim's Rest for stealing gold from a tent, after which he was tarred and feathered and chased out of town; the man foolishly returned and was shot dead. He was buried where he fell, and the area around his grave became the town's unofficial cemetery. To get here, follow the steep path that starts next to the picnic area, near the post office.

In 1930, 16 general dealers lined the streets of Pilgrim's Rest. By 1950, mine production had taken a nosedive and most of the businesses had shut down. The **Dredzen Shop and House Museum** re-creates the look of a general dealer during those lean years. The attached residence focuses on life in Pilgrim's Rest in the years immediately following World War II. After you come down the hill from the cemetery, turn left on Main Street to get to the museum. ✉ *Main St., Uptown,* ☎ *no phone.* 💳 *R5 combined ticket good also for the Pilgrim's and Sabie News Printing Museum and the House Museum. Tickets available at Information Center (☞ above).* ⊙ *Daily 9–1 and 1:30–4.*

You can also take a guided tour of **Alanglade,** the beautiful home of Transvaal Gold Mining Estates' (TGME) mine manager, set in a forested grove 2 km (1 mi) north of town. The huge house was built in 1916 for Richard Barry and his family and is furnished with pieces dating from 1900 to 1930. Look carefully at the largest pieces—you will see that they are segmented, so they could be taken apart and carried on ox wagons. ✉ *Vaalhoek Rd., off R533,* ☎ *no phone.* 💳 *R20 for a* *guided tour (including refreshments). Tickets available at Information Center (☞ above). ☉ Tours Mon.–Sat. at 11 and 2, reserve 30 mins in advance.*

At the **Diggings Museum,** in the creek where the alluvial gold was originally panned, you'll find displays of a water-driven stamp battery and some of the tents and wattle-and-daub huts typical of the early gold-rush years. The tour lasts about an hour and is more enjoyable than actually informative. The retired prospector who conducts the tours enlivens the proceedings with yarns about the old days. You'll also see a display of gold-panning and get to poke around in some of the old diggings. The museum is about 2 km (1 mi) south of Pilgrim's Rest on R533. ⊠ *R533,* ☎ *no phone.* ⊠ *R5. Tickets available at Information Center (☞ above). ☉ Tours daily at 10, 11, noon, 2, and 3.*

For a close-up view of the old gold mining works at Beta Mine (the original Pilgrim's Rest gold mine), take one of the **Peach Tree Creek Gold Panning Tours.** These informative tours cover the history of the gold rush and take visitors back in time to those heady days. Peach Tree Creek is where it all started, and the ruins of the old refinery, the ore bins, and the cocopans can all still be seen. In addition, you can pan Peach Tree Creek and keep any gold you find. It's mainly gold dust these days; nevertheless, it's thrilling to see the glittering flecks left behind when you've finished panning a sample of dirt. Tours start at Jubilee's Restaurant and take about 1½ hours. ⊠ *Jubilee's Restaurant, Main St., Downtown,* ☎ *013/768–1296.* ⊠ *R25. ☉ Tours daily at 10, noon, and 2 or by appointment.*

Dining and Lodging

$ ✕ **Scott's Café.** Visit this delightful restaurant to try one of its dozens of varieties of specialty pancakes. Both savory (stir-fried chicken) and sweet (fried nuts and cinnamon with chocolate sauce) are on the menu. Meals can be eaten outside on the pleasant wide veranda. ⊠ *Main St.,* ☎ *013/768–1061. AE, DC, MC, V. ☉ Daily 9–5.*

$ ✕ **Vine Restaurant and Pub.** In a former trading store dating from 1910, the Vine uses antique sideboards, sepia photos, and country-style wood furniture to capture a gold rush–era feeling. The food is straightforward and hearty. Try traditional South African *bobotie* (curried ground-mutton pie), *potjiekos* (stew), or oxtail and *samp* (corn porridge). The pub in the back is a good place to meet the locals and is also the only place in town offering regular sports coverage on television. ⊠ *Main St., Downtown,* ☎ *013/768–1080. DC, MC, V.*

$$$ ☷ **Royal Hotel.** Established in 1873, this hotel dates back to the very beginning of the gold rush in Pilgrim's Rest—you'll see its corrugated-iron facade in sepia photos displayed around town. The hotel is spread out over 10 quaint wood-and-tin buildings and rooms are decorated with reproduction four-poster beds, wood ceiling fans, sumptuous deep baths, and marble-and-oak washstands. Activities arranged by the hotel include horseback riding, gold panning, hiking, golf, museum visits, and trout fishing. ⊠ *Main St., Uptown (mailing address: Box 59, Pilgrim's Rest 1290),* ☎ *013/768–1100,* ☎ *013/768–1188. 50 rooms with bath. Restaurant, bar. BP. AE, DC, MC, V.*

$ ☷ **District 6 Miners' Cottages.** On a hill above Pilgrim's Rest, these self-catering cottages are the best value in town. The cottages are all miners' homes dating back to 1920, and they're delightful. From their verandas there are spectacular views of the town and surrounding mountains. The interiors are furnished with period reproductions, complete with wood floors, brass bedsteads, and claw-foot tubs. Each cottage consists of a small living room, two double bedrooms, a fully equipped kitchen and pantry, and a bathroom. You can walk to the two restaurants in town in five minutes. If you arrive after hours, pick up keys from Royal Hotel. ⊠ *District 6, Pilgrim's Rest (mailing address: Private Bag X516, Pilgrim's Rest 1290),* ☏ *013/768–1211. 7 cottages with bath and kitchen. No credit cards.*

Hiking

The **Golden Trail,** a self-guided hiking trail, takes two to three hours to complete and guides you through historic areas around town and on part of the Prospector's Hiking Trail, which requires an overnight excursion on its own. The walk begins at the Pilgrim's Rest Cemetery and ends at the Diggings Museum and takes in proteas, rolling grassland, indigenous forest, and the remains of Pilgrim's Rest's mining sights, such as the Jubilee Orebin, the Reduction Works, and the old cocopan railway line. There are beautiful views over town and of Black Hill, the region's highest point. *Book reservations and obtain maps at the Information Center (☞ above). Guided walks available for groups of 6 people or more—book in advance at the Information Center (☞ above).* ☏ *R15.*

The 1,225-acre **Mount Sheba Nature Reserve** contains one of the last stands of indigenous forest in the Transvaal Drakensberg. Fourteen trails of varying difficulty run through the reserve, each taking from 1½ to 2½ hours to complete. Some walks lead to waterfalls hidden in the bush or to pools where you can swim. A map is available from the reception desk at Mount Sheba Hotel. A word of warning: the dirt access road to Mount Sheba is not in very good condition. ⊠ *Follow the brown signs to Mount Sheba from Robber's Pass—the R533 to Lydenburg.*

Graskop

⑨ *20 km (13 mi) southeast of Pilgrim's Rest.*

In the 1850s, the farm Graskop—so named because of the vast tracts of grassveld and singular lack of trees in the area—was owned by Abel Erasmus, who later became the local magistrate. The little town was declared a township in 1914, and in 1918 the first school was built. Graskop considers itself the "Window on the Lowveld," and several nearby lookouts do have stunning views over the edge of the escarpment. Even if the town itself is largely forgettable, it does make a good base for exploring. It's also where you'll find amenities such as a post office, public telephones, a selection of shops and eateries, and a garage. The nearby Blyde River Canyon is spectacular; farther afield, you can get in a day of game viewing beyond Abel Erasmus Pass at Tshukudu.

⑩ The **Pinnacle** is a 100-ft-high quartzite "needle" that rose dramatically out of the surrounding fern-clad ravine countless millennia ago. Beneath and to the right of the viewing platform, there is a plateau that you can see only from the topmost of eight waterfalls: the watercourse drops down some 1,475 ft in a series of alternating falls and cascades. From Graskop, take the R532 north and turn right after 2½ km (1½ mi) onto the R534, marked "God's Window." Continue 1½ km (1 mi) and look for a brown sign to "The Pinnacle," indicating the parking area on the right.

⑪ Part of the Blyde River Canyon Nature Reserve, **God's Window** is the most famous of the Lowveld lookouts. As such it is geared for tourists, with toilet facilities, paved parking areas, curio vendors, and marked walking trails. The altitude here is 5,700 ft, just a little lower than Johannesburg. But you still feel as though you're standing on top of the world, because the escarpment drops away almost vertically to the Lowveld. Paved walking trails lead to various lookouts. The God's Window lookout has a view back along the escarpment framed between towering cliffs. For a broader panorama, follow the paved track up through the rain forest to a small, unfenced area that offers sweeping views of the entire Lowveld. On sunny days carry water—it's a 10-minute climb. From the Pinnacle, turn right onto R534, pass two overlooks, and after 4½ km (2¾ mi) turn into the parking area on the right.

⑫ Set in a bowl between hills, **Lisbon Falls** cascade 120 ft onto rocks below, throwing spray over a deep pool. You can hike down to the pool on a path from the parking area. From God's Window, turn right onto the R534 and continue 6 km (4 mi). At the T-junction with R532, turn left (toward Graskop); after 1 km (½ mi) turn right onto the road marked Lisbon Falls.

A small stream, Waterfall Spruit, runs through a broad expanse of grassland to **Berlin Falls.** The cascade itself is a thin stream that drops 150 ⑬ ft into a deep-green pool surrounded by tall pines. Berlin Falls is a little over 2 km (1 mi) north of Lisbon Falls off of the R532.

Leaving Graskop, traveling toward Hazyview, you'll enter the lovely **Koewyns Pass.** Unfortunately, there are few vista viewing points, but you'll still get sweeping views of Graskop Gorge. Look for the turnoff to **Graskopkloof** on your left as you leave town, and stop to get a closer view into this deep, surprisingly spectacular gorge. In the rainy season, two waterfalls plunge to the river below.

Dining and Lodging

$ ✕ **Harrie's Pancake Bar.** Harrie's was the original pancake bar in the area, and it's still the best. (Tour groups know this, too, so you might have to stand in line on weekends and during high season.) If the weather's fine, take a seat on the veranda overlooking the street. Otherwise, warm yourself by the fire inside and listen to classical music while mulling over the selection of pancakes and infusion coffees. Pancakes in South Africa are a thicker version of crepes, stuffed with either dessert fillings or savories like ground beef, Dutch bacon, ratatouille, or spinach and feta. Harrie's is open daily 8–5, although the restaurant stays open longer during peak season. ⊠ *Louis Trichardt Ave. and Kerk St.,* ☎ *013/767–1273. AE, MC, V.*

$$ 🏨 **Graskop Hotel.** If you don't want to self-cater or go the bed-and-breakfast route, this hotel is an attractive alternative—the only one in town, in fact. The public areas are decorated with an interesting collection of African art. Zulu baskets brighten long corridors, avant-garde metal ostriches flank the foyer, and Swazi pots and sculpture dot the lounge. Rooms are light and airy, with white walls, green wicker furniture, and lots of blond wood. Unfortunately, the walls are too thin to keep out noise from neighboring rooms. If you want something quieter, ask for one of the new garden rooms. ⊠ *Main St. (mailing address: Box 568, Graskop 1270),* ☎ 🖷 *013/767–1244. 24 rooms, 18 with bath; 5 family cottages; 10 garden rooms. 2 restaurants, bar, coffee shop, pool. CP. AE, DC, MC, V.*

$$ 🏨 **Lisbon Hideaway.** In a peaceful meadow overlooking a small stream, ★ this self-catering establishment makes a great base from which to explore the escarpment. Graskop, several waterfalls, and the magnificent viewpoints of God's Window are minutes away. Accommodation is in modern, comfortable wood cabins, done in wicker and floral patterns. Each cabin sleeps a maximum of six, with two bedrooms, a living-dining room, and a fully equipped kitchen. Don't let the self-catering put you off. Talkative owner Phillip Flischman runs the Spar supermarket in Sabie and will stock the kitchen for you on request. ⊠ *Lisbon Falls Rd. off R532, 10 km (6 mi) from Graskop (mailing address: Box 43, Graskop 1270),* ☎ *013/767–1300. 3 log cabins with bath. MC, V.*

$$ **West Lodge.** If you're looking for an upmarket accommodation close to town and easily accessible to the R532 (which takes you to the scenic delights around Graskop) this attractive B&B has it all. Newly established at press time, West Lodge's rooms are decorated with pastels and crisp, white linens that give the rooms a light, airy feel. Two rooms are located in the main house and face an area known as the Fairyland, which exists as a communal farm area. It was here that Sir Percy Fitzpatrick set up camp on his way to Lydenburg. The two other rooms are in spacious annex. Formal English country gardens, public areas filled with interesting objects, and warm hospitality make this a comfortable place to stop for the night. ⊠ *12–14 Hugenot St., Graskop 1270 (mailing address: Box 2, Graskop 1270),* ☎ *013/767–1390. 4 rooms with bath. Minibars, library. BP. AE, DC, MC, V.*

Blyde River Canyon Nature Reserve

60 km (40 mi) northeast of Graskop.

As you head north from Graskop, after passing Lisbon and Berlin Falls, the dense plantations of gum and pine fall behind, and the road runs through magnificent grass-covered peaks. Once inside the nature reserve, **⑭** turn off to **Bourke's Luck Potholes.** Named after a gold prospector, the potholes are holes carved into the rock in the gorge where the Treur and Blyde rivers converge. The holes were created over eons by the abrasion of pebbles suspended in the swirling water. How these two rivers came to be named is part of Mpumalanga lore: Pioneer (Voortrekker) leader Hendrik Potgieter led an expedition to Lorenco Marques (now Maputo) in 1840, leaving the womenfolk behind near Graskop. The men took so long to return that the women gave them up for dead, naming the river beside which they camped the *Treur* (sorrow), and set off for home. En route, they were met by the returning men as they were about to wade across a river, and so overjoyed were they that they named the river the *Blyde* (joy). Here, too, is the headquarters for the **Blyde River Canyon Nature Reserve,** one of South Africa's scenic highlights. The canyon begins here and winds northward for nearly 30 km (20 mi). Several long canyon trails start from here (☞ Hiking, *below*), and an interesting nature center explains the geology and ecology of the canyon. The canyon proper begins some 27 km (19 mi) north of Berlin Falls. ⊠ *15 km (9 mi) northeast from Graskop on the R532,* ☎ *013/769–6019.* ☒ *R5.50.* ☉ *Reserve daily 7–5, visitor center daily 7:30–4.*

Continuing north from Bourke's Luck Potholes, you get occasional glimpses of the magnificent canyon and the distant cliffs of the escarpment. Nowhere, however, is the view better than from the **Three Rondawels** (Drie Rondawels), 14 km (9 mi) from the Potholes. This is one of the most spectacular vistas in South Africa—you'll find it in almost every travel brochure. The Blyde River, hemmed in by towering buttresses of red rock, snakes through the bottom of the canyon. The Three Rondawels are rock formations that bear a vague similarity to the round, thatched African dwellings known as rondawels.

Before Europeans moved into the area, the indigenous local people named the Three Rondawels "The Chief and His Three Wives." The flat-topped peak to the right is *Mapjaneng* (The Chief), named in honor of a Mapulana chief, Maripe Mashile, who routed invading Swazi at the battle of *Moholoholo* (the very great one). The three wives, in descending order from right to left, are Maseroto, Mogoladikwe, and Magabolle.

⑯ The descent down the escarpment through **Abel Erasmus Pass** is breathtaking. (From the Three Rondawels, take the R532 to a T-junction and turn right onto the R36.) Be careful as you drive this pass—the local African population has taken to grazing cattle and goats on the verges and you may be surprised by animals on the tarmac as you round a bend. The **J. G. Strijdom Tunnel,** burrowing through the mountainside, serves as the gateway to the Lowveld. At the mouth of the tunnel are curio and fruit stalls where you can buy clay pots, African masks, wooden giraffes, and subtropical fruit. As you emerge from the dark mouth of the tunnel, the Lowveld spreads out below, and the views of both it and the mountains are stunning. On the left, the Olifants River snakes through the bushveld, lined to some extent by African subsistence farms.

Once on the flat plains of the Lowveld, the road cuts east through bushveld scrub, alternating with plantations of mango and citrus. Keep an eye out for a lovely example of a baobab tree, on the right-hand side next to a fruit stand. These weird and wonderful trees don't grow much farther south than this.

Hiking

The **Blyde River Canyon Trail** is a 56-km (35-mi) hike that runs from God's Window right along the edge of the escarpment to the Sybrand van Niekerk Resort. The mountain scenery is spectacular, making it one of the most popular trails in the country. Several shorter trails explore the canyon from trailheads at Bourke's Luck Potholes. The number of hikers on these trails is controlled, so it's essential to reserve far in advance. To do so, contact the **Blyde River Canyon Nature Reserve** office (☎ 013/769–6019).

Hoedspruit

63 km (39 mi) northeast of Graskop.

Hoedspruit itself is a nondescript place, little more than a supply depot for the surrounding farms.

From Hoedspruit, turn left onto R40 and drive 4 km (2½ mi) to ⑱ **Tshukudu.** This 12,350-acre game farm bills itself as a safari lodge, but it's more like an animal park. Go somewhere else for a two- or three-night big-game adventure, but stop here for a day visit where you can do a bush walk, followed by breakfast (R60) or a morning game drive (R75), and then stay for lunch (R70). A package including all three costs around R145. The highlight of the day is the chance to meet some of the farm's orphaned animals, many of them completely tame. Don't be surprised if you're ambushed by a tame, gentle lion; nudged by a wildebeest; or accompanied by two young elephants on your bush walk. Advance reservations are essential. ⊠ *On R40, north of Hoedspruit,* ☎ *015/793–2476,* ℻ *015/793–2078.* ✆ *R145.* ☯ *By appointment only.*

Lodging

$$$ ⊡ **Mohlabetsi Safari Lodge.** Situated in Balule (an area adjoining Kruger National Park), this small, relaxed game lodge offers a true, hands-on bush experience. It's unlikely that you'll see all the Big Five—although elephants, lions, and buffalo have been known to wander through camp—but you *will* experience true Africa. Game drives and long bush walks, all accompanied by experienced game rangers, are the main feature of the lodge. Learn about trees and plants and track animals by day, or stargaze in the evening. The public area of the lodge consists of informal cane furniture and a bar area on a wide, thatched veranda, where you can relax and look out over surprisingly green lawns to a water hole. Guests stay in spacious, thatched *rondawels* (round huts modeled after traditional African dwellings) with decor that echoes the colors and themes of the bushveld. Delicious cuisine is served in a tranquil *boma* (outdoor eating area). Although informal, the lodge is extremely personal: rangers and staff are always on hand to offer you a drink or identify a bird you've seen. ⊠ *On R40, north of Hoedspruit (mailing* *address: Box 862, Hoedspruit 1380),* ☏ *015/793–2166. 7 rondawels with bath. 2 bars, 2 lounges, pool. MAP. AE, DC, MC, V.*

Hazyview

93 km (57 mi) south of Hoedspruit.

The town itself is nothing to write home about—it's the main commercial center for the local African population and has a tendency to be crowded and littered. However, you'll pass through en route to the Numbi and Paul Kruger gates to the Kruger National Park or to reach the Sabi Sand Private Reserve gate. Despite the less-than-idyllic downtown, there are some attractive places to stay in the area, particularly if you'll be arriving too late to reach reserve gates by closing time.

Dining and Lodging

$$$ ✕🏨 **Umbhaba Lodge and Restaurant.** This exquisite establishment is accessed from the R40, just past the main shopping area of Hazyview. Lush, beautifully landscaped gardens are a big feature of Umbhaba, starting with a man-made waterfall cascading off the roof of the reception area into a lily pond. There are panoramic views from most public areas, which are sumptuously and strikingly decorated. Guest stay in one of seven thatched, whitewashed chalets, arranged in a horseshoe around the gardens, where waterfalls, pools, and lush, green vegetation predominate. Enormous windows let in lots of light, and white walls and tile floors set off rich velvet drapes and luxurious silk brocade and leather furniture. The restaurant has sliding glass doors that highlight the beautiful view; and when the weather is warm the doors are opened and you can enjoy your breakfast or lunch alfresco on the terrace. Umbhaba dinner specialties include fish potjie; panfried sole served with mushroom quenelles and shrimp velouté; and warthog pie. Umbhaba can arrange activities into the Kruger National Park and surrounding areas, including day and night safaris, golf, helicopter and hot-air-balloon excursions, fishing, horseback riding, and river rafting. ✉ *On R40, east of Hazyview (mailing address: Box 1677, Hazyview 1242),* ☏ *013/737–7636,* 🖷 *013/ 737–7629. 7 suites. Restaurant, bar, pool. CP. AE, DC, MC, V.*

$–$$ 🏨 **Chilli Pepper Lodge.** Set among rolling hills with emerald-green views, this attractive B&B is a lovely place to stop if you're headed to the Kruger National Park or the Sabi Sand Private Reserve from Sabie. Green lawns slope down to a man-made dam and swimming pool where ornamental birds and animals watch you from the water's edge. Accommodation is in five fantastically furnished suites, each with a different theme and unique features—a crocodile light fitting over the bed in the African Suite, a huge iron bedstead in the Victorian Room, red poppies romping across the bedspreads in the Cottage Room. No children under 14. ✉ *On the R536, between Sabie and Hazyview (mailing address: Box 193, Kiepersol 1241),* ☏ *013/737–8373,* 🖷 *013/737– 8258. 5 suites. Pool, kitchenettes. CP. AE, DC, MC, V.*

Kiepersol

⑱ *28 km (17½ mi) east of Sabie.*

This one-road town used to be a trading station. Bananas were grown nearby. There's little here beyond its church and hotel.

Dining and Lodging

$$$$ ✕🏨 **Blue Mountain Lodge.** A member of Small Luxury Hotels of the World, this exclusive retreat focuses on creating a fantasy getaway for jaded city dwellers. The owners, Valma and Kobus Botha, both worked in the film industry, and their lodge has a setlike quality. Artificial moss adds instant age to stonework, and sponge-painting creates an illusion of fading murals on palace walls. The eight Victorian suites are huge, impeccably maintained, and of better value than those in other similar establishments. Each room follows a theme, ranging from English country to American Colonial, and all have fireplaces, verandas, and minibars but no TVs. The best is the *Out of Africa* Suite, done all in white, with billowing mosquito netting, white bedspreads, lots of wood, and a claw-foot bathtub in the center of the room. Avoid the less-expensive Quadrant suites, however. Set in a cobbled courtyard reminiscent of Old Europe, they feel too sharp and angular, a flaw not helped by gaudy stripes painted on the walls. Meals are a refreshing departure from the traditional offerings of other lodges. The cuisine is lighter, with a nouvelle California style that pairs sweet and savory, Western and Asian tastes. Look for dishes like a quenelle of lobster and mussels on a bed of roasted peppers, papaya salad with peanut sauce, or *cabeljou* (a local sea fish) with litchi sauce. Presentation and service are superb. ⊠ *Off R536, 10 km (6 mi) east from Kiepersol (mailing address: Box 101, Kiepersol 1241),* ☎ 🅵🅰🆇 *013/737–8446. 13 rooms with bath. Restaurant, bar, pool, fishing. MAP. AE, DC, MC, V.*

$$$$ ✕🏠 **Cybele Forest Lodge.** Cybele started the whole concept of the
★ country lodge in Mpumalanga, and to a large extent it still sets the pace, as its awards suggest. Cybele's service separates it from its competitors, and that's essentially what you pay for. The staff has achieved a fine mix of professionalism and friendliness, and they go out of their way to make you feel special. The English-country decor of the main lodge complements the service. The two living rooms, warmed by fires and cluttered with attractive bric-a-brac and books, have a reassuring, lived-in feel. Guest rooms are separate from the public areas—which makes for privacy, but less intimacy. Rooms have recently been refurbished, and bathrooms have also been completely rebuilt. The cottage and studio rooms are small and undistinguished. The larger Garden and Courtyard suites, decorated in a classic style, are more comfortable. The magnificent Paddock Suites, with thatched roofs and spectacular views over the forested hills, have their own garden and swimming pool and a private outdoor shower hidden in the foliage— sort of a Blue Lagoon scene for the over-40 crowd. Cybele built much of its reputation on the quality of its food, and it certainly keeps customers coming back. The traditional dinner melds classic French and traditional English country cooking. A light mushroom broth might be followed by risotto with ratatouille, then a choice of rack of lamb or trout fillets with a light lemon-cream sauce. For dessert, a rich gâteau with chocolate sauce is typical. ⊠ *Off R40 between Hazyview and White River (mailing address: Box 346, White River 1240),* ☎ *013/764–1823,* 🅵🅰🆇 *013/764–1810. 12 rooms with bath. Restaurant, bar, pool, horseback riding, fishing. MAP. AE, DC, MC, V.*

White River

⑲ *35 km (22 mi) southeast of Sabie.*

The R40 runs south through Lowveld thornscrub, with the distant barrier of the escarpment visible on the right. It passes through the service town of Hazyview before continuing on to White River, a pleasant farm town with several interesting arts-and-crafts shops.

Dining and Lodging

$$$$ ✕🏠 **Highgrove House.** On a hillside overlooking avocado and banana
★ orchards, this former farmhouse is considered one of the very best lodges in the country. Rooms are in white cottages scattered about lovely gardens, and each has a veranda, sitting area, and fireplace. The decor, both in the main lodge and the cottages, has colonial overtones, with

plenty of gathered curtains and floral upholstery. The atmosphere here tends to be rather formal but pays dividends, as the lodge is immaculate. Highgrove serves an excellent Anglo-French dinner. A typical meal might be a melange of Knysna oysters, quail eggs, and caviar with a sour-cream dressing followed by slivers of guinea fowl and foie gras with a port and cranberry sauce. One heavenly dessert is tartlets of fresh figs and almonds. Weather permitting, lunch and breakfast are served in the gazebo by the pool. Nonguests must reserve ahead for meals. ⊠ *R40, between Hazyview and White River (mailing address: Box 46, Kiepersol 1241),* ☎ *013/764–1844,* 𝐅𝐀𝐗 *013/764–1855, 8 suites. Restaurant, bar, pool. MAP. AE, DC, MC, V.*

$$$ ✕🏠 **Huala Lakeside Lodge.** This attractive lodge sits on a forested promontory, surrounded on three sides by a large dam. All rooms have water views, and the majority of activities involve swimming or boating on the lake. Guest rooms, in sandy yellow cottages, have a warm, comfortable feel, thanks to overhead beams, ivory stucco walls, and matching bedspreads and curtains. If you can, book the Malachite Suite, in a lovely cottage set apart from the main buildings, with a four-poster bed and its own swimming pool. The lodge's five-course dinner is served in an elegant, candlelit room and is a delicious affair; start with an appetizer of chicken liver parfait served with homemade apricot and orange chutney on brioche toast or a delicate soup of carrot with lime, coriander, coconut, and spinach; then move on to a main course like a hot Mediterranean vegetable gâteaux, served with basil pesto. A changing array of delectable desserts may include almond meringues filled with chocolate mousse and topped with chantilly cream. Breakfast and light lunches are served on the veranda under large umbrellas, overlooking the pool and lake. ⊠ *Off R40, between Hazyview and White River (mailing address: Box 1382, White River 1240),* ☎ *013/764– 1893,* 𝐅𝐀𝐗 *013/764–1864. 21 rooms with bath. Restaurant, bar, room service, pool, hiking, fishing. MAP. AE, DC, MC, V.*

$$$ ✕🏠 **Kirby Country Lodge.** This is one of those relaxed places where you can kick back and not worry about appearances. If the rooms aren't as fancy as those at some of the other lodges, they're not as expensive either. The fact that 70% of its guests are repeat or referral visitors is an indication that this lodge is doing something right. Owners John and Jennifer Ilsley personally welcome you to their thatched, whitebrick farmhouse set in pleasant gardens shaded by enormous trees. Spacious, comfortable rooms have phones and fans but no air-conditioning. A seasonal table d'hôte menu is served for dinner. The four-course meal focuses on creative use of homegrown produce, and for those with special dietary requirements, a vegetarian menu is available on request. Choose South African wines to complement the meal from the lodge's extensive wine list. Lunch is for residents only, and nonguests must book for dinner. ⊠ *Off R538, between White River and Plaston (mailing address: Box 3411, White River 1240),* ☎ *013/751–2645. 8 rooms with bath. Restaurant, bar, pool. MAP.*

Nelspruit

19 km (12 mi) southwest of White River on the R40.

Although it serves as the capital of Mpumalanga, Nelspruit has little to offer other than the **Lowveld National Botanical Gardens.** Set on the banks of the Crocodile River, these gardens display more than 500 plant species indigenous to the valley, including a spectacular collection of cycads and ferns. Several trails wind through the gardens, one leading to a pleasant waterfall. ⊠ *3 km (2 mi) outside Nelspruit on White River Rd.,* ☎ *013/ 752–5531.* 🖾 *R7.* ☉ *Oct.–Apr., daily 8–6; May–Sept., daily 8–5:15.*

Barberton

㉑   *50 km (31 mi) south of Nelspruit on the R40.*

The history of the southern Lowveld and Middleveld—between the southern boundary of Kruger National Park, the Swaziland border, and the village of Badplaas to the west—begins in the hills and valleys of the region, where Bushman rock paintings, archaeological ruins, wagon trails, and early gold diggings are all easily accessible. Routes to the Lowveld via Badplaas and Barberton pass through beautiful mountain scenery on quiet country roads.

The Barber family and its significant gold discoveries in the 1880s named this historical town, among the oldest in the area. It was the seat of South Africa's first gold stock exchange. Yet two years after gold was discovered, Barberton was all but deserted by prospectors who moved to the Witwatersrand, where Johannesburg's mining continues to this day. Barberton is now a thriving agricultural center and a tourist haven with a number of memorials linked to its pioneering days. The town has several hiking trails following the paths of early miners. The requisite statue of Jock of the Bushveld stands proudly in the center of town, along with a statuesque town hall. Here you'll also find the Garden of Remembrance, marking the fallen soldiers of both the South African War and World War II.

Barberton makes for an easy day trip from Sabie or Nelspruit. When you get into town, look for the **Market Square**'s information bureau and the **Victorian Tea Garden** for a cup of tea.

The **Barberton Museum**'s best exhibits cover gold-mine culture and history. Some of that culture has to do with colorful gold-rush characters like infamous Cockney Liz, a Phoenix Hotel (☞ *below*) barmaid and prostitute. ⊠ *Bias Building, Pilgrim St.,* ☎ *013/712–4281.* ☜ *Free.* ☼ *Daily 9–4.*

For a look at the lifestyle of a turn-of-the-century upper-middle-class Barberton family, visit the 1904 **Belhaven House Museum** whose late-Victorian–early-Edwardian furnishings seem a world apart from the rowdy gold-rush side of town. ⊠ *Town Square, Lee St.,* ☜ *R4 (includes Stopforth House).* ☼ *Guided tours only, weekdays at 10, 11, noon, 2, and 3.*

Baker and general dealer James Stopforth built the original wood-and-iron house and outbuildings (stable, woodwork shed, and outside bedroom) of **Stopforth House** in 1886. It was rebuilt in 1892, and the Stopforth family occupied it until 1983. ⊠ *18 Bowness St.* ☜ *R4 (includes Belhaven House).* ☼ *Guided tours only, Mon.–Sat. at 10, 11, noon, 2, and 3.*

For a brief period in the 1880s and '90s, Barberton's **De Kaap Stock Exchange** was a mainstay of the region's economy. It served as the country's first gold exchange. The region's gold mines still operate—and all are more than 100 years old. The exchange's facade has been preserved as a National Monument since 1965. ⊠ *Pilgrim St.* ☜ *Free.*

The **Fortuna Mine Hiking Trail,** in the southern part of Barberton, is nestled in the foothills of Lone Tree Hill, one of the better-known peaks of the Makonja range. The 2-km (1½-mi) trail passes through an area populated by some 80 tree species. After a little more than ¼ km (¹⁄₁₀ mi), the trail reaches an old mining tunnel, which was driven through the rocky hillside in the early 1900s for the transport of gold-bearing ore to the Fortuna Mine. Insufficient quantities of gold were found for the mining operation, but the rock formations here are estimated at

400 million years old, which dates them as the oldest sedimentary rock formations yet found on earth. Allow 1½ hours for the hike.

A visit to **De Brug Ostrich Farm** will show you how ostriches are bred and how these flightless birds live. There is an interesting gift shop on the premises, selling a variety of decorated ostrich eggs and items made from them. ⊠ *Off R40 (from Nelspruit) on the Kaapsehoop road,* ☎ *013/712–5265.* ⬚ *R15.* ☉ *Tues.–Sun., entry at 10 AM and 3 PM only.*

Gold Panning Expeditions leave from the Diggers Retreat Hotel, outside Barberton on the Kaapmuiden road. The tours explore one of the area's rivers—Louws Creek, Honeybird Creek, Revolver Creek, or Kaap River—where alluvial gold was once panned. Watch gold-panning demonstrations, try panning yourself, or learn about the region's gold-mining history from an informative guide. ⊠ *Off R40 (from Nelspruit) on the Kaapsehoop road,* ☎ *013/712–6289.* ⬚ *R50 (including lunch).* ☉ *Daily 10–2.*

A relatively new innovation at Barberton are the **4x4 Sunset Tours.** Guests are driven through the mountainous countryside surrounding Barberton in a 4x4 vehicle to watch the sunset from one of the region's rugged aeries. Tours last two to three hours. At press time these tours were still very new; phone ahead for more information (☎ 013/712–6950).

All three of the above activities can be arranged through the Barberton Information Bureau (☎ 013/712–2121).

Mpumalanga A to Z

Arriving and Departing

BY BUS

Greyhound (☎ 013/753–2100) runs daily between Johannesburg and Nelspruit (Panorama Hotel, opposite Joshua Doore Centre). The trip takes five or six hours.

BY CAR

It takes approximately four hours to drive the 350 km (220 mi) from Johannesburg to Nelspruit, capital of Mpumalanga and a major gateway to the region. The best route is north from Johannesburg on the N1 to Pretoria East, then east on the N4, passing the towns of Witbank and Middelberg.

Note: The N4 has recently become an expensive toll road—and there is no real alternative route, so it's difficult to avoid paying the high fees. Expect to pay at least R150 on a one-way trip from Johannesburg to Nelspruit or Malelane. Take cash for the purpose: you will be charged between R20 and R30 per toll.

BY PLANE

Nelspruit Airport is a one-hour hop from Johannesburg, about half that from other points in Mpumalanga. It is served by **S.A. Airlink** (☎ 013/741–3557 or 013/741–3558).

BY TRAIN

Spoornet's **Komati train** (☎ 011/773–2944) travels between Johannesburg and Nelspruit via Pretoria daily. The trip takes about 12 hours. The luxury *Blue Train* (☞ Rail Travel *in* Smart Travel Tips A to Z) also makes occasional runs from Pretoria to Nelspruit; Rovos Rail (☞ Train Travel *in* Smart Travel Tips A to Z), the Edwardian-era competitor of the *Blue Train,* travels from Pretoria to Komatipoort, just outside Kruger National Park. Most passengers combine a journey on Rovos Rail with a package trip to a game reserve or one of the exclusive lodges on the escarpment.

Getting Around

BY CAR

Renting a car is the only option if you really want to explore Mpumalanga.

BY MINIBUS

Public bus service is limited or nonexistent in Mpumalanga. If you don't have your own car, you're dependent on one of the tour companies to get around the escarpment and into the game reserves (☞ Guided Tours, *below*). Many of these companies also operate shuttle services that transfer guests between the various lodges and to the airport. It's usually possible to hire these chauffeured minibuses on an hourly or daily rate.

Contacts and Resources

CAR RENTAL

Avis (☎ 013/741–1087 or 013/741–1088), **Budget** (☎ 013/741–3871), and **Imperial** (☎ 013/741–3210) all have offices at Nelspruit Airport. **Avis** (☎ 013/735–5651) also has a desk at Skukuza Airport, in Kruger National Park, while **Imperial**'s Nelspruit office (☎ 013/741–3210) will deliver cars to Skukuza for clients. If you're planning to drive from Johannesburg, *see* Johannesburg A to Z *in* Chapter 2.

EMERGENCIES

In case of an emergency, contact the police at ☎ 10111. In the event of a serious medical emergency, contact **MRI** (☎ 0800118811), which offers emergency helicopter services.

The best-equipped hospitals in the Lowveld are in Nelspruit: **Nelspruit Private Hospital** (☎ 013/744–7150) and **Rob Ferreira Hospital** (☎ 013/741–3031).

GUIDED TOURS

➤ Flight Seeing: **National Airways Corporation** offers all types of helicopter charters, including lodge hopping. Deserving special mention is the "Misty Mountain" experience, during which the guest is taken on a helicopter journey from one waterfall and site to another, stopping off at the Pinnacle, near Graskop, for a picnic breakfast. ☎ *013/ 741–4651*.

➤ Orientation: All tour operators offer a package of trips that cover the major sights of the escarpment, as well as game-viewing trips into Kruger National Park and private reserves. The most reputable operators in the area are **Dragonfly Safaris** (⊠ Box 1042, White River 1240, ☎ 013/764–1823, 𝖥𝖠𝖷 013/764–1810) and **Welcome Tours** (⊠ Box 2191, Parklands 2121, ☎ 011/328–8050, 𝖥𝖠𝖷 011/442–8865).

VISITOR INFORMATION

Barberton Information Bureau. ⊠ *Market Sq.,* ☎ *013/712–2121,* 𝖥𝖠𝖷 *013/712–5120.* ☼ *Weekdays 8–4:30, Sat. 8:30–noon.*

Graskop Information and Reservations. ⊠ *Spar Center, Pilgrim's Rd.,* ☎ *013/767–1833,* 𝖥𝖠𝖷 *013/767–1855.* ☼ *Weekdays 8–4:30, Sat. 9–1.*

Pilgrim's Rest Information Centre. ⊠ *Main St.,* ☎ *013/768–1060.* ☼ *Daily 9–12:45 and 1:15–4:30.*

Sondelani Travel & Info, the SATOUR office in Sabie, provides information on the area and hires out mountain bikes. ⊠ *Woodsman Center, Main St., Sabie,* ☎ *013/764–3492.* ☼ *Daily 8–5.*

KRUGER NATIONAL PARK

Kruger lies in the hot Lowveld, a subtropical section of Mpumalanga and Northern Province that abuts Mozambique. The park cuts a swathe 80 km (50 mi) wide and 320 km (200 mi) long from Zimbabwe and the Limpopo River in the north to the Crocodile River in the south. Along the way, it crosses 14 different ecozones, each supporting a great variety of plants, birds, and animals.

The southern and central sections of the park are where you will probably see the most game. Riverine forests, thorny thickets, and large, grassy plains studded with knobthorn and marula trees are typical of this region and make ideal habitats for a variety of animals, including black and white rhino (once on the verge of extinction), leopard, and giraffe. The most consistently rewarding drive in the park is along the road paralleling the Sabie River from Skukuza to Lower Sabie.

As you head north to Olifants and Letaba, you enter major elephant country, although you're likely to spot any number of other animals as well, including lions and cheetahs. North of Letaba, however, the landscape becomes a monotonous blur of mopane, nutrient-poor land that supports a smaller numbers of animals. Some species, most notably tsessebe and roan antelope, thrive up here nevertheless. Elephants are partial to mopane and there's a good chance of seeing these huge beasts here, too. If you have a week in Kruger, it's worth driving north to check it out—there are also fewer people up there, if you want to avoid the crowds during the busy seasons. With less than that, you should stick to the southern and central sections of the park.

Summer in Kruger can be uncomfortably hot—temperatures of 100°F are common—and many northern European visitors become simpering puddles of discontent. If you feel the heat, come at another time or stay in the cool uplands of the Mpumalanga Drakensberg and visit Kruger just for game drives. Whatever you do, *avoid the park during school vacations.* During the July and Christmas holidays, Kruger looks more like summer camp than a game reserve. Reservations are hard to obtain (book a year in advance), and hour-long traffic jams at game-sightings are not uncommon.

Park entrance fees in recent years have fluctuated dramatically—increases of up to 15% per annum have suddenly become the norm. You will need to pay admission per person and per car. Service standards have, unfortunately, deteriorated somewhat, despite the price increases. Enormous staff turnovers and cuts in government spending have taken their toll. Don't expect wonders, and tell the national parks or the camp manager if you experience problems.

Park Activities

See Kruger A to Z, *below,* for information about reservations and fees.

Bush Drives

First-time visitors sometimes feel a little lost driving themselves through the park: they don't know what to look for, and they can't identify the animals they do find. An affordable solution is to hire a game ranger to show you the park and its animal inhabitants. The rest camps at Berg-en-Dal, Letaba, and Skukuza all offer ranger-led bush drives in open-air Land Rovers (minimum of two people). Not only can rangers explain the finer points of what you're seeing, but they can also take you into areas off-limits to the public. They may even take you on short walks through the bush, something else you can't do on your own. Day

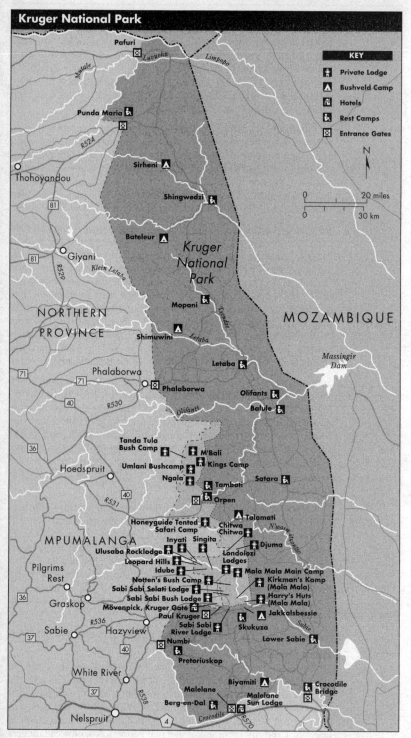

Kruger National Park

KEY

🛏 Private Lodge
⛺ Bushveld Camp
🏨 Hotels
🛖 Rest Camps
⊠ Entrance Gates

N

0 ———— 20 miles
0 ———— 30 km

Pafuri ⊠

Luvuvhu · *Limpopo*

Matale

Punda Maria 🛏
⊠

R524

Sirheni ⛺

Thohoyandou ○

Shingwedzi 🛖

Bateleur ⛺

81
81

Giyani ○

Kruger National Park

R529

Klein Letaba

NORTHERN PROVINCE

Mopani 🛖

Shimuwini ⛺

Letaba · *Tsendze*

MOZAMBIQUE

71

Phalaborwa

Letaba 🛖

Massingir Dam

71

40 *R530*

Phalaborwa ⊠

Olifants 🛖

Balule 🛖

36

Olifants

Tanda Tula Bush Camp 🛏

M'Bali 🛏
Kings Camp 🛏

Hoedspruit ○

Umlani Bushcamp 🛏

40

Ngala 🛏
Tamboti 🛏
Orpen ⊠🛖

Satara 🛖

R531

Honeyguide Tented Safari Camp 🛏

Talamati ⛺

Chitwa Chitwa 🛏

MPUMALANGA

Ulusaba Rocklodge 🛏

Inyati 🛏
Singita 🛏

Djuma 🛏

N'waste Hoopsi

Pilgrims Rest ○

Leopard Hills 🛏
Idube 🛏

Londolozi Lodges 🛏

36

Notten's Bush Camp 🛏

Mala Mala Main Camp 🛏

Graskop ○

Sabi Sabi Selati Lodge 🛏
Sabi Sabi Bush Lodge 🛏

Kirkman's Kamp (Mala Mala) 🛏

R536

Mövenpick, Kruger Gate 🛏

Harry's Huts (Mala Mala) 🛏

37

Sabie ○

Paul Kruger ⊠

Jakkalsbessie ⛺

Hazyview ○

Sabi Sabi River Lodge 🛏

Skukuza 🛖

Sabie

Numbi ⊠🛖

Lower Sabie 🛖

37

White River ○

Pretoriuskop 🛖

Biyamiti ⛺

40

Malelane 🛏

Crocodile Bridge 🛖⊠

R538

Berg-en-Dal 🛖

Malelane Sun Lodge 🛏
⊠

Nelspruit ○

4

Crocodile · *R570*

excursions cost about R150 per person, less than renting a car for a day. Book drives at least a week in advance.

Night Drives

★ Even if you tour the park by yourself during the day, be sure to go on a ranger-led night drive, when the park is closed to regular visitors. Passengers sit in large, open-air vehicles, and rangers use powerful spotlights to pick out animals, including nocturnal creatures that you would never see otherwise, such as bush babies, servals, civets, and, if you're really lucky, aardvarks. Night is also the time when hyenas, lions, and leopards hunt. These opportunities alone make a night drive an unmissable experience. The major rest camps offer these drives, with the exception of Lower Sabie and Olifants. The three- to four-hour trip leaves the rest camps half an hour before the gates close. Night drives cost about R75 per person, and it's advisable to reserve in advance.

Wilderness Trails

★ Spend a few days hiking through the wilds of Africa and you'll probably never be satisfied driving around a game reserve again. On foot, you gain an affinity for the animals and the bush that's impossible in the confines of a car. Kruger has seven wilderness trails, each of which can accommodate eight people. Led by an armed ranger, you'll spend the day walking through the bush, returning each day to the same trail camp. These trails are not get-fit hikes but slow meanders, the point being to learn about your surroundings: the medicinal purposes of trees, the role of dung beetles in the ecology, even how to recognize animals by their spoor. In general, you can't get as close to animals on foot as you can in a vehicle. You *will* see animals, though, and many hikers can recount face-to-face encounters with everything from rhino to elephant and lion. It's a heart-pumping thrill you won't soon forget. Hikes last three nights and two days (starting on Sundays and Wednesdays), and you should be prepared to walk as much as 19 km (12 mi) a day. No one under 12 or over 60 is allowed. Hikers sleep in rustic, two-bed huts and share a reed-wall bathroom with flush toilets and showers. Meals are simple bush fare, including stews and barbecues; you must provide your own booze and soft drinks. These trails are incredibly popular—try to reserve 13 months in advance, when bookings open. The cost is approximately R935 per person per trail.

Bushman Trail. Situated in the southwestern corner of the park, this trail takes its name from the San rock paintings and sites found in the area. The trail camp lies in a secluded valley dominated by granite hills and cliffs. Game sightings frequently include white rhino, elephant, and buffalo. Check in at Berg-en-Dal.

Metsimetsi Trail. The permanent water of the nearby N'waswitsontso River makes this one of the best trails for winter game viewing. Midway between Skukuza and Satara, the trail camp hunkers in the lee of a mountain in an area of gorges, cliffs, and rolling savanna. Check in at Skukuza.

Napi Trail. Sightings of white rhino are common on this trail, which runs through mixed bushveld between Pretoriuskop and Skukuza. Other frequent sightings include black rhino, cheetah, leopard, and elephant. If you're lucky, you may also see nomadic wild dogs. The trail camp hides in dense riverine forest at the confluence of the Napi and Biyamiti rivers. Check in at Pretoriuskop.

Nyalaland Trail. They don't come much more remote than this trail camp, in pristine wilderness in the far north of the park. Bird-watching is the big thrill in this land of huge baobabs and fever trees. The camp lies on the bank of the Madzaringwe Spruit, near the Luvuvhu

River. You're almost sure to see hippo, crocodiles, nyala, and elephant. Check in at Punda Maria.

Olifants Trail. East of Olifants rest camp, this trail camp commands a great view of the Olifants River and affords regular sightings of elephant, lion, buffalo, and hippo. The landscape varies from riverine forest to the rocky foothills of the Lebombo Mountains. Check in at Letaba.

Sweni Trail. East of Satara, this trail camp overlooks the Sweni Spruit and savanna dotted with marula and knobthorn trees. The area attracts large herds of zebra, wildebeest, and buffalo—with their attendant predators, lion and spotted hyena. Check in at Satara.

Wolhuter Trail. If you want to come face-to-face with a white rhino, choose this trail midway between Berg-en-Dal and Pretoriuskop. The undulating bushveld, interspersed with rocky *kopjes* (hills), is ideal habitat for these tremendous prehistoric beasts, but you're also likely to see elephant, buffalo, and lion. Check in at Berg-en-Dal.

National Parks Lodging

It's necessary to book a year in advance if you want a room during peak seasons (December–January and July). Reservations must be made directly with the **National Parks Board** (✉ Box 787, Pretoria 0001, ☎ 012/343–1991, ⅏ 012/343–0905).

Rest Camps

For a couple staying in an en suite rondawel expect to pay around R350 per night. Costs increase for additional beds. A site to pitch your own tent costs R65 for up to two people throughout the park. All camps except Balule and Tamboti have gas stations and stores on-site.

$–$$ 🏠 **Balule.** On the bank of the Olifants River, this rustic camp differs radically from the others and will appeal to those who want to experience the true feel of the bush. There are no shops or restaurants, and there's no electricity—only lanterns. Accommodations are in basic, three-bed huts with no windows (vents only) and shared bathroom facilities. Cooking is done in a communal kitchen. Visitors must check in at Olifants (☞ *below*), 11 km (7 mi) away.

$–$$ 🏠 **Berg-en-Dal.** Built in 1984, this rest camp lies at the southern tip of the park, in a basin surrounded by rocky hills. Berg-en-Dal is known for its white rhino, leopard, and wild dog, but it lacks the tremendous game density of some of the camps farther north. A small dam runs by one side of the perimeter fence, offering good game viewing, including a close look at cruising crocodiles. Berg-en-Dal itself is one of the more attractive camps, drawing great benefit from its thoughtful landscaping, which has left much of the indigenous vegetation intact. The strategic positioning of accommodations among bushes and trees affords more seclusion than any of the older camps. Berg-en-Dal has two types of accommodations: three-bed chalets and family cottages that sleep six in two bedrooms. All huts come with fully equipped kitchens, including pots, pans, and cutlery. *Restaurant, cafeteria, pool, coin laundry.*

$–$$ 🏠 **Crocodile Bridge.** In the southeastern corner of the park, this small rest camp doubles as an entrance gate and makes a convenient stopover for visitors who arrive too late to reach another camp. Although the Crocodile River provides the scenic backdrop for the camp, any sense of being in the wild is quickly shattered by views of power lines and farms on its south side. The road leading from the camp to Lower Sabie is well known for its sightings of general game as well as buffalo, rhino, cheetah, and lion. A hippo pool lies just 5 km (3 mi) away. Accommodations are in two- or three-bed huts with fully equipped kitchenettes and bathrooms en suite. Newly introduced—and very popular—are six East African–style safari tents. *Coin laundry.*

$–$$ ▣ **Letaba.** Overlooking the frequently dry Letaba River, this lovely camp sits in the middle of elephant country in the central section of the park. Excellent game-viewing sites in the area are the Engelhardt and Mingerhout dams. The camp itself has a real bush feel: all the huts are thatched, and the grounds are overgrown with apple leaf trees, acacias, mopane, and lala palms. The restaurant and snack bar, with attractive outdoor seating, look out over the broad, sandy river bed. Even if you aren't staying at Letaba, stop in for the superb exhibit on elephants at the Environmental Education Centre. The display examines the social and physical characteristics of the huge animals, from their development in the womb to their death from starvation as a result of tooth loss. Accommodations are in large cottages and two-, three-, and four-bed rondawels, some without bathrooms and kitchenettes. Cooking utensils are not provided. Unfortunately, dense local foliage means that few rooms have views. Attractive alternatives are the large, East African–style safari tents furnished with four beds, tables and chairs, a refrigerator, and a fan. The campground, on the fence perimeter, offers lots of shade. *Restaurant, cafeteria, coin laundry.*

$–$$ ▣ **Lower Sabie.** This is one of the most popular camps in Kruger for good reason: it commands tremendous views over a broad sweep of the Sabie River and sits in one of the best game-viewing areas of the park (along with Skukuza and Satara). The camp is well known for white rhino, lion, and cheetah, and elephant and buffalo frequently come down to the river to drink. The vegetation around the camp consists mainly of grassland savanna interspersed with marula trees and knobthorn, and there are plenty of watering holes within a few minutes' drive. Lower Sabie is small compared with minitowns like Skukuza, and you get a pretty good feel for the surrounding bush. Accommodations are in five-bed cottages and one-, two-, three-, and five-bed huts, some of which lack kitchens and bathrooms. Cooking utensils are also not provided. *Restaurant, cafeteria, coin laundry.*

$–$$ ▣ **Mopani.** Built in the lee of a rocky kopje overlooking a dam, this huge settlement is the newest and most attractive of Kruger's rest camps. The dam and the camp are an oasis for both animals and people amid the numbing monotony of the mopane shrubveld in the northern section of the park. You will probably see more game from the rest camp than you will in hours of sweaty driving through the surrounding country. Constructed of rough stone, wood, and thatch, the camp merges well into the thick vegetation. Shaded wood walkways connect the public areas, all of which overlook the dam—the view from the open-air bar is outstanding. The restaurant is à la carte (you must reserve before 6) and the food far superior to the buffet-style fare served at other rest camps. The cottages, too, are better equipped and much larger than their counterparts elsewhere in Kruger. Units with kitchenettes come with a full complement of crockery, cutlery, and cooking utensils, and six-bed family cottages are nothing less than fully furnished houses. *Restaurant, cafeteria, bar, pool, coin laundry.*

$–$$ ▣ **Olifants.** In the central section of the park, Olifants has the best setting of all the Kruger camps. It sits high atop cliffs on a rocky ridge, with panoramic views over the distant hills and the Olifants River below. A lovely, thatch-sheltered terrace allows visitors to sit for hours with a pair of binoculars and pick out the animals below. Lions often make kills in the river valley, and elephant, buffalo, giraffe, kudu, and other game come down to drink and bathe. Do whatever it takes to secure one of the thatched rondawels overlooking the valley. It's worth reserving these rondawels for at least two nights (book a year in advance) so you can hang out on the veranda and watch Africa unfold below—

you won't be disappointed. Olifants offers a lot more than a good view, however. It's a charming old camp, graced with wonderful indigenous trees like sycamores and knobbly figs, mopane, and sausage trees. Accommodations are in two- and three-bed thatched rondawels, some with fully equipped kitchens. The camp has a big drawback in that it has no swimming pool—a must during summer, when temperatures soar. *Restaurant, cafeteria, coin laundry.*

$–$$ 🏠 **Orpen.** Little needs to be said about this tiny rest camp, which lies just yards from Orpen Gate, in the central section of the park. The only reason to stay here is if you arrive at the gate too late to make it to another camp before the roads are closed. None of the two-bedroom units have bathrooms or cooking facilities. The rooms, arranged in a rough semicircle around a large lawn, look out toward the perimeter fence, about 150 ft away. More recently, family cottages have been added to the camp, and these are equipped with cooking supplies.

$–$$ 🏠 **Pretoriuskop.** This large rest camp, conveniently close to the Numbi Gate in the southwest corner of the park, makes a good overnight stop for new arrivals. The landscape here consists of rocky kopjes and steep ridges that provide an ideal habitat for mountain reedbuck and klipspringers. The area's sourveld vegetation also attracts browsers like giraffe and kudu, as well as white rhino, lion, and wild dog. Like several other Kruger camps, Pretoriuskop is laid out so guests see less of the surrounding bush than of their neighbors grilling *boerewors* (coarse farmer's sausages) and chops. Accommodations are in typical thatched rondawels and cottages, some of which lack bathrooms and kitchens. The campground enjoys some shade, but sites lack privacy. *Restaurant, cafeteria, pool, coin laundry.*

$–$$ 🏠 **Punda Maria.** Few foreign visitors make it to this camp in the far northern end of the park, near Zimbabwe. This is a shame, for in many ways it offers the best bush experience of any of the major rest camps. It's a small enclave, with whitewashed, thatched cottages arranged in terraces on a hill. The camp lies in the sandveld, a botanically rich area notable for its unique plant life and birds. An interesting nature trail winds through the rest camp. Two-bed huts all come with bathrooms en suite, and many have fully equipped kitchenettes. *Restaurant.*

$–$$ 🏠 **Satara.** Second in size only to Skukuza, this camp sits in the middle of the hot plains between Olifants and Lower Sabie, in the central section of Kruger. The knobthorn veld surrounding the camp provides the best grazing in the park and attracts large concentrations of game, which in turn attract plenty of lion. Just standing at the perimeter fence, you often see giraffe, zebra, waterbuck, and other antelope. Despite its size, Satara has far more appeal than Skukuza, possibly because of the privacy it offers—the huts aren't all piled on top of one another—and possibly because of the tremendous birdlife that flies in from the bush. The restaurant and snack bar are very pleasant, with shady seating overlooking the lawns and the bush beyond. Accommodations are in large cottages and two- or three-bed thatched rondawels, some with kitchenettes (no cooking utensils). The rondawels, arranged in large circles, face inward onto a central, parklike space. Campsites are secluded, with an excellent view of the bush, although none of the sites enjoy much shade. *Restaurant, cafeteria, coin laundry.*

$–$$ 🏠 **Shingwedzi.** This camp lies in the northern section of the park, amid the blistering plains of mopane shrubveld. The camp benefits enormously from the riverine growth associated with the Shingwedzi River and Kanniedood Dam. As a result, you will probably find more game right around the camp than anywhere else in the region. Among the species that thrive in the harsh mopane environment are elephant, roan antelope, Sharpe's grysbok, and tsessebe. The use of thatch and unworked tree trunks as roof supports gives the camp a rugged, pioneer feel. Both the restaurant (à la carte) and outdoor cafeteria have views over the Shingwedzi River. Accommodations are of two types, A and B. Choose A. These whitewashed units have steeply pitched thatched roofs that accommodate an additional two-bed loft; some also have fully equipped kitchenettes. The B units, painted a dull beige, are built of brick and roofed with unsightly tile; while most have bathrooms, none have kitchenettes. It's anyone's guess why all of the huts face each other across a mopane grove, ignoring the lovely views of the bush beyond the perimeter fence. The campground is large but barren, with almost no shade. *Restaurant, cafeteria, pool, coin laundry.*

$–$$ 🏠 **Skukuza.** By far the largest camp in Kruger, it serves as the park's headquarters. It's large enough to pass for a small town—with a gas station, police station, post office, car rental, grocery store, and library—and as a result it has completely lost all bush feel. At times you wonder if you're in a game reserve at all. Skukuza is popular for good reason, though. It's easily accessible by both air and road, and it lies in a region of thorn thicket that supports a high density of game, including lion, cheetah, and hyena. The camp itself sits on a bank of the crocodile-infested Sabie River, with good views of thick reeds and grazing waterbuck. A museum and education center offer an interesting look at the history and ecology of the park. There are both bush drives and night drives to see game. Accommodations are in two- or three-bed rondawels and four-bed cottages, as well as four- and six-bed family cottages. Most units are equipped with cooking utensils and kitchen facilities. Some rondawels lack kitchens, but all have refrigerators. Guests also have the option of staying in permanent tents of the sort used on luxury East African safaris. Sited on a concrete platform, each tent comes with two or four beds, a cupboard, refrigerator, and fan. *Restaurant, cafeteria.*

$–$$ 🏠 **Tamboti.** Kruger's first tented camp, and also its newest, has a name with the romantic ring of a traditional East African safari, but communal facilities can make it a bit like an upmarket campsite. Nevertheless, it is one of Kruger's most popular camps, boasting an average annual occupancy rate of around 90%. Its position on the banks of the frequently dry Timbavati River is superb, among apple leaf trees, sycamore figs, and jackalberries. From your tent, it isn't uncommon to see elephants just beyond the barely visible electrified fence digging in the riverbed for moisture, which is why you need to book well ahead to get a place. Each of the walk-in tents has its own deck overlooking the river, but the ones to make a beeline for are those that enjoy the deep shade of large riverine trees—something to value highly in the midsummer sweat. All kitchen, washing, and toilet facilities are in two shared central blocks, and you have to bring all your own cooking and eating utensils.

Bushveld Camps

If you're prepared to cook for yourself, Kruger's bushveld camps are infinitely more attractive than the major rest camps. They're small and intimate—you can't get lost the way you can at Skukuza—and access is restricted to residents only. As a result, you experience more of the bush and less of fellow travelers. These camps do not have restaurants, gas pumps, or grocery stores, but all huts have fully equipped kitchens. The only drawback is that most of the cottages are intended for four or more people. Because of the four-bed minimum requirement, most bushveld camps cost R615–R760 per night. The handful of one-bedroom cottages at Biyamiti, Shimuwini, Sirheni, and Talamati go for R355 and understandably get snapped up fast.

$$$ ⬚ **Bateleur.** Hidden in the northern reaches of the park, this is one of the most remote destinations in Kruger. Shaded by tall trees, the camp overlooks the dry watercourse of the Mashokwe Spruit. A raised platform provides an excellent vantage point from which to view game coming to drink from rainy-season pools, and two nearby dams draw a variety of animals. The camp accommodates a total of 34 people in seven family cottages. Each thatched cottage has two bathrooms, a fully equipped kitchenette, and veranda. There are bush drives and night drives.

$$$ ⬚ **Jakkalsbessie.** You couldn't ask for a better game-viewing location, along the Sabie River near Skukuza. The game density here is among the highest in the region. The only drawback is the noise from aircraft landing at Skukuza airport. Eight family cottages can house a maximum of 32 visitors. Each of the thatched cottages has two bedrooms, two bathrooms, a fully equipped kitchen, and a veranda. An added bonus is the camp's proximity to the big grocery store at Skukuza.

$$–$$$ ⬚ **Biyamiti.** Close to the park gate at Crocodile Bridge, this large camp overlooks the normally dry sands of the Byamiti River. The vegetation is mixed combretum woodland, which attracts healthy populations of kudu, impala, and elephant, as well as lion and black and white rhino. The camp consists of 15 thatched cottages, which can accommodate 70 people. All cottages have large verandas and fully equipped kitchens.

$$–$$$ ⬚ **Shimuwini.** Bird-lovers descend in droves on this isolated camp, set on a lovely dam on the Letaba River. Towering jackalberry and sycamore fig trees offer welcome shade, as well as refuge to a host of local and migratory birds. Away from the river, the riverine forest quickly gives way to mopane—bushwillow woodland, not typically known for supporting large amounts of game. Even so, roan and sable move through the area, and in the peak of summer elephants arrive to browse on the mopane. The camp can house 71 guests in one-, two-, and three-bedroom cottages, all with verandas and kitchens. There are bush drives and night drives.

$$–$$$ ⬚ **Sirheni.** Another major bird-watching camp, Sirheni sits on the edge of Sirheni Dam, in the far north of the park. A rewarding drive for birders and game-spotters alike runs along the Mphongolo River, but the area can't rival the game density of the Sabie and Crocodile river basins farther south. A maximum of 80 guests can stay in the camp's one- and two-bedroom cottages, all with their own verandas and fully equipped kitchens.

$$–$$$ ⬚ **Talamati.** On the banks of the normally dry N'waswitsontso River in Kruger's central section, this tranquil camp offers one of the best game-viewing experiences in the park. Grassy plains and mixed woodlands provide an ideal habitat for herds of impala, zebra, and wildebeest, as well as lion, cheetah, and elephant. Two hides (blinds) give guests a chance to watch birds and game from the camp itself. The camp can house 80 people in four- and six-bed cottages, all fully equipped.

Near Kruger National Park

$$$$ ⬚ **Malelane Sun Lodge.** This pleasant hotel offers a level of luxury that cannot be matched by rest camps inside the park. If you're prepared to pay the entrance fee to Kruger Park every day, you can have the best of Kruger and a comfortable base, too. The hotel sits just yards from the park's Malelane Gate, overlooking the Crocodile River. The focal point is a creatively sculpted swimming pool, edged with manicured lawns and served by a thatched bar area. Rooms are done in subtle greens and lit by faux miners' lanterns but lacks a bush feel. The lodge is in close proximity to Swaziland and the casino there. ⊠ *Off N4 toward Malelane Gate (mailing address: Box 392, Malelane 1320).*, ☎ *013/790–3304,* ℻ *013/790–3303. 102 rooms. Restaurant, bar, room service, pool, 9-hole golf course, tennis, squash. CP. AE, DC, MC, V.*

$$–$$$$ ⊞ **Mövenpick Kruger Gate.** This attractive hotel next to the Paul
★ Kruger Gate offers visitors a luxury alternative to the bare-bones ac-
commodation of Kruger's rest camps. The hotel has two major ad-
vantages: guests have quick access to the south-central portion of the
park, where game viewing is best; and the hotel *feels* likes it's in the
wilds of Africa. Dinner is served in a *boma,* a traditional reed enclo-
sure around a blazing campfire; rangers lead guided walks through the
surrounding bush; and guests can even sleep overnight in a tree house.
The rooms are connected by a raised wood walkway that passes
through thick indigenous forest. Rooms have Spanish-tile floors and
standard hotel furniture, as well as air-conditioning, cable TVs, and
minibars. ⊠ *R536, next to Paul Kruger Gate (mailing address: Box
54, Skukuza 1350),* ☎ *013/735–5671,* ℻ *013/735–5676. 96 doubles.
2 restaurants, 4 bars, room service, pool, tennis. CP. AE, DC, MC, V.*

Kruger A to Z

Arriving and Departing

For information about bus, train, and plane transport to Nelspruit, 50
km (31 mi) from Kruger's Numbi Gate and 64 km (40 mi) from Male-
lane Gate, *see* Mpumalanga A to Z, *above.*

BY CAR

From Johannesburg, drive north on the N1 to Pretoria East and then
head east on the N4 to Nelspruit, where you can choose which of the
park's entrances to use. The Malelane and Numbi gates, closest to Nel-
spruit, are about four to five hours from Johannesburg.

Note: The N4 has recently become an expensive toll road—and there
is no real alternative route, so it's difficult to avoid paying the high
fees. Expect to pay at least R150 on a one-way trip from Johannes-
burg to Nelspruit or Malelane. Take cash for the purpose: you will be
charged around R20–R30 per toll.

BY PLANE

Two airlines fly into the park or to nearby airports. **S.A. Express** (☎ 011/
978–5390) has three flights daily between Johannesburg and Skukuza,
the park headquarters and the largest rest camp in the park. One of these
goes via Hoedspruit, a small service town close to Kruger's Orpen Gate
that is also convenient for some of the private game lodges on the west
side of the national park. All passengers landing at Skukuza must pay a
R22 entrance fee to the park; if, however, you are not going to stay in
the park, this charge will be R66. **S.A. Airlink** (☎ 015/781–5823 or 015/
781–5833) sends at least one flight a day from Johannesburg to Phal-
aborwa, a mining town on the edge of the park's central section.

Getting Around

BY CAR

Avis (☎ 013/735–5651) is the only car rental agency with an office at
Skukuza, inside the park. However, the Nelspruit branch of **Imperial**
(☎ 013/741–3210) will deliver a car to Skukuza for you. If you have
five or more people in your group, consider hiring a minibus. Not only
do you get your own window, but you also sit much higher than in a
regular car—a big plus when you're searching for game hidden in
dense bush. **Avis** (☎ 015/24–5169), **Budget** (☎ 015/781–3169), and
Imperial (☎ 015/781–5404) have rental desks at Phalaborwa airport.

Depending on the month, rest-camp gates close between 5:30 and
6:30 at night and open again between 4:30 and 6:30 in the morning.
The driver of any vehicle caught on the roads between these hours is
liable to a fine or prosecution.

Reservations and Fees

Admission to the park is R24 per vehicle, plus R30 for each visitor, whether you're staying overnight or longer. Reservations for all accommodations, bush drives, and wilderness trails must be made through the **National Parks Board** (✉ Box 787, Pretoria 0001, ☎ 012/343–1991, FAX 012/343–0905).

Safari Operators

S.A. Express (✉ Box 101, Johannesburg International Airport, 1627, ☎ 011/978–5390, FAX 011/978–5429) is the biggest safari company in Kruger and the only commercial flight operator in the region. Visitors can choose from a variety of tour packages ranging from quickie overnight jaunts to five-day extravaganzas that also take in the scenic splendors of the Mpumalanga Escarpment. Visitors fly into Skukuza on one of S.A. Express's regularly scheduled flights, tour the park in minibuses, and sleep in rest camps, usually Skukuza. Tour leaders are knowledgeable about the park's ecosystems and usually know where to find animals you would probably miss on your own. Other operators offering minibus tours of Kruger Park are **Game Encounter** (✉ Box 48737, Roosevelt Park 2129, ☎ FAX 011/888–2100), **Springbok Atlas** (✉ Box 14884, Bredell 1623, ☎ 011/396–1053, FAX 011/396–1069), and **Welcome Tours** (✉ Box 2191, Parklands 2121, ☎ 011/328–8050, FAX 011/442–8865).

PRIVATE GAME RESERVES AND LODGES

CATEGORY	COST*
$$$$	over R2,200
$$$	R1,700–R2,200
$$	R1,000–R1,700
$	under R1,000

*All prices are per person sharing a double room, including all meals, bush walks, and game drives.

Mpumalanga is the heart of South Africa's big-game country, where you'll find the country's most famous private lodges and some of the best wildlife viewing in the world. All lodges reviewed below lie in game reserves adjoining the immense Kruger National Park (☞ *above*). In the last couple of years, most of the veterinary fences separating Kruger from these reserves have been dismantled, allowing game to roam freely back and forth.

The most famous and exclusive of these parks is the **Sabi Sand Game Reserve.** Collectively owned and managed, the 153,000-acre reserve is home to dozens of private lodges, including Mala Mala and Londolozi. The Sabi Sand fully deserves its exalted reputation, boasting perhaps the highest game density of any private reserve in southern Africa. North of the Sabi Sand lies the 59,000-acre **Manyeleti Game Reserve.** During the apartheid era, this park was reserved for blacks, who were not allowed into the country's major national reserves. It remains a public park today, although a couple of lodges have won private concessions. The **Timbavati Game Reserve,** also collectively owned and managed, lies north of the Manyeleti. The 185,000-acre Timbavati is renowned for its rare white lions, the product of a recessive gene that surfaces occasionally. Generally speaking, the Timbavati has plenty of lions and more elephant breeding herds than Sabi Sand, but it lacks a large rhino population—rumor has it that the rhinos keep crossing back into the Kruger National Park.

All lodges will arrange pickups from the airports at Skukuza, Nelspruit, Phalaborwa, or Hoedspruit. Some have their own private airstrips and can arrange for you to fly in by light aircraft. For information about arriving in Mpumalanga, *see* Mpumalanga A to Z, *above*.

Lodges covered below are marked on the Kruger National Park map.

Sabi Sand Game Reserve

Although not all lodges own vast tracts of land, most have traversing rights over anything from about 15,000 acres to around 45,000 acres of Sabi Sand land. With an average of 14–20 vehicles out looking for game and communicating via radio to ensure that guests see all the animals they want, the chances are very good that you will see the Big Five in an average two- to three-day stay in the region. Expect to see large herds of elephants, particularly in the fall, when they migrate from Kruger in search of water and better grazing. The Sabi Sand is also the best area for leopard sightings: game rangers have written books about these beautiful, elusive felines after a spell in the Sabi Sand. There are several lion prides, and, occasionally, the increasingly rare wild dogs will migrate from Kruger to den in the Sabi Sand. Privileged indeed is the lodge that is graced by a visit from these nomadic animals. White rhino may also be seen, along with giraffe, most antelope species, wildebeest, and zebra. It's also an excellent area for bird-watchers, and most game rangers will oblige you in your search for lilac-breasted rollers, francolins, guinea fowl, robins, or whatever else you fancy. (Try to go in a group or link up with other bird-watchers if you can—this seems to best way to spot the most birds.)

The program at almost every lodge rarely deviates from an accepted pattern: an early morning game drive, during which refreshments may be served, usually followed by a full English breakfast. After that, there's an optional bush walk with a ranger, where you can see the small creatures of the bush, although you could also happen upon giraffe, antelope, or even one of the Big Five. The rest of the day is spent at leisure, so don't forget to pack a good book or two. If it's hot, most establishments have at least a splash pool. One thing you won't do at these lodges is go hungry—some give you a full luncheon, while others serve a substantial tea before taking off for an afternoon game drive. Cocktails are then served, either as the sun goes down or at dusk (or later, if you're tracking down something interesting in the African bushveld). Then, it's time to see nocturnal animals: trackers and rangers use hand-held spotlights for the purpose. On a good night, you may see creatures such as leopards, lions (which hunt at night), hyenas, jackals, porcupines, pangolins, and serval or genet cats. On your return to the lodge, it's time for predinner drinks, followed by a three- or five-course dinner. These are usually served in a boma, around a crackling log fire.

Mala Mala is the only lodge in the Sabi Sand that appears to deviate from the theme. In winter, it's possible to go out looking for game for most of the day, pausing only briefly for lunch and a siesta.

The following two lodges are situated in the northern reaches of the Sabi Sand Reserve and are not accessed via the paved road in the south. Access is via a torturous dirt road, signposted from the town of Acorn-hoek on the R40, north of Hazyview. There are 64 km (25 mi) of potholes, corrugations, and washaways. The road is seldom graded and deteriorates quickly during the rainy season. Follow the signs carefully and don't go off onto side roads, which are worse. Check with the lodge about access if you're driving and be prepared to fly in if necessary.

Chitwa Chitwa

Chitwa Chitwa is a small camp in the isolated northern reaches of Sabi Sand Game Reserve. Run by a married couple, Charl and Maria Brink, this camp has a youthful spirit and places much emphasis on style. In fact, Chitwa Chitwa's whole operation resembles a beer commercial filled with beautiful people.

$$–$$$ **Chitwa Chitwa Game Lodge.** This is the main camp for Chitwa Chitwa and is situated on one of the largest lakes in the Sabi Sand. The spacious bar and lounge area has a high thatched roof and affords fabulous views across the lake, through picture windows. The swimming pool creates an interesting focal point. There's lots of wood, and the neutral color schemes are relaxed and informal. Accommodation is in stylish, individually decorated chalets, each of which has uninterrupted views of the surrounding bushveld. Minimalistic decor combines contemporary and African elements. All units have air-conditioning. Delicious cuisine is served in a traditional boma or at the indoor restaurant. ⊠ *Reservations: Box 781854, Sandton 2146,* ☎ *013/735–5357 (lodge), 011/883–1354, or 011/784–8131;* FAX *011/783–1858. 6 chalets, 3 suites (18 guests). Bar, pool, private airstrip. AE, DC, MC, V.*

$$–$$$ **Chitwa Chitwa Safari Lodge.** More relaxed and comfortable than main camp, this lodge is also slightly smaller, accommodating a maximum of 10 guests. Situated in a forest of knobthorn trees beside the enormous lake, Safari Lodge also boasts fantastic waterside views. The thatched roof of the lounge-bar area is supported on old tree trunks; a wood deck overlooks the dam and is often where meals are served. Spacious chalets are decorated in colonial style, with creamy colors, lots of wood, and billowing mosquito nets. All units have air-conditioning. As at the Game Lodge, the cuisine is superb. ⊠ *Reservations: Box 781854, Sandton 2146,* ☎ *013/735–5357 (lodge), 011/883–1354 or 011/784–8131 (reservations);* FAX *011/783–1858. 5 chalets (10 guests). Bar, pool, private airstrip. AE, DC, MC, V.*

Djuma

$$ Djuma abuts Chitwa Chitwa in the northeast corner of the Sabi Sand Game Reserve and uses the same entrance gate as its neighbor. The hosts are a husband-and-wife team, Jurie and Pippa Moolman, who are young, interesting, and passionate about their work (Jurie has a B.S. in ecology). Although there's a very good chance of seeing the Big Five during the bush walk after breakfast and two game drives per day, Djuma also caters to those with special bushveld interests, such as bird-watching or tree identification. Djuma's rangers and trackers are also adept at finding seldom-seen animals such as Cape wild dogs, spotted hyenas, and genet cats. You'll find none of the formality that prevails at larger lodges, and the staff eat all their meals with you and join you around the fire. The camp is unfenced, and it's quite usual to see kudu nibbling the lawns and flower beds or giraffes towering above the rooftops. Accommodations are in comfortable, thatched chalets that are beautifully decorated. However, fluorescent lights cast an ugly glow, and the wall between the bathroom and the bedroom doesn't go all the way to the ceiling. There are overhead fans and air-conditioning. ⊠ *Reservations: Box 338, Hluvukani 1363,* ☎ *013/735–5118,* FAX *013/735–5070. 7 chalets (14 guests). Bar, pool, private airstrip. AE, DC, MC, V.*
The following lodges are situated in the southern sector of the Sabi Sands and are accessed from the Kruger Gate road, via Hazyview.

Idube

$$ Tucked away in the Sabi Sand Game Reserve, this small lodge sits in a grassy clearing overlooking a dam. Idube prides itself on its personal attention and relaxed atmosphere, and it gets a lot of repeat business as a result. Guests eat together at long tables, on a wooden deck or round the fire in the boma, and the informal atmosphere generated by the staff makes this potentially awkward experience easy and fun.

Dinners in the bush are also arranged on occasion. The public rooms make effective use of thatch, wood, and African art to create a bush ambience. The guest rooms, however, are a disappointment, built of institutional brick with tile roofs and floors. They're very large, though, and huge sliding doors give guests a good view of the surrounding bush. ⊠ *Box 2617, Northcliff 2115,* ☎ *011/888–3713,* ℻ *011/888–2181. 9 rooms (18 guests). Bar, pool, private airstrip. AE, DC, MC, V.*

Inyati

$$ Set on a hillside in Sabi Sand, this lovely lodge presides over a broad sweep of lawns running down to the Sand River and a hippo pool. Life here unfolds on the thatched veranda, where guests use binoculars to scan the bush-covered hills for lion and other game. A wooden viewing deck, set under large trees by the river, offers an even better vantage point from which to see animals coming to drink. A special option for a unique wildlife experience is a trip on the Sand River on a large floating pontoon powered by a silent bass motor. Inyati delivers the animals and much, much more. The service is among the best of all the lodges, a welcome mix of professionalism and friendliness. A glass of champagne might materialize after a game drive, or a bottle of sherry may accompany sautéed mushrooms at lunch. The food at Inyati is excellent, head and shoulders above that at comparably priced lodges. Surprisingly, the guest rooms are nothing fancy: simple thatched cottages with rustic log furniture and African-inspired materials and curios; all have air-conditioning. ⊠ *Box 38838, Booysens 2016,* ☎ *011/880–5950,* ℻ *011/788–2406. 10 rooms (20 guests). Bar, pool, health club, private airstrip. AE, DC, MC, V.*

Leopard Hills

$$
★ Set on the edge of a rocky outcrop, this lodge commands an impressive view of the surrounding bushveld (although not to quite the same, extraordinary extent as Ulusaba; ☞ *below*). Leopard Hills' colonial-style decor is among the most impressive of all the lodges in the region: public areas are furnished in dark woods, and rich, deep colors predominate. The rooms themselves have lots of crisp, white linen and billowing mosquito nets, while bathrooms have the ultimate luxury of his-and-hers showers. The attention to detail is amazing, from the leopard tracks pressed into the steps as you enter the lodge to the ceramic chameleon running around the dressing table. Motifs on the floor even match the monograms on the bath towels. All rooms have air-conditioning, minibars, room safes, and telephones (connected on request). The lodge is designed to take full advantage of the bushveld panorama, whether you're relaxing in the public rooms, lazing by the pool, or enjoying a meal on the small deck. If you tire of the bush and would like to view some of the region's local culture, tours to a genuine Shangaan village can be arranged on request (R335 per person). ⊠ *Box 3619, White River 1240,* ☎ *013/751–2205,* ℻ *013/751–2204. 10 rooms (20 guests). Bar, pool, private airstrip. AE, DC, V.*

Londolozi

Londolozi is the youngest of the leading lodges in the Sabi Sand, having only started its operations in 1974 when the Varty family, the owners of the property, were obliged to pay death duties when the family patriarch passed away. They decided their best option was to start a lodge on the property—and so Londolozi was born. The lodge concept proved extremely successful, and Londolozi gradually evolved into the popular upscale place you see today. Its popularity has been greatly assisted by the massive publicity campaign by John Varty, who has filmed a series of popular wildlife videos here featuring stories of the animals in the Sabi Sand, Londolozi, and his family.

In the heart of Sabi Sand Game Reserve, Londolozi offers outstanding service and superior accommodations and food. Londolozi is part of CC Africa, previously the Conservation Corporation, one of the most highly regarded wildlife companies on the continent. All waste is recycled or composted, none of the rooms use air-conditioning, and rangers show enormous respect for the land. Acting as a focal point from all Londolozi's camps and adding to the game-viewing experience are the 19 km (12 mi) of Sand River that meander through the property. Londolozi comprises three camps, all within a few hundred yards of each other on a bank of the Sand River. Regular bush dinners and breakfasts make an interesting change from dining out on the wooden deck or in the boma. In keeping with its conservation-for-the-people approach, Londolozi has developed a craft village where items are produced by members of the local Shangaan community that borders the Sabie Sand Game Reserve, and proceeds go toward providing services and building roads, schools, and hospitals.

At press time, Londolozi was undergoing extensive redecoration at all its camps. The result, while purporting to be very African, is somewhat disappointing. ⊠ *Private Bag X27, Benmore 2010,* ☎ *011/735–5653,* ℻ *011/735–5100. AE, DC, MC, V.*

$$$$ **Bush Camp.** A step down from Tree Camp (☞ *below*), this lodge employs many of the same decorative devices as its upscale neighbor. The stone-and-thatch structure lies in a forest of ebony and boerbean and commands impressive views of the river. Dark beams, comfortable sofas, and African art set the tone for the main lounge, which opens onto a broad wooden deck supported on stilts above the riverbank. Rooms, in stone cottages hidden in the forest, differ little from those at Tree Camp. Each room has its own plunge pool. *8 rooms (16 guests). Bar, pool, private airstrip.*

$$$$ **Tree Camp.** Shaded by thick riverine forest, this magnificent lodge is
★   Londolozi's top-of-the-line camp. The lodge is built into the riverbank and makes clever use of the natural rock and indigenous forest. The main living area consists of a huge, thatched A-frame with a wooden deck on stilts jutting out over the river. Guest rooms, in thatched chalets, are an exquisite blend of modern luxury and *Out of Africa* chic: track lighting captures the glow of burnished Rhodesian teak; mosquito nets drape languidly over snow-white beds; and old railway sleepers, skillfully crafted into furniture and window frames, add to the rich textures of the room. All rooms also have their own plunge pools, and if you simply can't tear yourself away, private dinners may be arranged on request. From the central wraparound deck, you look out onto a world of cool green forest. *6 rooms (12 guests). Bar, pool, private airstrip. Strict no children policy.*

$$$ **Main Camp.** The largest of the three camps, Main Camp accommodates guests in chalets. The lodge is an enormous, thatched A-frame that extends out onto a broad wood deck above the riverbank. Fireplaces, comfy armchairs, and bookcases filled with wildlife literature give a warm, lived-in feel. Rising from below the deck are an enormous jackalberry tree provides cooling shade. Behind the deck are a group of thatched rondawels that were the original hunting camp owned by the Varty family. They now do duty as a reading room, a wine cellar, and an interpretive center where history talks, carving demonstrations, and other events are held. Chalet rooms are smaller than in the satellite camps but all have air-conditioning, minibars, and safes. Room decor is rather dull and uninspiring, featuring lots of black, beige, and brown. On the plus side, there are beautiful views from every room, and bathrooms have both indoor and outdoor showers. Two suites boast private swimming pools. Private dinners may be arranged on request. *10 chalets (20 guests). Bar, pool, private airstrip.*

Mala Mala

Mala Mala started the whole frenzy about the Big Five, and it still places a huge emphasis on delivering the big five—buffalo, leopards, lions, elephants, and rhinos. It has been operating for 30 years as a photo safari lodge, and much of the game is now completely habituated to the presence of the lodge's Land Rovers, allowing them to come extremely close. The biggest advantage Mala Mala has over its competition, however, is its size: 54,300 acres, a full third of the Sabi Sand Game Reserve, including a 32-km (20-mi) boundary with the Kruger National Park (☞ *above*). Another major bonus is the lodge's 53 km (33 mi) of river frontage, which attracts animals to the sweet grasses that grow on the banks. The dense riverine forest is an ideal habitat for leopards and birds.

Mala Mala enjoys a reputation as the best safari lodge in Africa. Its name carries a real cachet in jet-set circles, and international celebrities, politicians, and industry tycoons flock here. It's also one of the most expensive lodges in the country and intends to stay that way, catering to a clientele that equates stratospheric prices with quality. Without question, Mala Mala does offer a superb experience, but after many years the competition has caught up. Today, Mala Mala's guest rooms can't hold a candle to the glorious mix of bush and luxury offered by Londolozi's Tree Camp or Singita, and its food is no better than that of a half-dozen other lodges in Mpumalanga. Mala Mala's rangers are more than your guides to the game—they are your hosts and valets, hovering by your elbow to fetch you drinks and pool towels. They may eat meals with you, and it almost comes as a surprise when they don't follow you into the bedroom at the end of the day. Some visitors may find the constant attention irritating. Mala Mala operates three camps, ranging from the ultraexpensive Main Camp to the budget Harry's Camp, which was being rebuilt at press time. ✉ *Box 2575, Randburg 2125,* ☎ *011/789–2677,* 🅵🅰🆇 *011/886–4382. AE, DC, MC, V.*

$$$$　**Main Camp.** For first-time visitors to Africa, this large camp overlooking the Sand River offers a very gentle introduction to the bush. However, it won't give you much of true safari lodge feel: the hotel could conceivably be transported to a Johannesburg suburb without feeling out of place. The magnificently appointed guest rooms, in a mix of rondawels and larger suites, could be in any luxury hotel in the world. Each room has two bathrooms to make it easier for couples to prepare for early morning game drives, and such amenities as hair dryers, air-conditioning, and telephones. Beige wall-to-wall carpet adds to its generic hotel feel. Fortunately, the main public area is steeped in African lore. Drawing on the camp's history as a hunting lodge, the lounge displays a host of animal skins and heads, old hunting spears, and antique rifles. Massive elephant tusks frame a huge fireplace, and African sculptures and reference books dot the tables. *25 rooms (50 guests). Bar, pool, private airstrip.*

$$　**Harry's Camp.** This is Mala Mala's budget lodge, competitively priced with most of the other lodges in Sabi Sand. The huge advantage of staying here is that you get the Mala Mala game experience at a fraction of the cost of Main Camp, which explains why it's almost always full. At press time, the entire camp was being rebuilt: however, it is anticipated that it will be a small, intimate slice of Africa—probably along the lines of Sabi Sabi. *Bar, pool, private airstrip.*

$$　**Kirkman's Kamp.** This lodge is an absolute delight, with far more
★　　charm—at a much lower price—than Main Camp. The atmosphere is

also far more relaxed and friendly. At its core stands a 1920s farm-stead, a relic of the days when this area was a cattle ranch. With its corrugated-iron roof and deep verandas, it has a strong colonial feel that will appeal to Britons and those who've watched *Out of Africa* more than twice. The theme of the camp is Harry Kirkman, the man-ager of the cattle farm and one of the first game rangers at Kruger Na-tional Park. The main room, with high wood ceilings and creaking overhead fans, is lined with trophy heads, old maps of the Transvaal, sepia photos of Kirkman's hunting experiences, and antique rifles. It all spirits you back to another age, and the atmosphere is magical. The farmstead and guest rooms overlook a broad sweep of lawn leading down to the Sand River. The rooms, constructed in recent years, con-tinue the colonial theme, with claw-foot tubs in the bathrooms, white wood-slat ceilings, old photos, and French doors opening onto small verandas. *10 rooms (20 guests). Bar, pool, private airstrip.*

Notten's Bush Camp

Unlike many other lodges, Notten's has only one Land Rover, so the chances of finding the Big Five are slim. However, rangers impart a wealth of information about everything from trees to insects and birds.

$ You probably won't see the Big Five at this delightful little camp, but you may have the bush experience of your life. This means it's not ideal for a first trip to Africa unless you're combining it with other camps that can deliver game sightings. Sandwiched between Mala Mala, Lon-dolozi, and Sabi Sabi, Notten's family-run operation is the antithesis of the animal treasure hunts conducted by its more famous neighbors. Owners Gilly and Bambi Notten personally tend to their guests, and a stay at their camp is like a visit with good friends who happen to live in the bush. It's a measure of the Nottens' success that 70% of their guests are return visitors. The lodge sleeps 10 people in simple cottages lit only by paraffin lamps and candles. At night, flickering torches line the walkways and a hurricane lantern on your veranda guides you back to your room. The camp is rustic with no electricity and exteriors are a little old, but appearances can be deceptive and the inside of the cot-tages are comfortable and welcoming. After the evening game drive, guests meet for drinks in the boma and then dine together under the stars. Breakfast and tea are served in an open-sided shelter overlook-ing a grassy plain and a pan where animals come to drink. A lounge area is furnished with comfy chairs, bookshelves filled with wildlife literature, and a refrigerator where guests help themselves to drinks. For weekends and major holidays, you need to make reservations about six months in advance; at other times, two months is usually sufficient. ✉ *Box 622, Hazyview 1242,* ☎ *013/735–5105,* 𝔽𝔸𝕏 *013/735–5970. 5 rooms (10 guests). Bar, pool. No credit cards.*

Sabi Sabi

At the southern end of Sabi Sand Game Reserve, Sabi Sabi is the largest private safari operation in Mpumalanga and is among the most expensive. It was also one of the first lodges to offer photo safaris, along with Mala Mala. Bush and River lodges, the more capacious of its three camps, have large public spaces that make them more like hotels than any other in the Mpumalanga private reserves. On the other hand, the exclusive Selati Lodge, which takes only 16 people, has an intimate, "old-Africa" atmosphere. What draws guests to Sabi Sabi in such large numbers are its setting along the Sabie River—the only perennial water source in Sabi Sand—and the sheer density of game supported by its highly varied habi-tats. That's not to say Sabi Sabi is simply about bagging the Big Five. Although you do stand an excellent chance of seeing them, there's a strong emphasis here on ecology; guests are encouraged to broaden their experience to become aware of the birds, smaller animals, and myriad sounds and smells of the bush. ✉ *Box 52665, Saxonwold 2132,* ☎ *011/483–3939,* FAX *011/483–3799. AE, DC, MC, V.*

$$$$ **Selati Lodge.** Formerly a private hunting lodge, Selati is the most intimate and stylish of the Sabi Sabi accommodations, limited to just eight chalets. A turn-of-the-century atmosphere is created by the use of train memorabilia that recalls the now-defunct Selati railroad that once passed this way. There's no electricity, and the lodge flickers at night under the light of the original shunters' oil lamps; in one thatched chalet old leather suitcases serve as a table, while in another an antique sewing machine has a new lease on life as a vanity table. Deep-colored wood, cream fabrics, and mosquito nets draped over large double beds hark back to the traditional East African safari. As you'd expect with this level of luxury, each cottage is en suite but also has the added bonus of its own outdoor shower. *8 chalets (16 guests). Bar, pool.*

$$$ **Bush Lodge.** This large lodge overlooks a water hole and the dry course of the Msuthlu River. The reception area leads back through attractive open courtyards to a thatched and open-sided dining area, an airy bar, and a lounge where residents can watch nature videos. Public rooms are tastefully decorated with African art and artifacts, animal skulls, and African prints. An observation deck has magnificent views of game at the water hole, as does the pool. Chalets, all thatched, are connected by walkways that wend through manicured lawns and beneath enormous shade trees. The five thatched suites are lovely, decorated with wicker and pretty African-print bedspreads and upholstery. Each suite has a deck overlooking the dry river course, as well as air-conditioning. *21 chalets, 5 suites (54 guests). Bar, pool.*

$$$ ⌂ **River Lodge.** Shaded by giant jackalberry trees, this attractive lodge is smaller and more relaxed than Bush Lodge. It's popular among birders, who spend hours peering into the thick riverine forest that surrounds the camp. The lodge looks onto a dry riverbed, beyond which lies the perennial Sabie River. Guest rooms are spread out along the river. Otherwise, amenities are very similar to those at Bush Lodge. *24 rooms (48 guests). Bar, pool.*

Singita

★ This is undoubtedly the most luxurious lodge in Sabi Sand Game Reserve. For unfettered extravagance, Singita leaves lodges like Londolozi and Sabi Sabi far behind. Having been taken over from Conservation Corporation (CC Africa) some time ago, Singita now has two camps, both overlooking the Sand River. And while Singita offers much the same bush experience as the other lodges, its public areas and dining options help set it apart. Riverside breakfasts, picnic lunches, and starlit suppers in the bush are all popular and unique options. There are also reading rooms, wine cellars, and beautiful views over the bushveld.

$$$$ **Boulders Lodge.** If you've been to Great Zimbabwe (☞ Chapter 10), you'll immediately recognize Boulders as an exact replica of the exterior of the monument. Large ponds guard the entrance to the public areas, where decor combines the modern with the bushveld, although coffee tables mounted on imitation gemsbok horns can be a little kitschy. In the dining room the impossibly high walls and minimum of windows make the place dark during the day. Visit the incredible wine cellar—which stocks vintages you probably won't find anywhere else in the country—both to choose your wine for dinner and to do some wine tasting. Suites here are elegant and sumptuous without being over the top: four-poster beds festooned in yards of white mosquito netting and bathrooms with claw-foot baths and indoor and outdoor showers are just a few of the details. As at Ebony (☞ *below*), all units have private swimming pools. Picture windows in all units look out over the Sand River and the African bush, as does the enormous wooden deck beneath the trees where meals are served. ⊠ *Box 650881, Benmore 2010,* ☎ *011/234–0990,* ℻ *011/234–0535. 9 rooms (18 guests). Bar, pool, private airstrip. AE, DC, MC, V.*

$$$$ 🏨 **Ebony Lodge.** Each cottage or suite here has a double-sided fireplace, separate living room, enormous veranda—even an outside shower in case your inner Tarzan feels confined in the cavernous one in the bathroom. Furnishings are reminiscent of a country house, although a quick glance through enormous picture windows will remind you that you are, in fact, in the African bush. Mosquito nets, railway-sleeper furniture, masks, beads, and animal skulls round out the African decor. Luxury suites are fronted by walls of glass opening onto an expansive teak deck with a private pool that affords magnificent views of the Sand River. Rooms are lavishly furnished with a combination of antique and contemporary African pieces. In keeping with the uncompromising luxury, all accommodations have air-conditioning and private plunge pools. The main lodge consists of a giant, thatched A-frame and a large deck raised on stilts overlooking the river. An enormous fireplace, topped by a stuffed buffalo head, dominates the room, and zebra skins, skulls, and trophy horns complete the safari theme. At dinner, fine glass and china foster a colonial formality that works surprisingly well. More recently, an indoor dining facility has been added (mainly used when it's raining) with wooden tables, billowing curtains, hunting prints, and wall murals depicting the bush. ⊠ *Box 650881, Benmore 2010,* ☎ *011/234–0990,* ℻ *011/234–0535. 9 cottages, 6 suites (18 guests). Bar, pool, private airstrip. AE, DC, MC, V.*

Ulusaba Rocklodge

$$$ Perched atop a rocky hill in Sabi Sand Game Reserve, this magnificent aerie has all the makings of the finest private game reserves on the continent. Rocklodge is built into the side of a cliff, 850 ft above a water hole and the bushveld plains. The road leading up to the lodge is so steep that guests must be driven up in four-wheel-drive vehicles. A maze of stone walkways and steps gives the lodge a fortresslike feel. The view from the enormous wooden deck off the lounge is incredible: you'll feel like the king of the world, lord of all you survey. The rooms provide some of the finest accommodation you will find in a game lodge. Huge windows have panoramic views of the bush, and high thatched ceilings and white stucco walls create a light, airy effect. All rooms are air-conditioned. The three public areas—the pool deck, restaurant, and bar—are ingeniously built into a cliff face, and buffet meals are eaten at long tables. The atmosphere is congenial and informal. At the time of writing, Ulusaba had just been bought by Virgin Hotels, which aims to make it one of the most luxurious establishments in the Sabi Sand. The Virgin Hotels group recently renovated Safari Lodge—11 romantic, tree-house–style chalets under a canopy of trees, each with a private entrance and viewing deck—which is now part of the Ulusaba Private Game Reserve. Safari Lodge borders the Mabrak River and stands close to a busy watering hole. ⊠ *Box 239, Lonehill 2062,* ☎ *011/465–6646,* ℻ *011/465–6649. 11 rooms (22 guests). Bar, pool, private airstrip. AE, DC, MC, V.*

Manyeleti Game Reserve

The Manyeleti Game Reserve is a public park covering 59,280 acres and adjoining Kruger National Park, but it's amazingly underused, and you will see very few other vehicles while you're here. The park's grassy plains and mixed woodland attract good-size herds of general game and their attendant predators. You have a strong chance of seeing the Big Five here, but Manyeleti lodges tend to focus more on providing an overall bush experience than simply rushing after big game for the sake of it. You'll learn about trees, birds, and the bushveld ecosystems and will very often get the chance to walk in the bush. In fact, it's not unusual to be following a rhino on a game drive when your ranger stops and suggests that you follow it on foot as far as you can. Let your ranger know if there's any animal you *really* want to see and he'll endeavour to find it for you. Most rangers and lodges work together and are in contact with one another via radio, so if one vehicle sees something special, there's a good chance that you will too. It's common policy to have no more than three or four vehicles on a sighting at any one time, so you may have to wait your turn—but it's generally worth it.

Honeyguide Tented Safari Camp

This tented camp offers the best value of all the Mpumalanga lodges, especially if you stay at its budget Outpost Camp, which specializes in highly regarded foot safaris. The camp brilliantly achieves the delicate balance of combining professional service with a casual atmosphere— a welcome relief if the stuffy over-attentiveness of some of the more upscale lodges isn't to your taste. ⊠ *Box 781959, Sandton 2146,* ☎ *011/880–3912,* ꜰꜲꭓ *011/447–4326. AE, DC, MC, V.*

$ **Main Camp.** Honeyguide was one of the first lodges to use the luxury ★ East African–style safari tents that have since become so popular. But to call these comfortable canvas homes "tents" is really an insult, because they have everything a more conventional room does while giving guests the true feel of camping in the wild. Each one is large enough to accommodate two beds, a cupboard, clothing shelves, and battery-operated lights. A bathroom en suite, accessed through the back zip of the tent, provides complete privacy, as well as hot showers. Four of the 12 tents are larger and a little more expensive than the others and have baths as well. A shaded wood deck extends from the front of the tent and overlooks a dry riverbed and thick riverine forest. Despite its economy price tag, the camp has some true luxury touches: tea or coffee served in your tent at dawn, and a fully stocked bar on each vehicle for sundowner cocktails. *12 tents (24 guests). Bar, pool, private airstrip.*

$ **Outpost Camp.** Representing a growing trend among the Mpumalanga private game reserves, this intimate and thoroughly rustic camp is light-years away from the large, formal lodges of Sabi Sand. Don't expect smartly decked-out waiters, ethnic-chic decor, or pampering. But for a raw experience of the bush, you'll find this camp and its rock-bottom price tag hard to beat. Four two-bed tents have showers and toilets en suite that are open to the African sky, and meals are cooked by a chef over an open fire. If you've switched off your cell phone and want to leave civilization behind, the real joy here is that there are no vehicles. All your game outings are done on foot, and you can experience the thrill of sneaking around rhinos or lions, being charged by buffalo, or holding dung beetles in your hand. Rangers also teach guests about other, smaller aspects of the bushveld, including the habits and behavior of various animals, the medicinal (and other) uses of plants and trees, and some tips about animal tracking. *4 tents (8 guests). Bar, private airstrip.*

Timbavati Game Reserve

The Timbavati is the northernmost of the private reserves that are open to tourists. If you desperately want to see rhino, there's a good chance that you might miss them, as they are scarce in this region. However, the Timbavati has a relatively large lion population, and it's likely that you will also see leopard, buffalo, and spotted hyenas. Lodges here tend to have fewer vehicles in the field on average than in the Sabi Sand, although rangers work together to ensure that clients see all they want. The animals are relaxed in the presence of vehicles, and you may be able to follow a particular lion pride or leopard with cubs for a day or two. If you're lucky, you might see wild dogs, as these migrate irregularly to this region from Kruger. Rangers and staff are wildlife enthusiasts and several will regale you with tales of the bush.

M'Bali

M'Bali places a stronger emphasis on walking and enjoying the bush experience than do most lodges, and it encourages guests to do a long walk instead of a game drive at least once during their stay. In winter, guests encounter elephant almost every day on these walks. The rangers are all highly qualified and knowledgeable about the animals and the area's ecosystem.

$$ This beautiful tented camp lies at the northern tip of the Timbavati Game Reserve. Built on a hillside overlooking a dam, it enjoys the best view of any tented camp—elephants come to bathe below the lodge daily in winter, and on a clear day you can see all the way to the Mpumalanga Escarpment. Sand pathways run down the hillside to the guest tents, on raised wood platforms supported by stilts. Dismiss the image of some poky little tent in a campsite. These are huge, intended to re-create the spirit of the old East African hunting safaris. Mosquito nets shroud the beds, and each tent is equipped with bedside tables, a closet, and electric lights. An A-frame thatched shelter shields the tent from the sun and rain. The bathroom is located underneath the wood deck and reached by way of very steep stairs. The lodge now has electricity, so this shouldn't present a problem. ✉ *Box 67865, Bryanston 2021*, ☎ *011/463–1990*, 🖷 *011/463–1992. 9 tents (18 guests). Bar, pool, private airstrip. AE, DC, MC, V.*

Ngala

Ngala's main advantage over Sabi Sand is its proximity to four major ecozones—mopane shrubveld, marula combretum, acacia scrub, and riverine forest—which provide habitats for a wide range of animals.

$$$ This exclusive lodge lies in mopane shrubveld in the Timbavati Game Reserve. Part of CC Africa, previously the Conservation Corporation, Ngala offers the same level of professionalism and service as Londolozi (☞ *above*). The main lodge has a Mediterranean style and sophistication that are refreshing after the hunting-lodge decor espoused by so many lodges. Track lighting and dark-slate flooring and tables provide an elegant counterpoint to high thatched ceilings and African art. A massive, double-sided fireplace dominates the lodge, opening on one side onto a lounge filled with comfy sofas and chairs and on the other a dining room. Dinner at Ngala is more formal than at most lodges, served in a reed-enclosed boma or in a tree-filled courtyard lit by lanterns; crystal glasses and silver place settings enhance the sophisticated atmosphere. Guest cottages, set in mopane shrubveld with no views, contain two rooms, each with its own thatched veranda. Rooms make extensive use of hemp carpeting, thatch, and dark beams to create an appealing warmth. ✉ *Private Bag X27, Benmore 2010*, ☎ *011/*

775–0000, FAX *011/784–7667. 20 rooms, 1 suite (22 guests). Pool, meeting rooms. AE, DC, MC, V.*

Tanda Tula Bush Camp

$$
★
At this luxury tented camp in the Timbavati you'll be closer to the bush than at almost any other lodge. When lions roar nearby, the noise sounds like it's coming from under the bed. The reason is simple: guests sleep in East African safari-style tents with huge window flaps that roll up, leaving you staring at the bush largely through mosquito netting. The effect is magical and much more rewarding than sleeping in a conventional room. Of the tented camps in Mpumalanga, Tanda Tula is by far the most luxurious. Its 12 tents, all with bathrooms en suite and their own wood decks, overlook the dry bed of the Nhlaralumi River. Each tent is beautifully decorated with wicker chairs, bedspreads made from colorful African materials, and elegant side tables, a cupboard, and dresser. An oscillating fan and electric lights add a convenient modern touch. A large, open-sided thatched shelter serves as the main lounge, where breakfast and lunch are served. Of particular note are Tanda Tula's bush braais, held in the dry bed of the Nhlaralumi River with the moon reflecting off the bright sand. It's worth noting that, although the lodge can accommodate a maximum of 24 guests, it usually keeps numbers down to 16, a device that makes it easy to mix with people. For groups, however, the camp will open all 12 tents and cater for 24 people. ⊠ *Box 151, Hoedspruit 1380,* ☎ FAX *01528/3–2435. Reservations:* ⊠ *Constantia Uitsig, Box 32, Constantia 7848, Western Cape,* ☎ *021/794–6500,* FAX *021/794–7605. 12 tents (24 guests). Bar, pool, private airstrip. AE, DC, MC, V.*

Umlani Bushcamp

Umlani places a stronger emphasis on bush walks than other lodges, and an armed ranger usually hops off the vehicle and leads you in search of rhino or other game as often as he can during the morning game drive. Animals run from humans who are on foot, so don't expect to get up close and personal with an elephant. However, the visceral thrill of seeing big game while on foot, even from 150 ft away, more than compensates—plus you learn a tremendous amount about bushveld ecology. In the evening, a ranger takes guests on a conventional game drive.

$
Snoozing under enormous shade trees in the Timbavati, this superb bush camp offers visitors a very different experience from the other lodges. The focus here is on a bush experience, as opposed to the search for big game, and accommodations are accordingly rustic. Guests sleep in rondawels made from reeds and thatch, and the door is a wooden stable door. The bed—you do get one—is protected by a mosquito net, and each room has its own bathroom and shower en suite, exhilaratingly open to the sky and fenced in with bamboo. Communal facilities include a thatched covered boma facing a dry riverbed and a large boma and reed-walled dining area. There's no electricity here, but the kerosene lanterns and candles add to the bush ambience. Despite this, there are facilities to charge your video-camera battery. It's not everyone's cup of tea, but you really feel like you're out in the African wilds, and the atmosphere is fun and relaxed. ⊠ *Box 26350, Arcadia, Pretoria 0007,* ☎ *012/329–3765,* FAX *012/329–6441. 8 rondawels (16 guests). Bar, pool. AE, DC, MC, V.*

$$ **King's Camp.** One of the most comfortable and popular lodges in the area. The camp itself is unfenced, and it's quite usual to have warthogs and antelope grazing on the lawn; there's also a water hole close enough that you can view elephants coming to drink while you laze by the pool. A spotlight on the water after dark means that you can enjoy nocturnal sightings, too. Although luxurious, the lodge maintains a relaxed, informal air that soon has strangers chatting away like long-lost friends. Guests stay in thatched rondawels decorated with white linen, billowing mosquito nets, wood furniture, and sepia photographs. The bathrooms are enormous and contain both bath and shower. There's a glass-enclosed lounge and bar where you can relax on huge sofas and a dining area that extends outside onto a raised platform to allow for alfresco lunch and dinner. ⊠ *Box 427, Nelspruit 1200,* ☎ *015/793–3633,* ℻ *015/793–3634. 8 rooms, 3 suites (24 guests). Bar, pool. AE, DC, MC, V.*

4 CAPE TOWN AND THE PENINSULA

Backed by the familiar shape of Table Mountain, Cape Town presides over a coastline of unsurpassed beauty: of mountains edging the sea, miles of beaches, and 18th-century wineries napping under giant oaks. Modern South Africa was born here, and the city is filled with reminders of its historic role in overseas trade between Europe and the East. Today Cape Town is home to the country's best museums, restaurants, and hotels.

By Andrew
Barbour

Updated by
Jennifer Stern

I **F YOU VISIT ONLY ONE PLACE** in South Africa, make it Cape Town. Sheltered beneath the familiar shape of Table Mountain, this historic city is instantly recognizable, and few cities in the world possess its beauty and style.

A stroll through the lovely city center reveals Cape Town's three centuries as the sea link between Europe and the East. Elegant Cape Dutch buildings, with their whitewashed gables, abut imposing monuments to Britain's imperial legacy. In the Bo-Kaap neighborhood, the call to prayer echoes from minarets while the sweet tang of Malay curry wafts through the cobbled streets. And everywhere, whether you're eating outdoors at one of the country's best restaurants or sipping wine atop Table Mountain, you sense—correctly—that this is South Africa's most urbane, civilized city.

As impressive as all this is, though, what you will ultimately recall about Cape Town is the sheer grandeur of its setting—Table Mountain rising above the city, the sweep of the bay, and mountains cascading into the sea. You will likely spend more time marveling at the views than anything else.

The city lies at the northern end of the cape peninsula, a 75-km (44-mi) tail of mountains that hangs down from the tip of Africa, ending at the Cape of Good Hope. Drive 15 minutes in any direction and you may lose yourself in a stunning landscape of 18th-century Cape Dutch manors, historic wineries, and white-sand beaches backed by sheer mountains. Francis Drake wasn't exaggerating when he said this was "the fairest Cape we saw in the whole circumference of the earth," and he would have little cause to change his opinion today. You could spend a week exploring just the city and peninsula, and a lifetime discovering the nearby wonders of the Western Cape (☞ Chapter 5), including the Winelands, one of the great highlights of a trip to South Africa.

Capetonians know they have it good and look with condescending sympathy on those with the misfortune of living elsewhere. On weekends they hike, sail, and bike in their African Eden. At night they congregate at the city's fine restaurants, fortified with the Cape wine that plays such an integral role in the city's life. Laid-back Cape Town has none of the frenetic energy of hard-nosed Johannesburg. Maybe that's because Cape Town doesn't need to unearth its treasures—the beauty of the place is right in front of you as soon as you roll out of bed.

In this respect the city is often likened to San Francisco, but Cape Town has what San Francisco can never have—history and the mountain. Table Mountain is key to Cape Town's identity. It dominates the city in a way that's difficult to comprehend until you visit. In the afternoon, when creeping fingers of cloud spill over the mountain and reach toward the city, the whole town seems to shiver and hold its breath. Depending upon which side of the mountain you live on, it even dictates when the sun will rise and set.

Indeed, the city owes its very existence to the mountain. The freshwater streams running off its slopes were what first prompted early explorers to anchor here. In 1652, Jan van Riebeeck and 90 Dutch settlers established a revictualing station for ships of the Dutch East India Company (VOC) on the long voyage east. The settlement represented the first European toehold in South Africa, and Cape Town is still sometimes called the Mother City.

Those first Dutch settlers soon ventured into the interior to establish their own farms, and 140 years later the settlement supported a population of 20,000 whites as well as 25,000 slaves brought from distant lands like Java, Madagascar, and Guinea. Its position on the strategic cusp of Africa, however, meant that the colony never enjoyed any real stability. The British, entangled in a global dogfight with Napoléon, occupied the Cape twice, first in 1795 and then permanently in 1806. With them they brought additional slaves from Ceylon, India, and the Philippines. Destroyed or assimilated in this colonial expansion were the indigenous Khoikhoi (Hottentots), who once herded their cattle here and foraged along the coast.

For visitors used to hearing about South Africa's problems in black and white, Cape Town will come as a surprise—the city is black, white, and colored. Today more than 1 million coloreds—the term used to describe people of mixed race, or of Khoikhoi or slave descent—live in the city and give it a distinct spice.

Perhaps the greatest celebration of this colored culture is the annual Coon Carnival, when thousands of wild celebrants take to the streets in vibrant costumes to sing *moppies* (vaudeville-style songs), accompanied by banjos, drums, and whistles. The carnival is the most visible reminder of a way of life that saw its finest flowering in District Six, a predominantly colored neighborhood on the fringes of the city center whose destruction was a tragic result of apartheid in Cape Town. District Six was a living festival of music and soul, a vibrant community bound by poverty, hope, and sheer joie de vivre. In 1966 the Nationalist government invoked the Group Areas Act, rezoned District Six a whites-only area, and razed it. The scars of that event still run deep. A new museum seeks to recapture the mood of the lost community, and a move is afoot to build low-cost housing in the area, although it has been suggested that it be turned into some kind of living monument, instead.

Other legacies of apartheid fester. Each year for decades, thousands of blacks have streamed to the Cape in search of work, food, and a better life. They end up in the squatter camps of Crossroads and Khayelitsha, names that once flickered across TV screens around the globe. Many visitors never see this side of South Africa, but, as you drive into town along the N2 from the airport, you can't miss the pitiful shacks built on shifting dunes as far as the eye can see—a sobering contrast to the first-world luxury of the city center. A tour of these areas offers a glimpse of the old South Africa—and the enormous challenges facing the new one.

Pleasures and Pastimes

Beaches
The Cape's beaches on both the Atlantic and False Bay sides are truly legendary. They stretch endlessly and you can walk for miles without seeing a fast-food outlet or cool-drink stand. But you will see seagulls, dolphins, penguins, and whales (in season). Forget swimming in the Atlantic—even a dip will freeze your toes. The heat plus the scent of coconut-oiled beauties make for a heady atmosphere. The "in" crowd flocks to Clifton, a must for sunbathers. Although Camps Bay, Llandudno, and Sandy Bay have their attractions, if it's swimming you're into, take yourself to the warmer waters of St. James, Kalk Bay, Fish Hoek, and Simonstown. Windsurfers congregate at Blouberg, where several competitions are held. Don't miss Boulders or Seaforth for snorkeling among great rocks in secluded coves and pools.

History
Wherever you are, there's history in the air. Take a cultural tour of the townships and Bo-Kaap to see communities still struggling to emerge

from the yoke of apartheid. Take a tour of Robben Island, where Nelson Mandela and thousands of other political prisoners were imprisoned for so many long years. Cape Town's small, so walking tours are easy and you can pack in a lot in just a few hours.

Markets

Cape Town has the best markets in the country—informal, creative, artistic, with a good selection of the usual tatty or really splendid African curios. The Waterfont markets are tremendous, and serious goody hunters might strike gold at the Greenpoint open-air market on a Sunday. Greenmarket Square's terrific: Look out for the special rubber-tire sandals. The Rondebosch Park Craft Market on the first Saturday of the month has unusual items, as does the Constantia Market, held on summer weekends. Read the papers for up-to-date listings on these and other ephemeral markets, such as the Observatory Holistic Lifestyle Fair, held on the first Sunday of the month.

Outdoor Activities

Cape Town is an adventure capital with great surfing, wonderful diving, world-class climbing, excellent paragliding and hang gliding, horseback riding along lonely beaches or bright green vineyards, hectic mountain biking along trails, and fun bike riding, sailing, kite flying, and, of course, hiking and walking along the slopes of Table Mountain or the edge of the sea. Or, for something totally different, bungee-jump 300 ft from a cable car, hurtle earthward in a tandem skydive with Table Mountain as a backdrop, or fly upside down in an aerobatic plane. You'll be spoiled by all the choices.

Picnics

Cape Town is the ultimate picnic land. Pack a basket and head off to Rondevlei to bird-watch or to the top of Table Mountain to enjoy gorgeous views. Soon you'll also be able to picnic on Robben Island. Capetonians love evening beach picnics at the end of long summer days. Choose Bakoven, Clifton, or Llandudno and watch the pink sun turn crimson before it slips below the horizon.

EXPLORING CAPE TOWN

Cape Town is surprisingly small. The area between Table Mountain and Table Bay, including the city center and the nearby suburbs, is known as the City Bowl. In the city center, an orderly street grid and the constant view of Table Mountain make it almost impossible to get lost. Major arteries running toward the mountain from the sea are Adderley, Loop, and Long streets; among the major cross streets are Strand, Longmarket, and Wale, which, be warned, is alternately written as Wale St. and Waalst, on signs. The heart of the historic city—where you'll find many of the museums and major buildings—is Government Avenue, a pedestrian mall at the top of Adderley Street. St. George's Mall, another major pedestrian thoroughfare, runs the length of commercial Cape Town.

Cape Town has grown as a city, in a way that few others in the world have. Take a good look at the street names. Strand and Waterkant (meaning "waterside") streets are far from the sea. However, when they were named, they were right on the beach. An enormous program of dumping rubble into the ocean extended the city by a good few square miles. (This can, no doubt, be put down to the Dutch obsession with reclaiming land from the sea.) Almost all the city on the seaward side of Strand and Waterkant is part of the reclaimed area the city known as the Foreshore.

Once you leave the city center, orienting yourself becomes trickier. As you face Table Mountain from the city, the distinctive mountain on your left is Devil's Peak; on the right are Signal Hill and Lion's Head. Signal Hill takes its name from a gun fired there every day at noon. If you look carefully you will see that Signal Hill forms the body of a reclining lion, while the maned Lion's Head looks south past Table Mountain. On the other side of Signal Hill and Lion's Head lie the Atlantic communities of Sea Point, Clifton, and Camps Bay. Heading the other way, around Devil's Peak, you come to Cape Town's exclusive southern suburbs—Rondebosch, Newlands, Claremont, and Constantia. The happening Waterfront lies north of the City Bowl on the other side of the horrendous freeways that separate the docks from downtown.

The Cape Peninsula, much of which is included in the newly proclaimed Cape Peninsula National Park, extends 40 km (25 mi) below the city. The park comprises Table Mountain, most of the high-lying land on the Peninsula Mountain Chain that runs down the center of the peninsula and used to be known as the Cape Point Nature Reserve, and Boulders Beach. The steep mountain slopes leave little room for settlement in the narrow shelf next to the sea. The east side of the peninsula is washed by the waters of False Bay. Here, connected by a coastal road and railway line, lie the suburbs of Muizenberg, St. James, Kalk Bay, and Fish Hoek, as well as the naval base at historic Simonstown. The western shores of the peninsula are wilder and emptier, pounded by huge Atlantic swells. In addition to the tiny hamlets of Scarborough, Kommetjie, Noordhoek, and Llandudno, you'll find the fishing port of Hout Bay and the dizzying heights of Chapman's Peak, one of the most awe-inspiring drives in the world.

Great Itineraries

IF YOU HAVE 2 DAYS

Do an early morning city walk to see the sights or take in a half-day city tour. You will see the **Company's Gardens,** the **Castle of Good Hope, City Hall,** the **Bo-Kaap,** and other historical highlights.

For lunch, go to the **V&A Waterfront** and eat at one of the outside restaurants if the weather's good, inside if it's not. Visit the various waterfront attractions, including the **Aquarium** (a must), and the **SAS Somerset.** Then go to the **IMAX Cinema** to see a show. If you don't dine at the Green Dolphin and listen to terrific jazz, then move away from the waterfront and go uptown.

Perhaps have dinner in one of the city's many excellent restaurants and then go to the theater, ballet, or opera at the **Nico Theatre Centre,** or at the **Baxter Theatre Complex.** For a real taste of contemporary African–New Age Cape Town fusion, go to the Drum Cafe on Glynn Street to watch a performance and maybe join in a drum circle.

The next morning take a **Robben Island** tour, which takes 3½ hours. On your return, go straight to the **Lower Cableway** and ride to the summit of **Table Mountain.** Have lunch in the restaurant and hike one of the trails—walks can last from a few minutes to a few hours.

When you come down from the mountain, drive to **Camps Bay** and dine at a beach-view restaurant. Then kick off your shoes and walk on the beach. To round out the evening you might want to take in a show at the Playhouse Theatre in Camps Bay.

IF YOU HAVE 5 OR MORE DAYS

Spend the first day or two exploring Cape Town. There's a lot to see. Pop into museums and galleries, visit **Bo-Kaap,** and wander around this old Cape Malay area with its cobblestone streets and quaint buildings. On the afternoon of the second day, browse along the waterfront.

On the morning of Day 3, explore **Robben Island** and, on your return, lunch at the waterfront. In the afternoon you might visit the castle or have high tea at the **Mount Nelson hotel.** In the evening, head out to the vibey suburb of Observatory for dinner, and then wander down Lower Main Road, perhaps popping in for a drink or late-night coffee at a café.

On Day 4, drive out to **Constantia** and the **Winelands.** Visit the estates, enjoy the countryside, do a little wine tasting, have lunch, and then in the afternoon drive over Constantia Nek to Hout Bay. Go to the harbor and take an early afternoon cruise to Seal Island. For a more adventurous activity, maybe admire the sunset from the back of a horse on Noordhoek or Hout Bay Beach; or, if there's a moderate southwest wind blowing, why not opt for a paraglider flight off Lion's Head, landing at the popular La Med just in time for cocktails overlooking the beach. Even if you don't paraglide in here, have dinner on this side of the mountain, at Greenpoint, Sea Point, or Camps Bay.

Day 5 is penguin day. You simply have to take the trek—it's a fairly long drive—and wend your way along the False Bay coast to Boulders Beach in the Cape Peninsula National Park, where you'll find the penguins in profusion. This is one of the few sites in the world where these comical little creatures live and breed. Then go on a little farther for a seafood lunch at Millers Point. In the afternoon, grab your map and follow the road to the Cape of Good Hope, part of the national park (there's a separate admission fee) and, of course, Cape Point. You can take the steep walk to the point, or take the funicular. It looks as if this is where the Indian and Atlantic oceans meet—sometimes there is even a line of foam stretching out to sea—but of course it's not. No matter, it's a dramatic spot.

If you still have a few days, drive up the west coast to Langebaan and into the interior to Darling, where Pieter Dirk Uys, South Africa's most beloved and wicked satirical actor, has a theater and restaurant, Evita se Peron, in the converted Darling railway station.

Table Mountain

Along with Victoria Falls (☞ Chapter 10), Table Mountain is one of southern Africa's most beautiful and impressive natural wonders. The views from its summit can reduce you to speechless awe. The mountain rises more than 3,500 ft above the city, its flat top visible to sailors 65 km (40 mi) out to sea. In summer, when the southeaster blows, moist air from False Bay funnels over the mountain, condensing in the colder, higher air to form a tablecloth of cloud. Legend attributes this low-lying cloud to a pipe-smoking contest between the devil and Jan van Hunks, a pirate who settled on Devil's Peak. The devil lost, and the cloud serves to remind him of his defeat.

The first recorded ascent of Table Mountain was made in 1503 by Portuguese admiral Antonio de Saldanha, who wanted to get a better sense of the topography of the Cape Peninsula. He couldn't have asked for a better view. In one direction you look down on today's city, cradled between Lion's Head and Devil's Peak. In another you see the crescent of sand at Camps Bay, sandwiched between the sea and the granite faces of the Twelve Apostles. Farther south the peninsula trails off toward the Cape of Good Hope, its mountains forming a ragged spine between False Bay and the empty vastness of the Atlantic. No matter where you look, you just can't get over how high you feel.

Despite being virtually surrounded by the city, Table Mountain is a remarkably unspoiled wilderness. Most of the Cape Peninsula's 2,200 species of flora are found on the mountain—there are about as many plant species in the Cape Peninsula as there are in the whole of North America and Europe combined—including magnificent examples of Cape Town's wild indigenous flowers, known as *fynbos*. The best time to see the mountain in bloom is between September and March, although you can be sure to find some flowers whatever the time of year. Long gone are the days when Cape lions, zebras, and hyenas roamed the mountain, but you can still glimpse *grysboks* (small antelopes) or baboons, and cute, rabbitlike *dassies* (rock hyraxes) congregate in large numbers near the upper cable station.

Atop the mountain, well-marked trails offering 10- to 40-minute jaunts crisscross the Western Table near the Cableway. Two excellent new wheelchair-friendly walks with spectacular views were opened to coincide with the launch of the new Cableway system in September 1997. Many other trails lead to the other side of Platteklip Gorge and into the mountain's catchment area, where you'll find reservoirs, hidden streams, and more incredible views. Be aware, though, that weather on the mountain can change quickly. Even if you're making only a short visit, take a sweater. If you're planning an extended hike, carry water, plenty of warm clothing, and a mobile phone.

During the warm summer months Capetonians are fond of taking picnic baskets up the mountain. The best time to do this is after 5: Some say sipping a glass of chilled Cape wine while watching the sun set from Table Mountain is one of life's great joys. Otherwise, you can eat at the large self-service restaurant, which offers an eclectic buffet, including some South African–style food, such as Malay curry, and a range of Mediterranean meze (appetizer) dishes. The hot breakfasts are great. The smaller bistro serves light snacks, cocktails, and a range of coffees and pastries. The restaurant is open from 8:30 to 3:30 and the bistro from 10 until the last cable car. As you might expect, both restaurants offer a good wine list with local wines predominating. For noshers, there's a convenient fast-food kiosk.

If you're feeling adventurous, try an abseil from the top—it's only 370 ft, but you're hanging out over 3,300 ft of air. Or opt for a bungee jump from the cable car—at press time one of only two such bungee jumps in the world.

You have only two ways of reaching the top of the mountain: Walk, or take the Cableway.

Riding the Cableway

Cable cars take three to five minutes to reach the summit. There used to be terrible congestion at the Lower Cable Station, but the building of the new Cableway, with two large, wheelchair-friendly revolving cars that give a 180 degree view, has eased things somewhat. You can't prebook for the cable car, but the longest you'll have to wait is about an hour, and then only in peak season (December 15–January 15). Several tour operators include a trip up the mountain in their schedules (☞ Guided Tours *in* Cape Town A to Z, *below*). ✉ *Tafelberg Rd.,* ☎ *021/424–8181.* ☎ *R50–R75 round-trip, R30–R40 one-way (depending on season).* ◷ *Dec.–May, daily 7:30 AM–9 PM; June–Aug., daily 8:30–5; Sept.–Nov., daily 8–6:30.*

The Lower Cableway lies on the slopes of Table Mountain near its western end. It's a long way from the city on foot, and you're better off traveling by car, taxi, or *riki* (a slow, low-tech minibus). To get there from the City Bowl, take Buitengracht Street toward the mountain. Once you cross Camp Street, Buitengracht becomes Kloof Nek Road. Follow Kloof Nek Road through the residential neighborhood of Gardens to a traffic circle; turn left on Tafelberg Road and follow signs to the Lower Cableway.

A taxi from the city center to the Lower Cableway (one-way) costs about R30–R55, and a riki costs R10 per person, but they are only available during the week.

Walking up the Mountain

More than 300 walking trails wend their way up the mountain, but the only route up the front section is via Platteklip Gorge. You can start at the Lower Cable Station, but remember that you need to walk about 3–4 km (2–2½ mi) to the left (east) before heading up. It is easier, but slightly less scenic, to walk along Tafelberg Road until the PLATTEKLOOF GORGE sign and then head up. Once on the right path, you shouldn't get lost. There is no water in Platteklip Gorge; you *must* take at least 2 liters (½ gallon) of water per person. Table Mountain can be dangerous if you're not familiar with the terrain. Many paths that look like good routes off the mountain end in treacherous cliffs. Do not underestimate this mountain. It may be in the middle of a city, but it is not a genteel town park. Always take warm clothes and a mobile phone, and let someone know of your plan. The mountain is quite safe if you stick to the known paths. If you are on the mountain and the weather changes dramatically (heavy rain, mist) and you can't tell where you are, just sit tight—you will be rescued as soon as the weather permits. Walking around in the mist is quite dangerous. There are several routes from Kirstenbosch National Botanic Gardens (☞ *below*) that are wonderful, easy, and scenic but that take you to a section of the mountain that is far from the front table and the cable station. There is still quite a long and very scenic but pretty challenging walk from the top of the Kirstenbosch routes to the front table.

If you don't feel comfortable tackling the mountain alone, contact **Cape Eco Trails** (☎ 021/785–5511), which offers guided walks to the top and all over the mountain. Alternately, you can contact one of the climbing schools listed in Outdoor Activities and Sports (☞ *below*), who escort hikes, but not too eagerly, as they tend to concentrate more on climbing. Expect to pay R100–R400 per person, which may include descent by cable car.

The City Center

Numbers in the text correspond to numbers in the margin and on the Cape Town map.

A Good Walk

Begin your walk at **Cape Town Tourism's Information Office** ①, on the corner of Burg and Castle streets (one block up from Strand Street). At no time during the walk will you be more than 15 minutes from this starting point. Head down Castle and turn right onto **Adderley Street** ②, directly opposite the **Golden Acre** ③ shopping center. Turn left on Darling Street and head toward the **Castle of Good Hope** ④ and the **Grand Parade** ⑤. Just across the way is the beautiful **City Hall** ⑥. Retrace your steps toward Adderley Street, turning left one block before you get there onto Parliament Street, to reach the austere **Groote Kerk** ⑦. The Groote Kerk faces Church Square, now a parking lot, where churchgoers used to unharness their oxen. On the skinny traffic island in the middle of Spin Street is a concrete plaque marking the **Slave Tree** ⑧. A brass plaque commemorating the slave tree and a cross section of the tree itself are on display in the **South African Cultural History Museum** ⑨, next door on Adderley Street. Here, Adderley swings to the right to become Wale Street (Waalst), but if you continue straight on, you'll be walking up Government Avenue, a wide and attractive squirrel-filled, tree-lined walkway that leads past many of the country's most important institutions and museums. On your right is the **South African Library** ⑩, the oldest in the country, and **Company's Gardens** ⑪. This is a great place to sit and watch the world go by. Buy a bag of peanuts from a vendor and feed the pigeons and squirrels. Continue along Government Avenue, and walk past Parliament to the **Tuynhuys** ⑫. The **South African National Gallery** ⑬ stands farther up Government Avenue, on your left, and opposite it on your right are the **South African Museum** ⑭ and the Planetarium. The temple in front of the South African Museum is the **Delville Wood Monument** ⑮. Walk through the alleyway on the left of the gallery onto Hatfield Street to reach the **South African Jewish Museum** ⑯, the Cape Town Holocaust Center, and the imposing **Great Synagogue** ⑰, South Africa's mother synagogue. Carry on up Hatfield toward the mountain and take the first small tree-lined lane to the right; this will lead you back to Government Avenue. Turn left to go to **Bertram House** ⑱ at the top of the avenue, and then backtrack and turn left to cut across the front of the South African Museum to Queen Victoria Street. For something completely different, head down Bloem to **Long Street** ⑲. Turn left on Wale Street and walk four blocks to the **Bo-Kaap** ⑳. Near the corner of Wale and Rose stands the **Bo-Kaap Museum** ㉑. Retrace your steps down Wale Street to **St. George's Cathedral** ㉒. Across Wale is the entrance to **St. George's Mall** ㉓. From there, turn left onto **Church Street** ㉔, where you'll find art galleries, African curio shops, a flea market, and a great coffee shop (Mozarts) in the short section between Burg and Long. It's worth turning left onto Long to see the attractive old buildings, but if you're short on time or energy, turn right (away from the mountain) onto Longmarket and then amble around **Greenmarket Square** ㉕, the center of the city since 1710. The **Old Town House** ㉖ faces the square on the mountain side. Work your way back to Long Street and walk away from the mountain—you can't see the sea but you can see the mountain. When you reach Strand Street, turn right to reach the **Koopmans–De Wet House** ㉗. Turn right again onto Burg and you'll be back at Cape Town Tourism.

Sights to See

❷ **Adderley Street.** Originally named Heerengracht after a canal that ran the length of the avenue, this street has always been Cape Town's principal thoroughfare. It was once the favored address of the city's leading families, and its oak-shaded sidewalks served as a promenade for those who wanted to see and be seen. By the mid-19th century the oaks had all been chopped down and the canal covered as Adderley Street became the main commercial street. By 1908 it had become such a busy thoroughfare that the city fathers paved it with wooden blocks in an attempt to dampen the noise of countless wagons, carts, and hooves.

⑱ **Bertram House.** Built around 1840, this is the only surviving Georgian brick town house in Cape Town. Once a common sight in the city, these boxlike, two-story houses were a response by the English community to Cape Dutch architecture. The projecting front porch was intended to shield the house from the worst effects of the frequent southeasters. The collection of furniture, silver, jewelry, and porcelain recaptures the look and feel of an early 19th-century home. The catalog available at the entrance describes the entire collection. ✉ *Government Ave. and Orange St.,* ☎ *021/424–9381.* 🎫 *R3.* ☉ *Tues.–Sat. 9:30–4:30.*

NEED A BREAK? Government Avenue ends opposite the famous gateway to the **Mount Nelson** hotel (✉ 76 Orange St., ☎ 021/423–1000), complete with two pith-helmeted gatekeepers, which was erected in 1924 to welcome the Prince of Wales on his visit to the Cape. The "Nellie" remains Cape Town's most fashionable and genteel social venue. More importantly, it

Cape Town

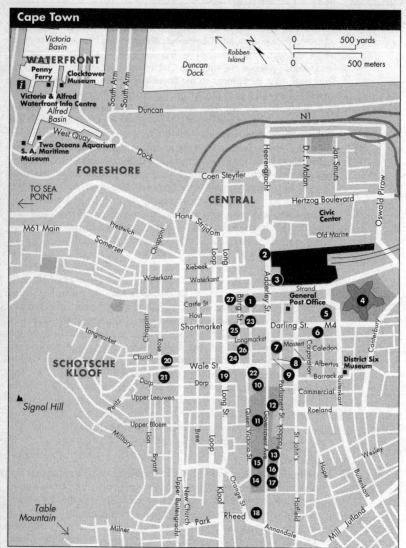

Adderly Street, **2**
Bertram House, **18**
Bo-Kaap, **20**
Bo-Kaap Museum, **21**
Cape Town Tourism
Information Office, **1**
Castle of Good
Hope, **4**
Church Street, **24**
City Hall, **6**
Company's
Gardens, **11**
Delville Wood
Monument, **15**
Golden Acre, **3**

Grand Parade, **5**
Great Synagogue, **17**
Greenmarket
Square, **25**
Groote Kerk, **7**
Koopmans-De Wet
House, **27**
Long Street, **19**
Old Town House, **26**
Slave Tree, **8**
South African
Cultural History
Museum, **9**
South African Jewish
Museum, **16**

South African
Library, **10**
South African
Museum, **14**
South African
National Gallery, **13**
St. George's
Cathedral, **22**
St. George's Mall, **23**
Tuynhuys, **12**

serves the city's best high tea, although the new Table Bay Hotel at the V&A Waterfront also provides a memorable version. Both hotels provide a pastry selection to tempt the most jaded palate.

★ ⓴ **Bo-Kaap.** In the late 17th and early 18th centuries, this district was the historic home of the city's Muslim population brought from the East as slaves. Today, the area remains strongly Muslim, and it's fascinating to wander the narrow cobbled lanes past mosques and colorful, flat-roof houses. Many of the homes combine elements of Cape Dutch and British architecture, and altogether they represent the largest collection of pre-1840 architecture in South Africa. The Bo-Kaap is also known as the Malay quarter, despite the fact that its inhabitants originated from all over, including the Indonesian archipelago, India, Turkey, and Madagascar.

㉑ **Bo-Kaap Museum.** Built in the 18th century, this museum was originally the home of Abu Bakr Effendi, a well-known member of the Muslim community. The house has been furnished to re-create the lifestyle of a typical Malay family in the 19th century. Since the exhibits aren't labeled, you might do better to visit the museum as part of a guided tour of the Malay quarter (☞ Guided Tours *in* Cape Town A to Z, *below*). ✉ *71 Wale St.,* ☎ *021/424–3846.* 🖭 *R3.* ⊘ *Mon.–Sat. 9:30–4:30.*

❶ **Cape Town Tourism Information Office.** Here you can pick up information on most of the major monuments and buildings associated with the settlement of Cape Town. Do the short walking tour of the city (R30), which gives you a good orientation. There is also a coffee bar and internet café (☞ Contacts and Resources *in* Cape Town A to Z, *below*).

★ ❹ **Castle of Good Hope.** Despite its name, the castle isn't one of those fairy-tale fantasies you find perched on a cliff above the Rhine. It is a squat fortress that hunkers into the ground as if to avoid shell fire. Built between 1665 and 1676 by the Dutch East India Company (VOC) to replace an earthen fort constructed by Jan van Riebeeck in 1652, it is the oldest building in the country. Its pentagonal plan, with a diamond-shape bastion at each corner, is typical of the Old Netherlands defense system adopted in the early 17th century. The design was intended to allow covering fire to be provided for every portion of the castle. As added protection, the whole fortification was surrounded by a moat, with the sea nearly washing up against its walls. The castle served as both the VOC headquarters and the official governor's residence and still houses the regional headquarters of the National Defence Force. Despite it bellicose origins, no shot has ever been fired from its ramparts, except ceremonially.

You can wander around on your own or join one of the guided tours that leave at 11, noon, or 2, at no extra cost. Also worth seeing is the excellent William Fehr Collection, housed in the governor's residence. The collection consists of antiques, artifacts, and paintings of early Cape Town and South African history. Conservationists should go upstairs to see John Thomas Baine's *The Greatest Hunt in Africa,* celebrating a "hunt" in honor of Prince Alfred when nearly 30,000 animals were driven together and slaughtered. ✉ *Buitenkant St.,* ☎ *021/469–1249.* 🖭 *R12.* ⊘ *Mid-Jan.–mid-Dec., Mon.–Sat. 9–4; mid-Dec.–mid-Jan., daily 9–4.*

| NEED A BREAK? | **Die Goeweneur Restaurant** (✉ Buitenkant St., ☎ 021/469–1249) is in the central courtyard of the Castle of Good Hope and, from the veranda, offers a pleasing view of the lawn and the buildings beyond. It is open 9–4 for light meals and teas and in the evenings for dinner. |

㉔ **Church Street.** The center of Cape Town's art and antiques business, the section between Burg and Long streets is a pedestrian mall, filled with art galleries, antiques dealers, and small cafés. This is the site of a daily antiques and flea market.

❻ **City Hall.** The old seat of local administration is home to the Cape Town Philharmonic Orchestra (which also holds performances at the Nico Theatre Centre) (☞ Nightlife and the Arts, *below*) and the City Library. It was from a balcony here, overlooking Darling Street, that Nelson Mandela gave his historic speech on his release from prison.

★ ⓫ **Company's Gardens.** These are all that remains of a 43-acre garden laid out by Jan van Riebeeck in April 1652 to supply fresh vegetables to ships on their way to the Dutch East Indies. By 1700, free burghers were cultivating plenty of crops on their own land, and in time the VOC vegetable patch was transformed into a botanic garden. It remains a delightful haven in the city center, graced by fountains, exotic trees, rose gardens, aviaries, and a pleasant outdoor café. At the bottom of the gardens, close to Government Avenue, look for an **old well** that used to provide water for the town's residents and the garden. The old water pump, engraved with the maker's name and the date 1842, has been overtaken by an oak tree and now juts out of the tree's trunk some 6 ft above the ground. A huge **statue of Cecil Rhodes** looms over the path that runs through the center of the gardens. He points to the north, and an inscription reads "Your hinterland is there," a reference to Rhodes's dream of extending the British Empire from the Cape to Cairo.

⓯ **Delville Wood Monument.** The monument honors South Africans who died in the fight for Delville Wood during the great Somme offensive of 1916. Of the 121 officers and 3,032 soldiers who participated in the three-day battle, only 5 officers and 750 soldiers survived unhurt. Facing the memorial is a **statue of Brigadier-General Lukin,** who commanded the South African Infantry Brigade during World War I.

❸ **Golden Acre.** Until earlier in the century, this part of the city was all at sea—literally. The land was reclaimed as part of a program to expand the docks. If you look at old paintings of the city, you will see that originally waves lapped at the very walls of the castle (☞ *above*), now more than half a mile from the ocean. At the bottom of the escalator leading from the railway station into the Golden Acre is a solid black line that marks the approximate position of the shoreline in 1693. A bit farther on, enclosed in glass, are the remains of Cape Town's first reservoir, which was uncovered when the foundations of the Golden Acre were being dug.

❺ **Grand Parade.** Once a military parade ground, this is now just a bleak parking lot. A statue of Edward VII serves as a parking attendant. It was here, upon his release on February 11, 1990, after 27 years in prison, that Nelson Mandela addressed an adoring crowd of more than 100,000 supporters. Today this is the site of South Africa's oldest flea market, which has been held on Wednesday and Saturday mornings for decades. It's not particularly tourist oriented, but it is the best place to see some of the "real" Cape Town, as it's here that many locals in the know get all manner of goods at bargain prices. Also, pop into one of the rather kitschy food stalls and try a *gatsby* (a sandwich on a long roll filled with french fries, lettuce, tomato, and a choice of fresh or pickled fish, curry, or steak), a *salomie* (roti, or soft round bread, wrapped around a curry filling), or a few samosas (fried, filled dough triangles) for a cheap lunch and a genuine cultural experience. And finish off with some *koeksusters* (sweet, plaited, lightly spiced, deep-fried pastries) for dessert.

⑰ Great Synagogue. Built in 1903 in the baroque style, this synagogue has notable twin towers and a dome. The building is kept locked for security, but ask in the offices in the Albow Centre at 88 Hatfield Street to be let in. Services are held twice daily. This forms the center of a newly developed Jewish complex, which includes the South African Jewish Museum (☞ *below*) and the Cape Town Holocaust Centre, which is housed in the Albow Centre, next door. ☒ *84 Hatfield St.,* ☎ *021/465–1405.*

★ **㉕ Greenmarket Square.** For more than a century, this cobbled square served as a forum for public announcements, including the 1834 declaration abolishing slavery. In the 19th century, the square became a vegetable market as well as a popular watering hole—the city's hardest boozers used to drink themselves comatose at the nearby Old Thatched Tavern and London Hotel. Today, the square is a fun open-air market, with vendors selling a wide selection of clothing and sandals, as well as African jewelry, art, and fabrics. For present buying, it's virtually unbeatable.

❼ Groote Kerk (Great Church). One of the most famous churches in South Africa, Groote Kerk was built in 1841 on the site of an earlier Dutch Reformed church dating from 1704. The adjoining clock tower is all that remains of that earlier building. Among the building's interesting features are the enclosed pews, each with its own door. Prominent families would buy their own pews—and lock the doors—so they wouldn't have to pray with the great unwashed. The enormous pulpit is the work of the famous sculptor Anton Anreith and carpenter Jan Jacob Graaff. The lions supporting it are carved from local stinkwood; the upper portion is Burmese teak. The organ, with nearly 6,000 pipes, is the largest in the Southern Hemisphere. Approximately 200 people are buried beneath the Batavian soapstone floor, including eight governors. There are free guided tours on request. ☒ *43 Adderley St. (enter on Church Sq.),* ☎ *021/461–7044.* ☒ *Free.* ☉ *Weekdays 10–2. Services Sun. at 10 AM and 7 PM.*

㉗ Koopmans–De Wet House. Now a museum, this lovely 18th-century home is a haven of peace in the city center. The structure you see today dates largely from the period 1771–93. It is notable for its neoclassical facade, which has been variously attributed to Anton Anreith and Louis Thibault. The house enjoyed its heyday under Maria de Wet (1834–1906), a Cape Town socialite who entertained most of the major figures in Cape society, including Boer presidents and British governors. The furnishings date to the early 19th century, when the house belonged to Maria's grandmother. The collection includes a stunning selection of antiques, carpets, paintings, and porcelain. It's worth buying the excellent guide to the museum, which describes every item in the collection. ☒ *35 Strand St.,* ☎ *021/424–2473.* ☒ *R3.* ☉ *Tues.–Sat. 9:30–4:30.*

⑲ Long Street. The section of Long between Orange and Wale streets is lined with magnificently restored Georgian and Victorian buildings. Wrought-iron balconies and fancy curlicues on these colorful houses create an impression reminiscent of the French Quarter in New Orleans. During the 1960s, Long Street did a good imitation of the Big Easy, including a host of bars, prostitutes, and sleazy hotels. Today, antiques dealers, secondhand-book stores (Clarke's is a must; ☞ Shopping, *below*), pawn shops, the Pan-African Market (☞ Shopping, *below*), and funky and vintage clothing outlets make it the best browsing street in the city. There's also a good selection of backpackers' lodges. At the mountain end is Long Street Baths, an indoor swimming pool and old Turkish hamam.

㉖ Old Town House. For 150 years this was the most important civic building in Cape Town. Built in 1755 as a guardhouse, it also saw duty as a meeting place for the burgher senate, a police station, and from 1840 to 1905 as Cape Town's city hall. The building is a beautiful example of urban Cape Dutch architecture, with thick whitewashed walls, green-and-white shutters, and small-paned windows. Today the former city hall is home to the Michaelis Collection, an extensive selection of brooding Dutch landscape paintings, as well as changing exhibits. ⊠ *Greenmarket Sq.*, ☎ *021/424–6367.* ⌂ *Free.* ☉ *Weekdays 10–5, Sat. 10–4.*

NEED A BREAK? The **Ivy Garden** (⊠ Greenmarket Square, ☎ 021/424–6367), in the courtyard of the Old Town House, serves light lunches and teas in a leafy, green setting. Seating on the veranda overlooks the hustle and bustle of Greenmarket Square.

8 Slave Tree. Slaves were auctioned under the tree that once stood here. A cross section of the enormous Canadian pine is displayed at the South African Cultural History Museum (☞ *below*). Slavery began in the Cape Colony in 1658, when free burghers petitioned the government for farmhands. The first group of 400 slaves arrived from Guinea, Angola, Batavia (modern Java), and Madagascar. During the first British occupation of the Cape (1795–1803), 17,000 slaves were brought from India, Ceylon, and the Philippines, swelling the total slave population to 30,000. Slavery was abolished by the British in 1834, an act that served as the final impetus for one of South Africa's great historical events, the Great Trek, when thousands of outraged Afrikaaners set off in their covered wagons to establish a new state in the hinterland where they would be free from British taxation and laws.

★ **9 South African Cultural History Museum** (also known as the Slave Lodge). Built in 1679 by the Dutch East India Company to house slaves, this building, although beautiful, has a pretty nasty history. Currently, the museum offers an excellent overview of South Africa's early settler history. Displays detailing the settlement and colonization of the Cape are superb; letters, coins, paintings, clothes, and furniture bring the period almost palpably to life. The museum also has minor collections of Roman, Greek, Egyptian, and Asian antiquities, as well as displays of antique silver, musical instruments, glass, ceramics, weapons, and coins. From 1815 to 1914 the building housed the supreme court. At press time, the future of the museum was under debate, and it may soon be turned into a slavery museum. ⊠ *Adderley and Wale Sts.*, ☎ *021/ 461–8280.* ⌂ *R5.* ☉ *Mon.–Sat. 9:30–4:30.*

16 South African Jewish Museum. The SAJM is due to reopen in July 2000, housed in a new building, with the original museum (which was the oldest synagogue in Cape Town) as its entrance. The museum captures the story of South African Jewry from its early beginnings, spanning 150 years. "Themes of Memories" (immigrant experiences), "Reality" (integration into South Africa), and "Dreams" (visions) are dynamically portrayed, represented by high-tech multimedia and interactive displays, reconstructed sets, models, and Judaica artifacts. Plans are also afoot for a computerized Discovery Center with a roots bank, a temporary gallery for changing exhibits, a museum restaurant and shop, and an auditorium. ⊠ *84 Hatfield St.*, ☎ *021/465–1546.* ⌂ *About R25.* ☉ *Not available at press time.*

10 South African Library. The National Reference Library, as it is also known, owes its existence to Lord Charles Somerset, governor of the Cape Colony, who in 1818 imposed a wine tax to fund the creation of a library that would "place the means of knowledge within the reach of the youth of this remote corner of the Globe." In 1860 the library moved into its current home, a neoclassical building modeled after the Fitzwilliam Museum in Cambridge, England. The library has an extensive collection of Africana, including the works of many 18th- and 19th-century explorers. ⊠ *Botanical Gardens*, ☎ *021/424–6320*. 🖃 *Free.* ⊙ *Weekdays 9–5.*

⑭ South African Museum. This is a natural history museum with some interesting cultural hangovers. Probably the strangest is the section on ethnography and archaeology, which, many argue, should be in the Cultural History Museum. Far more interesting is the section on the fossil remains of prehistoric reptiles and other animals, and the quite spectacular Whale Well—where musical recitals are often held, under suspended life-size casts of enormous marine mammals. The adjoining planetarium stages a variety of shows throughout the week and, at noon on Saturday and Sunday, a special children's show. ⊠ *25 Queen Victoria St.*, ☎ *021/424–3330*, ℻ *021/424–6716.* 🖃 *Museum R5, planetarium R7.* ⊙ *Museum daily 10–5; planetarium shows Tues.–Fri. at 1, weekends at noon, 1, and 2:30.*

★ ⑬ South African National Gallery. Don't miss this art gallery. The museum houses a good collection of 19th- and 20th-century European and British works, but it's most interesting for its South African works, many of which reflect the country's traumatic history. The director is known for innovative, brave, and sometimes controversial exhibitions. The museum café serves salads, sandwiches, pastas, and cakes. Free guided tours are given on Wednesday at 1 and Saturday at 3. ⊠ *Government Ave., Gardens*, ☎ *021/465–1628.* 🖃 *Free.* ⊙ *Tues.–Sun. 10–5.*

㉒ St. George's Cathedral. The cathedral was once the religious seat of one of the most recognizable faces—and voices—in the fight against apartheid, Archbishop Desmond Tutu. In his position as the first black archbishop of Cape Town, he vociferously denounced apartheid and relentlessly pressed for a democratic government. The present Anglican cathedral was designed by Sir Herbert Baker in the Gothic Revival style; construction began in 1901, using sandstone from Table Mountain. The structure contains the largest stained-glass window in the country, some beautiful examples of late-Victorian stained glass, and a 1,000-year-old Coptic cross. If you want to hear the magnificent organ, go to the choral evensong at 5:30 on Wednesday evenings, the 9:15 AM or 7 PM mass on Sunday, or the 11 AM mass on the last Sunday of every month. ⊠ *Wale St.*, ☎ *021/424–7360.* 🖃 *Free.* ⊙ *Daily 8–5. Services weekdays at 7:15 and 1:15; Tues. and Fri. also at 5:30 PM; Sat. at 8 AM; Sun. at 7, 8, 9:15, and 7 PM.*

㉓ St. George's Mall. This promenade stretches almost all the way to the Foreshore. Shops and cafés line the mall, and street vendors hawk everything from T-shirts to African arts and crafts. Buskers and dancers gather daily to entertain the crowds.

⑫ Tuynhuys (Town House). Parts of the Tuynhuys date to the late 17th and early 18th centuries. The building contains the offices of the state president and is not open to the public.

The Victoria & Alfred Waterfront

The Victoria & Alfred Waterfront is the culmination of a long-term project undertaken to breathe new life into the historical dockland of the city. It is one of Cape Town's most vibrant and exciting attractions and is the focus of the city's nightlife and entertainment scene. Hundreds of shops, cinemas, restaurants, and bars share quarters in restored warehouses and dock buildings, all connected by pedestrian plazas and promenades. It's clean, it's safe, and it's car-free.

A Good Walk

It makes sense to begin your walk at the **Victoria & Alfred Waterfront Information Centre** (which you should visit before you do anything else, to get the latest news on this constantly changing part of the city). Leave the Information Centre on the Dock Road side (away from the sea), turn right, and walk down Dock Road to the long, narrow stone shed that once housed the **Rocket Life-Saving Apparatus.** Next door is **Mitchell's Waterfront Brewery.** The heady smell of malt emanating from Mitchell's will be enough to send anyone with a thirst into the adjoining **Ferryman's Tavern.** Facing Ferryman's Tavern is the **AGFA Amphitheatre.** From the amphitheater, walk over to Quay 5 (in front of Tequila Cantina) and the **Victoria Basin,** where you can see the historic, but not particularly aesthetic, Robben Island embarkation point where prisoners were shipped to the prison and relatives boarded the ferry to visit their loved ones. Walk back past the red Fisherman's Choice restaurant to Market Square and the mustard-color **Union-Castle House.** Walk past the National Sea Rescue Institute (NSRI) shed and around the bottom of Alfred Mall, between the Green Dolphin and the Hildebrand and over the Swing Bridge to what used to be called Berties Landing (and still is by most Capetonians). You can't miss it—head for the bright orange clock tower. Here you may see seals resting on a platform just near the embarkation point for the Robben Island Ferries. Also here is the ticket office for Robben Island and a small shop selling island memorabilia. A museum is planned, but at press time details were still a bit vague. From here you can backtrack over the swing bridge, but it's much more interesting to walk past the Fish Quay and turn right along the rather tacky-looking road, where you are bound to see a few boats up on the hard, being painted or serviced. This is the unprettified section of the harbor, but it is quite safe. Follow the road up to the traffic circle and then turn right and head toward the Cape Grace Hotel, in front of which is the **S.A.S. Somerset.** The ship is part of the **South African Maritime Museum.** Head back toward the Alfred Mall, looking left as you cross the second bridge, to see if there is a ship in dry dock. Slip to the left of the mall and visit the SA Maritime Museum. Then amble around the Craft Market, which is designed to spit you out the other end, right in front of the **Two Oceans Aquarium.** Then head back toward the Information Centre, taking the stairs on the left up to Portswood Ridge, where there are several late-19th-century buildings once used by the harbor administration. At the top of the stairs stands the brick Time Ball Tower, the **Harbour Master's Residence,** and the Dragon Tree. Take the stairs back down and cross Dock Road to return to your starting point.

Sights to See

AGFA Amphitheatre. This popular outdoor performance space mounts shows almost daily, ranging from concerts by the Cape Town Philharmonic Orchestra to gigs by jazz and rock bands. Check with the **Information Centre** (☞ *below*) for the schedule of events. The amphitheater stands on the site where, in 1860, the teenage Prince Alfred inaugurated the construction of a breakwater to protect shipping in the harbor. Table Bay was never an ideal natural harbor. In winter, devastating northwesterly winds pounded ships caught in the exposed waters. Between 1647 and 1870 more than 190 ships went down in Table Bay. Since the breakwater was built, only 40 ships have foundered here.

Ferryman's Tavern. With the heady smell of malt emanating from Mitchell's Brewery (☞ *below*) adjoining the pub, you won't have to wait long for a nice cool one. Constructed in 1877 of bluestone and Table Mountain sandstone, this is one of the oldest buildings in the harbor. Before 1912 the temperance movement in Cape Town had managed to force a ban on the sale of alcohol within the docks. As a result, a host of pubs sprang up just outside the dock gates, particularly along Dock Road. ⊠ *Market Plaza,* ☎ *021/419–7748.*

Harbour Master's Residence. Built in 1860, in front there is a beautiful, century-old dragon tree, a native of the Canary Islands. The resin of this tree species, known as "dragon's blood," was used in Europe to treat dysentery and is still used in all manner of Asian medicines.

Mitchell's Waterfront Brewery. This is one of a handful of microbreweries in South Africa. The brewery produces four beers: Foresters Draught Lager, Bosuns Bitter, Ravenstout, and Ferryman's Ale. The brewery offers tours, which include beer-tasting and a look at the fermentation tanks, for which reservations are essential. ⊠ *Dock Rd.,* ☎ *021/ 418–2461.* ▣ *Tour R20.* ☉ *Daily 11–3.*

★ **Robben Island.** Made famous by its most illustrious inhabitant, Nelson Rolihlahla Mandela, this island, whose name means "seals" in Dutch, has a long and mostly sad history. At various times a prison, leper colony, mental institution, and military base, it is finally fulfilling a positive, enlightening, and empowering role in its new incarnation as a museum. As well as Mandela, Robert Sobukwe, and Walter Sisulu, there have been some fascinating (reluctant) inhabitants of this at once formidable and beautiful place. One of the first prisoners was Autshumato, known to the early Dutch settlers as "Harry the Hottentot." He was one of the main interpreters for Jan van Riebeeck in the mid-17th century, as was his niece, Krotoa, who was also imprisoned on the island when she fell into disfavor. In 1820, the British thought they could solve some of the problems they were having on the Eastern Cape frontier by banishing the Xhosa leader Makhanda to the island. Both Autshumato and Makhanda (also spelled Makana) escaped by rowboat, but Makhanda didn't make it. Notice when you go to the island that the two new, sleek high-speed ferries are called *Autshumato* and *Makana.*

Tours of the island are organized by the Robben Island Museum, and visitors are taken around the island and the prison by guides who were themselves political prisoners (mostly.) Tours leave from the jetty in front of Seekers, near the Fish Quay ("Berties"), on the hour every hour between 9 and 3, except 1. The boat crossing takes 30 minutes. The island tour itself lasts 2½ hours, during which time you walk through the prison and see the cell in which Mandela was imprisoned, as well as the quarry where the former president pounded rocks for so many years. During peak season (mid-December–mid-January) it may get pretty crowded, so reserve in advance.

The Robben Island Museum is constantly working on new and interesting ways to visit the island. At press time it was planning to offer longer, self-guided tours. These will be available only on the older, slower, not-so-comfortable but very seaworthy traditional island ferries (the ones the prison services used). You will be dropped off on the island and allowed to walk around, picnic, swim (in the icy water, if you are brave), and generally amuse yourself. A few overnight trips have been run by ex-prisoners; you get to spend the night on the island sharing stories around a campfire. This is a very African way of imparting information, but it is a little disorganized. Future plans include formal overnight accommodation in the existing buildings, but no, you won't be able to sleep in Nelson Mandela's bed. The tour offered by the **Robben Island Museum** (☎ 021/419–1300) is the only one that actually visits the island; several operators advertise Robben Island tours and just take visitors on a boat trip *around* the island (☞ Guided Tours *in* Cape Town A to Z, *below.*

S.A.S. Somerset. The *Somerset* is the only surviving boom-defense vessel in the world. During World War II, harbors were protected against enemy submarines and divers by booms, essentially metal mesh curtains drawn across the harbor entrance. The *Somerset* (then named the H.M.S. *Barcross*) controlled the boom across Saldanha Bay, north of Cape Town. You can explore the entire ship, including the bridge and the engine room. The ship is part of the South African Maritime Museum (☞ *below*).

South African Maritime Museum. The museum provides a look at ships and the history of Table Bay, including a model of Cape Town harbor as it appeared in 1886. In the model workshop you can watch modelers build scale replicas of famous ships. ✉ *Dock Rd.,* ☎ *021/419–2505.* ✆ *R5, S.A.S. Somerset R3.* ⊙ *Daily 10–5.*

Time Ball Tower. The tower was built in 1894, before the advent of modern navigational equipment, when ships' crews needed to know the exact time to help them calculate longitude. Navigators set their clocks by the time ball, which fell every day at 1 PM, much like the ball that marks the stroke of midnight in New York's Times Square on New Year's Eve.

★ **Two Oceans Aquarium.** The aquarium is thought to be one of the finest in the world. Stunning displays show the marine life of the warm Indian Ocean and the cold Atlantic Ocean. It's a hands-on place with a touch pool for children and opportunities for certified divers to explore the vast, five-story kelp forest or the predator tank, where you share the water with a couple of large ragged-tooth sharks (*Carcharias taurus*). The latest, nonpermanent exhibit is "Fangs," which will be in place until 2002. It's a display of all the really scary underwater beasts, including brightly colored sea snakes and shocking electric eels. The aquarium also runs "the most fun baby-sitting service in the world." Drop your children (ages 7–12) off anytime after 6:30 with a sleeping bag, and head off to the waterfront to party. They will be fed, given a gift pack, taken on a tour, shown a video, led in games, and, after all the excitement, given a chance to "sleep with the fish." There is full-time supervision, and security is tight. If you like, you may pick them up after midnight, but they probably won't want to leave. This service is subject to demand. ✉ *Dock Rd., Waterfront,* ☎ *021/418–3823.* ✆ *R40; dives R300 (R225 with own gear).* ⊙ *Daily 9:30–6.*

Union-Castle House. Designed in 1919 by Sir Herbert Baker, the house was headquarters for the famous Union-Castle shipping line. Before World War II many English-speaking South Africans looked upon England as home, even if they had never been there. The emotional link between the two countries was symbolized most strongly by the mail steamers, carrying both mail and passengers, that sailed weekly between South Africa and England. In 1977, amid much pomp and ceremony, the last Union-Castle mail ship, the *Windsor Castle,* made its final passage to England. Even today, older South Africans like to wax lyrical about the joys of a voyage on one of those steamers. Union-Castle House is now home to several banks and small businesses. Inside Standard Bank you can still see the iron rings in the ceiling from which mailbags were hung. ✉ *Quay 4.*

Victoria & Alfred Waterfront Information Centre. The center, opposite the V&A Hotel, has the lowdown on everything happening in the area, including upcoming events and shows. Here you can arrange walking tours of the waterfront, book accommodations, and get information about the whole Western Cape. A scale model shows what the waterfront will look like when it's finished. ✉ *Pierhead,* ☎ *021/418–2369,* ℻ *021/21–2565.* ⊙ *Oct.–Apr., daily 9–6; May–Sept., daily 8–5.*

Victoria Basin. The basin was constructed between 1870 and 1905 to accommodate the huge increase in shipping following the discovery of diamonds at Kimberley and gold on the Witwatersrand. Across the basin is the South Arm, used as a debarkation point for British troops, horses, and material during the Boer War (1899–1902). Much of the fodder for the British horses was shipped in from Argentina and catastrophically infested with rats and fleas. As a result, bubonic plague broke out in Cape Town in February 1901, creating wholesale panic in the city. African dockworkers, suspected of harboring the disease, were forbidden to leave the city and ultimately confined to specific quarters. During the epidemic, 766 people contracted the plague; 371 died.

The Peninsula

This driving tour takes you south from Cape Town on a loop of the peninsula, heading through the scenic southern suburbs before running down the False Bay coast to Cape Point. It's a magnificent drive back to the city along the wild Atlantic coast. Plan a full day to travel the entire loop, more if you want to stop along the way.

Numbers in the text correspond to numbers in the margin and on the Cape Peninsula map.

A Good Drive

Take the N2 or De Waal Drive (M3) out of the city center. The two highways merge near Groote Schuur Hospital and split again soon after. Bear right, taking the M3 (signposted Southern Suburbs/Muizenberg), and look up at the mountain—you will see zebras, gnu, and eland grazing peacefully. After 1 km (½ mi) you'll pass **Mostert's Mill** ㉙, one of two remaining windmills in the Cape on the left, and, on your right, the beautifully situated campus of the University of Cape Town, nestled against the slopes of Devil's Peak. Continue on the M3 for another kilometer (½ mi) to the exit marked with a sign to the **Rhodes Memorial** ㉚. Return to the M3 and head south toward Muizenberg. After 1½ km (1 mi), exit right onto Rhodes Avenue (M63). This leafy road winds through large trees to the **Kirstenbosch National Botanic Gardens** ㉛, one of the most beautiful spots in the Cape. Turn right as you leave the Botanic Gardens. When you reach a T-junction, turn right again and begin the winding climb to the pass at Constantia Nek. From the traffic circle at the top you can either cut over the mountains and down into Hout Bay (☞ *below*) or turn left onto the M41 (the sign reads WYNBERG AND GROOT CONSTANTIA) and begin the snaking descent into Constantia and **Groot Constantia** ㉜. Leaving Groot Constantia, turn right on Main Road and then right again onto Ladies Mile Extension (a sign points you to Muizenberg and Bergvliet). Another right at the first traffic light puts you on Spaanschemat River Road, and a further right turn funnels you onto Klein Constantia Road. Follow this to **Buitenverwachting** ㉝. Turn left out of Buitenverwachting and continue for ½ km (¼ mi) to **Klein Constantia** ㉞. Head back down Klein Constantia Road, and turn right into Spaanschemat River Road. After about 3 km (2 mi) turn left onto Tokai Road and right again at the PORTER SCHOOL sign and drive 1 km (½ mi) to **Tokai Manor** ㉟. Return to the junction and continue straight on Tokai Road, through the traffic circle, and to Steenberg Country Hotel, Golf Estate and Vineyards on your right. On the left is Pollsmoor Prison, where Nelson Mandela stayed after he was moved from Robben Island. Turn left at the T-junction and continue to the Main Road (M4) and turn right again. After ½ km (¼ mi), Boyes Drive leads off the M4. The M4, or Main Road, on the other hand, takes you through **Muizenberg** ㊱, where the Main Road runs parallel to the sea. Watch on your right for a De Post Huys, a small thatched building with rough, whitewashed walls, and the imposing facade of the Natale Labia Museum. Continue to Rhodes Cottage Museum. From Muizenberg, Main Road heads down the peninsula, hugging the shore of False Bay. Strung along this coastline are a collection of small villages that long ago merged to form a thin suburban belt between the ocean and the mountains. **Kalk Bay** ㊲, **Fish Hoek** ㊳, and **Simonstown** ㊴ are all on this stretch. Simonstown is the last community of any size before you reach Cape Point. From here the road traverses a wild, windswept landscape as beautiful as it is desolate. You can stop at tiny **Boulders Beach** ㊵ to look at the colony of African penguins. The mountains, covered with rugged fynbos, descend almost straight into the sea. Don't be surprised to see troops of baboons lounging beside the road as you approach the **Cape of Good Hope** ㊶ section of the Cape Peninsula National Park. Close the windows of your car and don't attempt to feed the baboons. They are dangerous. Before you reach the Cape Point gate, look left and you will see the almost outrageously beautiful settlement of Smitswinkel Bay—accessible only on foot, via a steep and narrow path. Turn left out of the Cape Point gate onto the M65 to **Scarborough** ㊷ and **Kommetjie** ㊸. From Kommetjie the M65 leads to a major intersection. Turn left onto the M6 (Hout Bay), go through one set of lights, and then turn left again, following the signs to Hout Bay. The road passes through the small community of **Noordhoek** ㊹ before beginning its treacherous climb around **Chapman's Peak Drive** ㊺. From Chapman's Peak you descend into the attractive suburb and fishing center of **Hout Bay** ㊻. Turn left to stay on the M6 (a sign reads CITY AND LLANDUDNO). After less than a kilometer (½ mi), turn right on Valley Road to the **World of Birds** ㊼. From Hout Bay the M6 climbs past the exclusive community of Llandudno and then runs along the coast to **Camps Bay** ㊽. Follow Victoria Road (M6) out of Camps Bay and turn right at the sign reading KLOOF NEK ROUND HOUSE. This road snakes up the mountain until it reaches a five-way intersection at Kloof Nek. Make a sharp left onto the road leading to **Signal Hill** ㊾. For more great views of the city, return to the Kloof Nek intersection and take **Tafelberg Road** ㊿.

Sights to See

㊵ **Boulders Beach.** This series of small coves lies on the outskirts of Simonstown among giant boulders. Part of the Cape Peninsula National Park, the beach is best known for its resident colony of African penguins. You must stay out of the fenced-off breeding beach, but the birds will probably come waddling up to you to take a look. ✍ *R10.* ☉ *Daily 9–6.*

Boyes Drive. If you prefer scenic views to historical sites, Boyes Drive is probably a better option than the main highway. The drive runs high along the mountains, offering panoramic views of False Bay and the Hottentots Holland mountains, before rejoining the M4 at Kalk Bay (☞ *below*).

㉝ **Buitenverwachting.** A gorgeous winery that was also once part of Van der Stel's original Constantia farm, Buitenverwachting means "beyond expectation," and its setting certainly surpasses anything you might have imagined: An oak-lined avenue leads past the Cape Dutch homestead to the thatched modern cellar. Acres of vines spread up hillsides flanked by more towering oaks and the rocky crags of the Constantiaberg.

Buitenverwachting's wine is just as superb as its setting. The largest seller is the slightly dry Buiten Blanc, an easy-drinking blend of a few varieties. The best red is Christine, which until the 1991 vintage was known as Grand Vin; it's a blend of mostly cabernet sauvignon and

The Cape Peninsula

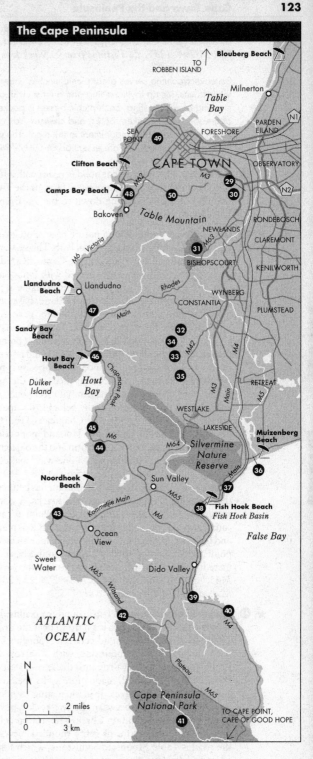

30% merlot. The winery's restaurant (☞ Dining, *below*) is probably the finest in the Cape. ⊠ *Off Klein Constantia Rd.*, ☎ *021/794–5190*, FAX *021/794–1351*. ☎ *Tastings free.* ⊙ *Weekdays 9–5, Sat. 9–1.*

NEED A
BREAK?
Buitenverwachting serves great picnic lunches under the oaks on the estate's lawns. It's an idyllic setting and a most civilized way to cap a morning of wine tasting. Each picnic basket is packed with a selection of breads, meat, chicken, pâtés, and cheeses. You can buy a bottle of estate wine as an accompaniment to the meal. The **picnic** costs R55 per person, and reservations are essential. ☎ *021/794–1012. Closed Sun.*

㊽ Camps Bay. This is a popular holiday resort with a long beach and plenty of restaurants and bars. The craggy faces of the Twelve Apostles, huge granite buttresses reaching down to the sea from the mountains behind, loom over the town.

★ **㊶ Cape of Good Hope.** Once a nature reserve on its own, this now forms part of the Cape Peninsula National Park. This section covers some 19,100 acres, including Cape Point and the Cape of Good Hope. Much of the park consists of rolling hills covered with fynbos and laced with miles of walking trails, for which maps are available at the park entrance. It also has beautiful deserted beaches. Eland, baboons, ostrich, and bontebok are among the animals that roam the park. A tarred road runs 14 km (8 mi) to the tip of the peninsula. A turnoff leads to the Cape of Good Hope, a rocky cape on the southwesternmost point of the continent. A plaque marks the spot—otherwise you would never know you're standing on a site of such significance. The opposite is true of Cape Point, a dramatic knife's edge of rock that slices into the Atlantic. Looking out to sea from the viewing platform, you feel you're at the tip of Africa, even though that honor officially belongs to Cape Agulhas, about 160 km (100 mi) to the southeast (☞ Chapter 5). From Cape Point the views of False Bay and the Hottentots Holland mountains are breathtaking. The walk up to the viewing platform and the old lighthouse is very steep; a funicular (R21 round-trip, R13 one-way) makes the run every three to four minutes. Take an anorak or sweater—the wind can take your breath away. A large sit-down restaurant has better views than food (but that is saying a lot) and a kiosk sells snacks. A gift shop completes the picture. During peak season, visit Cape Point as early in the day as you can; otherwise you'll be swamped by horrendous numbers of tourist buses and their occupants. Fun alternatives include an escorted bike trip to the point and an overnight hike with comfortable basic accommodation and incredible views, which is booked through the parks board. ⊠ *Off the M65*, ☎ *021/780–9526 or 021/780–9204.* ☎ *R20 per person.* ⊙ *Oct.– Mar., daily 7–6; Apr.–Sept., daily 7–5.*

★ **㊺ Chapman's Peak Drive.** A trip around the peninsula exhausts anyone's supply of superlatives, but it's hard to beat the dramatic beauty of the 10-km (6-mi) stretch of road between Noordhoek and Hout Bay. The road clings to the mountainside, with a narrow retaining wall separating you from a sheer drop into the sea—528 ft down at its highest. It's dizzyingly beautiful, made more so by the fact that the road constantly ducks and weaves. It is interesting to note that the road follows the contact line between the two rock types that make up most of the Peninsula Mountain Chain. The section below the road is built on Cape Granite and forms softly rounded curves. The section above the road is Table Mountain Sandstone, which forms positive vertical edges and displays conspicuous layering. (Bearing this in mind, you can also see where the contact is on Table Mountain and, especially, Lion's Head.) Follow the signs to Chapman's Peak Drive from Hout Bay on the Atlantic side and from Noordhoek from the False Bay side. Note: At press time the drive was temporarily closed due to rock slides.

Constantia. Backed by the rugged mountains of the Constantiaberg and overlooking the Cape Flats and False Bay, Constantia is an idyllic spot to while away a day—or a week. Vineyards carpet the lower slopes, while plantations of pine predominate higher up. This is very much the domain of the suburban gentry. If you don't have time to visit the Winelands (☞ Chapter 5), Constantia is a must. Here you'll find five excellent estates, Buitenverwachting, Groot Constantia, Klein Constantia, Constantia Uitsig, and the relatively new Steenberg.

De Post Huys. One of the oldest buildings in the country, it was constructed in 1673 as a lookout post and signal station. ⊠ Main Rd., ☎ 021/788–7035. ☜ Free. ⊙ Weekdays 8–3:30, Sat. 7:30–1, Sun. 1–5.

㊳ Fish Hoek. This is one of the most popular resort towns on the False Bay coast, with a smooth, sandy beach that is protected on the south side from the summer southeasters by Elsies Peak. It's one of the best places to see whales during calving season—from approximately August to November, though there have been whale sightings as early as June and as late as January. Until recently, Fish Hoek was the only teetotaling town in the country. In 1810 Lord Charles Somerset issued the first grant of Crown land in Fish Hoek on condition that no wine house should ever exist on the property. Somerset was evidently alarmed by the excesses associated with a wine house near Kommetjie, where wagon drivers would become too drunk to deliver their supplies to the Royal Navy at Simonstown. Jagers Walk, from the south side of Fish Hoek Beach to Sunny Cove, is a pleasant, scenic pathway that meanders through the rocks, giving access to some sheltered natural rock pools that are just great for swimming. The snorkeling is good, too.

★ ㉜ Groot Constantia. Constantia takes its name from the wine estate founded here in 1685 by Simon van der Stel, one of the first Dutch governors of the Cape. After his death in 1712 the land was subdivided, with the heart of the estate preserved at Groot Constantia. The enormous complex enjoys the status of a national monument and is by far the most commercial and touristy of the wineries. Van der Stel's magnificent homestead, the oldest in the Cape, lies at the center of Groot Constantia. It's built in traditional Cape Dutch style, with thick whitewashed walls, a thatched roof, small-pane windows, and ornate gables. The house is a museum furnished with exquisite period pieces. The old wine cellar sits behind the manor house. Built in 1791, it is most famous for its own ornate gable, designed by sculptor Anton Anreith. The cellar houses a wine museum, with displays of wine-drinking and storage vessels dating to antiquity.

In the 19th century the sweet wines of Groot Constantia were highly regarded in Europe and especially favored by King Louis Philippe and Bismarck. Today Groot Constantia is known for its splendid red wines. The best is the excellent Gouverneurs Reserve, made from mostly cabernet sauvignon grapes with smaller amounts of merlot and cabernet franc. Full of tannin and fruit, this big, robust wine will be at its best in 8 to 10 years. The Pinotage is consistently good, too, reaching its velvety prime in about five years. The estate operates two restaurants: the elegant Jonkershuis (☞ Dining, *below*) and the Tavern, which serves light meals at picnic tables on the lawn. You can also bring your own picnic and relax on the lawns behind the wine cellar. ⊠ Off Main Rd., ☎ 021/794–5128 (winery), 021/794–5067 (museum). ☜ Museum R5, wine tasting R11, cellar tour R10. ⊙ Daily 10–4:30. Cellar tour hourly 10–4.

NEED A
BREAK? The **Old Cape Farmstall** (✉ Near entrance to Groot Constantia, ☎ 021/794–7062) is worth a visit and has lovely homemade goodies and a huge range of local and imported cheeses, meats, preserves, spices, and various deli goods. It's a great place to fill a picnic basket. The **Old Cape Bistro** (☎ 021/794–7058) next door is open daily 8:30–5 and serves teas and lunches.

Groote Schuur Hospital. Dr. Christian Barnard performed the world's first heart transplant here in 1967. Just off Main Road, you'll see this visible landmark on the slopes of Table Mountain below the scenic De Waal Drive. The Transplant Museum and Educational Center is worth a visit, if you're interested in medical history or techniques. ☎ 021/404–5232. ✎ R5. ⊙ Weekdays 9–2.

㊻ Hout Bay. Cradled in a lovely bay and guarded by a 1,000-ft peak known as the Sentinel, Hout Bay is the center of Cape Town's crayfishing industry, and the town operates several fish-processing plants. Mariner's Wharf is Hout Bay's salty answer to the waterfront in Cape Town, a collection of bars and restaurants on the quayside. You can buy fresh fish at a seafood market and take it outside to be grilled. You should also try *snoek*—a baracuda-like fish, which is traditionally eaten smoked. Cruise boats depart from Hout Bay's harbor to view the **seal colony** on Duiker Island (☞ Cape Town A to Z, *below*).

The **Irma Stern Museum** is dedicated to the works and art collection of Stern (1894–1966), one of South Africa's greatest painters. The museum is administered by the University of Cape Town and occupies the Firs, the artist's home for 38 years. She is best known for African studies, particularly her paintings of indigenous people inspired by trips to the Congo and Zanzibar. Her collection of African artifacts, including priceless Congolese stools and carvings, is superb. ✉ Cecil Rd., Rosebank, ☎ 021/685–5686. ✎ R2. ⊙ Tues.–Sat. 10–5.

★ ㊲ Kalk Bay. The name of Kalk Bay recalls that seashells were once baked in large kilns near the shore to produce lime (kalk). This is one of the most fascinating destinations on the peninsula. A small harbor, where you can buy fish so fresh it wriggles, shelters a weathered fishing fleet, and tiny cottages crowd up the narrow cobbled streets, clinging to the mountain. Funky crafts shops, galleries, antiques shops, and cozy bistros can fill a whole day of rambling. Gnarled fishing folk rub shoulders with Rastafarians, surfers, yuppies, new-age trendies, and genteel ladies with blue hair rinses. The Brass Bell is a great place to down a few beers in the sun while local surfers strut their stuff on Kalk Bay Reef—a nice hollow left—barely yards from your comfortable table. You can walk up one of the many steep stairways to Boyes Drive and from there up the mountain. Escorted trips are led into the Kalk Bay Caves (☞ Outdoor Activities and Sports, *below*).

★ ㉛ Kirstenbosch National Botanic Gardens. The gardens extend up the eastern slopes of Table Mountain, overlooking the Cape Flats and distant Hottentots Holland Mountains. Walking trails meander through the gardens, and grassy banks are ideal for a picnic or afternoon nap. The plantings are limited to species native to southern Africa, including fynbos—hardy, thin-leaved plants that proliferate in the Cape. Among these are proteas, including silver trees and king proteas, ericas, and restios (reeds). Highlights include a large cycad garden, the Bird Bath (a beautiful stone pool built around a crystal clear spring), and the fragrance garden, which is wheelchair friendly and has a tapping rail and braille interpretive boards. Those who have difficulty walking can take a comprehensive tour lasting between 45 minutes and an hour (R12) by six-person cart. There is also a wheelchair trail that goes off

Finally, a travel companion that doesn't snore on the plane or eat all your peanuts.

When traveling, your MCI WorldCom Card is the best way to keep in touch. Our operators speak your language, so they'll be able to connect you back home—no matter where your travels take you. Plus, your MCI WorldCom Card is easy to use, and even earns you frequent flyer miles every time you use it. When you add in our great rates, you get something even more valuable: peace-of-mind. So go ahead. Travel the world. MCI WorldCom just brought it a whole lot closer.

You can even sign up today at www.mci.com/worldphone or ask your operator to make a collect call to 1-410-314-2938.

EASY TO CALL WORLDWIDE

1 Just dial the WorldPhone access number of the country you're calling from.
2 Dial or give the operator your MCI WorldCom Card number.
3 Dial or give the number you're calling.

China	
Available from most major cities	108-12
For a Mandarin-speaking Operator	108-17
Hong Kong	**800-96-1121**
Japan ◆	
To call using JT	0044-11-121
To call using KDD	00539-121▶
To call using IDC	0066-55-121
South Africa	**0800-99-0011**

For your complete WorldPhone calling guide, dial the WorldPhone access number for the country you're in and ask the operator for Customer Service. In the U.S. call 1-800-431-5402.

◆ Public phones may require deposit of coin or phone card for dial tone.
▶ Regulation does not permit Intra-Japan calls.

EARN FREQUENT FLYER MILES

MCI WorldCom, its logo and the names of the products referred to herein are proprietary marks of MCI WorldCom, Inc. All airline names and logos are proprietary marks of the respective airlines. All airline program rules and conditions apply.

The first thing you need overseas is the one thing you forget to pack.

FOREIGN CURRENCY DELIVERED OVERNIGHT

Chase Currency To Go® delivers foreign currency to your home by the next business day*

It's easy–before you travel, call 1-888-CHASE84 for delivery of any of 75 currencies

Delivery is free with orders of $500 or more

Competitive rates– without exchange fees

You don't have to be a Chase customer–you can pay by Visa® or MasterCard®

CHASE

THE RIGHT RELATIONSHIP IS EVERYTHING.®

1•888•CHASE84
www.chase.com

the main paths into the wilder section of the park and gets close to the feel of the mountain walks. Concerts are held here on summer Sundays at 5. With Table Mountain as a magnificent backdrop and the gardens all around, you can catch the best of South Africa's entertainment with everything from classical music to township jazz to rock and roll. There is a newly built center that leads into the conservatory and houses a restaurant, bookstore, and coffee shop. ⊠ *Rhodes Ave., Newlands,* ☎ *021/ 762–1166.* ⊠ *R15.* ☉ *Apr.–Aug., daily 8–6; Sept.–Mar., daily 8–7.*

34 **Klein Constantia.** Klein (rhymes with "stain") means "small" in Afrikaans and indicates the relative size of this portion of van der Stel's original Constantia estate. The winery has an impressive modern cellar, deliberately unobtrusive so as not to detract from the vine-covered mountain slopes. Its Cape Dutch homestead, visible as you drive in, was built in the late 18th century. This estate also produces wines of superb quality, as awards displayed in the tasting area attest. The excellent sauvignon blanc is used as a point of reference by many South African connoisseurs and vintners. Whereas early vintages were particularly opulent, more recent ones have been a little racy upon first release. The closest you'll come to the famous Constantia wine of the 18th century is the Vin de Constance, a sweet wine made from predominantly muscat de Frontignan grapes. The cabernet sauvignon is one of the best produced in the Cape—a collector's wine that will develop wonderfully over time. ⊠ *Klein Constantia Rd.,* ☎ *021/794– 5188,* FAX *021/794–2464.* ⊠ *Free.* ☉ *Weekdays 9–5, Sat. 9–1. Cellar tours by appointment.*

43 **Kommetjie.** A pleasant, somewhat isolated suburb, Kommetjie has a scenic 45-minute walk down Long Beach that leads to the wreck of the *Kakapo,* a steamship that ran aground on her maiden voyage in 1900. This is surfer's paradise, with some really big wave spots and a few gentler breaks. The nearby Imhoffs Gift complex is a must, especially if you have children. There is a nature park, with loads of birds, a snake park, camel rides, horse rides, a petting farm, crafts shops and, of course, a coffee shop.

29 **Mostert's Mill.** Built in 1796, this thatched wheat mill consists of a tower with a rotating cap to which sails were attached. Mills like this were once common in the area. Inside is the original mechanism, but it's not necessarily worth pulling off the highway to see. ⊠ *Rhodes Dr., Mowbray,* ☎ *no phone.* ☉ *Daily 9–5.*

36 **Muizenberg.** At the turn of the century this was the premier bathing resort in South Africa, attracting many of the country's wealthy mining magnates, as the many mansions along Baden Powell Drive attest. Long gone, though, are the days when anyone thought of Muizenberg as chic. A drab complex of shops and fast-food outlets, complete with kiddie pools and miniature golf, blights the beachfront, and the views of mountains and sea cannot make up for it. The whole area is in a state of not-so-genteel decay, and many beautiful Art Deco beachfront buildings have become slums. That doesn't stop beginner surfers and keen dog-walkers from utilizing the still wonderful beach, but, quite honestly, give the area on the sea side of the railway line a miss.

44 **Noordhoek.** Noordhoek is another popular beach community with stunning white sands that stretch forever. The bordering village has become a retreat for the arts-and-crafts community, and there are lots of galleries and boutiques selling unusual items. You can walk all the way between Kommetjie and Noordhoek on the aptly named Long Beach. It's also very popular with horseback riders (☞ Outdoor Activities and Sports, *below*) and surfers.

Rhodes Cottage Museum. Considering the great power wielded by Cecil John Rhodes (1853–1902), one of Britain's great empire builders, his seaside cottage was surprisingly humble and spare. Yet this is where the man who was instrumental in the development of present-day South Africa chose to spend his last days in 1902, preferring the cool sea air of Muizenberg to the stifling opulence of his home at Groote Schuur. The cottage, including the bedroom where he died, has been completely restored. Other rooms display photos documenting Rhodes's life. His remains are buried in the Matopos Hills in Zimbabwe (☞ Chapter 10). ⊠ *246 Main Rd., Muizenberg,* ☎ *021/788–1816.* 🎟 *Free.* ☉ *Tues.–Sun. 10–1 and 2–5.*

★ ⑳ **Rhodes Memorial.** Rhodes served as prime minister of the Cape from 1890 to 1896. He made his fortune in the diamond rush at Kimberley, but his greatest dream was to forge a Cape–Cairo railway, a tangible symbol of British dominion in Africa. The classical-style granite memorial sits high on the slopes of Devil's Peak, on part of Rhodes's old estate, Groote Schuur. A mounted rider symbolizing energy faces north toward the continent for which Rhodes felt such passion. A bust of Rhodes dominates the temple—ironically, he's leaning on one hand as if he's about to nod off. ⊠ *Off Rhodes Dr., Rondebosch,* ☎ *021/ 689–9151.* 🎟 *Free.*

NEED A BREAK?	The **Rhodes Memorial Tea Garden,** tucked under towering pines behind the memorial, is a pleasant spot for tea or a light lunch. ☉ *Daily 9–5.*

④② **Scarborough.** The town is a tiny holiday community with one of the best beaches on the peninsula. Scarborough is becoming popular with artists and craftspeople, and you'll find their offerings exhibited at informal galleries. From Scarborough the road hugs the shoreline, snaking between the mountains and the crashing surf (this part of the shore is considered unsafe).

★ ④⑨ **Signal Hill.** Here the road swings around the shoulder of Lion's Head, then runs along the flank of Signal Hill. The views of the city below and Table Mountain are superb. The road ends at a parking lot overlooking Sea Point and all of Table Bay. Be careful around here, especially if it is deserted. There have been incidents of violent crime.

★ ③⑨ **Simonstown.** Because Simonstown is a naval base, and has been for many years, a large part of the seafront is out of bounds. Even worse, defense force personnel knock off at 4 during the week, when the single-lane road going out of Simonstown is stop-start traffic (as it is in the morning). Despite this, it is an attractive town with many lovely old buildings and is close to what are possibly the peninsula's best swimming beaches, Seaforth and Boulders. Simonstown has had a long association with the Royal Navy. It was here in 1795 that British troops landed before defeating the Dutch at the Battle of Muizenberg, and the town served as a base for the Royal Navy from 1814 to 1957, when the naval base was handed over to the South African Navy.

Jubilee Square, a dockside plaza that serves as the de facto town center, is just off the Main Road (St. George's Road). Next to the dock wall stands a sculpture of **Just Nuisance**, a Great Dane adopted as a mascot by the Royal Navy during World War II. Just Nuisance apparently liked his pint of beer and would accompany sailors on the train into Cape Town. He had the endearing habit of leading drunken sailors— and only sailors—that he found in the city back to the station in time to catch the last train. The navy went so far as to induct him into the service as an able seaman attached to the H.M.S. *Afrikander.* He died at the age of seven in April 1944 and was given a military funeral. Just below Jubilee Square is the newly built Simonstown Waterfront Centre with numerous artsy shops, including a Just Nuisance store where you can buy a present for your pooch back home.

NEED A
BREAK?

Berthas Restaurant (✉ Wharf's Rd., Simonstown, ☎ 021/786–2138) serves excellent meals overlooking the jetty, where charter boats take off for whale-watching (in season) and trips to Cape Point. The attached coffee shop has just as good a view and serves light lunches and teas.

Penguin Point Cafe (☎ 021/786–1758) has a huge veranda with views over False Bay. It serves hearty breakfasts, light lunches, teas, and dinner. There's a full bar, and it's a great place to watch the sun set—if you're sharp, you'll remember that you're facing east, not west, but don't let that deter you. False Bay sunsets are spectacular. Consisting mostly of reflected light, they are pastel pink, pale blue, lavender, and gold, as opposed to the more common red and orange variety.

50 **Tafelberg Road.** The road crosses the northern side of Table Mountain before ending at Devil's Peak. From the Kloof Nek intersection you can descend to Cape Town directly or return to Camps Bay and follow the coastal road back to the city. This route takes you through the beautiful seaside communities of Clifton (☞ Beaches, *below*) and Bantry Bay and then along the seaside promenade in Sea Point.

35 **Tokai Manor.** Built in 1795, this is one of the finest Cape Dutch homes in the country. Famed architect Louis Michel Thibault designed its facade. The homestead is reputedly haunted by a horseman who died when he tried to ride his horse down the curving front steps during a drunken revel. You can stop for a look, but the house is not open to the public.

47 **World of Birds.** Here you can walk through aviaries housing 450 species of indigenous and exotic birds, including eagles, vultures, penguins, and flamingos. No cages separate you from most of the birds, so you can get some pretty good photographs; however, the big raptors are kept behind fences. ✉ *Valley Rd., Hout Bay,* ☎ *021/790–2730,* ℻ *021/790–4839.* 💴 *R13.* 🕙 *Daily 9–6.*

OFF THE
BEATEN PATH

District Six Museum. Housed in the Buitenkant Methodist Church, this museum preserves the memory of one of Cape Town's most vibrant multicultural neighborhoods and of the district's destruction in one of the cruelest acts of the apartheid Nationalist government. District Six was proclaimed a white area in 1966 and existing residents were evicted from their homes, which were razed to make way for a white suburb. The people were forced to resettle in bleak, outlying areas on the Cape Flats and, by the 1970s, all the buildings, except churches and mosques, had been demolished. Huge controversy accompanied the proposed redevelopment of the area, and only a small housing component, Zonnebloem, and the campus of the Cape Technicon have been built, leaving much of the ground still bare—a grim reminder of the past. There are plans to bring former residents back into the area and reestablish the suburb; however, the old swinging District Six can never be re-created. The museum consists of street signs, photographs, life stories of the people who lived there, and a huge floor plan, where former residents can identify the site of their homes. ✉ *25A Buitenkant St., Cape Town,* ☎ *021/ 461–4735 or 021/465–8009.* 💴 *Donation suggested.* 🕙 *Mon.–Sat. 9–4.*

BEACHES

With panoramic views of mountains tumbling to the ocean, the sandy beaches of the Cape Peninsula are stunning and are a major draw for Capetonians and visitors alike. Beautiful as the beaches may be, don't expect to spend hours splashing in the surf. The water around Cape Town is very, very cold, but you get used to it. Beaches on the Atlantic are washed by the Benguela Current flowing up from the Antarctic, and in midsummer the water hovers around 10°C–15°C (50°F–60°F). The water on the False Bay side is usually 5°C (9°F) warmer. Cape beaches are renowned for their clean, snow-white powdery sand. Beachcombers will find every kind of beach to suit them, from intimate coves to sheltered bays and wild, wide beaches stretching forever. If you are looking for more tropical water temperatures, head for the warm Indian Ocean waters of KwaZulu-Natal (☞ Chapter 8) or the Garden Route (☞ Chapter 7).

The major factor that affects any day at a Cape beach is wind. In summer, howling southeasters, known as the Doctor, are all too common and can ruin a trip to the beach; during these gales you're better off at Clifton or Llandudno on the Atlantic side, or the sheltered but very small St. James Beach on the False Bay side, and maybe even the southern corner of Fish Hoek Beach, or one of the pools along Jagers Walk. Boulders and Seaforth are also often sheltered from the southeaster. However, not all Atlantic beaches are sheltered in a southeaster— you'll get blown out to sea at Camps Bay, while some False Bay beaches are absolutely wind-free.

Every False Bay community has its own beach, but most are not reviewed here. In comparison with Atlantic beaches, most of them are rather small and often crowded, being sandwiched between the sea and the commuter rail line, with Fish Hoek a major exception. South of Simonstown, the beaches tend to be more wild and less developed, except for the very popular Seaforth and Millers Point beaches. At many beaches, there may be powerful waves, strong undertow, and dangerous riptides. Lifeguards work the main beaches, but only on weekends and during school holidays, while many beaches are unpatrolled. Although it is nice to stroll along a lonely beach, remember it is risky to wander off on your own in a deserted area.

Atlantic Coast

The beaches below are listed from north to south and are marked on the Cape Peninsula map in the Exploring section.

Blouberg. Make the 25-km (16-mi) trip north from the city to the other side of Table Bay and you'll be rewarded with an exceptional (and the most famous) view of Cape Town and Table Mountain. It is divided into two parts: Big Bay, which hosts surfing and sailboarding contests; and Little Bay, better suited to sunbathers and families. It's frequently windy here, which is fine if you want to fly a kite but a nuisance otherwise. (Buy a brightly colored high-tech number at the Kite Shop in Victoria Wharf at the waterfront and relive your childhood.) Swim in front of the lifeguard club. The lawns of the Blue Peter Hotel are a favorite sunset cocktail spot, especially with tired boardsailers. ⊠ *Follow N1 north toward Paarl, and then R27 to Milnerton and Bloubergstrand.*

Clifton. This is where the "in" crowd comes to see and be seen. Some of the Cape's most desirable houses cling to the slopes above the beach, and elegant yachts often anchor in the calm water beyond the breakers. Granite outcroppings divide the beach into four segments, imaginatively known as First, Second, Third, and Fourth beaches. Fourth

Beach is popular with families, while the others support a strong social and singles scene. Swimming is reasonably safe here, although the undertow is strong and the water, again, freezing. Lifeguards are on duty. On weekends and in peak season Clifton can be a madhouse, and your chances of finding parking at these times are nil. If you plan to visit the beaches in midsummer, consider renting a scooter or motorcycle instead of a car (☞ Getting Around *in* Cape Town A to Z, *below*) or taking a shuttle from your hotel. ⊠ *Off Victoria Rd., Clifton. Hout Bay bus from OK Bazaars on Adderley St.*

Camps Bay. The spectacular western edge of Table Mountain, known as the Twelve Apostles, provides the backdrop for this long, sandy beach, which slopes gently to the water from a grassy verge. The surf is powerful and there are no lifeguards, but sunbathers can cool off in a tidal pool or under cool outdoor showers. The popular bars and restaurants of Camps Bay lie only yards away across Victoria Road. One drawback is the wind, which can blow hard here. ⊠ *Victoria Rd. Hout Bay bus from OK Bazaars on Adderley St.*

Llandudno. Die-hard fans return to this beach again and again, and who can blame them? Its setting, among giant boulders at the base of a mountain, is glorious, and sunsets here attract their own aficionados. The surf can be very powerful on the northern side of the beach (where you'll find all the surfers, of course), but the southern side is fine for a quick dip—and in this water that's all you'll want. Lifeguards are on duty on weekends and in season. If you come by bus, brace yourself for a long walk down (and back up) the mountain from the bus stop on the M6. Parking is a nightmare, but most hotels run shuttles during summer. ⊠ *Llandudno exit off M6 and follow signs. Hout Bay bus from OK Bazaars on Adderley St.*

Sandy Bay. Backed by wild dunes, Cape Town's unofficial nudist beach is also one of its prettiest. Sunbathers can hide among rocky coves or frolic on a long stretch of sandy beach. Shy nudists will appreciate its isolation, 20 minutes on foot from the nearest parking area in Llandudno. Wind, however, can be a problem: If you're caught in the buff when the southeaster starts to blow, you're in for a painful sandblasting. Getting here by bus means a very long walk going down and up the mountain; parking is very difficult. ⊠ *Llandudno exit off M6 and follow signs to Sandy Bay. Hout Bay bus from OK Bazaars on Adderley St.*

Hout Bay. This beach appears to have it all: a knockout view of the mountains, gentle surf, and easy access to the restaurants and bars of Mariner's Wharf. The reality is not quite so stunning, with the town's industrial fishing harbor and its mini–oil slicks and other waste products nearby. ⊠ *Off the M6, Hout Bay. Hout Bay bus from OK Bazaars on Adderley St.*

Long Beach. This may be the most impressive beach on the peninsula, a vast expanse of white sand stretching 6½ km (4 mi) from the base of Chapman's Peak to Kommetjie. It's also one of the wildest and least populated, backed by a lagoon and private nature reserve. Because of the wind, it attracts horseback riders and walkers rather than sunbathers and the surfing is excellent. There is no bus service. ⊠ *Off M6, Noordhoek.*

False Bay

Muizenberg. Once the fashionable resort of South African high society, this long, sandy beach has lost much of its glamour and now appeals to families and beginner surfers. A tacky pavilion houses a swimming pool, water slides, toilets, changing rooms, and snack shops. The beach is lined with colorful bathing boxes of the type once popular at British resorts. Lifeguards are on duty, and the sea is shallow and reasonably safe. ⊠ *Cape Metro train on Simonstown line.*

Fish Hoek. With the southern corner protected from the southeaster by Elsies Peak, this sandy beach attracts retirees, who appreciate the calm, clear water—it may be the safest bathing beach in the Cape. The middle and northern end of the beach is also popular with catamaran sailors and sailboarders, who often stage regattas offshore. Jager Walk, a pathway that runs along the rocky coastline, begins at the beach's southern end.

DINING

By Myrna
Robins

Cape Town is the culinary capital of South Africa. Nowhere else in the country is the populace so discerning about food, and nowhere else is there such a wide selection of restaurants. Western culinary history here dates back more than 300 years—Cape Town was founded specifically to grow food—and that heritage is reflected in the city's cuisine. A number of restaurants operate in historic town houses and 18th-century wine estates.

Many restaurants are crowded in high season, so it's best to book in advance whenever possible. With the exception of the fancier restaurants in hotels—where a jacket is required—the dress code in Cape Town is casual (but no shorts). For a description of South African culinary terms, *see* Pleasures and Pastimes *in* Chapter 1. For price ranges, *see* Dining *in* Smart Travel Tips A to Z.

City Bowl

$$$$ ✕ **Atlantic Grill Room.** This flagship restaurant of the luxurious Table Bay Hotel (☞ Lodging, *below*) holds a prime position at the city's waterfront development. The room is decorated with updated colonial elegance, and seating on the terrace has stunning views of working docks against a mountain backdrop. Executive chef Marcus Koessler presents menus that combine elements from Asia, Europe, and California with local ingredients like crayfish and ostrich. First courses favor seafood, but eggplant rolled in rice paper with shiitake mushrooms also makes a great starter. Main-course specialties include roast rack of lacquered lamb paired with elephant garlic and crisp potato and a tower of seared tuna with a warm fennel salad. Artistically plated desserts offer light, fruity creations and heritage Cape favorites like brandied pudding. The extensive wine list presents a vast choice of the best of the Cape. ⊠ *Table Bay Hotel, Prince Alfred Breakwater, V&A Waterfront,* ☎ *021/406–5688. AE, DC, MC, V.*

$$$$ ✕ **Blue Danube.** Chef Thomas Sinn gives free rein to his considerable talent on the ground floor of a tall, turn-of-the-century house on the city perimeter. The tastes of his Austrian homeland are apparent in updated classics from Western and Central Europe. Complimentary appetizers precede starter dishes like smoked *kudu* (venison) lasagna with creamed spinach, or duck liver parfait with smoked duck breast. Robust main courses include lamb knuckle in red wine with pureed potato and onion, ostrich fillet with a cashew nut crust, and Viennese *tafelspitz* (beef simmered in broth, then sliced) with horseradish. For dessert you might choose apple strudel with cinnamon ice cream or dark and white Belgian chocolate mousse, or a platter of local and imported cheeses. Unhurried, professional service and a carefully selected wine list are hallmarks here. ⊠ *102 New Church St., Tamboerskloof,* ☎ *021/423–3624. AE, DC, MC, V. Closed Sun. No lunch Mon. or Sat.*

Cape Town Dining and Lodging

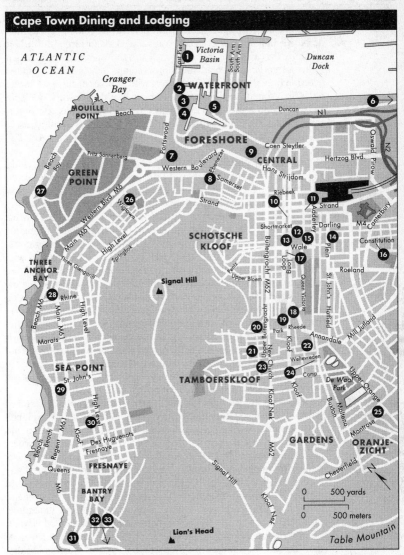

Dining

Atlantic Grill Room, **1**
Blue Danube, **23**
Bukhara, **15**
Cape Colony Restaurant, **22**
Floris Smit Huijs, **13**
Nando's Tasca, **2**
Ocean Basket, **18**
Panama Jack's, **6**
Quay West, **3**
Rozenhof, **19**
San Marco, **28**
Wangthai, **26**
Yellow Pepper Deli and Eaterie, **17**

Lodging

Best Western Cape Suites Hotel, **16**
Breakwater Lodge, **7**
The Cape Grace Hotel, **3**
Cape Sun Inter-Continental, **11**
City Lodge, **9**
Clarens Manor, **30**
Cullinan Cape Town Waterfront, **5**
Ellerman House, **31**
Holiday Inn Garden Court–Greenmarket Square, **12**
La Splendida, **27**

Lady Hamilton Hotel, **24**
Metropole Hotel, **10**
Mijlof Manor Hotel, **20**
Monkey Valley, **32**
Mount Nelson, **22**
Peninsula All Suites Hotel, **29**
Place on the Bay, **33**
Protea Victoria Junction, **8**
Table Bay Hotel, **1**
Townhouse Hotel, **14**
Underberg Guest House, **21**
Victoria & Alfred Hotel, **4**
Villa Belmonte, **25**

$$$$ ✕ **Bukhara.** Set above a pedestrian mall lined with antiques shops and stalls, this hugely popular restaurant presents delectable and authentic North Indian fare. Even red walls and dark furniture do little to minimize the cavernous interior, which also showcases an open kitchen. Delicious garlic nan bread starts proceedings, which could include a selection from the tandoor oven, along with a choice of curries. Chicken tikka, in a tomato and cashew nut gravy, is addictive stuff, while the lamb vindaloo is incendiary. Vegetarians have a delicious selection to contemplate. Go in a small group and mix and match menu items. ⊠ *33 Church St.,* ☎ *021/424–0000. Reservations essential. AE, DC, MC, V. Closed Sun.*

$$$$ ✕ **Cape Colony Restaurant.** Tall bay windows, a high domed ceiling, and a giant trompe-l'oeil mural—an inventive evocation of Table Mountain in the days of yore—are a befitting setting in the city's most historic and unashamedly colonial hotel. Ingredients from southern Africa, Asia, and the Mediterranean along with flavor-sparked touches of Cape Malay add up to the ultimate in fusion fare. Both springbok (venison) and crocodile appear as smoked delicacies on the starter menu. Other outstanding appetizers include ostrich carpaccio sparked with tandoori spices and roasted pear and Camembert tortellini with red cabbage. Karoo lamb, both cutlet and noisette, are served with a delicious vegetable tian topped with tabbouleh. Other main courses include honey-roasted duck with Asian greens; beef fillet with a potato feta galette; and risotto with roasted butternut squash and arugula, finished with sautéed mushrooms and truffle oil. Visually stunning desserts include ginger crème brûlée with biscotti and lemon and passion-fruit tart. A pricey but authoritative wine list offers the best South African vintages supplemented by French champagnes. ⊠ *Orange St., Gardens,* ☎ *021/423–1000. Reservations essential. AE, DC, MC, V.*

$$$$ ✕ **Floris Smit Huijs.** This appealing restaurant occupies a restored 18th-century town house in the city center and draws a devoted lunch crowd of office workers and gourmets. The menus reflect Asian and European influences gathered during the extensive travels of owners Steve Moncrieff and Piero Romero, but African emphasis, particularly in the form of game and local seafood, is also apparent. Cape Malay chicken salad with garlic, ginger, and coriander is a perennial and popular starter, while many regulars stay with one of the colorful and flavorful vegetarian pastas, which come in two sizes at lunchtime. Rack of lamb is teamed with a blue cheese and thyme sauce, while venison medallions are perched on a dense prune and port game sauce. A small dessert list stars an inspired combination of chocolate millefeuilles with crème brûlée and crème de cacao. The wine list is small but carefully chosen. Street parking is a nightmare at lunch, but there is a garage one block up the hill. ⊠ *55 Church St.,* ☎ *021/423–3414. Reservations essential. AE, DC, MC, V. Closed Sun. and mid-July–mid-Aug. No lunch Sat.*

$$$$ ✕ **Quay West.** The restaurant of the Cape Grace Hotel (☞ Lodging, ★   *below*) overlooks the bascule bridge gateway to the new international yacht basin at the waterfront. The decor is cool, uncluttered, and inviting, with comfortable wicker chairs and crisp table settings. The cuisine is contemporary and delectable, with quality local produce given star treatment. You could start with langoustine samosas with a melon and balsamic reduction or carpaccio of springbok (venison) loin with apple and walnut pesto. Main courses include an excellent breast of guinea fowl with wild mushroom ravioli, a beef fillet with oxtail praline paired with creamed leeks and rosti, or a sophisticated seasonal pasta. Dessert can be as simple as a fresh fruit platter or as inventive as the Thai spiced ice cream and green-tea anglaise. The carefully compiled wine list is well annotated. A shorter lunch menu is less expensive, and breakfast is a bargain. ⊠ *Cape Grace Hotel, West Quay, V&A Waterfront,* ☎ *021/418–0520. AE, DC, MC, V.*

$$$$ ✕ **Rozenhof.** Within easy walking distance of the hotels in Gardens,
★ this late-18th-century town house offers stylish fare and one of the best wine selections in town. Yellowwood ceilings and brass chandeliers provide historical Cape touches, and works by local artists adorn the walls. The menu is inspired by Asia and the Mediterranean and supplemented with time-honored local dishes. Summer salads make delectable first courses, and the cheese soufflé with herbed mustard cream has become a classic. Linefish comes with a choice of sauces, and crispy duck is teamed with fig and marsala sauce. Layers of local Gorgonzola and mascarpone paired with preserved figs and a glass of port make a savory-sweet alternative to contemporary Cape-style and Italian desserts. ⊠ *18 Kloof St.,* ☎ *021/424–1968. AE, DC, MC, V. Closed Sun. No lunch Sat.*

$$$–$$$$ ✕ **Panama Jack's.** In this raw-timber structure in the heart of the docks, the music is loud, the tables are crowded, and the decor is nonexistent, but nowhere in town will you find bigger crayfish. Choose one from the large, open tanks and combine it with other shellfish in a generous seafood platter if you like. You can also stick to less expensive fare like mussels, calamari, and local fish. It can be difficult to find this place at night, so you may want to come for lunch if it's your first visit. ⊠ *Royal Yacht Club basin, off Goliath Rd., Docks,* ☎ *021/447–3992. AE, DC, MC, V. No lunch Sat.*

$$$ ✕ **Nando's Tasca.** Hemmed in by a plethora of ethnic and fast-food restaurants, this spot in the heart of the waterfront offers authentic tastes of Portugal's robust peasant cuisine. The restaurant is noisy, cheerful, and informal, and the bar counter, blue wall, tiles, and banners contribute to the atmosphere of a taberna Portugesa. When the so-called Doctor—a strong southeaster—prevails, avoid the tables near the door. In balmy weather, sit outside and watch maritime activities against the backdrop of Table Mountain. Portions are generous: Warm Madeira bread with garlic butter makes a good accompaniment to first courses of chicken livers or giblets, *chourico* (spicy Portuguese sausage), or mussels in red wine sauce. Calamari comes in various guises, and there's a good selection of other seafood and of Portuguese beef dishes. If you like your food fiery, order chicken or prawns peri-peri, but stipulate that your order be basted with the chili sauce during grilling, so that it soaks into the meat and becomes fiery. Desserts are run-of-the-mill. The wine list includes a few Portuguese labels. ⊠ *154 V&A Waterfront,* ☎ *021/419–3009. AE, DC, MC, V.*

$$ ✕ **Wangthai.** Thai restaurants are flourishing in South African cities, and this is one of the best. *Satays* (grilled meats with a spicy peanut dip) make a good starter, as do prawns wrapped in rice pastry with sweet chili sauce. Tom Kha Gai is an aromatic chicken and coconut milk broth scented with *galangal,* a type of ginger. Colorful stir-fries combine chicken, pork, or beef with coriander leaves and sweet basil or the fire of roasted chilies. Pungent red and green curries are tempered by coconut milk and mounds of sticky rice. The restaurant, which recently relocated to the city perimeter, has acquired an open-plan kitchen and sports an attractive Asian decor. ⊠ *105 Paramount Pl., Main Rd., Green Point,* ☎ *021/439–6164. AE, DC, MC, V. No lunch Sat.*

$ ✕ **Ocean Basket.** On restaurant mile along the city fringe, this informal venue has few competitors in the field of bargain-priced, ocean-fresh, well-cooked seafood. You can sit facing the street or find a table in the courtyard at the back. Calamari—stewed, curried, pickled, or in a salad—features prominently among the starters. The catch of the day is listed on the many blackboards lining the mustard-yellow walls, but delicately flavored hake-and-chips is the budget draw card at R16.

Tartare, chili, and garlic sauces come on the side, and Greek salads are authentic. Desserts are average. ⊠ *75 Kloof St.,* ☎ *021/422–0322. Reservations not accepted. AE, DC, MC, V. No lunch Sun.*

$ ✕ **Yellow Pepper Deli and Eaterie.** For good, home-cooked food at bargain prices, this popular outlet has few rivals. Diners can order from a chalkboard menu or select what they fancy from dishes displayed behind a glass counter. Sophisticated Greek *mezes* (appetizers) and Mediterranean salads precede hearty dishes like vegetarian lasagna, bobotie, chicken and pasta bake, and peasant sausage casserole. Arrive early to claim a portion of malva pudding, an outstanding version of this traditional Cape baked dessert—fluffy, syrupy, and topped with cream. Try to sit in the high-ceiling, artsy interior: Outdoor diners suffer from the noise and fumes of traffic. ⊠ *138 Long St.,* ☎ *021/24–9250. AE, DC, MC, V. Closed Sun. No dinner Mon.–Tues.*

Atlantic Coast

$$$$ ✕ **Blues.** Doors open to frame an inviting vista of palms, sand, and azure sea from the balcony of this popular restaurant in Camps Bay. The mood and menu are Californian, the clientele young and sophisticated. Appetizers inspired by Thailand and the Mediterranean are juxtaposed with local smoked salmon trout and West Coast mussels. The pasta is deservedly popular, and the quality of fresh line- and shellfish is virtually guaranteed. Crisp stir-fried vegetables add color to generous portions that are attractively presented. For dessert, try chocolate brownies or sticky toffee pudding with ginger ice cream. ⊠ *The Promenade, Victoria Rd., Camps Bay,* ☎ *021/438–2040. Reservations essential. AE, DC, MC, V.*

$$$ ✕ **Kronendal.** It lacks a sea view, but its classic Cape architecture and history will command your attention. Hout Bay's most beautiful Cape Dutch manor house comes with a friendly 19th-century ghost called Elsa, who has a table set for her and her long-lost lover every night. The restaurant, operated by three Austrian brothers, presents a menu that includes touches of their homeland cuisine, along with an Occidental cosmopolitan selection. Red meat is treated with respect, and the chef makes a good classic consomme. Alfresco lunches and teas are served in the courtyard, but the dinner menu is usually a better bet. ⊠ *Main Rd., Hout Bay,* ☎ *021/790–1970. AE, DC, MC, V. No lunch Mon.–Thurs.*

$$$ ✕ **San Marco.** Restaurants open and close in Cape Town with alarming speed, but this Italian institution in Sea Point is a happy exception, a meeting place for generations of diners since it first opened its doors as a gelateria. Come here not for the decor but for the consistency and authenticity of dishes that are all cooked to order. Start with superb grilled calamari; then move to homemade pasta or one of the veal dishes—escalopes cooked with sage and white wine are especially good. If one of the less common Cape linefish such as elf (shad) is offered, don't miss it. Finish with a selection of the house's renowned ice creams and sorbets, which are dressed with a splash of liqueur. ⊠ *92 Main Rd., Sea Point,* ☎ *021/439–2758. Reservations essential. AE, DC, MC, V. Closed Tues. and 1 month in midwinter. No lunch Mon.–Sat.*

Southern Suburbs

$$$$ ✕ **Au Jardin.** Tucked away in a corner of the historic Vineyard hotel
★   in Newlands (☞ *below*), complete with fountain and views of Table Mountain, talented French chef Christophe Dehosse and his team imbue classic French cuisine with subtle Cape and Mediterranean accents. Appetizers might include panfried quail salad with toasted almonds or carpaccio of fresh Cape salmon with walnut oil and coriander.

Dining
Africa Cafe, **3**
Au Jardin, **5**
Bertha's Restaurant and Coffeehouse, **17**
Blues, **1**
Brass Bell, **15**
Buitenverwachting, **11**
Constantia Uitsig, **12**
Emily's Bistro, **2**
Jonkershuis, **10**
Kronendal, **20**
La Colombe, **13**
Novelli at the Cellars, **6**
Parks, **9**

Lodging
Alphen Hotel, **8**
Bay Hotel, **1**
Boulders Beach Guest House, **19**
British Hotel Apartments, **18**
Cellars-Hohenort Country House Hotel, **6**
Constantia Uitsig, **12**
De Ouderkraal Hotel, **21**
Koornhoop Manor Guest House, **4**
Quayside Lodge, **16**
Palm House, **7**
Steenberg Country Hotel, **14**
The Vineyard, **5**

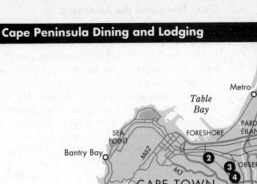

Cape Peninsula Dining and Lodging

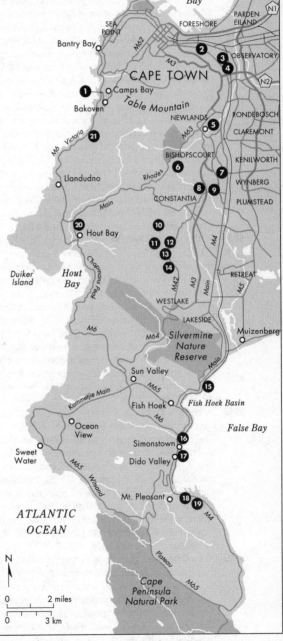

Entrées often include choices such as local linefish teamed with braised fennel and a pernod sauce or paired with cabbage and crispy bacon. Guinea fowl, beef fillet, and lamb are also given stellar Gallic treatment. For dessert try the banana and pistachio parfait with caramel and rum-poached bananas. There's a menu dégustation, and the lighter à la carte menu at lunch is a good value. The wine list presents the best of the Cape, but there are also French labels for conservative tastes. ⊠ *Vineyard Hotel, Colinton Rd., Claremont,* ☎ *021/683–1520. AE, DC, MC, V. Closed Sun. No lunch Sat. or Mon.*

$$$$ ✕ **Buitenverwachting.** On a historic wine estate in Constantia, this su-
★   perb restaurant is consistently rated among the country's top 10. Window-side tables provide views of the vineyards sloping up toward the mountains. Executive chef Edgar Osojnik continues the tradition of presenting meticulously prepared dishes with artistic flair. Imaginative starters include house-smoked duck breast and duck liver parfait dressed with raspberry walnut vinaigrette and served with bacon brioche or pecorino gratinated crayfish with a trio of tapenades. Look for dishes based on local seafood and Karoo lamb and game. Try pan-fried kabeljou with pepperonata, ricotta and pine-nut ravioli with saffron sauce, or grilled loin of lamb au jus with a baked olive risotto. Dessert masterpieces include a banana soufflé with praline ice cream set on a pool of passion-fruit coulis. ⊠ *Klein Constantia Rd., Constantia,* ☎ *021/794–3522. Reservations essential. AE, DC, MC, V. Closed Sun.–Mon. and July. No lunch Sat.*

$$$$ ✕ **Constantia Uitsig.** This restaurant in a restored farmstead attracts
★   a large, loyal following. Reserve a table on the enclosed veranda for tremendous views of the mountains. The menu is a pricy and harmonious blend of northern Italian and Provençal cuisines. Tomato tart with basil and fontina sings with Mediterranean flavor, as does the excellent homemade pasta. For something more substantial, there's wild duck braised with mushrooms in red wine, teamed with mashed potatoes or polenta, grilled springbok (venison) served with honey and lemon sauce, or chef Frank Swainston's classic butter-tender Florentine tripe braised in tomato-and-vegetable sauce. From a quartet of desserts, heart-shaped homemade cheese set on a berry coulis is recommended. ⊠ *Spaanschemat River Rd., Constantia,* ☎ *021/794–4480. Reservations essential. AE, DC, MC, V. No lunch Mon.*

$$$$ ✕ **Emily's Bistro.** In a down-market neighborhood minutes from the city, this unpretentious boîte serves substantial fare with artistic flair. The flamboyant menu highlights innovative dishes with Cape Malay accents, as well as updated versions of traditional South African cooking. A terrine of ox tongue and oxtail with grape marmalade and spiced sultanas could precede deboned quail with a farce of duck liver and Kalahari truffles on a wild mushroom and demiglace sauce. Finish with pumpkin dumplings in orange sauce with almond flakes, paired with passion-fruit ice cream and brandy snaps. ⊠ *77 Roodebloem Rd., Woodstock,* ☎ *021/448–2366. AE, DC, MC, V. Closed Sun.–Mon. No lunch Tues. or Sat.*

$$$$ ✕ **La Colombe.** The Uitsig farm is home to a comparative newcomer that has quickly attracted devotees of Provençal fare. The walls and woodwork of this small restaurant are painted sunshine yellow and sky blue, and French doors in the dining room open onto a courtyard. The menu is chalked on one blackboard, a limited wine list on another. Youthful chef Franck Dangereux transforms local produce into a menu that sings of his native French province: Expect flavorful renderings of *pan bagna* (salad niçoise sandwiched into French bread), gazpacho enhanced with crayfish and fresh mint, or warm potato and French sausage salad with a red wine jus to precede items like slow-cooked duck leg with roast potatoes and a confit of garlic, or guinea-fowl breast stuffed with black olive pulp and teamed with basil sauce. Cape line-fish is given star treatment and paired with a choice of sauces. Desserts range from fruity sorbets to puff pastry filled with caramelized pears on vanilla toffee sauce. ⊠ *Uitsig Farm, Spaanschemat River Rd., Constantia,* ☏ *021/794–2390. Reservations essential. AE, DC, MC, V. Closed Tues. No dinner Sun.*

$$$$ ✕ **Novelli at the Cellars.** Classic table settings and highly professional service complement artfully presented fare at this restaurant in the historic Cellars-Hohenhort Hotel in Constantia (☞ *below*). Renowned London-based chef and restaurateur Jean-Christophe Novelli has put his stamp on the dinner menu with earthy Gallic creations like pot-roasted guinea fowl paired with a wild mushroom and truffle bouillon and braised cabbage. Lighter options include prettily presented starters such as home-smoked salmon with cardamom orange dressing and an herb salad or local black mussels, which come baked with ginger, lemongrass, and coconut. Delectable desserts include a pear tart Tatin with bourbon vanilla ice cream. Diners are also offered a three-course table d'hôte dinner menu, which changes daily. The wine list has won several awards. A sister restaurant, the Cape Malay Kitchen, presents table d'hôte heritage fare. ⊠ *15 Hohenort Ave., Constantia,* ☏ *021/794–2137. Reservations essential. AE, DC, MC, V.*

$$$$ ✕ **Parks.** This restored Victorian villa in Constantia has been jam-packed since it opened three years ago. The reasons are twofold: The elegant decor is convivial, not intimidating, and Michael Olivier's zesty contemporary cuisine strikes the right chord with local and out-of-town patrons. Starters of gravlax of salmon trout with horseradish cream and pickled ginger, and deep-fried Cajun potato skins with chili jam and tomato-cilantro salsa are typical of the eclectic menu. Ostrich fillet is served with a confit of beetroot, potato rosti, and a prune and wine sauce while chargrilled beef fillet is paired with pommes frîtes and onions with a red wine, mustard-paprika sauce. For dessert don't pass up a rose-scented crème caramel with a spiral tuile and white-chocolate rose leaves. ⊠ *114 Constantia Rd., Constantia,* ☏ *021/797–8202. Reservations essential. AE, DC, MC, V. Closed Sun. No lunch Sat.*

$$$ ✕ **Africa Cafe.** Locals and tourists crowd this Observatory restaurant, the country's first to serve indigenous dishes from across the continent. Multicolored cloths and stunning hand-glazed crockery brighten the ocher interior of the old terrace house, complementing an equally vibrant cuisine. Fresh fruit cocktails accompany a communal feast, with dishes originating from Ethiopia to Zambia, Kenya to Angola. Along with a tasty mélange of patties, dips, puffs, and pastries accompanied by an addictive chili dip, dishes like Malawi chicken macadamia and *Sik-Sik wat,* an Ethiopian lamb stew, are favorite main choices. Vegetarians applaud the Senegalese stuffed papaya. Most diners choose the R80 set menu. Parking can be tricky along narrow streets. ⊠ *213 Lower Main Rd., Observatory,* ☏ *021/447–9553. AE, DC, MC, V. Closed Sun. No lunch.*

$$$ ✕ **Jonkershuis.** This establishment offers classic Cape hospitality in a 19th-century building adjoining the gracious manor house at Groot Constantia, the Cape's oldest wine estate. Fresh linefish and roast loin of lamb keep company on the menu with classic bobotie-spiced beef mince studded with dried fruit and nut slivers and topped with a savory baked custard, and *smoorsnoek,* a popular Cape fish braised with onion, potato, and chili and served with baked sweet potatoes in fresh orange sauce. The traditional chicken pie is made from a recipe handed down through generations of Dutch settlers. If you want to taste all of these dishes, ask for a Cape sampler. Jonkershuis also serves hearty breakfasts and light refreshments. ⊠ *Groot Constantia Estate, Main Rd., Constantia,* ☏ *021/794–6255. Reservations essential. AE, DC, MC. No dinner Sun.–Mon.*

False Bay

$$$ ✕ **Bertha's Restaurant and Coffeehouse.** Alfresco dining at this recently opened waterfront venue offers a feast for both palate and eye. Boating activities from the naval dockyard on one side and yacht club on the other enliven vistas of sparkling water against a mountain backdrop. The contemporary menu makes good use of local produce, such as Atlantic black mussels, which come in three guises as starters, and snoek pate, which is paired with watermelon preserve. Although standard fare of steak and ribs is popular, seafood, pasta, and a choice of chicken sates make tempting alternatives. From a small dessert list, the lemon tart with mascarpone cream cheese gets rave reviews. Lunch here is popular, so it's a good idea to reserve in advance. ⊠ *1 Wharf Rd., Simons Town,* ☎ *021/786–2138. AE, DC, MC, V.*

$$ ✕ **Brass Bell.** Whether diners choose to eat in the main restaurant, in the cabin, on the terrace, or in the gazebo, they enjoy views of False Bay, frolicking surfers, and fishing boats heading for the harbor. This cheerful, informal place can get crowded and noisy. There's a choice of three menus—the main restaurant presents a more formal menu, while the other areas share a lighter, more casual menu—both of which offer good value for money. The emphasis is on fish and seafood, but vegetarians and carnivores alike will find sufficient items to please them. The fare is mostly straightforward, enlivened by a few traditional Cape and Mediterranean dishes. ⊠ *Waterfront, Kalk Bay,* ☎ *021/788–5456. Reservations essential in season. AE, DC, MC, V.*

LODGING

Finding lodging in Cape Town can be a nightmare during high season (December–January), as much of the more reasonable accommodation is booked up. It is worth traveling between April and August, if you can, to take advantage of the "secret season" discounts. If you arrive in Cape Town without a reservation, head for **Cape Town Tourism's Information Centre** (☞ Contacts and Resources *in* Cape Town A to Z, *below*), which has a helpful accommodation desk.

Hotels in the city center are a good option if you're here on business. During the day the historic city center is a vibrant place. At night, though, it's shut up tight; night owls may prefer a hotel amid the nonstop action of the redeveloped waterfront. Hotels and B&Bs in the southern suburbs, especially Constantia, offer unrivaled beauty and tranquillity and make an ideal base if you're exploring the peninsula. You'll need a car, though, and should plan on 15–30 minutes to get into town. Atlantic Coast hotels provide the closest thing in Cape Town to a beach-vacation atmosphere, in spite of the cold ocean waters.

Keep in mind that international flights from the United States and Europe arrive in the morning and return flights depart in the evening. Since most hotels have an 11 AM checkout, you may have to wait for a room if you've just arrived; if you're leaving, you will be hauled kicking and screaming out of your room hours before your flight. Most hotels will try to accommodate you, but they often have no choice in peak season. Some of the larger hotels have residents-only lounges where you can spend the hours awaiting your flight. Note that many small luxury accommodations either do not permit children or have minimum age restrictions. It's a good idea to inquire in advance if this will be an issue.

Cape Town is regarded as one of the top backpackers' destinations in the world, with more than 50 hostels. Contact **Backpacker Tourism, South Africa** (BTSA; ☎ 021/564–1688) for information.

The most reliable source of good B&B establishments is **Bed & Breakfast Bureau** (☎ 021/794–0030, FAX 021/794–0031). Or try the **Portfolio of Places** (☎ 011/880–3414, FAX 011/788–4802) brochure.If you don't like tiptoeing around someone's house, or you want to save money, consider taking a fully furnished apartment, especially if you're staying two or more weeks. Contact **Holiday Booking Services** (✉ Box 514, Cape Town 8000, ☎ 021/424–3693, FAX 021/424–1907), with more than 500 high-quality, furnished, self-catering apartments on its books.

Waterfront Villas, Cape Town's first and only guest street with an entire little community of houses to rent, are unusual, trendy, classy, and quite charming and are near the harbor, as the name implies. There are 30 beautifully restored, small, self-catering houses, with daily housekeeping services. ✉ *1 Loader St., Cape Town 8000,* ☎ *021/409–2500,* FAX *021/418–6082. AE, DC, MC, V.*

For price ranges, *see* Lodging *in* Smart Travel Tips A to Z.

City Bowl

$$$$ 🏨 **Cape Sun Inter-Continental.** One of the top hotels in the city center, this 32-story tower dominates the skyline and is near the Cape Town Tourism office and St. George's Mall. The lobby, with marble floors, a paneled ceiling, and green-marble pillars, sets the tone for the hotel. Rooms reflect a Cape Dutch influence: They are done in pale yellows and blues and light- and dark-wood paneling and are decorated with Cape Dutch furniture and line drawings of Cape Dutch estates. Guests can opt for a room facing the sea or Table Mountain. Both views are spectacular, but request a room on a high floor—the sea view from lower rooms is partially obstructed by other buildings. ✉ *Strand St. (Box 4532), Cape Town 8000,* ☎ *021/488–5100,* FAX *021/423–8875. 350 rooms. 2 restaurants, bar, room service, sauna, exercise room, travel services. AE, DC, MC, V.*

$$$$ 🏨 **Mount Nelson.** This distinctive pink landmark is the grande dame
★ of Cape Town. Since it opened its doors in 1899 to accommodate passengers of the Union-Castle steamships, it has been the focal point of Cape social life. Its guest book reads like a *Who's Who* of South African history, and it's still the favorite locale for Cape Town society functions. Named by *Tatler* and *Harpers & Queen* magazines as one of the best hotels in the world, it retains an old-fashioned charm and gentility that other luxury hotels often lack. High tea is served in the lounge, to piano accompaniment; the Grill Room offers a nightly dinner dance; and the staff almost outnumbers the guests. The hotel stands at the top of Government Avenue, but, surrounded as it is by 7 acres of manicured gardens, it might as well be in the country. For peak season, December–March, it's advisable to book a year in advance. ✉ *76 Orange St., Cape Town 8001,* ☎ *021/423–1000,* FAX *021/424–7472. 226 rooms. 3 restaurants, bar, 2 pools, exercise room, 2 tennis courts, squash. AE, DC, MC, V.*

$$$ 🏨 **Best Western Cape Suites Hotel.** This is a village-style hotel, with low buildings and adjoining individual units, 5 minutes from the center of Cape Town, near Parliament, and a 15-minute walk from the waterfront. Comfortably luxurious, each suite has a fully equipped kitchen, a plus if you're traveling as a family. Rooms are spacious and pleasantly furnished. Some rooms have mountain views, and others look into the city. Although it's on a corner site, the hotel is well insulated, so traffic noise is not a major problem; inner rooms tend to be quieter. If you have a car, you can park it virtually outside your room. A free shuttle takes guests to popular sights within about 13 km (8 mi) of the hotel, for example to Clifton beach. ✉ *Constitution and de Villiers Sts.*

(Box 51085, Waterfront), Cape Town 8002, ☎ *021/461–0727,* FAX *021/462–4389. 126 rooms. 2 restaurants, bar, 2 pools, exercise room, recreation room, free parking. AE, DC, MC, V.*

$$$ 🏨 **Villa Belmonte.** In a quiet residential neighborhood on the slopes above the city, this small guest house offers privacy and luxury in an attractive Dutch Revival residence. Owners Tabea and Cliff Jacobs have sought to create the feeling of an Italian villa through the use of marbling, molded ceilings, and natural wood floors. Wide verandas command superb views of the city, Table Mountain, and Devil's Peak. Rooms, each with air-conditioning and decorated according to a theme, make effective use of colorful draperies, wicker furniture, and small-pane windows. It's a 20-minute walk to the city center. ⊠ *33 Belmont Ave., Oranjezicht 8001,* ☎ *021/462–1576,* FAX *021/462–1579. 14 rooms. Restaurant, bar, room service, pool. CP. AE, DC, MC, V.*

$$ 🏨 **Holiday Inn Garden Court–Greenmarket Square.** Facing historic Greenmarket Square, this minimum-service hotel has one of the best locations in the city, especially for those who don't have a car. All rooms were recently refurbished and have cable TV and air-conditioning. Mountain-facing rooms overlooking the square are pleasant, but the dawn chorus of vendors setting up their stalls may drive you to distraction. The outdoor section of the restaurant, Cycles on the Square, is a popular choice with great views of the market. Parking is a major headache in this part of town. ⊠ *10 Greenmarket Sq. (Box 3775), Cape Town 8000,* ☎ *021/423–2040,* FAX *021/423–3664. 170 rooms. Restaurant, bar. AE, DC, MC, V.*

$$ 🏨 **Mijlof Manor Hotel.** The Mijlof is a comfortable retreat from the city center (15 minutes away on foot). In a residential neighborhood below Signal Hill, this mid-range hotel is built around a 1710 Tamboerskloof farmhouse, most of which is concealed now by a modern wing. Cape Dutch–style rooms are large and well equipped. The wood-paneled bar is a popular watering hole. ⊠ *2A Milner Rd., Tamboerskloof, Cape Town 8001,* ☎ *021/426–1476,* FAX *021/422–2046. 70 rooms. Restaurant, 2 bars, room service, pool, beauty salon. AE, DC, MC, V.*

$$ 🏨 **Townhouse Hotel.** Its proximity to government buildings and its easy-going atmosphere (not to mention extremely competitive rates) make the Townhouse a popular choice. Rooms are decorated in gentle pastels with soft, warm curtaining. Request a view of the mountain. There's a free shuttle to the Waterfront and the Southern Suburbs. ⊠ *60 Corporation St. (Box 5053), Cape Town 8000,* ☎ *021/465–7050,* FAX *021/465–3891. 104 rooms. Restaurant, bar, room service, health club. AE, DC, MC, V.*

$$ 🏨 **Underberg Guest House.** In a restored Victorian farmhouse in Tam-
★   boerskloof, this guest house caters primarily to businesspeople, who appreciate the privacy and location, a 20-minute walk from the city center. The rooms are airy and light, thanks to high ceilings and large windows, and have an elegance seldom found in conventional hotels. Each room has a a TV, minibar, and tea/coffeemaker. ⊠ *6 Tamboerskloof Rd., Tamboerskloof, Cape Town 8001,* ☎ *021/426–2262,* FAX *021/424–4059. 10 rooms, 1 suite. Bar, dining room. BP. AE, DC, MC, V.*

$ 🏨 **Lady Hamilton Hotel.** You get both good value and an excellent location at this hotel on a peaceful residential street in Gardens, 15 minutes on foot from the city center. Rooms are attractive and bright, decorated with blond wood furniture and African-print bedspreads. ⊠ *10 Union St., Gardens, Cape Town 8001,* ☎ *021/423–3888,* FAX *021/423–7788. 52 rooms. Restaurant, bar, room service, pool. AE, DC, MC, V.*

$ 🏨 **Metropole Hotel.** More than 100 years old and showing it a bit, this basic hotel in the center of town has probably seen it all. The lobby centers on a teak-paneled elevator, the second-oldest in Cape Town.

Unfortunately, standard rooms are very dull and nondescript, but the price is right. The Mandarin suite, with rosewood paneling and understated Chinese decor, is far more attractive, but for the extra money you may be better off at the Townhouse Hotel (☞ *above*). Street noise may be a problem during the day. ⊠ *38 Long St. (Box 3086), Cape Town 8000,* ☎ *021/423–6363,* 𝔽𝔸𝕏 *021/423–6370. 33 rooms. Bar, coffee shop, room service. CP. AE, DC, MC, V.*

Waterfront

$$$$ 🖫 **The Cape Grace Hotel.** It's not a surprise that this well-appointed,
★ exclusive hotel at the V&A Waterfront became an instant success. Built on a spit of land jutting into a working harbor, the Cape Grace offers views of seals frolicking in the surrounding waters and seagulls soaring above. The large guest rooms have harbor or mountain views. Elegant and understated with both French period decor and a wonderful modern design, it's owned and run by one of the country's leading hotelier families, the Brands. The attention to detail throughout is outstanding, from the antique pieces to the fresh flowers in the rooms. There's a wonderful well-stocked library for browsing and a superb restaurant, Quay West, which serves local and international cuisine. Guests have free use of the nearby health club and the hotel's courtesy car for service into the city. Booking well in advance is essential. ⊠ *West Quay, V&A Waterfront, Cape Town 8002,* ☎ *021/410–7100,* 𝔽𝔸𝕏 *021/419–7622. 122 rooms. Restaurant, bar, pool, library. AE, DC, MC, V.*

$$$$ **Cullinan Cape Town Waterfront.** Just opposite the entrance to the waterfront, this sparklingly white, brand-new hotel stands out with its asymmetrical stepped tower. The spacious marble-tiled lobby has huge picture windows, draped in rose and gold, leading out to the pool. An enormous, double-curving gilt staircase completes the picture. The rooms are quite restrained, with muted green carpets and floral notes; bathrooms are well laid out with separate showers and are quiet and understated in white tiles and gray marble. ⊠ *1 Cullinan St., V&A Waterfront, Cape Town, 8001,* ☎ *021/418–6920,* 𝔽𝔸𝕏 *021/418–3559. 416 rooms. Restaurant, bar, room service, pool, health club. AE, DC, MC, V.*

$$$$ 🖫 **Protea Victoria Junction.** This is South Africa's first loft hotel, and with its spot on Main Road, Greenpoint, adjacent to the waterfront, and its distinctly funky and art deco–style decor, it's popular with those looking for something different. The spacious loft rooms have high ceilings and beds on special platforms, but be warned: You have to be nimble to climb to your large double bed in the upstairs section of the room. You'll be pleased to hear the standard rooms have ordinary knee-level beds but are still pretty funky and chic. The Set is a trendy restaurant for business lunches and has a great range of salads and quite innovative fare, and the bar always jumps at happy hour. ⊠ *Somerset and Ebenezer Rd., Greenpoint (Box 51234, Waterfront), Cape Town 8002,* ☎ *021/418–1234,* 𝔽𝔸𝕏 *021/418–5678. 172 rooms. Restaurant, coffee shop, bar, pool. AE, DC, MC, V.*

$$$$ 🖫 **Table Bay Hotel.** This hotel is new, glitzy, and on arguably the best spot, at the tip of the V&A Waterfront. It's the top pick for celebrities—Michael Jackson and Richard Branson stayed here—which, no doubt, gives it a distinct buzz. The decor is sunny and eclectic, with picture windows, marble mosaic and parquet floors, and lots of plants, including the hotel's trademark orchid arrangements, containing more than 1,000 blooms. In the lounge, you can browse through the selection of international newspapers as you sit by the fireside, relaxing to live chamber music. The rooms, while understated, are colorful and bright, with comfortable marble and tile bathrooms with roomy showers. The suites, especially Lion's Head, are huge and exquisitely furnished in an eclectic style. The hotel has recently acquired its own helicopter for airport transfers and scenic flights. ✉ *Quay 6, V&A Waterfront, Cape Town 8002,* ☎ *021/406–5000,* FAX *021/406–5767. 239 rooms, 15 suites. 3 restaurants, 2 bars, lobby lounge, pool, beauty salon, spa, health club, business services, meeting room. AE, DC, MC, V.*

$$$$ ⬚ **Victoria & Alfred Hotel.** You couldn't find a better location for this upmarket hotel, in a converted warehouse smack in the middle of the waterfront, surrounded by shops, bars, and restaurants. Rooms are huge, furnished in neo–Cape Dutch style, and decorated in muted rust and sea colors. Views from the costlier mountain-facing rooms are spectacular, encompassing not only Table Mountain but the city and docks as well. Waterfront buses leave regularly for the city center, a five-minute ride away. ✉ *Pierhead (Box 50050), Waterfront, Cape Town 8002,* ☎ *021/419–6677,* FAX *021/419–8955. 68 rooms. Restaurant, bar, room service. AE, DC, MC, V.*

$$ ⬚ **City Lodge.** Location is everything at this no-frills chain hotel, a 5-minute walk from the waterfront and 10 minutes from the city center. Rooms are standard, decorated with ship prints and blond wood furniture, and all have TVs and tea/coffeemakers. ✉ *Dock and Alfred Drs., Waterfront (Box 6025, Roggebaai), Cape Town 8012,* ☎ *021/419–9450,* FAX *021/419–0460. 164 rooms. Bar, breakfast room, pool. AE, DC, MC, V.*

$ ⬚ **Breakwater Lodge.** You won't find another hotel this close to the waterfront offering rates so low. Built in a converted 19th-century prison on Portswood Ridge, the Breakwater certainly won't win any awards for charm or coziness. Its history is quite evident in the long, narrow corridors, which lead to tiny, sparsely furnished cells (sorry rooms). Nevertheless, the rooms are clean and have TVs, phones, and tea- and coffeemakers. Ask for a room with a view of Table Mountain. ✉ *Portswood Rd., Waterfront, Cape Town 8001,* ☎ *021/406–1911,* FAX *021/406–1070. 327 rooms, 110 with shared bath. 2 restaurants, bar. AE, DC, MC, V.*

Atlantic Coast

$$$$ ⬚ **Bay Hotel.** Of the luxury hotels in and around Cape Town, this beach hotel in Camps Bay is the most relaxed and unpretentious. The three-story structure is across the road from a white-sand beach and is backed by the towering cliffs of the Twelve Apostles. From the raised pool deck, guests look out over sea and sand, far from the hurly-burly of Cape Town. Cane furniture, colorful paintings, and attractive peach and sea tones make the rooms bright. Service is excellent, with an emphasis on privacy. Ask for a premier room if you want a sea view. ✉ *Victoria Rd. (Box 32021), Camps Bay 8040,* ☎ *021/438–4444,* FAX *021/ 438–4455. 76 rooms with bath. Restaurant, bar, room service, pool. AE, DC, MC, V.*

$$$$ ⬚ **De Oudekraal Hotel.** This luxurious hotel has the most fantastic location—which has turned out to be a mixed blessing. Built amid great controversy, it is the only building between Camps Bay and Llandudno, bordering on the Cape Peninsula National Park (it was built just before the park's status was proclaimed), and is uncomfortably close to a historical Muslim Kramat (holy burial site). Despite the vociferous objections of the Muslim community and conservationists, here it stands. And it is a really nice hotel. All the rooms are comfortably and stylishly decorated in shades of blue, for the sea facing, and brown and green for the mountain facing. Built high up, it has a spectacular sea view, and the busy Victoria Road is totally out of sight beneath you. ✉ *Victoria Rd. (Box 32117), Camps Bay 8040,* ☎ *021/437–9000,* FAX *021/437–9001. 48 rooms, 22 suites. Restaurant, bar, pool, meeting rooms, travel services. AE, DC, MC, V.*

$$$$ ★ **Ellerman House.** Without a doubt, this is one of the finest (and most expensive) hotels in South Africa. Built in 1912 for shipping magnate Sir John Ellerman, the hotel sits high on a hill in Bantry Bay and enjoys stupendous views of the sea. Broad, terraced lawns fronted by elegant balustrades step down the hillside to a sparkling pool. The drawing and living rooms, decorated in Regency style, are elegant yet not forbiddingly formal. Guest rooms benefit from enormous picture windows, high ceilings, and spacious tile bathrooms. Of particular note is the Africa-theme room, decorated with cane furniture, ostrich-egg lamps, and African sculptures. The hotel accommodates only 22 guests, and a highly trained staff caters to their every whim. In the kitchen, four chefs prepare whatever guests request—whether it's on the menu or not. All drinks except wine and champagne are included in the rates. ⊠ *180 Kloof Rd., Bantry Bay 8001 (Box 515, Sea Point 8060),* ☎ *021/439–9182,* FAX *021/434–7257. 11 rooms. Restaurant, bar, room service, pool, sauna, exercise room. CP. AE, DC, MC, V.*

$$$$ **Place on the Bay.** These luxury self-catering apartments are on the beachfront in Camps Bay, within easy walking distance of a host of restaurants and bars. Apartments are tasteful, modern affairs that make extensive use of glass. Many units have good sea views from their balconies. If you really want to have it all, take the magnificent penthouse, which occupies the entire top floor and comes with its own swimming pool. All units have daily housekeeping service. ⊠ *Fairways and Victoria Rds., Camps Bay 8001,* ☎ *021/438–7060,* FAX *021/438–2692. 21 apartments. Restaurant, bar, pool. AE, DC, MC, V.*

$$$ **Clarens Manor.** This beautiful guest house is at once invigorating and extremely restful. Original art, antique furniture, and a few African artifacts stand out against the soft sunshine-yellow walls. While still retaining some of the influence of its creator, François Ferreira, it is now under the management of Laurel Rutherford, who was born in Jamaica and has lived in New York, New Zealand, the Philippines, and Uganda and has brought the influence of her eclectic international background to bear on this lovely old house overlooking the Atlantic. The refurbished upstairs rooms are grand in size and decor, and the downstairs lounges and dining room are warm and comfortable. Forget the sea view—it's nothing compared to the magnificent spectacle of Lion's Head looming over you as you gaze from the mountain-facing rooms. Lovingly prepared meals are served around one huge table and resemble private dinner parties. Laurel holds elegant soirées two or three times a month with classical or jazz performances or poetry readings, accompanied by a three-course meal. If driving, enter Clarens Road from High Level Road, not Regent Street, as it is a one-way. ⊠ *35 Clarens Rd., Sea Point, Cape Town 8060,* ☎ *021/434–6801,* FAX *021/434–6845. 7 rooms. Dining room, 2 lounges, pool, laundry service. BP. AE, DC, MC, V.*

$$$ **La Splendida.** Designed to look like a Miami South Beach Art Deco hotel, this trendy all-suites addition to the Cape Town scene has a great location on Beach Road, Mouille Point. Ask for a sea- or mountain-facing room, either of which has great views. Well-proportioned rooms are zanily decorated with bright colors and natural fabrics, and the overall feeling is light and airy. Cafe Faro, the outstanding hotel restaurant with interesting eclectic cuisine, is a favorite with local yuppies. The V&A Waterfront is a seven-minute walk. You have a choice of executive or penthouse suites (slightly larger and a bit more expensive), but whichever you choose, you'll be very comfortable. ⊠ *121 Beach Rd., Mouille Point 8001,* ☎ *021/439–5119,* FAX *021/439–5112. 22 suites. Restaurant, lap pool. AE, DC, MC, V*

$$$ **Peninsula All Suites Hotel.** Housed in an 11-story building just across the road from the the ocean, this exclusive self-catering establishment is ideal for families or groups of friends. Guests can choose from a variety of suites that sleep four to eight people and command incredible views of the sea. The larger suites are the most attractive, full of light and air, thanks to picture windows, sliding doors, wide balconies, and white tile floors. Small studio suites look more like conventional hotel rooms. Each suite has a fully equipped kitchen with microwave oven. The hotel is a time-share property, so booking during the busy December holiday could be a problem. ⊠ *313 Beach Rd., Sea Point 8001 (Box 768, Sea Point 8060),* ☎ *021/439–8888,* FAX *021/439–8886. 110 suites. Restaurant, bar, room service, 2 pools, sauna, exercise room. AE, DC, MC, V.*

$$ 🏨 **Monkey Valley.** This secluded resort is one of the best places on the
★ peninsula for families and is very popular for small conferences. Built on stilts, each of the self-catering thatched log cottages lies in an indigenous milkwood forest overlooking a nature reserve and the white sands of Noordhoek Beach. Cottages have two or three bedrooms, fully equipped kitchens, and large balconies. The wood interiors are attractive and rustic, brightened by floral fabrics, cottage-style furniture, and fireplaces. Rooms are similarly decorated, and some have pretty Victorian bathrooms. The resort has its own restaurant, and there is a large grocery store 5 km (3 mi) away. Owner Judy Sole runs an outstanding establishment and is a character in her own right. ⊠ *Mountain Rd. (Box 114), Noordhoek 7985,* ☎ *021/789–1391,* FAX *021/789–1143. 34 rooms, 17 cottages. Restaurant, bar, pool, playground, convention center. AE, DC, MC, V.*

Southern Suburbs

$$$$ 🏨 **Cellars-Hohenort Country House Hotel.** It's easy to forget the out-
★ side world at this idyllic getaway in Constantia. Set on 9 acres of gardens on the slopes of Constantiaberg, this luxury hotel commands spectacular views across Constantia Valley to False Bay. The 18th-century cellars of the Klaasenbosch wine estate and the Hohenort manor house form the heart of the hotel. Guest rooms are large and elegant, furnished in English-country style with brass beds, flowery valances, and reproduction antiques. Rooms in the manor house have the best views of the valley. Although the hotel lacks the historical significance of the Alphen (☞ *below*), it offers a level of luxury and tranquillity that its more famous competitor cannot match. The Presidential Suite sleeps a family of six. ⊠ *93 Brommersvlei Rd. (Box 270), Constantia 7800,* ☎ *021/794–2137,* FAX *021/794–2149. 55 rooms, 1 suite. 2 restaurants, 2 bars, room service, 2 pools, beauty salon, tennis court. AE, DC, MC, V.*

$$$$ 🏨 **Steenberg Country Hotel.** This is a relatively new addition to the collection of fine country establishments in Cape Town. One of the oldest estates in the area, the original farm "Swaaneweide aan den Steenberg" was granted to the four-time widow Catherina Ustings by her lover Simon van der Stel, the governor of the Cape, in the late 17th century, and so she became the first woman to own land in South Africa. The original buildings have been painstakingly restored, the gardens manicured to perfection, and the vineyards replanted higher up on the mountain. The original vineyards, have been converted to a championship golf 18-hole course. The buildings are spectacular and are all furnished in antiques, as are guest rooms which have a Provencal style with yellow painted wood and salvaged barn floorboards. ⊠ *Steenberg and Tokai Rds., Tokai 7945,* ☎ *021/713–2222,* FAX *021/713–2221. 23 rooms, 1 suite. Restaurant, bar, 2 pools, beauty salon, 18-hole golf course. AE, DC, MC, V.*

$$$ ⊞ **Alphen Hotel.** If you want a taste of gracious Cape living and his-
★ tory, stay at this elegant Constantia hotel. Built sometime between 1750
and 1770 in Cape Dutch style, the former manor house is now a na-
tional monument and one of the Cape's historical treasures. The own-
ers are descendants of the distinguished Cloete family, which has
farmed the land around Constantia since 1750. Cloete paintings and
antiques, each with a story to tell, adorn the public rooms. Rooms range
in size from compact to pretty large. A small drawback is the slight
traffic noise from the nearby highway in rush hour. Only luxury rooms
have air-conditioning. ⊠ *Alphen Dr. (Box 35), Constantia 7848,* ☎
021/794–5011, 𝔽𝔸𝕏 *021/794–5710. 34 rooms. Restaurant, bar, room
service, pool. AE, DC, MC, V.*

$$$ ⊞ **Constantia Uitsig.** This 200-acre winery has an enviable setting, backed
by the magnificent mountains of the Constantiaberg and overlooking
the vineyards of Constantia Valley. Rooms, in whitewashed farm cottages set amid manicured lawns and gardens, are comfortable and inviting. Wicker headboards, timber ceilings, and bright floral patterns add
a rustic feeling. The restaurant in the original farmhouse draws diners from all over the Cape. If you value peace and quiet, this is a great
place to stay. ⊠ *Spaanschemat River Rd. (Box 32), Constantia 7848,*
☎ *021/794–6500,* 𝔽𝔸𝕏 *021/794–7605. 16 rooms. Restaurant, room service, 2 pools. AE, DC, MC, V.*

$$–$$$ ⊞ **Palm House.** Towering palms dominate the manicured lawns of this
peaceful guest house straddling the border of Kenilworth and Wynberg, a 15-minute drive from the city. The house is an enormous, stolid
affair, built in the early 1920s by a protégé of Sir Herbert Baker and
filled with dark-wood paneling, wood staircases, and fireplaces. Guest
rooms are large and decorated with bold floral fabrics and reproduction antiques. Upstairs rooms benefit from more air and light. Guests
often meet for evening drinks in the drawing room. ⊠ *10 Oxford St.,
Wynberg 7800,* ☎ *021/761–5009,* 𝔽𝔸𝕏 *021/761–8776. 10 rooms. Bar,
pool. BP. AE, DC, MC, V.*

$$ ⊞ **The Vineyard.** Set in 6 acres of rolling gardens overlooking the
Liesbeek River in residential Newlands, this comfortable hotel is built
around the 18th-century weekend home of Lady Anne Barnard. The
lobby is paved in worn terra-cotta tiles and revolves around the leafy
breakfast room. The views of the back of Table Mountain are spec-
tacular, but at a better rate, a courtyard-facing room offers views of a
veritable rain forest growing amid gurgling waters. The hotel is 10 min-
utes by car from the city but within walking distance of the Newlands
sports arenas and the shops of Cavendish Square. Au Jardin (☞ *Din-
ing, above*), the classic French restaurant, is very well regarded. ⊠ *Col-
inton Rd. (Box 151), Newlands 7725,* ☎ *021/683–3044,* 𝔽𝔸𝕏 *021/
683–3365. 160 rooms. 2 restaurants, bar, room service, pool, exercise
room. AE, DC, MC, V.*

$ ⊞ **Koornhoop Manor Guest House.** This is one of the best values in
Cape Town. A lovely Victorian house set in a pretty garden, Koorn-
hoop is best described as extremely nice and totally unpretentious. The
rooms, which vary in size, are simply decorated in pretty florals, all
en-suite, and have tea and coffee stations. It's very central and is within
safe walking distance of a huge range of restaurants in the vibey young
suburb of Observatory, five minutes' drive from the city, UCT or
Groote Schuur Hospital, and conveniently close to the railway station.
A communal TV room with an honor bar is a convivial meeting place.
You need to book quite far in advance to take advantage of this little
gem. ⊠ *Wrench and Nuttal Rds., Observatory 7925,* ☎ 𝔽𝔸𝕏 *021/448–
0595. 8 rooms, 1 three-bedroom apartment. BP. No credit cards.*

False Bay

$$ 🏨 **Boulders Beach Guesthouse.** Positioned just a few steps away from the beautiful Boulders Beach—the best swimming beach in Cape Town—this comfortable guest house is a winner. The understated rooms are decorated with elegant black wrought-iron furniture and snow-white linen, creating a restful, minimalist feel. The adjacent restaurant and pub are a bit more boisterous. ⊠ *4 Boulders Pl., Boulders, Simonstown 7975,* ☎ *021/786–1758,* ℻ *021/786–1826. 13 rooms. Restaurant, bar. AE, DC, MC, V.*

$$ 🏨 **British Hotel Apartments.** In a stone Victorian building in historic
★ Simonstown, these self-catering apartments offer a good value for the money. The apartments are huge, with fully equipped kitchens, two or three bedrooms, two sitting rooms, and wide Victorian balconies overlooking the harbor. Suites, decorated in similar style, consist of a bedroom, small lounge with coffee station, and a bathroom. High ceilings, wood floors, and giant windows create a sense of space and elegance. The decor differs from unit to unit but draws much of its inspiration from the turn of the century. Ask for Number 2, a two-bedroom apartment that perfectly balances the old-fashioned and the modern, with claw-foot bathtubs, cane furniture, and sponge-painted walls. ⊠ *90 St. George's Rd. (Main Rd.), Simonstown,* ☎ ℻ *021/786–2214. 4 apartments, 4 suites. AE, DC, MC, V.*

$$ 🏨 **Quayside Lodge.** This limited-service hotel has wonderful views over Simon's Bay, the harbor, and the yacht club. Situated on Jubilee Square, and part of the newly built Simonstown Waterfront, it's right in the action. Only five rooms are not sea facing, and all are light and airy, combining lime-washed wood with white walls and pale blue finishes. "Room Service" can be arranged from the adjacent Bertha's restaurant or coffee shop. ⊠ *Jubilee Sq., Main Rd., Simonstown,* ☎ *021/ 786–3838,* ℻ *021/786–2241. 25 rooms, 3 suites. AE, DC, MC, V.*

NIGHTLIFE AND THE ARTS

Although *SA City Life* also lists events in Durban and Johannesburg, along with *Cape Review,* it's the best monthly roundup of entertainment in Cape Town. For weekly updates, try "Friday," the entertainment supplement of the *Mail & Guardian,* or the "Top of the Times" in Friday's *Cape Times.* Both are informed, opinionated, and up-to-date. The *Argus* newspaper's "Tonight" section gives you a complete daily listing of what's on, plus contact numbers. Tickets for almost every cultural and sporting event in the country (including movies) can be purchased at **Computicket** (☎ 021/430–8000), with more than 18 outlets around the city. Two of the most convenient are in Sun Gallery, below the Cape Sun Inter-Continental, and at the waterfront. You can also book by phone with Computicket using any major credit card. For information on the gay scene, contact Africa Outing (☎ 021/671–4028 or 083/273–8422).

The Arts

The **Nico Theatre Centre** (⊠ D. F. Malan St., Foreshore, ☎ 021/21–7839), a huge and unattractive theater complex, is the hub for performing arts and other cultural activities. Cape Town City Ballet and the Cape Town Philharmonic Orchestra, as well as the city's theater and opera companies, make their homes in the Nico's three theaters. Since 1994 there's been a conscious effort throughout the country to make the performing arts more representative and multicultural. The formerly Eurocentric emphasis has subsided, and today there's a palpable African-arts excitement in the air. Classics are still well represented, as are the latest contemporary worldwide trends. During summer, when the weather's good, Cape Town has its own version of Central Park's Shakespeare in the Park at **Maynardville Open-Air Theatre** in Wynberg. Booking is through Computicket. Theatergoers often bring a picnic supper to enjoy before the show.

Classical Music

The **Cape Town Philharmonic Orchestra,** which recently merged with the Cape Town Symphony Orchestra, alternates performing at City Hall and the Nico Theatre Center (☞ *above*). The **Spier Summer Festival** (☎ 021/434–5423, FAX 021/434–0845), which takes place between November and February, has a varied program, and performances are held under the stars in an amphitheater at the Spier Wine Estate. You can take Spier's own vintage steam train out to the estate, wine and dine at one of the three restaurants or have a picnic dinner prepared by the estate, then enjoy the show, and return to Cape Town on the train. And, in October, the attractive village of Franschhoek (☞ The Winelands *in* Chapter 5) hosts the Fête de la Musique, featuring many visiting artists, mostly from France. As part of its program to introduce classical music to the general public, the Philharmonic Orchestra also stages a series of lunchtime concerts in the foyer of the Nico complex. Far more exciting, though, would be to watch the orchestra at one of its two appearances at the Kirstenbosch Gardens open-air concerts (☞ *above*). They always do the first and last concerts of the season. The orchestra has hosted several guest conductors from Europe and the United States and has an active program, which includes a summer program of free concerts at the outdoor AGFA Amphitheatre at the waterfront.

Film

Ster-Kinekor and Nu Metro screen mainstream movies at cinema complexes all over the city. The waterfront alone has two cinemas with 16 screens altogether, which gives you a huge choice. Check newspaper listings for what's playing. At Cavendish Square and the waterfront, the Cinema Nouveau concentrates on showing foreign and art films.

The **Labia** (✉ 68 Orange St., Gardens, ☎ 021/424–5927) is an independent art cinema that screens quality mainstream and alternative films, including the works of some of the best European filmmakers. There are three screens. A small coffee bar serves snacks.

IMAX Cinema (✉ BMW Pavilion, Waterfront, ☎ 021/430–8025), with a giant, nearly hemispherical, five-story screen and six-channel wraparound sound, makes viewers feel as if they're participating in the filmed event. Movies usually concentrate more on visuals than story line, such as wildlife, extreme sports, underwater marine life, or even rock concerts.

Theater

The **Baxter Theatre Complex** (✉ Main Rd., Rondebosch, ☎ 021/685–7880) is part of the University of Cape Town and has a reputation for producing serious drama, whacky comedy shows, and pretty experimental stuff, too. The complex features a 657-seat theater, a concert hall, a smaller studio, and a restaurant and bar.

Nightlife

The city's nightlife is concentrated in the revitalized harbor. You will always find something to do at the waterfront, when you consider that you have more than a dozen cinema screens, 40 restaurants, and 10 bars from which to choose. The rest of the city center, except for isolated restaurants and bars, empties out after business hours, and lone couples may not feel safe walking these deserted streets at night. The big exception is the few square blocks around the intersection of Long and Orange streets, which have become a cauldron of youth-oriented nightclubs, bars, and restaurants. Even here, though, exercise caution late at night. Sea Point, once a major after-dark scene, has lost much of its business to the waterfront. Depending on your outlook, however, you might relish the opportunity to visit here and see a bit of contemporary black South African culture and partake in some good music and nightlife.

Bars and Pubs

The **Perseverance Tavern** (⊠ 83 Buitenkant St., Gardens, ☎ 021/461–2440), which dates to 1836, claims to be the oldest tavern in the city. The facade has been beautifully restored, but you may feel claustrophobic in the small, interconnected rooms; the clientele here is pretty rowdy. The wood-lined pub at **Mijlof Manor Hotel** (⊠ 5 Military Rd., ☎ 021/426–1476) in Tamboerskloof is a popular watering hole for the after-work crowd. The popular **Obz Cafe** (⊠ 115 Lower Main Rd., Observatory, ☎ 021/448–5555), is a big and funky bar/café with excellent coffee, good food, and cocktails. **Long Street Cafe** (⊠ 259 Long St, Cape Town, ☎ 021/424–2464) is a favorite with locals, serving up light tasty dishes, coffee, and, of course, cocktails.

The **Sports Bar** (⊠ Victoria Wharf, Waterfront, ☎ 021/419–5558) is a huge place with large-screen TVs. The bar gets into the spirit of major foreign sporting events like the Super Bowl and the FA Cup Final (England's soccer championship) and is undoubtedly the best place to watch sports in the city. **Quay Four** (⊠ Quay 4, ☎ 021/419–2008), also at the waterfront, is big with the after-work suit-and-tie brigade, which clogs picnic tables on the wooden deck overlooking the harbor. **Ferrymans** (⊠ Dock Rd. at the V&A Waterfront, ☎ 021/419–7748) has a roaring fire inside on winter nights in addition to an outdoor deck area and a suit-and-tie crowd. Just outside the entrance to the waterfront is the **Fireman's Arms** (⊠ Buitengracht and Mechau Sts., ☎ 021/419–1513), a great old bar that serves pizzas cooked in a wood-fired oven. The restrained but fairly funky crowd lean toward **Cafe Erte** (⊠ 265 Main Rd., Three Anchor Bay, ☎ 021/434–6624) which is very gay-friendly. Serious party animals can go wild at **Fat Boys** (⊠ 9 Alfred Rd., Greenpoint, ☎ no phone)—it often has unlimited drink specials for R30. You have been warned.

Clubs

Nightclubs in Cape Town change faster than the weather. The area bounded by Loop, Long, Wale, and Orange streets is the best place to get a feeling for what's going on in town. An old die-hard is **Corner House** (⊠ Glynn and Canterbury Sts., ☎ no phone), which plays music from the 1980s onward.

For clubs with live music your best bet is **Mama Africa** (⊠ Long St., ☎ 021/424–8634), with live music Monday through Saturday and usually a marimba band on Wednesday nights, authentic African food, authentic African music, authentic African pulse. The **Jam** (⊠ Top of de Villiers Rd., ☎ 021/462–2105) is a relaxed place with pool tables and a good vibe. It is owned by the Springbok Nude Girls (who are not girls and do not play rugby but wear clothes). It is one of Cape Town's top bands, so there is often good live music and sometimes just a jam session. Probably the best spot in town is the **Drum Cafe** (⊠ Glynn St., ☎ 021/461–1305), which features live performances by percussionists from all over Africa. On Wednesdays there is a drum circle and, on Mondays, a women's drum circle (men are welcome but may not drum). **Café Camissa** (⊠ 80 Kloof St., Garden, ☎ 021/424–2289), with live music most nights, frequent jam sessions, and an open-mike session for local (amateur and professional) poets on Monday, is a great place. Loads of board games contribute to the laid-back atmosphere.

Jazz

Many of the mainstream jazz clubs in the city double as restaurants. Cover charges range from R10 to R25. The **Green Dolphin Jazz Restaurant** (✉ Waterfront, ☎ 021/421–7471) attracts some of the best mainstream musicians in the country as well as a few from overseas. The cover charge is R15–R20 and there's a food and beverage minimum of R65 (which includes cover charge) for a seat at a table (the kitchen specializes in pasta and seafood). **Jazz Cafe** (✉ 41 The Drive, Camps Bay, ☎ 021/438–2686) is an intimate club in an old Cape Dutch building in Camps Bay. Come here to listen to small groups that won't completely dominate your dinner or drinks. **Winchester Mansions Hotel** (✉ Beach Rd., Sea Point, ☎ 021/434–2351) does a mellow Sunday brunch in the courtyard for R85 with some of the city's best jazz musicians livening the scene. One of the best venues is the **Blue Note** (✉ Cine 400 Building, College Rd., Rylands, ☎ 021/683–9133). Other than the above, the hot venues change so quickly, it's best to get info when you're there. Cape Town Tourism is compiling a list of good jazz venues and will attempt to keep up with the frequent changes.

OUTDOOR ACTIVITIES AND SPORTS

Cape Town is the adventure capital of the universe. Whatever you want to do—dive, paddle, fly, jump, run, slide, fin, walk, or clamber—this is the city to do it in. As well as those listed below, **Adventure Village** (☎ 021/424–1580) books a range of activities.

Participant Sports

Abseiling

Abseil Africa (☎ 021/424–1580) offers abseiling off Table Mountain, Chapmans Peak, and over a waterfall in the mountains about an hour's drive away. Costs range from R250 to R400.

Aerobatic Flight

Fly upside down in an aerobatic flight over the vineyards in a Pitts Special. Contact **Mike Fagan** (☎ 083/462–0570); costs range from R600 to R800.

Canoeing and White-Water Rafting

The most accessible river close to Cape Town is the Breede, where you can do one- or two-day trips. Contact **Felixe Unite River Adventures** (☎ 021/683–6433), **River Rafters** (☎ 021/712–5094), **Wild Thing Adventures** (☎ 021/461–1653). For real white water, which is only possible in late winter, the Doring and the Palmiet are your best bets. Contact **Steep Creek** (☎ 021/685–4040) or **Gravity River Tours** (☎ 021/689–3698). A good half-day's drive from Cape Town is the Orange River, which has the most dependable paddling. Trips range from family-style meanders to serious white water. Contact any of the above operators as well as **Walkers Augrabies Canoe Trails** (☎ 054/451–0177) or **Intrepid Rafting** (☎ 021/461–4918 or 082/555–0551).

Caving

Escorted trips are run by **Abseil Africa** (☞ *above*) to the Kalk Bay Caves. These trips involve some Single Rope Technique, lots of scrambling, and squirming along on your belly—good dirty fun. Cost is R250.

Climbing

Cape Town has hundreds of bolted sport routes around the city and peninsula, ranging from an easy 10 to a hectic 30. Both Table Mountain Sandstone and Cape Granite are excellent hard rocks. There are route guides to all the major climbs and a number of climbing schools in Cape Town. The following are recommended: **Cape Town School of Mountaineering** (☎ 021/671–9604), **Guided Ascents in Africa** (GAIA; ☎ 021/448–2697 or 082/494–9635), the **Leading Edge** (☎ 021/797–3386 or 803/309–1554), and **High Adventure** (☎ 021/447–8036).

Diving

The diving around the Cape is excellent, with kelp forests, cold-water corals, very brightly colored reef life, and numerous wrecks. An unusual experience is a dive in the Two Oceans Aquarium (☞ V&A Waterfront, *above*). CMAS, NAUI, and PADI dive courses are offered, from about R1,300, at **Iain's Scuba School** (☎ 021/439–9322 or 082/894–6054) and **Underwater World** (☎ 021/461–8290).

Fly-fishing

You will find no captive-bred, corn-fed trout lurking in sluggish dams near Cape Town. But, in the mountains, just an hour or so away, you'll encounter wild and wily fish in wild and wonderful rivers. The season runs from September 1 to May 31. Outfitter **Tim Rolston** (☎ 083/626–0467) has escorted trips, all equipment, and advice.

Golf

Most golf clubs in the Cape accept visitors, but prior booking is essential. Expect to pay R200–R350 for 18 holes. Most clubs offer equipment rental. The Winelands in particular have some spectacular courses (☞ Chapter 5). **Clovelley Country Club** (☎ 021/782–6410) near Fish Hoek is a tight course that requires masterful shot placement from tee to green. **Durbanville Golf Club** (☎ 021/96–8121) may not be the most challenging course in the Cape but has tremendous views and bird life. **King David Country Club** (☎ 021/934–0365) is famous for its layout, with undulating fairways and elevated tees; the 12th hole plays into the wind and is probably the toughest par-3 in the Cape. **Milnerton Golf Club** (☎ 021/552–1047), sandwiched between the sea and a lagoon, is the Western Cape's only links course and can be difficult when the wind blows. **Mowbray Golf Club** (☎ 021/685–3018), with its great views of Devil's Peak, is a magnificent parkland course that has hosted several major tournaments; there are a number of interesting water holes. Unfortunately, noise from the highway can spoil the atmosphere. Founded in 1885, **Royal Cape Golf Club** (☎ 021/761–6551) in Wynberg is the oldest course in Africa and has hosted the South African Open many times. Its beautiful setting and immaculate fairways and greens make a round here a must for visitors. The club does not rent equipment. **Westlake Golf Club** (☎ 021/788–2020) is laid out around a large lake in the shadow of rocky mountains; the 7th and 14th holes are extremely difficult. **Steenberg Golf Estate** (☎ 021/713–2233) is the most exclusive club on the peninsula and is open to only members and guests of the Steenberg Country Hotel (☞ *above*).

Hiking and Kloofing

Cape Town and the surrounding areas offer some of the finest hiking in the world, mostly through the spectacularly beautiful mountains. Kloofing, known as canyoning in the United States, is the practice of following a mountain stream through its gorge, canyon, or "kloof," by swimming, rock hopping, and jumping over waterfalls or cliffs into deep pools. There are some exceptional kloofing venues in the Cape; contact **Daytrippers** (☞ *below*) and **Abseil Africa** (☞ *above*). **Cape Eco Trails** (☞ Table Mountain, *above*) has various escorted hikes.

Horseback Riding

Sleepy Hollow Horse Riding (☎ FAX 021/789–2341) offers 1½- and 2-hour rides down Long Beach, a 6-km (4-mi) expanse of sand that stretches from Noordhoek Beach to Kommetjie.

Skydiving

Do a tandem sky dive (no experience necessary) and have your photograph taken hurtling earthward with Table Mountain in the background with **Cape Parachute Club** (☎ 082/800–6290).

Spectator Sports

It's easy to get tickets for ordinary club matches and Inter-Provincial tickets. Getting tickets to an international test match is more of a challenge; however, there's always somebody selling tickets at a price, of course.

Cricket and Rugby

The huge sporting complex off Boundary Road in Newlands is known countrywide simply as Newlands. It's the home of the **Western Province Cricket Union** (☎ 021/683–6420) and the **Western Province Rugby Football Union** (⊠ Newlands, ☎ 021/689–4921). Next door, in the South African Sports Science Institute, is the **SA Rugby Museum** (☎ 021/685–3038), open weekdays 9–4.

Football

Football (the sport known as soccer in the United States) is much more grassroots than cricket or rugby and is very big in the townships. Amateur games are played from March to September at many venues all over the peninsula. Call the **South African Football Association** (SAFA; ☎ 082/456–2137) for details. Professional games are played from October to April at Greenpoint Stadium, Athlone Stadium, and even in the hallowed grounds of Newlands—a new development that didn't result in the end of the world as many rugby fans and longtime residents of the surrounding suburbs predicted.

SHOPPING

A number of stores in Cape Town sell African art and crafts, much of which comes from Zululand or neighboring countries. Street vendors, particularly on St. George's Mall and Greenmarket Square, often sell the same curios for half the price.

Markets

Greenmarket Square. You can get good buys on clothing, T-shirts, handcrafted silver jewelry, and locally made leather shoes and sandals. It's lively and fun whether or not you buy anything. ☉ *Mon.–Sat. 9–4:30.*

Red Shed Craft Workshop. Here you can watch craftspeople blowing glass, knitting sweaters, and weaving rugs. All of the work is for sale. ⊠ *Victoria Wharf, Waterfront.* ☉ *Mon.–Sat. 9–7, Sun. 10–6.*

Waterfront Art and Craft Market. In this indoor market, more than 140 artists show their work: an assortment of handcrafted jewelry, rugs, glass, pottery, and leather shoes and sandals. ⊠ *Waterfront,* ☎ *021/418–2850.* ☉ *Weekends 8:30–6.*

Specialty Stores

AFRICAN ART

African Image. Look here for traditional and contemporary African art and curios, colorful cloth from Nigeria and Ghana, plus West

African masks, Malian blankets, and beaded designs from southern African tribes. A variety of Zulu baskets are also available at moderate prices. ⊠ *Burg and Church Sts.,* ☎ FAX *021/423–8385.* ⊙ *Weekdays 8:45–5, Sat. 9–1:30.*

The Collector. Serious buyers with unlimited spending power favor this museumlike shop, with its small, select assortment of works ranging from West African ornamental beads to hand-painted Tuareg leather pillows and Zairian Kuba knives. Tags describe the place of origin and uses of all pieces. It's an interesting place to learn about African artifacts. ⊠ *52 Church St.,* ☎ *021/423–1483.* ⊙ *Weekdays 10–1 and 2:15–4, Sat. 10–1.*

The Pan-African Market. The market extends over two floors of a huge building and is a jumble of tiny stalls, traditional African hairdressers and tailors, potters, artists, musicians, and drummers. There is also a small, very African restaurant. If you're not going to visit countries to the north, go here. You'll get an idea of what you're missing. ⊠ *76 Long St.,* ☎ *021/424–2957.* ⊙ *Weekdays 9–5, Sat. 9–3.*

AFRICAN CLOTHING AND FABRICS

Mnandi Textiles. Here you'll find a range of African fabrics, including traditional West African prints and Dutch wax prints. The store sells ready-made African clothing for adults and children. You can also have items made to order. ⊠ *90 Station Rd.,* ☎ *021/447–6814,* FAX *021/447–7937.* ⊙ *Weekdays 9–5, Sat. 9–1.*

N.C.M. Fashions – African Pride. This is the place to go for traditional clothing from all over Africa. One of the most striking outfits is the brightly colored *bubu,* a loose-fitting garment with a matching head wrap, or try a traditional Xhosa outfit, complete with braiding, beads, and a multilayer wraparound skirt. You can buy off the rack or order a custom outfit from a wide selection of fabrics. ⊠ *173 Main Rd., Claremont,* ☎ *021/683–1022.* ⊙ *Weekdays 9–5:30, Sat. 9–1:30.*

BOOKS

Clarke's Bookshop. A local favorite, you'll find a fantastic collection of Africana books here as well as a good selection of antiquarian titles, and some esoterica. ⊠ *211 Long St.,* ☎ *021/423–5739.* ⊙ *Weekdays 9–5, Sat. 9–1.*

Exclusive Books. This is one of the best all-around bookshops in the country. The chain carries a wide selection of local and international periodicals and coffee-table books on Africa. An integrated coffee bar allows you to browse at a comfortable table with an espresso or cappuccino. Be prepared, though, to pay at least twice as much for books as you would in the United States or Britain. ⊠ *Shop 225, Victoria Wharf, Waterfront,* ☎ *021/419–0905,* FAX *021/419–0909.* ⊙ *Mon.–Thurs. 9 AM–10:30 PM, Fri.–Sat. 9 AM–11 PM, Sun. 10–9.* ⊠ *Lower Mall, Cavendish Square, Claremont,* ☎ *021/674–3030,* FAX *021/683–5053.* ⊙ *Mon.–Thurs. 9–9, Fri.–Sat. 9 AM–11 PM, Sun. 10–9.*

CAPE TOWN A TO Z

Arriving and Departing

By Bus

All intercity buses depart from the station complex on Adderley Street. **Greyhound** (⊠ 1 Adderley St., ☎ 021/418–4310) offers daily overnight service to Johannesburg and Pretoria; the one-way fare is about R360. **Intercape Mainliner** (⊠ 1 Adderley St., ☎ 021/386–4400) operates a far more extensive network of routes in the Western Cape than does

Greyhound, with daily service up the N7 to Springbok (R230) and Windhoek (R350), along the Garden Route to George (R120) and Port Elizabeth (R165); a bus also travels daily to Johannesburg (R325). **Translux Express Bus** (⊠ 1 Adderley St., ☎ 021/449–3333) offers a similar network of routes at comparable prices.

The **Baz Bus** (☎ 021/439–2323, ℻ 021/439–2343) offers service aimed mostly at backpackers who don't want to travel vast distances in one day and don't have transportation to get to train or bus stations.

By Car

Parking in the city center can be a hassle. Parking spaces are so scarce that most hotels charge extra for the service, and even then you won't be guaranteed a space. You can usually find parking out on the "Pay and Display" lots on Buitengracht Street or on the Grand Parade. Wherever you park, you will be accosted by an informal (or semiformal) parking attendant. It's a good idea to pay them a rand in advance and then another rand or two if you return to find your car safe. The Sanlam Golden Acre Parking Garage on Adderley Street offers covered parking, as does the Parkade on Strand Street.

The main arteries leading out of the city are the N1, which runs to Paarl and, ultimately, Johannesburg; and the N2, which heads to the Overberg and the Garden Route. The N7 goes up to Namibia and leads off the N1. The M3 (colloquially and rather loosely referred to as the Top Highway, the Top Freeway, or the Blue Route) leads to Constantia, Muizenberg, and the small towns of the peninsula; it splits from the N2 just after Groote Schuur Hospital, in the shadow of Devil's Peak.

CAR RENTAL

Most of the large car-rental agencies offer similar rates; expect to pay through the nose if you rent by the day. A Nissan Sentra or Toyota Corolla 1600cc with a radio-tape player and air-conditioning costs about R160 a day plus a whopping R1.20 to R1.40 per kilometer, but you can get a no-frills 1300cc VW Golf or Opel Corsa for about R65 per day and R1.05 per kilometer. If you rent for five days or more, you get 200 km–300 km (124 mi–186 mi) free per day with a daily rate of about R260 or R156. You must take out insurance. Cape Town drivers are considered the worst in the country for disregarding traffic rules. There's also been an increase in car theft over the last few years.

Among the major rental agencies in Cape Town proper are **Avis** (⊠ 123 Strand St., ☎ 021/424–1177); **Budget** (⊠ 120 Strand St., ☎ 021/418–5232); **Europcar** (☎ 021/418–0670); and **Hertz** (⊠ 139 Buitengraght St., ☎ 021/422–1515). You can obtain rates about a third lower at budget agencies like **Economy Car Hire** (⊠ 6 Three Anchor Bay Rd., ☎ 021/434–8304) and **Elite Car Hire** (⊠ 346B Victoria Rd., Salt River, ☎ 021/448–5294), but these companies usually offer limited breakdown support and you must return the car in Cape Town.

By Plane

Cape Town International Airport, formerly known as D. F. Malan, lies 22½ km (14 mi) southeast of the city in the Cape Flats. For flight arrival and departure information call 021/934–0407. International airlines flying into Cape Town include **Air France** (☎ 021/934–8818 or 021/418–8180), **Air Namibia** (☎ 021/934–0757 or 421–6685), **British Airways** (☎ 021/934–4729), **Delta Airlines** (021/011/482–4582), **KLM** (☎ 021/670–2500), **Lufthansa** (☎ 021/425–1490), **Singapore Airlines** (☎ 021/419–6226), **South African Airways** (☎ 021/936–1111), and **Swissair** (☎ 021/421–4938).

The major domestic carriers serving Cape Town are **British Airways/Comair** (☎ 0800/961–1196 toll-free), **Sabena/Nationwide** (☎ 021/936–2050, 021/936–2051, or 021/936–2052), and **South African Airways** (☎ 021/936–1111).

Cape Town International Airport is tiny: The domestic and international terminals are no more than 200 yards apart. In addition to a VAT refund office (☞ Taxes *in* Smart Travel Tips A to Z), there is a Western Cape Tourism Board booth and an accommodations hot line, open daily 7–5, that provides information on guest houses around the city. Trust Bank exchanges money weekdays 9–3:30 and Saturday 8:30–10:30; it stays open later for international arrivals and departures.

BETWEEN THE AIRPORT AND CAPE TOWN

Intercape Shuttle (☎ 021/934–0802) operates a minibus service between the city and the airport for R30 per person. Buses drop passengers off at the station on Adderley Street. Buy tickets at the Intercape Shuttle desk in the domestic arrivals terminal or, after hours, from the bus driver. Buses depart every hour. A door-to-door service with the same company costs between R80 and R100. Cape Town Tourism (☞ Visitor Information, *below*) runs a shuttle to and from the information center for R30.

Taxis are available at stands outside the terminals. Only those with airport licenses are allowed to pick up arriving passengers, and drivers must use the meter. Expect to pay about R130 for a trip to the city center.

Or travel in comfort in a stretch limo from **Cape Limo Services** (☎ 021/785–3100) for about R350 an hour.

Avis (☎ 0800/002–1111 or 021/934–0808), **Budget** (☎ 0860/016622 or 021/934–0216), **Imperial** (☎ 0800/131000 or 021/386–3239), and **Tempest** (☎ 0800/031666 or 021/934–3845) have car-rental offices at the airport (☞ Arriving and Departing by Car, *above*).

By Train

Cape Town's **train station** is in the heart of the city. Mainline Passenger Services' *Trans-Karoo* runs daily between Cape Town and Johannesburg; the trip takes about 25 hours and costs R375 first-class. The *Southern Cross* makes the 24-hour trip to Port Elizabeth on Fridays and back on Sundays (R235 first-class); it's a night ride, so forget about seeing the splendors of the Garden Route. The luxury *Blue Train* (☞ Train Travel *in* Smart Travel Tips A to Z) makes the Cape Town–Johannesburg run three times per week and the Cape Town to Port Elizabeth run once a month; call 021/449–2672 for information and reservations. The *Rovos Rail Pride of Africa* (☎ 021/421–4020), another luxurious train, also travels from Cape Town to Johannesburg and up the Garden Route. ⊠ *Cape Town Station, Adderley St.,* ☎ *021/449–3871.* ⊘ *Reservations office Mon.–Thurs. 8–4:30, Fri. 8–4, Sat. 8–noon. AE, DC, MC, V.*

Getting Around

If you confine yourself to the city center you won't need a car—in fact, the shortage of parking spaces makes having a car in the city a nightmare. A rental car is your only feasible option, however, if you want to explore the peninsula or the Winelands and are not on a guided tour. Another fun and practical option is to rent a scooter (which eliminates parking problems) from **African Buzz** on Long Street, ☎ 021/423–0052, FAX 021/423–0056 (R160 per day unlimited kilometers), or a motorcycle from **Mitaka** in Seapoint, ☎ 021/439–6036 (R350–R450 per day, includes 250 km/155 mi).

By Bus

The only bus that visitors are likely to use is the waterfront shuttle. It runs every 10 minutes between the waterfront and the station complex on Adderley Street. The fare is about R2. However, the bus is not recommended, as it is very slow. It is more efficient to take a minibus taxi (☞ *below*).

Golden Arrow (☎ 080/121–2111) operates an extensive network of local buses serving the City Bowl and outlying suburbs. Generally, service is infrequent and slow.

By Taxi

Taxis are metered and reasonably priced and offer an easy, quick way to get around a city, where parking is such trouble. Don't expect to see the throngs of cabs you find in London or New York. You may be lucky enough to hail one on the street, but your best bet is to summon one by phone or head to a major taxi stand—Greenmarket Square, the top of Adderley Street, or the bottom, opposite the station. **Sea Point Taxis** (☎ 021/434–4444), probably the most reliable of the companies, starts the meter at R2 and charges R6 per kilometer. Another reputable company is **Marine Taxis** (☎ 021/434–0434). Expect to pay R20–R25 for a trip from the city center to the waterfront.

You will also see local **minibus taxis** tearing around town at high speed, stuffed to capacity with hapless commuters. These buses ply routes all over the city and suburbs, but you can flag them down anywhere along the way. The depot is on top of the train station. For the modest fare of R3–R5, you'll have an opportunity to experience some local atmosphere, and incidentally get to where you're going quite efficiently—but not elegantly.

By Train

Cape Metro (☎ 080/065–6463) is Cape Town's commuter line and offers regular but infrequent service to the southern suburbs and the towns on the False Bay side of the peninsula, including Muizenberg, St. James, Kalk Bay, Fish Hoek, and Simonstown.

All trains depart from Cape Town Station on Adderley Street. The trip to False Bay takes 45–60 minutes and costs about R10 one-way, first-class. Cape Metro also serves Paarl, Stellenbosch, and Somerset West in the Winelands (☞ Chapter 5).

The trains do not run after 7 PM during the week or after about 2 PM on Saturday. There is one train an hour between about 7:30 and 11 and 3:30 and 7:30 on Sunday. If you travel the train off-peak periods, choose as crowded a compartment as you can, and be alert of your surroundings when the train is at stations, as agile young bag-snatchers can slip in and out pretty quickly and target "dreamy" passengers or those engrossed in a book. Strange as it sounds, you may be safer standing in a cramped third-class carriage than sitting comfortably in splendid isolation in an empty first-class one.

Contacts and Resources

Changing Money

Don't even think about changing money at your hotel. The rates at most hotels are outrageous, and the city center is swamped with banks and bureaux de change that give much better rates. **American Express**'s (⊠ Thibault Sq., ☎ 021/421–5586; ⊠ Shop 11A Alfred Mall, ☎ 021/419–3917) downtown office is open 8:30–5 weekdays and 9–noon Saturdays; at the waterfront, 9–7 weekdays and 9–5 weekends.

Rennies Travel's (⊠ 2 St. George's Mall, ☎ 021/418–1206; ⊠ Upper Level, Victoria Wharf, Waterfront, ☎ 021/418–3744) downtown office is open weekdays 8:30–5 and Saturdays 9–noon. The waterfront location is open until 9 daily.

Consulates

Australian High Commission. ⊠ *Thibault Sq., BP Centre, 14th floor,* ☎ *021/419–5425.*

Canadian High Commission. ⊠ *Reserve Bank Building, 19th Floor, St. George's Mall,* ☎ *021/423–5240.*

U.K. Consulate. ⊠ *8 Riebeeck St.,* ☎ *021/425–3670.*

U.S. Consulate. ⊠ *Broadway Building, Heerengracht (bottom of Adderley St.),* ☎ *021/421–4280.*

Emergencies

Ambulance (☎ 10177), **police** (☎ 10111). The police also operate a **Tourist Assistance Unit** (⊠ Tulbagh Sq., ☎ 021/421–5115) for foreign visitors who are robbed or experience other trouble. The unit can provide translators and will help you contact your embassy or consulate if need be.

DOCTORS AND DENTISTS

Emergency Medical Service (☎ 021/671–3634 or 021/671–2924) is a 24-hour referral service. They will page doctors or dentists (but very few dentists work after hours), and even veterinarians.

PRIVATE CLINICS

While public hospital emergency rooms do offer good service, they are hopelessly understaffed and underfunded and have to deal with a huge number of local people, most of whom cannot afford any alternative. As a visitor, you should contact one of the private clinics; make sure you have medical insurance.

City Park Hospital (⊠ 181 Longmarket St., Constantiaberg, ☎ 021/480–6111), **Medi-clinic** (☎ 021/799–2911), **Claremont Hospital** (⊠ Harfield and Main Rds., Claremont, ☎ 021/674–4050), **Newlands Surgical Clinic** (⊠ Pick and Pay Center, corner Main Rd. and Keurboom Rd, Claremont, ☎ 021/682–1220), **Panorama Medi-clinic** (⊠ Rothchild Blvd., Panorama, ☎ 021/938–2111).

Guided Tours

BOAT TOURS

Until the middle of the 20th century most travelers' first glimpse of Cape Town was from the sea, and that's still the best way to get a feeling for the city, with its famous mountain as a backdrop. Several companies offer trips in a variety of vessels. The tours, all of which leave from the waterfront, are essentially the same: a one-hour to 90-minute tour of Table Bay (about R60–R90). The last cruise of the day usually includes free sparkling wine. It is advisable to take a jacket (☞ Robben Island, *above*) for trips to the island. The **Spirit of Victoria** (☎ 021/425–4062 is a lovely, traditional gaff-rigged schooner with red sails; and **Tigresse** (☎ 021/419–7746) is a big, fast, sleek sailing catamaran.

Drum Beat Charters (☎ 021/790–4859) offers one-hour trips (R28) from Hout Bay marina at 1:30 daily to see the Cape fur seals in their natural habitat on scenic Duiker Island.

HELICOPTER TOURS

Court Helicopters (⊠ Waterfront, ☎ 021/425–2966) and **Civair Helicopters** (⊠ Waterfront, ☎ 021/419–5182) offer tours of the city and surrounding area ranging from 20 minutes to several hours. Custom tours can be arranged. The Table Bay Hotel (☞ Lodging, *above*) offers tours for guests of the hotel.

ORIENTATION

A host of companies offer guided tours of the city, the peninsula, the Winelands, and anyplace else in the Cape you might wish to visit. Among the most reliable operators are **Classic Cape Tours** (☎ 021/686–6310, FAX 021/686–9216), **Hylton Ross Tours** (☎ 021/511–1784, FAX 021/511–2401), **Mother City Tours** (☎ 021/448–3817, FAX 021/418–2581), **Platinum Tours** (☎ 021/683–1590), **Springbok Atlas** (☎ 021/460–4700), and **Welcome Tours & Safaris** (☎ 021/510–6001, FAX 021/22–1816).

A cheaper and more casual way to see the sights is with **Topless Tours** (☎ 021/418–5888, FAX 021/418–5872), which runs two-hour tours of the city (R35) aboard topless double-decker buses. On city tours, passengers can hop off at designated points, then catch a later bus. In high season, buses leave hourly from the station on Adderley Street from 9:40 to 2:40 and the Waterfront Information Centre, every hour on the hour from 10 to 3. In the off-season there are three tours per day, at 10, noon, and 2.

ROBBEN ISLAND TOURS

Boat trips to Robben Island (☞ Boat Tours, *above*) don't actually land on the famous island. If you want to tour the island where Nelson Mandela spent a good chunk of his life, you need to organize a tour through the **Robben Island Museum** (☞ Exploring, *above*).

TOWNSHIP TOURS

For R75, **One City Tours** (☎ 021/387–5351, FAX 021/387–1338) offers eye-opening tours of the Cape's black townships. Tours are safe, conducted in minivans, and led by a well-spoken, knowledgeable guide. Visitors are introduced to District Six, a multiracial neighborhood razed to satisfy the Group Areas Act, and to some of the country's most notorious townships and squatter camps, including Langa, Nyanga, Gugulethu, Crossroads and Khayelitsha. You'll visit the cramped living quarters of a hostel, a spaza shop, and a *shebeen* (a vibrant township bar). The three-hour tour is well worth the time and money: It reveals a side of the country that most white South Africans have never seen.

Legend Tours (☎ 021/697–4056, FAX 021/697–4090) offers Walk to Freedom tours that cover District Six, Bo-Kaap, the townships, and Robben Island. The well-informed guides lead the tours, casting a strong historical and political emphasis.

Muse-Art Journeys (☎ 021/919–9168) conducts fascinating tours covering the cultural life of Cape Town, including art, music, crafts, and architecture. The graffiti tour is a real eye-opener and includes an introduction to hip-hop art and music. Cost is about R160.

Travel Agencies

American Express Travel Service changes money, books trips and airline tickets, and offers a range of other services to cardholders, including holding mail (☞ Changing Money, *above*).

Rennies Travel, which represents Thomas Cook in South Africa, has several branches throughout the city, but the main office is in the city center on St. George's Mall. In addition to providing the usual services of a travel agent, the office operates a bureau de change (☞ Changing Money, *above*).

Visitor Information

Cape Town Tourism is the city's official tourist body and offers information on tours, hotels, restaurants, rental cars, and shops. It also has a coffee shop and Internet café. The staff also makes hotel, tour, travel, and walking-tour reservations. ⊠ *The Pinnacle at Burg and Castle Sts. (Box 1403), Cape Town 8000,* ☎ *021/426–4260,* FAX *021/426–4263.* ⊙ *Weekdays 9–6, Sat. 8:30–2, Sun. 9–1.*

5 THE WESTERN CAPE

The wonders of the Western Cape are nearly endless. The jagged mountains, elegant estates, and delicious vintages of the Winelands; the pristine, mountain-edged beaches and historic towns of the Overberg; and the glorious wildflowers, old fishing villages, and interior ranges of the West Coast provide some of South Africa's most memorable experiences.

By Andrew
Barbour

Updated
by Andrew
Bergman and
Myrna Robbins

ANCHORED BY CAPE TOWN in the southwest, the Western Cape is South Africa's most delightful province, a sweep of endless mountain ranges, empty beaches, and European history dating back more than three centuries. In less than two hours from Cape Town you can reach most of the province's highlights, making the city an ideal regional base.

The historic Winelands, in the City's backyard, produce fine wine amid the exquisite beauty of rocky mountains, serried vines, and elegant Cape Dutch estates. By South African standards this southwestern region of the Cape is a settled land, with a sense of tradition and continuity lacking in much of the rest of the country. Here, farms have been handed down from one generation to another for centuries, and old-name families like the Cloetes have become part of the fabric of the region.

Even first-time visitors may notice subtle differences between these Cape Afrikaners and their more conservative cousins in the hinterland. For the most part, they are descendants of the landed gentry and educated classes who stayed in the Cape after the British takeover in 1806 and the emancipation of slaves in 1834. Not for them the hard uncertainties of the Great Trek, when ruddy-faced Boers (farmers) outraged at British intervention loaded their families into ox wagons and set off into the unknown, a rifle in one hand and a Bible in the other.

The genteel atmosphere of the southwestern Cape fades quickly the farther from Cape Town you go. The Overberg, separated from the city by the Hottentots Holland Mountains, presides over the rocky headland of Cape Agulhas, where the Indian and Atlantic oceans meet at the tip of the continent. Unspoiled beaches and coastal mountains are the lure of this remote area. North of Cape Town on the West Coast, civilization drops away altogether, bar a few lonely fishing villages and mining towns. Each spring, though, the entire region, stretching up into Namaqualand in the Northern Cape province (☞ Chapter 7), explodes in a spectacular wildflower display that slowly spreads inland to the grassy Hantam Plateau and the *Cedarberg* (Cedar Mountains).

Wildflowers are one extraordinary element of a region truly blessed by nature. The Western Cape is famous for its *fynbos* (pronounced "*feign-boss*"), the hardy, thin-leafed vegetation that gives much of the province its distinctive look. Fynbos composes a major part of the Cape floral kingdom, the smallest and richest of the world's six floral kingdoms. More than 8,500 plant species are found in the province, of which 5,000 grow nowhere else on earth. The region is dotted with nature reserves where you can hike through this profusion of flora, admiring the majesty of the king protea or the shimmering leaves of the silver tree. When the wind blows and mist trails across the mountainsides, the fynbos-covered landscape takes on the look of a Scottish heath.

Not surprisingly, people have taken full advantage of the Cape's natural bonanza. In the Overberg and along the West Coast, rolling wheat fields extend to the horizon, while farther inland jagged mountain ranges hide fertile valleys of apple orchards, orange groves, and vineyards. At sea, hardy fishermen battle icy swells to harvest succulent crayfish (clawless lobsters), delicate perlemoen (a type of abalone), and a variety of line fish, such as the delicious kabeljou.

For untold centuries, this fertile region supported the Khoikhoi and San, indigenous peoples who lived off the land as pastoralists and hunter-gatherers. With the arrival of European settlers, however, they were

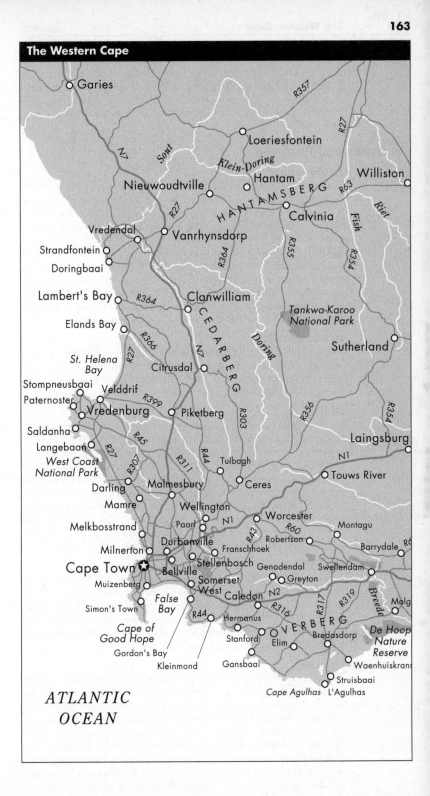

Garies

Loeriesfontein

R357

R27

Klein-Doring

Nieuwoudtville

Hantam

H A N T A M S B E R G

Williston

Calvinia

Riet

Fish

R63

Sout

N7

R27

Vredendal

Vanrhynsdorp

Strandfontein

Doringbaai

R364

R355

R354

Lambert's Bay

R364

Clanwilliam

Tankwa-Karoo
National Park

Elands Bay

R366

C E D A R B E R G

Doring

Sutherland

St. Helena
Bay

R27

Citrusdal

N7

R356

R354

Stompneusbaai

Velddrif

R399

Paternoster

Vredenburg

Piketberg

R303

Laingsburg

Saldanha

Langebaan

West Coast
National Park

R27

R307

R45

R311

R44

Tulbagh

N1

Touws River

Darling

Malmesbury

Ceres

Mamre

Wellington

Paarl

N1

Worcester

Montagu

Melkbosstrand

R43

R60

Robertson

Barrydale

R6

Milnerton

Durbanville

Franschhoek

Cape Town ★

Bellville

Stellenbosch

Genadendal

Swellendam

Muizenberg

Somerset
West

Greyton

Breede

Malg

Simon's Town

False
Bay

R44

Caledon

N2

R316

O V E R B E R G

R317

R319

De Hoop
Nature
Reserve

Cape of
Good Hope

Hermanus

Waenhuiskrans

Gordon's Bay

Stanford

Elim

Bredasdorp

Kleinmond

Gansbaai

Struisbaai

Cape Agulhas

L'Agulhas

*ATLANTIC
OCEAN*

chased off, killed, or enslaved. In the remote recesses of the Cedarberg and along the West Coast, you can still see the fading rock paintings left by the San (Bushman), whose few remaining clans have long since retreated into the Kalahari Desert. The population of the Western Cape today is largely "colored," a catchall term to describe South Africans of mixed race and descendants of imported slaves, the San, and the Khoikhoi.

Pleasures and Pastimes

Architecture

The most visible emblem of local culture is Cape Dutch architecture. As you travel from estate to estate, you will see a number of 18th- and 19th-century manor houses that share certain characteristics: thick white-washed walls, thatched roofs curving around elegant gables, and small-pane windows framed by wooden shutters. It's a classic look—a uniquely Cape look—ideally suited to a land that is hot in summer and cold in winter. The Cape Dutch style developed in the 18th century from traditional long houses: simple, rectangular sheds capped by thatch. As farmers became more prosperous, they added the ornate gables and other features. Several estates, most notably Vergelegen and Boschendal, have opened their manor houses as museums.

Art and Crafts

The well-respected galleries throughout this region could surprise you with anything from protest paintings from the apartheid era to high-quality ceramics and pewter work. Also keep an eye open for smaller local crafts shops, which can provide you with unique souvenirs.

Dining

South African cuisine at its finest can be found in the Western Cape. If silver service is not your cup of tea, however, local, laid-back country-style cooking can be just as satisfying. The area is home to some of the country's best Cape Malay cuisine, characterized by mild, slightly sweet curries and the use of aromatic spices. Be prepared for fluctuations in the level of service. Generally, South Africans are still trying to get this right, but there are some remarkable exceptions to what appears to be a general go-slow rule of thumb. For a description of South African culinary terms, *see* Pleasures and Pastimes *in* Chapter 1. For price ranges, *see* Dining *in* Smart Travel Tips A to Z.

Golf

Fourteen golf courses lie within a 45-minute drive of the center of the Winelands, and four are situated within the Winelands themselves. All accept foreign visitors and most rent clubs. Greens fees for 18 holes average R70–R195. You shouldn't have a problem finding a course to your liking, the very best being situated in Somerset West, where you will find the Gary Player–designed Erinvale.

Lodging

The Winelands are sufficiently compact that you can make one hotel your touring base for your entire stay. Stellenbosch and Paarl offer the most flexibility, situated close to dozens of wineries and restaurants, as well as the major highways to Cape Town. Franschhoek is comparatively isolated, which many visitors consider a blessing. Tourist offices (☞ Contacts and Resources *in* Winelands A to Z, *below*) have extensive information on bed-and-breakfasts and self-catering options, many of which are less expensive than hotels and often give you a more personal taste of life in the Winelands. For price ranges, *see* Lodging *in* Smart Travel Tips A to Z.

Scenery

Few places in the world can match the drama of the Winelands, where African mountains rise sheer above vine-covered valleys and 300-year-old homesteads snooze in the shade of giant oaks. It's a place of such enviable beauty that you catch yourself glancing through the local real-estate pages.

Wine

Buried for years by sanctions, South African wines were largely unknown on the international scene. With the demise of the apartheid era, South African wine exports soared. No one could have expected such interest; as a result, the best are now in short supply in their country of origin, and South African wine lovers are peeved at the price they have to pay for a bottle of good local vino. Armed with foreign currency and a favorable rate of exchange, you will, however, still be able to get a good value for your money. While the quantity of South African wines remains a problem until the extensive new vine plantings come of age and the supply increases, the quality is improving with each vintage. Cape reds have recently won a slew of international awards. You must taste Pinotage, South Africa's own grape variety, a hybrid of pinot noir and Cinsaut (or Hermitage, as it was once called in the Cape). If you're really serious about wine, arm yourself with *John Platter's Wine Guide,* an annual pocket guide, or buy a copy of *WINE* magazine, a monthly publication that specializes in detailed features on local wineries. Keep in mind that many wineries close at lunchtime on Saturday and don't open at all on Sunday. For more information on shipping wine home, *see* Customs and Duties *in* Smart Travel Tips A to Z.

Exploring the Western Cape

As you move from Cape Town in the northwest to the southeast, there are five major areas of interest for the visitor. North of Cape Town, the West Coast and the neighboring interior are renowned for seafood and wildflowers, respectively. To the south are the important wine-producing centers of Paarl, Stellenbosch, and Franschhoek and to the east the historically significant and scenic Swellendam area. The southern tip of Africa, Cape Agulhas, can be reached by leaving the inland region and traveling south to the coast. The southern coastal area incorporates the small towns or villages of Gansbaai, Hermanus, Kleinmond, and Gordon's Bay.

Great Itineraries

Many people spend their entire vacations in the Western Cape after getting a big-game fix in Mpumalanga (☞ Chapter 3). Although it's possible to explore Cape Town and the Winelands in three or four days—the area is compact enough to allow it—you need six or seven to do it justice. You can get a good sense of either the Overberg or the West Coast on a three- or four-day jaunt, but set aside a week if you plan to tackle any more than one or two of the regions in this chapter. The most practical and enjoyable way to explore the region is by car.

Numbers in the text correspond to numbers in the margin and on the Winelands map.

IF YOU HAVE 3 DAYS

From Cape Town, take the N1 to **Paarl** ㉖, gliding off the highway at the ⊡ **Franschhoek** ㉒ turnoff. Book in and off-load your luggage at L'Auberge du Quartier Français before setting off to the Cabrière estate for a prearranged tour. Enjoy lunch at the **Haute Cabrière** ㉓ cellar or La Petite Ferme, both of which are on the Franschhoek pass and have great views. After lunch, visit **La Motte** ㉑, **Boschendal** ⑱, or **L'Or-**

marins ⑲ estate. In the late afternoon explore the antiques shops and art galleries in the main street of Franschhoek or visit the Huguenot Museum. On the second day, head for Paarl on the R45. Along the way visit **Backsberg** ㉚, **Fairview** ㉙, **Nederburg** ㉔, the **KWV** ㉗, or **Rhebokskloof** ㉕. Stop for lunch at the Grande Roche Hotel. If you've had a surfeit of wine-tasting, take a walk up Paarl Mountain, wander down the main street for a bit of shopping, soak up some old Cape architecture, or spend the afternoon on the front veranda at the Grande Roche and enjoy the view. Overnight, really splurge and spend a night at the 🏨 **Grande Roche Hotel.** Next morning head for **Stellenbosch** ⑥ via the N2 and the R44, en route back to Cape Town. Stop at **Vergelegen** ① for lunch, at the Lady Phillips Tea Garden. Allow plenty of time—it would be a shame to leave this vast estate without wandering around the gardens.

IF YOU HAVE 5 DAYS

Leaving Cape Town on the first day, take the N7 and head north to the 🏨 **Bushmans Kloof** game lodge in the Cedarberg. This drive will take you through Clanwilliam and the Swartland, the beginning of the wildflower route, which is best in spring. Try to reach the lodge by 3 PM, giving yourself time to unpack, enjoy a sumptuous tea, and be ready for the late-afternoon game drive. Spend the second day here, taking in all that the lodge and its inspiring environment have to offer. On the third morning head west to 🏨 **Lambert's Bay.** This coastal town certainly has charm, and the Marine Protea Hotel on the harborside will be more than adequate as a base from which to explore. After breakfast and a stroll on the fourth morning, set off on the R27 (mostly good gravel) south to 🏨 **Langebaan**'s lagoon and West Coast National Park. Overnight at the Farmhouse, on the hill overlooking the lagoon, and absorb the tranquil sights and sounds that make Langebaan famous. It is a comfortable, 90-minute drive back to Cape Town on the fifth day.

IF YOU HAVE 7 DAYS

The first two days of this tour follow the schedule described in either of the two itineraries above. The third day, however, takes you northeast toward the coast, your destination being 🏨 **Bartholomeus Klip Game Lodge** and farm. From Clanwilliam take the N7 to Piketberg, and then the R44 to Wellington, passing through the hamlets of Riebeek-West and Riebeek-Kasteel (try the Village Taverna in the latter for lunch). Once again, try to get to the lodge in time for tea and the afternoon game drive or a walk around the farm. Spend the following day here, allowing ample time to take it all in. On day five, travel over the Franschhoek Pass, and join the R43 at Villiersdorp, circumnavigating the extensive Theewaterskloof Dam. Head on to 🏨 **Grootbos** game lodge, where you'll spend the next day. On the seventh day retrace your route to the N2 and head back to the city.

When to Tour the Western Cape

The high season in the Western Cape is, of course, summer, and you will seldom visit major places of interest without the presence of busloads of fellow visitors. The weather is warm and dry, and although strong southeasterly winds can be a nuisance, they do keep the temperature bearable. If soaking up the sun is not of primary importance and you prefer to tour during quieter times, spring (September and October) and autumn–early winter (late March through May) are ideal. The weather is milder and the lines shorter. Spring also brings southern right whales close to the shores of the Western Cape to calve, and late August–October are the months to see the wildflowers explode across the West Coast. If the Winelands are high on your list of must-dos, remember that the busiest time in the vineyards and cellars is January–March.

THE WINELANDS

Frank Prial, wine critic for the *New York Times,* wrote that he harbored "a nagging suspicion that great wines must be made in spectacular surroundings." If that's true, the French may as well rip up their vines and brew beer, because the Cape Winelands are absolutely stunning.

All of this lies only 45 minutes east of Cape Town in three historic towns and valleys. Founded in 1685, Stellenbosch is a gem; it's also a vibrant university community. Franschhoek, enclosed by towering mountains, is the original home of the Cape's French Huguenots, whose descendants have made a conscious effort to reassert their French heritage. Paarl lies beneath huge granite domes, its main street running 11 km (7 mi) along the Berg River past some of the country's most elegant historical monuments. Throughout the region you will find some of South Africa's best restaurants and hotels.

It's no longer entirely accurate to describe these three valleys as *the* Winelands. Today, they make up only 35% of all the land in the Cape under vine. This wine-growing region is now so vast that you can trek to the fringes of the Karoo Desert in the northeast and still find a grape. There are altogether more than 10 wine routes, as well as a newly established brandy route, in the Western Cape, ranging from the Olifants River in the north to the coastal mountains of the Overberg (☞ *below*).

Each of the wine-producing areas has its own wine route where member wineries throw open their estates to the public. They maintain tasting rooms where you can sample their vintages either gratis or for a nominal fee. Happily, no one expects you to be a connoisseur, or even to buy the wines. Just relax and enjoy yourself, and don't hesitate to ask tasting room staff which flavors to expect in what you're drinking. Some wineries have restaurants; at others, you can call ahead to reserve a picnic basket to enjoy on the estate grounds.

The secret of touring the Winelands is not to hurry. Dally over lunch on a vine-shaded veranda at a 300-year-old estate; enjoy an afternoon nap under a spreading oak; or sip wine while savoring the impossible views. This may not be the Africa of *National Geographic,* but no one's complaining. Nowhere in South Africa is the living more civilized and the culture more self-assured.

The Winelands encompass scores of wineries and estates. The ones listed below are chosen for their great wine, their beauty, or their historic significance. It would be a mistake to try to cover them all in less than a week. You have nothing to gain from hightailing it around the Winelands other than a headache. The vineyards fan out around three major towns, Stellenbosch, Franschhoek, and Paarl. If your interest is more aesthetic and cultural than wine-driven, you would do well to focus on the historic estates of Stellenbosch and Franschhoek, after which you might head south into the Overberg. Most of the Paarl wineries on this tour stand out more for the quality of their wine than for their beauty.

Somerset West

40 km (25 mi) southeast of Cape Town on the N2.

Somerset West is on the edge of the Winelands. Just before you reach the center of town you'll see the turnoff to Lourensford Road, which runs 3 km (2 mi) to **Vergelegen.** This first winery may well spoil you for the rest. It is one of the most gracious, peaceful, and beautiful places in the Cape. Wine-tasting is a major reason to visit here, but you would be mad to leave without touring the grounds.

The Winelands

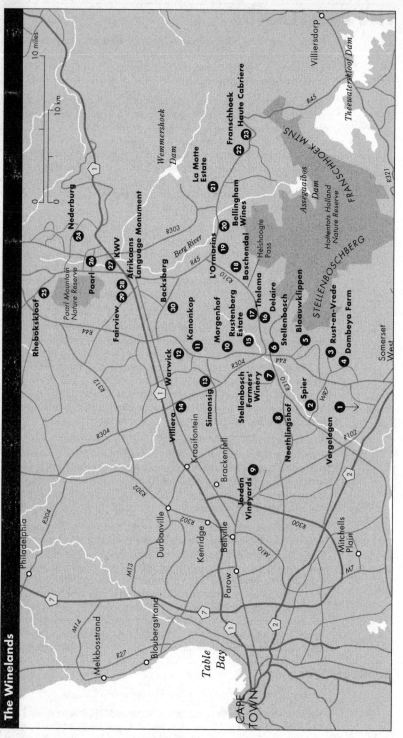

10 miles

10 km

Theewaterskloof Dam

Villiersdorp

R45

R321

FRANSCHHOEK MTNS.

Haute Cabriere 23

Franschhoek 22

Wemmershoek Dam

La Motte Estate 21

Bellingham Wines 20

Boschendal 19

L'Ormarins 18

Hottentots Holland Nature Reserve

Assegaaibos Dam

STELLENBOSCHBERG

Helshoogte Pass

Afrikaans Language Monument

Nederburg 24

KWV

Paarl 26 27

Fairview 29 28

Rhebokskloof 25

Paarl Mountain Nature Reserve

Berg River

R303

R45

Backsberg

R310

Thelema 17

Delaire 16

Kanonkop 30

Morgenhof

Rustenberg Estate

Blaauwklippen

Rust-en-Vrede 3

Dombeya Farm 4

Stellenbosch 6

5

Somerset West

Warwick 12

11

10 15

Villiera 14

Simonsig 13

Stellenbosch Farmers' Winery 7

Spier 2

Vergelegen 1

Neethlingshof 8

Kraaifontein

Brackenfell

Jordan Vineyards 9

R304

R302

R212

R44

R304

R300

R102

M2

Durbanville

Kenridge

Bellville

Parow

M10

Mitchells Plain

M7

Philadelphia

M13

Melkbosstrand

M14

R27

Bloubergstrand

Table Bay

CAPE TOWN

1

2

7

R302

Vergelegen was established in 1700 by Willem Adriaan van der Stel, who succeeded his father as governor of the Cape. His classic Cape Dutch homestead, with thatched roof and gables, looks like something out of a fairy tale. An octagonal walled garden aflame with flowers surrounds it, and huge camphor trees, planted almost 300 years ago, stand as gnarled sentinels. The estate was purchased for Lady Phillips by her husband, Sir Lionel, in 1917 and she spent vast sums on the restoration of the homestead, library, and gardens. The homestead is now a museum and is furnished in period style. Other historic buildings include a magnificent library and the old stables, now the reception area and interpretive center. Behind the house, Lady Phillips Tea Garden serves lunch and tea (☞ Dining and Lodging, *below*), and the Rose Terrace café looks onto a formal rose garden. Much of the fresh produce is supplied by the Margaret Roberts Herb and Vegetable Garden, which is next to the reception area.

Although Vergelegen still buys grapes from neighboring farms, the vineyards that were planted in 1989, during what is described as the renaissance of the farm, are beginning to give an inkling of some very good wines to come. You really should taste the merlot, with its ripe, plumy flavors. The chardonnay has touches of wood fermentation and maturation. ⊠ *Lourensford Rd., Somerset West,* ☎ *021/847–1334,* ☎ *021/847–1608.* ☞ *R7.50, tastings free.* ☉ *Daily 9:30–4 (no tastings Sun.). Library Mon.–Sat. 11–3. Cellar tours Mon.–Sat. at 10:30, 11:30, and 2:30 (reservations essential).*

➋ Describing **Spier** as simply a wine estate is doing Spier Home Farms an enormous disservice. The vast new complex comprises a manor house, wine cellars, wine and farm shop, rose garden, restaurants, conference center, open-air amphitheater, cheetah park, and equestrian facilities. It's all designed in Cape-country style, with whitewashed walls and thatched roofs, set along the verdant north bank of the Eerste River. You can even get to Spier's own little railway station by vintage locomotive from the V&A Waterfront in Cape Town. So, yes, it's seriously touristy, but still delightful. Try the sauvignon blanc (a local award winner), chardonnay, and cabernet sauvignon from the 1996 vintage to get a feel of the type of wines to come from this vast estate. ⊠ *R310, Stellenbosch,* ☎ *800/220–282 or 021/809–1100,* ☎ *021/881–3634.* ☞ *Free, tasting R10, train ride R75.* ☉ *Daily 9–5.*

➌ Nestled against the base of the Helderberg and shaded by giant oaks, the peaceful **Rust-en-Vrede** winery looks over steep slopes of vines and roses. Owned by former Springbok rugby great Jannie Engelbrecht, it's a comparatively small estate that specializes entirely in red wine—and produces some of the very best in South Africa. Rust-en-Vrede Estate is the flagship wine, a blend of predominantly cabernet sauvignon, shiraz, and just over 10% merlot grapes. It has already won several awards both locally and abroad, but it would do well to mature in the bottle for another 10 years or more. Another interesting wine is the shiraz, which has an inviting bouquet with the vanillin sweetness that American oak imparts; it will age for five to eight years. Rust-en-Vrede is one of the few estates that opens its historic winery and beautifully restored Cape Dutch homestead for tours. It also has a short birding trail that meanders through indigenous, riverine forest. ⊠ *R44, between Stellenbosch and Somerset West,* ☎ *021/881–3881,* ☎ *021/881–3000.* ☞ *Free.* ☉ *Weekdays 8:30–12:30 and 1:30–4:30, Sat. 9–1. Cellar tours on request.*

➍ Next door to Rust-en-Vrede is **Dombeya Farm,** one of the few places in the Western Cape to see spinning and hand weaving. The farm makes jerseys, blankets, and wool rugs, all in the bright, floral patterns that are Dombeya's hallmark. The shop also sells patterns and wool. A garden tearoom serves light lunches and snacks. ⊠ *Annandale Rd., Stellenbosch,* ☎ FAX *021/881–3746.* ☉ *Daily 9–5.*

❺ Established in the late 17th century, **Blaauwklippen** sits at the foot of the Stellenboschberg, shaded by oaks. It's a large winery that is well equipped to handle tour buses and will keep even non-oenophiles entertained. From October to April, you can take carriage rides (R2) through the vineyards, and there is also a free museum of old coaches, furniture, and kitchen utensils. If you arrive between noon and two, consider settling down on the veranda for a Coachman's Lunch of cold meats, cheeses, and pâté. Blaauwklippen produces a good range of both red and white wines. Its zinfandel is by far the best of the four produced in the Cape, and it has fared extremely well in competition with American zinfandels. The shiraz and cabernet sauvignon are also most commendable. For easy drinking right now, Red Landau, a blend of cabernet sauvignon and merlot grapes, is good value. A country shop sells souvenirs, as well as jams, Cape Malay chutneys, and *weinwurst* (a salami-like sausage). ⊠ *R44, between Stellenbosch and Somerset West,* ☎ *021/880–0133,* FAX *021/880–1036.* ⊠ *R1.70 for 5 tasting tickets.* ☉ *Weekdays 9–5, Sat. 9–1. Cellar tours Dec.–Jan. on request; Feb.–Nov., weekdays at 11 and 3, Sat. at 11.*

Dining and Lodging

$$$$ ✕ **L'Auberge du Paysan.** Come to this little cottage near Somerset West for classic French cuisine, formally presented. Tall upholstered chairs, small brass table lamps, and snowy linen set the tone for dishes from several Gallic provinces. Specialties include snails Provençale, rabbit casserole, and roast duck, but don't dismiss the excellent Cape crayfish bisque and braised quail in white wine with grapes. For dessert, meringue nests filled with vanilla ice cream and fresh fruit come with creme chantilly and raspberry coulis, and the crème brûlée is one of the Winelands' best. ⊠ *Raithby Rd., off R45, between Somerset West and Stellenbosch,* ☎ *011/842–2008. AE, DC, MC, V. Closed Sun. and 1 month in winter. No lunch Mon.*

$$$ ✕ **Lady Phillips Restaurant.** In summer you need to reserve a table three weeks in advance at this idyllic country restaurant on the Vergelegen estate. Whether dining inside or alfresco on the terrace, you will savor a luncheon of classy simplicity but presented with panache. Start with smoked salmon on herbed rösti with horseradish cream and follow with Cajun line fish teamed with apple and fennel butter; or try one of their renowned pies of the day, such as venison and apricot. The tangy citrus flan served with Greek yogurt makes a refreshing finale. If you can't get a reservation, head to the Rose Terrace during summer for light meals. ⊠ *Vergelegen Estate, Lourensford Rd., Somerset West,* ☎ *021/847–1334. Reservations essential Nov.–Apr. AE, DC, MC, V. No dinner.*

$$$$ 🏠 **Willowbrook Lodge.** This lodge, a member of the prestigious Relais & Châteaux group, makes a good base for exploring the entire southwestern Cape, including the peninsula, the Winelands, and the Overberg. The lodge lies hidden among beautiful gardens that extend down to the Lourens River; in the distance, the peaks of the Helderberg are visible. It's a very peaceful place, with large, airy, comfortable rooms with sliding doors opening onto the gardens. The cuisine is of an equally high standard, starring Provençale dishes using local ingredients. ⊠ *Morgenster Ave., Box 1892, Somerset West 7129,* ☎ *021/851–3759,* FAX *024/514–152. 11 rooms. Restaurant, bar, pool. No children under 12. AE, DC, MC, V.*

Golf

Somerset West Golf Club (✉ Rue de Jacqueline, ☎ 021/852–2925, ℻ 021/852–5879) is an easy course (💳 R85 for 18 holes) with plenty of leeway for errant tee-shots. **Erinvale Golf Club** (✉ Lourensford Rd., Somerset West ☎ 021/847–1144) is a Gary Player–designed course (💳 R250 for 18 holes) nestled beneath the Hottentots Holland Mountains.

Stellenbosch

★ ❻ *15 km (9½ mi) north of Somerset West.*

Stellenbosch may be the most delightful town in South Africa. It's small, sophisticated, and beautiful, and you could easily while away a week here. The second-oldest town after Cape Town, it actually *feels* old, unlike so many other historic towns in South Africa. Wandering the oak-shaded streets, which still have open irrigation furrows, you'll see some of the finest examples of Cape Dutch, Georgian, Victorian, and Regency architecture in the country. The town was founded in 1679 by Simon van der Stel, first governor of the Cape, who recognized the agricultural potential of this fertile valley. Wheat was the major crop grown by the early settlers, but vineyards now blanket the surrounding hills. The town is also home to the University of Stellenbosch, the country's first and most prestigious Afrikaans university.

A brief walking tour of the town starts at the corner of Dorp Street and the R44, where you first enter Stellenbosch. The **Rembrandt van Rijn Art Museum** occupies the historic Libertas Parva manor house, which displays the "H" shape so typical of Cape Dutch architecture. Built in 1780, the house has hosted some of the biggest names in South African history, including Cecil Rhodes and Barry Herzog. The art museum displays the work of some major South African artists, including Irma Stern, Willie Bester, and sculptor Anton van Wouw. ✉ *31 Dorp St.,* ☎ *021/ 886–4340,* ℻ *021/887–1645.* 💳 *Free.* ☉ *Weekdays 9–12:45 and 2– 5, Sat. 10–1 and 2–5.*

The **Stellenryk Wine Museum** is housed in the 18th-century wine cellars behind Libertas Parva. The cellar setting is appropriate for the museum's collection of wine-related artifacts, including presses, vats, and an interesting collection of wine vessels ranging from antiquity to the 18th century. ✉ *Off Dorp St.,* ☎ *021/888–3588.* 💳 *Free.* ☉ *Mon.– Sat. 9–12:45 and 2–5.*

Stroll up oak-lined Dorp Street, Stellenbosch's most historic avenue. Almost the entire street is a national monument, flanked by lovely, restored homes from every period of the town's history. Redolent with tobacco, dried fish, and spices, **Oom Samie Se Winkel** is a Victorian-style general store and one of Stellenbosch's most popular landmarks. In addition to the usual Cape kitsch, Oom Samie's sells some genuine *boere* (farmers') products, including *witblitz* and *mampoer,* the Afrikaner equivalent of moonshine. The shop operates a wine-export business and restaurant, too. ✉ *82/84 Dorp St.,* ☎ *021/887–0797,* ℻ *021/883– 8621.* ☉ *Weekdays 8:30–5:30, Sat. 9–5.*

As you continue up Dorp Street, keep an eye out for the historic **La Gratitude** home, built in the early 18th century in traditional Cape-Dutch town house style, and still a private home (✉ 95 Dorp St.); the all-seeing eye of God on its gable will be doing the same for you. **Voorgelegen** (✉ 176 Dorp St.) and the houses on either side of it form one of the best-preserved Georgian ensembles in town.

When you reach Andringa Street, turn left and then right onto Kerk (Church) Street. On your left is **d'Ouwe Werf,** possibly the country's oldest boardinghouse (☞ Dining and Lodging, *below*), which first took in paying guests as long ago as 1802.

At the corner of Kerk and Ryneveld streets is the **Stellenbosch Village Museum,** which is well worth a visit. The museum comprises four dwellings scattered within a two-block radius. These houses date from different periods in Stellenbosch's history and have been furnished to reflect changing lifestyles and tastes. The oldest of them is the very basic Schreuderhuis, which dates from 1709. The others date from 1789, 1803, and 1850, respectively. ⊠ *18 Ryneveld St.,* ☎ *021/887–2902.* ☞ *R10.* ☉ *Mon.–Sat. 9:30–5, Sun. 2–5.*

Continue down Ryneveld to Plein Street. Turn left and walk to the **Braak,** the grassy town square. Some of Stellenbosch's most historic buildings face the square, which is a national monument. At the southern end is the **Rhenish Church** (⊠ Bloem St.), erected by the Missionary Society of Stellenbosch in 1823 as a training school for slaves and blacks.

St. Mary's Church stands at the far end of the Braak. Built in 1852, it was consecrated by Bishop Robert Gray in 1854 and reflects the growing influence of the English in Stellenbosch. Across Bloem Street from St. Mary's is the **Burgher House,** built in 1797. Today, it houses the offices of Historical Homes in South Africa.

Next to the Burgher House, on an island in Market Street, stands the **V.O.C. Arsenal.** It took 91 years for the Political Council to hammer out the decision that Stellenbosch needed its own magazine. With the hard part behind them, it took just six months in 1777 to complete the structure. ⊠ *Bloem St.,* ☎ *no phone.* ☞ *R1.* ☉ *Aug.–May, weekdays 9:30–1:30 and 2–5.*

Walk down Market Street past the Tourist Information Bureau (☞ Winelands A to Z, *below*). On your left, facing a large lawn, is the **Rhenish Complex,** one of the most impressive restoration projects ever undertaken in South Africa. The complex consists of the old Cape Dutch Rhenish parsonage (1815); the Leipoldt House, which melds elements of English and Cape architecture; and a two-story building that is typically English.

Continue down Market and turn left on **Herte Street.** The whitewashed cottages along this street were built for freed slaves after the Emancipation Act of 1834. Although they were originally thatched, the houses are still evocative of 19th-century Stellenbosch. From here, follow Herte back to Dorp Street, where the walking tour began.

From Stellenbosch, wine routes fan out like spokes of a wheel, making excellent day trips if you're staying in town. Several excellent wineries lie nearby off the R310. To reach them, get back in your car, follow Dorp Street across the R44, and turn left at the Shell station.

Around Stellenbosch

❼ It's less than a mile from town to the **Stellenbosch Farmers' Winery** (SFW). Founded by a Kentuckian, William Charles Winshaw, SFW is the largest wholesale wine producer-merchant in South Africa and is responsible for almost 40% of the country's table wine. SFW also produces fortified wines, several brandies, and very good fruit juices and ciders. The SFW flagship is the Zonnebloem range of reds and whites, including among others a good shiraz (particularly those from the early 1980s). The Lanzerac Pinotage was the first of the variety ever made in South Africa (back in 1961), and it's still a good wine.

The **Farmers' Winery Center,** where tours begin, stands directly opposite the winery above a vineyard of cabernet sauvignon grapes. Here you'll find the wine-tasting center and salesroom. Each summer, concerts ranging from African jazz to opera and ballet are staged at the **Oude Libertas Amphitheatre,** a delightful open-air venue. ⊠ *Adam Tas Rd., off R310,* ☎ *021/808–7569 or 021/808–7474 Computicket,* ℻ *021/887–2506 or 021/886–4568 Computicket.* ☞ *Tastings R3.50, cellar tours R6.* ⊙ *Weekdays 8:30–5, Sat. 10–12:30. Cellar tours Mon.–Thurs. 10–2:30, Fri. at 10, Sat. by request only.*

❽ A long avenue of pines and oaks leads to the lovely estate of **Neethlingshof,** which traces its origins back to 1692. The magnificent 1814 Cape Dutch manor house looks out across formal rose gardens to the Stellenbosch Valley and the Hottentots Holland Mountains. The wines produced on this estate and those from its sister farm, Stellenzicht, are highly regarded both locally and abroad, and so be prepared for a rush of tour buses during the high season. The gewürztraminer is an off-dry, very elegant wine with rose-petal and spice aromas, while the Weisser Riesling is a good example of the few virtually dry wines made from this grape variety. Neethlingshof also produces an excellent Noble Late Harvest sweet dessert wine. Do not, however, leave the tasting room, without trying the pièce de résistance, the Stellenzicht Syrah. ⊠ *R310,* ☎ *021/883–8988,* ℻ *021/883–8941.* ☞ *Tastings R20 for 8 tastings.* ⊙ *Weekdays 9–5, weekends 10–4. Cellar tours by appointment.*

There are number of established estates, such as Overgaauw and Uiterwyk, on Stellenbosch Kloof Road. They are certainly worth a visit, but **❾** set your sights on **Jordan Vineyards,** a newer winery at the end of this road. Flanked by the hills of the Bottelaryberg and overlooking a vision of rolling vineyards and jagged mountains, it enjoys an enviable setting at the head of Stellenbosch Kloof. Gary and Cathy Jordan are a husband-and-wife team who studied at the University of California at Davis and worked at California's Iron Horse Winery. Although they produced their first vintage only in 1992, they have already established their reputation as producers of quality wines. The sauvignon blanc and chardonnay are delicious in their own ways, the former with lots of gooseberry fruit, the latter elegant and toasty. Also look for a combination of the two in the versatile Chameleon dry white, a flavorful, well-priced buy. Wine critics are also keeping their eyes on the Jordans' spicy cabernet sauvignon. ⊠ *Stellenbosch Kloof Rd.,* ☎ *021/881–3441,* ℻ *021/881–3426.* ☞ *Tastings R5.* ⊙ *Weekdays 10–4:30, Sat. 9:30–2:30. Cellar tours by appointment.*

Some of the Cape's most important wineries are on the stretch of the **❿** R44 that runs north from Stellenbosch. **Morgenhof** lies in the lee of a steep hill covered with vines and great pine trees. It's a beautiful Cape Dutch estate, with a history stretching back 300 years. In 1993, Morgenhof was acquired by the Huchon-Cointreaus of Cognac, France. They have spared nothing to make this one of the jewels of the Winelands, and behind the glamour there is an extremely talented wine maker and distinguished wines. Jean Daneel's award-winning 1992 merlot, for example, is a bold mouthful of a red wine, but his Morgenhof Chenin Blanc is the one currently making waves in the Cape. This workhorse wine tastes like a fine chardonnay. Apart from these celebrity wines, try the sauvignon blanc, chardonnay, and Pinotage. Morgenhof is an excellent place to stop for lunch. From October through April, you can reserve picnic baskets and dine on the lawns under a huge tree. The rest of the year, there are light lunches of homemade soup, freshly baked bread, cheese, and quiche. Reservations are advisable in summer. ⊠ *R44, between Paarl and Stellenbosch,* ☎ *021/889–*

5510, FAX 021/889–5266. ☜ *Tastings R2.50.* ⊙ *Weekdays 9–4:30, Sat. 10–3; Nov.–Apr., also Sun. 10–3. Cellar tours by appointment.*

In the days when ships of the Dutch East India Company used Cape Town as a revictualing station on the way to the East, they would fire a cannon as they entered the harbor to let farmers know they needed provisions. A relay cannon was then fired from a hill on this farm; *Kanonkop* is Afrikaans for Cannon Hill. The beauty of **Kanonkop** is not in its history or its buildings but in its wine. Since the early 1980s, wine making has been in the hands of legendary Beyers Truter. In 1991 he won the "Winemaker of the Year" award and the Robert Mondavi Trophy at the International Wine & Spirit Competition in London. No one would argue that Kanonkop's Pinotage is the best new-style Pinotage produced in South Africa. It's more wooded than most and shows excellent complexity and fruit; it will age for 8 to 15 years. Paul Sauer is a very good blend of about 80% cabernet sauvignon with the balance made up of equal parts merlot and cabernet franc. The 1995 vintage won a gold medal at the 1998 International Wine & Spirit Competition. ⊠ *R44, between Paarl and Stellenbosch,* ☎ *021/884–4656,* FAX *021/884–4719.* ☜ *Tastings free.* ⊙ *Weekdays 9–5, Sat. 8:30–12:30. No cellar tours.*

 Warwick is not a member of the Stellenbosch Wine Route, and you should visit this estate only if you're very keen to taste and buy wine; the tasting area is in a tiny cellar room cluttered with wine-making equipment (if possible, make an appointment first). Wine maker Norma Ratcliffe is very traditional in her approach to wine. She spent a couple of vintages in France perfecting her techniques and is now producing first-rate reds. Trilogy is one of the finest blended reds in the Cape, a stylish and complex wine made predominantly from cabernet sauvignon, with about 20% merlot and 10% cabernet franc. The cabernet franc is undoubtedly the best wine made from this varietal in the Winelands. The 1992 vintage is a particularly fruity wine, a real standout. ⊠ *R44, between Paarl and Stellenbosch,* ☎ *021/884–4020,* FAX *021/884–4025.* ☜ *Tastings R5.* ⊙ *Weekdays 8:30–4:30, Sat. by appointment. Cellar tours by appointment.*

 Simonsig sits in a sea of vines with tremendous views back toward Stellenbosch and the mountains. Its range of 15 white and red wines covers the whole taste and price spectrum. The Kaapse Vonkel is one of South Africa's best Méthode Cap Classique sparkling wines. Tiara is among the best cabernet blends in the Winelands, and the Pinotage is an excellent example of how well this varietal fares with no wood aging. You can bring your own picnic to enjoy at tables by the small playground. ⊠ *Kromme Rhee Rd.,* ☎ *021/882–2044,* FAX *021/882–2545.* ☜ *Tastings R3.50–R9 (depending on number of wines).* ⊙ *Weekdays 8:30–5, Sat. 8:30–4. Cellar tours weekdays at 10 and 3, Sat. 10.*

 Villiera is actually part of the Paarl Wine Route, but its location in the open flats near the N1 motorway makes it just as close to Stellenbosch as to Paarl. In a little more than 15 years of wine making, the Grier family has notched up numerous successes—such as Jeff Grier's late-1997 honor as the coveted "Winemaker of the Year" for his Bush Vine Sauvignon Blanc, the best in the Cape out of 72 entries. Jeff's merlot also ranks among the top five in the country, with excellent depth of fruit. ⊠ *R101 and R304 (Old Paarl and Stellenbosch Rds.), Koelenhof,* ☎ *021/882–2002,* FAX *021/882–2314.* ☜ *Tastings free.* ⊙ *Weekdays 8:30–5, Sat. 8:30–1. No cellar tours.*

A narrow lane runs through cattle pastures and groves of oak and birch to **Rustenberg Estate,** a Cape Dutch homestead (1811) and vision of bucolic bliss. Unlike some of the more touristy wineries, Rustenberg feels like a working farm. The estate is known for red wine, its Rustenberg Cabernet Sauvignon having enjoyed an unblemished record since it was first bottled more than 50 years ago. It's a lovely, unblended wine that will age for a decade or two. Try buying five bottles and drinking one every five years. ⊠ *Off R310 (Rustenberg Rd.), Ida's Valley,* ☎ *021/887–3153,* FAX *021/887–8466.* 🖃 *Tastings free.* ☉ *Weekdays 9–4:30, Sat. 9–12:30.*

⑯ Perched high above the valley, **Delaire** enjoys one of the most spectacular settings of any winery in the country. Sit on the terrace of the tasting room or restaurant and look past a screen of oaks to the valley below and the majestic crags of the Groot Drakenstein and Simonsberg mountains. It's an ideal place to stop for lunch, or even a short breather. The restaurant (open Tuesday–Saturday noon–2) serves light lunches and will provide picnic baskets to visitors who want to follow one of the scenic trails through the estate (open September 15–April 15). The tasting room is unpretentious and casual. ⊠ *R310, between Stellenbosch and Franschhoek (Helshoogte Rd.),* ☎ *021/885–1756,* FAX *021/885–1270.* 🖃 *Tastings R5.* ☉ *Mon.–Sat. 10–4. No cellar tours.*

⑰ On the slopes of the Simonsberg, **Thelema** is an excellent example of the exciting developments in the Cape Winelands since the early 1980s. When Gyles and Barbara Webb bought the farm in 1983, there was nothing here but very good soil and old fruit trees. It's a testament to their efforts that the winery has had regular prize-winners ever since. The 1992 cabernet sauvignon–merlot blend won Gyles Webb the Diner's Club "Winemaker of the Year" title in 1994. Two years later he took the award again with the '94 cabernet. Not to say that his white wines do not win accolades—Thelema's sauvignon blanc and chardonnay are certainly among the Cape's best. To cap it all off, the view of the Groot Drakenstein Mountains from the tasting room is unforgettable. ⊠ *R310, between Stellenbosch and Franschhoek (Helshoogte Pass),* ☎ *021/885–1924,* FAX *021/885–1800.* 🖃 *Tastings free.* ☉ *Weekdays 9–5, Sat. 9–1.*

Dining and Lodging

$$$$ ✕ **Jonkershuis.** The culinary influences that have contributed to traditional Cape cuisine—Cape Malay, Dutch, French, and German—are all celebrated here with a gargantuan buffet feast that you can savor under venerable oaks or inside the well-restored 18th-century homestead. Start with the soup of the day and farm breads or head for the cold table, laden with chicken satay in peanut sauce, lamb *frikkadels* (patties), excellent pickled fish, and well-dressed mussels. Cape chicken pie and roasts complete with a curry or two are among the main dishes. Look for the time-honored desserts *melktert* (a sweet milk tart sprinkled with cinnamon and sugar), *koeksister* (a plaited doughnut served with a gingery syrup), and brandy pudding. For lighter fare, try the Spier Café and the Taphuis. ⊠ *Spier Estate, Lynedoch Rd.,* ☎ *021/809–1172. AE, DC, MC, V. No dinner Sun. and Mon.*

$$$ ✕ **Lord Neethling.** In an 18th-century Cape Dutch manor on the historic Neethlingshof (☞ *above*) estate, this lovely restaurant overlooks a patchwork of vineyards and the Stellenbosch Mountains. The menu stays with cosmopolitan fare for the most part but includes Cape flavors such as *biltong* (jerky) soup with port wine and ostrich fillet with Cape gooseberries. Heritage dishes like bobotie and lamb bredie are also popular. A selection of fruity sorbets makes an agreeable summer dessert. ⊠ *Neethlingshof Estate, R310,* ☎ *021/883–8966. AE, DC, MC, V. No dinner Sun. and Mon.*

$$$ ✕ **Wijnhuis.** In the heart of the village, this small complex exudes a Continental air. Climb the stairs from an enclosed courtyard to reach the Italian-style restaurant and wine-tasting center. Have a drink at the bar or in the comfortable lounge area and then enjoy your meal either inside or on the marble-floored terrace. Antipasti include ostrich *bresaola* (air dried and salted thinly sliced meat) and good grilled baby calamari, while the choice of pasta dishes is extensive. Red meat and seafood are also quite popular, but the desserts are not always up to the same high standard. The wine list is a connoisseur's delight. ⊠ *Church and Andringa Sts.,* ☎ *021/887–5844. Reservations essential. AE, DC, MC, V.*

$$$$ ✕⊞ **Lanzerac Manor.** For generations, this hotel was "home" to students from Stellenbosch University, who knew that the best cheese platter in the Winelands and a jolly good afternoon's respite could be enjoyed after a morning's serious wine tasting. In 1991, however, Lanzerac was acquired by a Cape businessman and his family, and since then some R35 million has gone into remodeling, renovation, and refurbishment. Now Lanzerac Manor and Winery boasts state-of-the-art facilities of all kinds, and the 48 guest rooms, including five suites, have been tastefully redecorated in a luxurious style. A sense of history, dating back to 1692, still remains, and the sheer beauty of the setting has been left untouched: a classic Cape Dutch manor house flanked by the rolling vineyards and mountains of the Jonkershoek Valley. A casual lunch spot overlooks the manor house and serves a small à la carte menu. Those with heartier appetites have a lunchtime alternative at the Kombuis restaurant, where a cheese and Cape Malay buffet is served. ⊠ *Jonkershoek Rd., 1 km (½ mi) from Stellenbosch (mailing address: Box 4, Stellenbosch 7599),* ☎ *021/887–1132,* FAX *021/887–2310. 48 rooms. 3 restaurants, bar, room service, pool. BP. AE, DC, MC, V.*

$$$ ⊞ **De Goue Druif Guest House.** On Stellenbosch's most historic street, this tiny inn occupies an 1811 Georgian home that is also a national monument. Now settled in beautiful Stellenbosch, Belgian owners Catharina Cools and Yvan van Maercke go out of their way to make guests feel welcome in their gracious guest house with its high ceilings, wooden floors, and collection of antiques. Since taking over the business in 1995, the Van Maerckes have upgraded the entire guest house; added a swimming pool, a sauna, and gym facilities; overhauled the garden; and redecorated the guest rooms. Not surprisingly, the rejuvenated lodge was classified by SATOUR as the first three-star, silver-classified guest house in Stellenbosch. ⊠ *110 Dorp St., Stellenbosch 7600,* ☎ FAX *021/883–3555. 5 rooms, 1 cottage. BP. MC, V.*

$$$ ⊞ **d'Ouwe Werf Country Inn.** A national monument, this attractive 1802 inn is thought to be the oldest in South Africa. From the street, guests enter the original living room, a beautiful space enlivened by wood floors, a lofty beamed ceiling, and elegant antiques. The hotel is divided into two parts: the old inn with luxury rooms on its Georgian second story and a new wing with more standard rooms. All luxury rooms are furnished with antiques, including four-poster beds, draped sash windows, and bronze bathroom fittings. The standard rooms have reproductions only. A lovely coffee garden in a brick courtyard shaded by trellised vines is opens for meals and drinks throughout the day. ⊠ *30 Church St., Stellenbosch 7600,* ☎ *021/887–1608 or 021/887–4608,* FAX *021/887–4626. 25 rooms. Restaurant, room service, pool. BP. AE, DC, MC, V.*

Golf

Stellenbosch Golf Club (⊠ Strand Rd., ☎ 021/880–0103) has long, tree-lined fairways that will pose a problem if you don't hit the ball straight. Green fees are R160 for 18 holes.

Horseback Riding

Several riding outfits offer a range of rides for beginners and experts. Most lead standard one- and two-hour rides, as well as more interesting trips, including moonlight and sunset rides, wine-tasting trails, and even overnight camping. In Stellenbosch, contact **Amoi Riding Trails** (☎ 082/650–5794) or **Wine Valley Riding Club** (☎ 082/981–6331 or 083/226–8735).

Franschhoek and the Franschhoek Valley

22 km (14 mi) northeast of Stellenbosch.

From Thelema, the road runs down Helshoogte Pass into the fruit orchards and vines that mark the beginning of the Franschhoek Valley. This is the most isolated and spectacular of the three wine routes, a long valley encircled by towering mountain ranges and fed by a single road. Franschhoek takes its name from its first white settlers, French Huguenots who fled to the Cape to escape Catholic persecution in France. By the early 18th century, 270 of them had settled in the Cape, but their descendants—with names like de Villiers, Malan, and Joubert—now number in the tens of thousands. With their experience in French vineyards, the early Huguenots were instrumental in nurturing a winemaking culture in South Africa. As spectacular as the valley is today, it must have been even more so in the late 17th century when it teemed with game. In calving season, herds of elephants would migrate to the valley via the precipitous Franschhoek Mountains. The last wild elephant in the valley died in the 1930s. Some leopards still survive.

⓲ **Boschendal** lies at the base of Helshoogte Pass. With a history dating back three centuries, this lovely estate competes with Groot Constantia as one of the Cape's major attractions; you could easily spend half a day here. Cradled between the Simonsberg and Groot Drakenstein mountains, the farm "Bossendaal" was originally granted to Jean le Long, one of the first French Huguenot settlers in the late 17th century.

Boschendal runs one of the most pleasant wine tastings in the region: You can sit inside at the Taphuis, a Cape Dutch longhouse and the oldest building on the estate, or outside at wrought-iron tables under a spreading oak. In 1978, Boschendal was the first to pioneer a Cape blanc de noir, a pink wine made in a white-wine style from black grapes. The Boschendal Blanc de Noir remains the best-selling wine of this style. If you prefer sparkling wines, try the extremely popular Boschendal Brut, a blend of pinot noir and chardonnay made by the Méthode Cap Classique. From the Taphuis, it's a two-minute drive through vines and fruit trees to the main estate complex. The excellent Boschendal Restaurant (☞ Dining and Lodging, *below*) serves a buffet of Cape specialties. Le Café serves light meals at tables under the oaks leading to the manor house. And Le Pique Nique (open November–April) provides picnic baskets for visitors to enjoy on the lawns. Calling ahead for the restaurant and the picnic is essential. A gift shop sells wine, locally made rugs, preserves, and other Cape kitsch. ⊠ *R310, between Franschhoek and Stellenbosch (Pniel Rd., Groot Drakenstein)*, ☎ *021/870–4224,* 𝖥𝖠𝖷 *021/ 874–1531.* 🖃 *Tastings R5, cellar tours R5.* ☉ *Dec.–Jan., Mon.–Sat. 8:30–4:30, Sun. 8:30–12:30; Feb.–Nov., weekdays 8:30–4:30, Sat. 8:30–12:30. Cellar tours by appointment. Vineyard tours weekdays at 10:30 and 11:30, Sat. 10:30.*

⓳ Even in a region where superlatives seem to fall short, **L'Ormarins** stands out as something special. The 1811 manor house, approached through a tunnel of oaks, is spellbinding: a classic Cape Dutch building festooned with flowers and framed by majestic peaks. The huge tasting room is modern and slick, in great contrast to the manor house—which indicates the modern wine-making style here. Using classic grape varieties, the wine makers produce big, complex red wines, ready for early drinking but with excellent maturation potential. Optima is such a wine. A blend of predominantly cabernet sauvignon and merlot, it has great complexity that will improve in the bottle for 10 to 15 years. The straight cabernet is just as pleasing; among whites, try the Rhine Riesling. ⊠ *R45 (Franschhoek Rd.), Groot Drakenstein,* ☎ *021/874–1026,* FAX *021/ 874–1361.* ⌨ *Tastings R5.* ☉ *Weekdays 9–4:30, Sat. 9–12:30. Cellar tours weekdays at 10, 11:30, and 3; Sat. at 11.*

㉑ Bellingham Wines lies deep in the shadows of old oaks, its Cape Dutch manor house almost completely hidden from view. The house is off-limits, but you can stroll unaccompanied through the vineyards, which run up the slope toward the craggy base of the mountains. From December to January, you can also order light luncheon platters to eat under the trees. There has been a renaissance here in recent years: Much money and oodles of talent have turned this estate's wines around. Ignore the also-ran range and head straight for the wines with the Premium and Vintage labels. Don't miss the cabernet franc, a big, rich, spicy wine, and the sweetish, fruity Pinotage, or the value priced Sauvenay (a sauvignon blanc–chardonnay blend) among the whites. ⊠ *R45,* ☎ *021/874–1011,* FAX *021/874–1712.* ⌨ *Tastings R5.* ☉ *Weekdays 9–5, Sat. 10–12:30. No cellar tours.*

The R45 shares a narrow bridge over the Berg River with the railway **㉑** line. Less than 2 km (1 mi) beyond the bridge is the **La Motte Estate,** owned by a branch of the same Rupert family that owns L'Ormarins. The elegant and rather formal tasting room looks into the cellars through a wall of smoked glass. Visitors sit at a long, marble-topped table and sample five to seven wines. The shiraz is one of the biggest and boldest that you'll taste of this variety, full of rich flavors; it needs four to eight years to reach its peak. The Millennium is a very good blend of just over 50% cabernet sauvignon with the balance consisting of merlot and a little cabernet franc. This wine needs time to develop, coming into its own in 5 to 10 years. ⊠ *R45 (Huguenot Rd.),* ☎ *021/876–3119,* FAX *021/876–3446.* ⌨ *Tastings R2.60.* ☉ *Weekdays 9–4:30, Sat. 9–noon. No cellar tours.*

㉒ The village of **Franschhoek** lies at the base of the Franschhoek Mountains, which seal off the eastern end of the valley. It's a delightful village, with a pleasant, slow pace that belies the extraordinary number of restaurants, cafés, and small inns in town. It's makes a great stop for lunch or overnight.

The **Huguenot Memorial** (⊠ Lambrecht and Huguenot Sts.) stands at the end of the main road through Franschhoek. It was built in 1943 to commemorate the contribution of the Huguenots to South Africa's development. The three arches symbolize the Holy Trinity, the sun and cross form the Huguenots' emblem, and the female figure in front represents Freedom of Conscience.

Next to the memorial is the **Huguenot Memorial Museum.** Its main building is modeled after Thibault's 1791 Saasveld in Cape Town. The museum traces the causes of the Huguenots' flight from France and the life they carved out for themselves in the Cape. Wall displays profile some of the early Huguenot families. Exhibits also focus on other aspects of the region's history: One explains the development of Cape Dutch architecture; another explores the culture and life of the Khoikhoi, also known as Hottentots. ⊠ *Lambrecht St.,* ☎ *021/876–2532.* ⌨ *R4.* ☉ *Weekdays 9–5, Sat. 9–1 and 2–5, Sun. 2–5.*

Built in 1994 on the lower slopes of the Franschhoek Mountains, **㉓ Haute Cabrière** is the brainchild of Achim von Arnim, one of the Cape's most colorful wine makers. To avoid scarring the mountain, the complex hunkers into the hillside. In the restaurant, you can see the underground cellar through a large window—a very avant-garde touch for the Cape. Von Arnim makes five sparkling wines strictly according to the methods used in champagne. It is said that his fruity, mouth-filling '94 pinot noir set the standard by which Cape pinot noirs are judged. Also delicious is the chardonnay–pinot noir blend, an ideal, extremely quaffable wine to enjoy at lunchtime. ⊠ *R45,* ☎ *021/ 876–2630,* ℻ *021/876–3390.* ✆ *Tastings R5, cellar tours and tastings R10 (by appointment only).* ☉ *Weekdays 8–5, Sat. 11–1.*

Dining and Lodging

$$$$ ✕ **Boschendal Restaurant.** Reserve well in advance for the buffet lunch here at one of the Cape's most beautiful and historic wineries. A wide selection of soups, quiches, and pâtés prefaces a bewildering array of cold and hot main dishes, including pickled fish, roasts, and imaginative salads; traditional Cape dishes are well prepared. End with a sampling of local cheeses and preserves or a classic Cape dessert like malva pudding. ⊠ *R310, between Franschhoek and Stellenbosch,* ☎ *021/870– 4274. Reservations essential. AE, DC, MC, V. No dinner.*

$$$$ ✕ **Haute Cabrière.** Dine here atop a working winery built into the mountainside. Try to secure a window table for views across the vine-clad valley as you select from a mix-and-match menu created to complement the estate wines maturing in the cellar beneath you. Order half or full portions of the region's homegrown salmon trout and salad greens or tomato and goat cheese ravioli with toasted pine nuts and a watercress dressing. Sample the rack of lamb teamed with truffle oil mashed potatoes, or grilled pork cutlet with balsamic glaze and red bell pepper chutney. Don't miss the warm chocolate tart with milk chocolate ice cream, or indulge in a savory finale of Brie with fruit and green fig preserve. ⊠ *R45, Franschhoek Pass, Franschhoek,* ☎ *021/876–3688. Reservations essential. AE, DC, MC, V. No dinner Tues.*

$$$$ ✕ **La Couronne.** In a town renowned for gastronomic abundance, this comparative newcomer has already garnered impressive awards. Whether you dine at windowside tables or sit on the spacious terrace, you will have panoramic views over the valley. Chef Peter Goffe-Wood presents trendy cosmopolitan cuisine that makes the most of valley produce: chilled bell-pepper soup is a crimson puree both delectable and dense in flavor, while ceviche of salmon trout comes topped with mesclun and teamed with tomato and cilantro salsa. Main courses of line fish served with a risotto and rack of lamb on a bed of caponata with roasted garlic aioli are both recommended. A mascarpone and ginger cheesecake vies with shortbread tartlets filled with ice cream and berries as the definitive summer dessert. ⊠ *Robertsvlei Rd., Franschhoek,* ☎ *021/876–2770. Reservations essential. AE, DC, MC, V.*

$$$$ ✕ **Le Quartier Français.** This restaurant in a 19th-century home has garnered impressive local and international awards. On summer nights, glass doors open onto a spotlighted garden; in winter, a log fire burns in the hearth. Chef Margot Janse's entrées include shiitake and beetroot cappuccino with hazelnut froth and smoked tomato tart Tatin with olive dressing and Parmesan crackling. Her double-baked blue cheese soufflé comes with watercress gnocchi and a red-pepper compote. Grilled ostrich fillet is teamed with leeks and citrus preserve. Creative desserts include *rooibos* (herb tea) honey and orange *granita* (ice) with a rosemary biscuit and an apricot brownie sandwich with honey frozen yogurt. ⊠ *16 Huguenot Rd., Franschhoek,* ☎ *021/876–2151. Reservations essential. AE, DC, MC, V. No dinner Sun.*

$$$$ ✕ **Topsi & Company.** Chef Topsi Venter, doyenne of the Cape culinary scene, is as renowned as a raconteur as she is for her innovative country fare. The decor is simple and rustic, and local art lines the white walls. The menus, written on a blackboard, change daily, and only local and fresh ingredients are used. Proceedings could start with a liver and pear terrine teamed with caramelized leeks and go on to Franschhoek trout fillets in vermouth on wilted spinach, or pot-roasted rabbit marinated in shiraz and juniper berries served with maize meal dumplings. Farm cheeses paired with cardamom-spiked quinces make a flavorful alternative to dessert. In this valley of wonderful wines, it's great to be able to BYOB. ⊠ *7 Reservoir St., Franschhoek,* ☎ *021/876–2952. Reservations essential. DC, MC, V. Closed Tues.*

$$$ ⌂ **Le Quartier Français.** In the center of town, this classy guest house is a Winelands favorite. Separated from the village's main drag by a courtyard bistro and a superb restaurant (☞ *above*), the guest house exudes privacy and peace. Rooms in two-story whitewashed cottages face a pool deck and central garden exploding with flowers. Decor is low-key, with rustic furniture, sponge-painted walls, and small fireplaces. Upstairs rooms have timber beams and mountain views, but they're hot in summer. Rooms have TVs and ceiling fans but no air-conditioning. ⊠ *Huguenot Rd. (mailing address: Box 237, Franschhoek 7690),* ☎ *021/876–2248 or 021/876–2151,* 𝔽𝔸𝕏 *021/876–3105. 14 rooms. 2 restaurants, bar, pool. AE, DC, MC, V.*

$ ⌂ **Le Ballon Rouge Guest House.** In an old homestead in the center of Franschhoek village, this colonial-style guest house offers good value for money. Rooms open onto a veranda directly fronting the street— ideal for watching the world go by—and are small and feminine, with pretty floral fabrics, brass bedsteads, and country armoires. ⊠ *7 Reservoir St., Box 344, Franschhoek 7690,* ☎ *021/876–2651,* 𝔽𝔸𝕏 *021/876– 3743. 7 rooms. Restaurant, room service, pool. BP. AE, DC, MC, V.*

Paarl

21 km (13 mi) northwest of Franschhoek.

Soon after you pass La Motte on the R45, turn right onto the R303, which runs into North Paarl. Cross under the N1 and continue for a couple of blocks. At the traffic lights, turn right onto Optenhorst Street and follow the signs to Nederburg, on the Paarl Wine Route.

㉔ **Nederburg** is the Cape's most established wine label; no restaurant's wine list would be complete without some of its wine. It's a vast estate, and it is easy to feel overwhelmed by the industrial white buildings. Fortunately, the tasting room is friendly and welcoming, and cellar tours lead visitors through the estate's fine Cape Dutch homestead, built in 1800. You can also reserve picnic baskets to enjoy on the estate's lawns (except during the buildup to the annual Nederburg Auction in March or April). The auction is one of the world's most glamorous wine events, when the very best wine from all over the Cape is sold to the highest bidders, nearly half to overseas buyers. Besides those produced specially for the auction, Nederburg produces about 20 wines under its regular label, covering the spectrum of reds and whites. The estate's Noble Late Harvest is exceptional. For an easy-drinking dry white wine, try Prelude, a successful blend of sauvignon blanc and chardonnay. Paarl Cabernet Sauvignon is a traditional unblended cabernet with subtle wood tones. It ages extremely well for 5 to 10 years. ⊠ *WR4 (Meaker Rd.), Huguenot,* ☎ *021/862–3104,* 𝔽𝔸𝕏 *021/ 862–3320.* ▨ *Tastings free.* ☼ *Weekdays 8:30–5, Sat. 9–1. Cellar tours (in English, Afrikaans, German, or French) by appointment.*

Drive back down Optenhorst and continue straight through the set of traffic lights. At the next light, turn right onto North Main Street and drive 5 km (3 mi) to **Rhebokskloof.** The winery sits at the head of a shallow valley, backed by hillsides covered with vines and fynbos. It's a lovely place for lunch on a sunny day. The Victorian Restaurant serves à la carte meals and teas on an oak-shaded terrace overlooking the gardens and mountains; in inclement weather, meals are served in the Cape Dutch Restaurant, as is a Sunday buffet lunch. The full-bodied cabernet sauvignon is the pick of the bunch, with good fruit, cassis, and cedarbox aromas that follow through to the palate. It will develop for four to six years. ⊠ *WR8,* ☎ *021/863–8386,* ℻ *021/863–8504.* ✑ *Tastings R5.* ◷ *Nov.–Apr., daily 9–5; May–Oct., daily 9–4:30. No cellar tours.*

㉖ **Paarl** takes its name from the granite domes of Paarl Mountain, which looms above the town—*Paarlpaarl* is Afrikaans for pearl. The first farmers settled here in 1687, two years after the founding of Stellenbosch. The town has its fair share of historic homes and estates, but it lacks the charm of its distinguished neighbor simply because it's so spread out. Main Street, the town's oak-lined thoroughfare, extends some 11 km (7 mi) along the western bank of the Berg River. You can gain a good sense of the town's history on a drive along this lovely street.

Main Street North doglegs to the right at Lady Grey Street before continuing as Main Street South. On your left, the **Paarl Museum** (formerly Oude Pastorie) occupies a gorgeous Cape Dutch home built as a parsonage in 1787. In fact, the building itself is of more interest than the collection, which includes odds and ends donated by local families, including silver, glass, and kitchen utensils. A pleasant café at the side of the museum serves tea and snacks at tables on the museum lawns. ⊠ *303 Main St.,* ☎ *021/807–3008.* ✑ *R2.* ◷ *Weekdays 8–5.*

From the Paarl Museum walk about 200 yards along Pastorie Street to the **Afrikaans Language Museum** (Afrikaanse Taalmuseum), in the Gideon Malherbe House. It was from here in 1875 that the Society of True Afrikaners launched their campaign to gain widespread acceptance for Afrikaans, hitherto considered a sort of inferior, kitchen Dutch. The museum will be of limited interest to many visitors, since the displays are entirely in Afrikaans. ⊠ *Pastorie St.,* ☎ *021/872–3441.* ✑ *R2.* ◷ *Weekdays 8–5.*

Continue along Main Street past the Paarl Publicity Office (☞ Winelands A to Z, *below*) to **Zeederberg Square,** a grassy park bordered by some excellent examples of Cape Dutch, Georgian, and Victorian homes. A little farther down Main Street on the left is the old **Dutch Reformed Church,** a thatched building dating back to 1805. The cemetery contains the tombstones of the Malherbe family, which was instrumental in the campaign to gain official recognition for Afrikaans.

Continue down Main Street until you see signs leading to KWV Cellars. **㉗** **KWV** is short for Ko-operatieve Wijnbouwers Vereniging (Cooperative Winegrowers' Association), which for nearly 80 years has regulated and controlled the Cape wine industry. KWV sells wine and spirits in more than 40 countries and more than 30 U.S. states, and its brandies, sherries, and fortified dessert wines regularly garner gold medals at the International Wine & Spirit Competition in London. It also offers one of the most popular and most crowded cellar tours in the Winelands. KWV's cellars are the largest in the world, covering some 55 acres. Among the highlights is the famous Cathedral Cellar, with a barrel-vaulted ceiling and giant vats carved with scenes from the history of Cape wine making. In an adjoining cellar, you can see under one roof the five largest vats in the world. The tour begins with a short audiovisual presentation and ends with a tasting of some of KWV's products. ✉ *André du Toit Bldg., Kohler St.,* ☎ *021/807–3007,* FAX *021/863–1942.* ☞ *Cellar tours and tastings R10 (reservations essential).* ☉ *Tours Mon.–Sat. at 9:30, 10:15, 11, and 2:15.*

Return to Main Street and turn left. After the N1 bridge, a sign on your right points the way to the **Afrikaans Language Monument** (Afrikaanse Taalmonument), set high on a hill overlooking Paarl. Like the Voortrekker Monument in Pretoria, this concrete structure holds a special place in the hearts of Afrikaners, who struggled for years to gain acceptance for their language alongside English. The rising curve of the main pillar is supposed to represent the growth and potential of Afrikaans. When it was erected in 1973, the monument was as much a gesture of political victory as a paean to the Afrikaans language. Ironically, it may become the language's memorial. Under the new South Africa, Afrikaans has become just one of 11 official languages and is gradually losing its dominance. The view from the top of the hill is incredible, taking in Table Mountain, False Bay, Paarl Valley, and the various mountain ranges of the Winelands. A short, paved walking trail leads around the hillside past impressive fynbos specimens, particularly proteas. ✉ *Afrikaans Taalmonument Rd.* ☞ *R2.* ☉ *Daily 9–5.*

Halfway down the hill from the monument is a turnoff onto a dirt road and a sign for the Paarl Mountain Nature Reserve. The dirt road is **Jan Philips Drive,** which runs 11 km (7 mi) along the mountainside, offering tremendous views over the valley. Along the way, it passes the **Mill Water Wildflower Garden** and the starting points for myriad trails, including hikes up to the great, granite domes of Paarl Mountain. The dirt road rejoins Main Street at the far end of Paarl.

㉙ Fairview is one of the few wineries where visitors might feel comfortable taking their families. Children will get a kick out of seeing peacocks roaming the grounds and goats clambering up a spiral staircase into a goat tower. Every afternoon at four the goats are milked. Fairview produces a superb line of goat cheeses, all of which you can taste gratis. If you want to put together a picnic for the lawn, a deli counter sells sausages and cold meats to complement the estate's wines and cheeses.

Don't let Fairview's sideshows color your judgment about the wines. Charles Back, a member of the family that sells Backsberg (☞ *below*), is one of the most successful and innovative wine makers in the Cape, and the estate's wines are excellent and often surprising. Back has produced a shiraz-merlot blend, a shiraz-gamay, a crouchen-chardonnay, a sauvignon blanc–chenin blanc, and an excellent sauvignon blanc–sémillon. ✉ *WR3, off R101 (Suid-Agter-Paarl Rd.),* ☎ *021/863–2450,* FAX *021/863–2591.* ☞ *Tastings free.* ☉ *Weekdays 8:30–5, Sat. 8:30–1. Cellar tours by appointment.*

㉚ For 80 years **Backsberg** winery (framed by the mountains of the Simonsberg) has been run by the Back family, well known for producing award-winning wines of good value. An unusual feature of the winery is the self-conducted cellar tour. Visitors follow painted lines around the cellars, pausing to watch video monitors that explain the wine-making process. It's a low-pressure introduction to wine making and an ideal starting point for novices. Backsberg produces a comprehensive range of red and white wines, a Méthode Cap Classique sparkling wine, and a fine brandy made from chenin blanc. The chardonnay is consistently one of the best made, a rounded, fruity wine that develops well in the bottle for five or more years. Backsberg is the only producer of a Malbec, full of fruity berry flavors; it won a Veritas Gold award.

✉ *WR1, between R44 and R45 (Simondium Rd.),* ☎ *021/875–5141,* FAX *021/875–5144.* ✒ *Tastings R5, cellar tours free.* ◎ *Weekdays 8:30–5, Sat. 8:30–1.*

Ballooning

Wineland Ballooning (☎ 021/863–3192) in Paarl makes one-hour flights over the Winelands every morning from mid-October until the end of April, weather permitting. The balloon holds a maximum of six people, and the trip costs R750 per person. After the flight, everyone returns to the Grand Roche Hotel for a champagne breakfast.

Dining and Lodging

$$$$ ✕ **Bosman's.** Set amid the heady opulence of the Grand Roche hotel, ★ this elegant restaurant and Relais & Châteaux member ranks as one of the country's finest. The level of service is extraordinary, commensurate with that of the finest European restaurants, although some diners may find the attention a little suffocating. After a complimentary *amuse-bouche* (literally something to entertain your mouth), diners can start with a smoked carpaccio of Karoo lamb with roasted garlic dressing, or chilled fruit soup flavored with port wine. Line fish with gratinéed crayfish and chervil mousseline, fillet of kudu with butternut-potato puree, and beef with coriander butter and green peppercorn sauce are all excellent main-course selections. Beautifully plated desserts like quince and white chocolate gateau teamed with mandarin salad or orange soufflé with white-chocolate yogurt sorbet finish the meal in sophisticated style. ✉ *Grand Roche hotel, Plantasie St.,* ☎ *021/863–2727. AE, DC, MC, V.*

$$$$ 🏨 **Grande Roche.** A member of the prestigious Relais & Châteaux group, ★ this establishment can stake a claim as the best hotel in South Africa. In a gorgeous Cape Dutch manor house that dates from the mid-18th century, the hotel sits amid acres of vines beneath Paarl Mountain, overlooking the valley and the Drakenstein Mountains. Suites are housed either in the historical buildings—slave quarters, stables, and wine cellar—or in attractive, new terrace buildings constructed in traditional Cape Dutch style. Rooms are a tasteful mix of the modern and the old: Reed ceilings and thatch comfortably coexist with heated towel racks and air-conditioning. The staff, many of whom trained in Europe, outnumber the guests two to one and offer a level of service extremely rare in South Africa. ✉ *Plantasie St., Box 6038, Paarl 7622,* ☎ *021/ 863–2727,* FAX *021/863–2220. 35 suites. Restaurant, bar, room service, 2 pools, 2 tennis courts, exercise room. BP. AE, DC, MC, V.*

$$$$ ✕ **Roggeland.** For an unforgettable Cape experience, make a beeline for this glorious Cape Dutch manor house on a farm outside Paarl. Meals are long, languid rituals, whether it's an alfresco lunch in the garden or a four-course dinner in the 18th-century dining room. An evening might start with butternut coconut soup infused with lemongrass. A second course of grilled salmon trout with spinach pasta and red onion lemon salsa may be followed by red currant–glazed duck with chive couscous and a Mediterranean vegetable gateau. A heritage finale of malva pudding is served with rose-geranium ice cream. A different wine, included in the price, accompanies each course. ✉ *Roggeland Rd., North Paarl,* ☎ *021/868–2501. Reservations essential. AE, DC, MC, V.*

$$$$ 🏨 **Roggeland Country House.** Dating back to 1693, this historic farm ★ is one of the most delightful lodgings in the Winelands. The setting in Dal Josaphat Valley is breathtaking, with stunning views of the craggy Drakenstein Mountains. Guest rooms in restored farm buildings have reed ceilings, country dressers, and mosquito nets (not just for effect). The 1779 manor house, which contains the dining room and lounge, is a masterpiece of Cape Dutch architecture. Dinner and breakfast in

the fine restaurant (☞ *above*) are included in the rates. Be prepared for the slightly jarring sight of Fairyland, a shantytown a few minutes down the road from the inn, in case you happen upon it. ☒ *Rogge-land Rd., Box 7210, Northern Paarl 7623,* ☎ *021/868–2501,* ℻ *021/868–2113. 10 rooms. Restaurant. MAP. AE, DC, MC, V.*

$$$ 🏨 **Bartholomeus Klip Farmhouse.** For a break from a long bout of wine tasting, head to this Victorian guest house near Wellington on a na-ture reserve and working farm. Its luxurious accommodations and ex-cellent food come in the middle of 9,900 acres of rare *renosterveld* scrubland that is home to the endangered geometric tortoise. There are also plenty of elands, zebras, wildebeests, springboks, rheboks, bon-teboks, bat-eared foxes, Cape buffalos, and bird life in and around the mountains, streams, and plains. A wander around the farm, amid the barking of sheepdogs, is also amusing, and you can hike, mountain bike, or swim, as well. Rates include all meals, teas, and game drives. ☒ *Box 36, Hermon, 7308,* ☎ *022/448–1820,* ℻ *022/448–1829. 5 rooms. AE, DC, MC, V.*

$ 🏨 **Lemoenkloof Guesthouse.** In the heart of Paarl and a national mon-ument, this house is decorated in sophisticated country style. While the modern accouterments such as television, air-conditioning, bar fridge, and tea/coffee-making facilities in each of the guest rooms make your stay comfortable, the swimming pool and art gallery add an element of fun. A full South African breakfast is included in the rate, and din-ner can be arranged. ☒ *396A Main St., Box 2726, Paarl 7620,* ☎ *021/872–7520 or 021/872–7532,* ℻ *021/872–3782. 20 rooms. Pool. BP. AE, DC, MC, V.*

$ 🏨 **Rodeberg Lodge.** Right on Main Street in the heart of Paarl, this homey inn is one of the best examples of Victorian architecture in town. There's nothing flashy about the place—its main attraction is the per-sonal attention of owners Brian and Julie Lundie. Rooms are simply furnished, with rustic pine furniture, plain bedspreads, and hardwood floors. Downstairs rooms, with their high ceilings and large windows, are a better choice than those upstairs, which feel as if they're in an attic. None of the rooms has TV. ☒ *74 Main St., Box 2611, Paarl 7620,* ☎ *021/863–3202,* ℻ *021/863–3203. 6 rooms. BP. DC, MC, V.*

Golf

Paarl Golf Club (☒ Wemmershoek Rd., ☎ 021/863–1140) is sur-rounded by mountains, covered with trees, and dotted with water hazards. The greens fee is R100 for 18 holes.

Winelands A to Z

Arriving and Departing

BY CAR

From Cape Town it shouldn't take more than 30 minutes to Somerset West, 45 minutes to Stellenbosch and Paarl, and an hour to Franschhoek. If you're heading to Paarl or Franschhoek, it's a straight shot up the N1 before the turnoff onto the R45. To reach Somerset West, take the N2 to the R44/Somerset West turnoff and then follow the signs onto Main Street, the town's main drag. If you continue straight up the R44 instead, you come to Stellenbosch. The quickest way to reach Stellen-bosch, however, is to leave the N2 at the Eerste Rivier/Stellenbosch exit and follow the R310 straight into town.

BY TRAIN

Cape Metro trains run from Cape Town to Stellenbosch and Paarl, but with the increase in violent muggings and robbery in the area, the trains should be avoided.

Getting Around

BY BICYCLE

As long as you stick to the valley floors, you shouldn't have too many problems touring the Winelands on a bike, although summers here are very, very hot. You can rent mountain bikes for R40–R50 a day at **Village Cycles** (☎ 021/872–8909) in Stellenbosch.

BY CAR

Traveling around the Winelands in your own car is a snap. The whole Winelands region is quite small, and it's almost impossible to get lost. To help you even further, most of the wineries, hotels, and major attractions are clearly signposted with large, brown road signs. If you've arrived in the Winelands without a car, call **Avis** (☎ 021/887–0492), **Budget** (☎ 021/887–6935), **Premier** (☎ 021/883–9103), or **Imperial** (☎ 021/883–8140) in Stellenbosch; in Paarl contact **Wine Route Rent-a-Car** (☎ 021/872–8513 or 083/225–7089).

BY TAXI

Roland's Tours and Taxis (☎ 021/887–7295, FAX 021/887–7293) in Stellenbosch will provide a minibus and driver for four to seven people to tour the Winelands for a half day at R135 per person or a full day at R165 per person. In Paarl, **Paarl Radio Taxis** (☎ 021/872–5671) will transport up to four people at R4 per kilometer (½ mi).

Contacts and Resources

EMERGENCIES

Police/Fire (☎ 10111). **Ambulance** (☎ 10177).

GUIDED TOURS

Vineyard Ventures (⊠ 5 Hanover Rd., Fresnaye, Cape Town 8001, ☎ 021/434–8888) is the best of several companies offering tours of the Winelands. Sisters Gillian Stoltzman and Glen Christie are knowledgeable and passionate about wine and will tailor tours to your interest. You can also opt for one of their standard one-day tours. All tours feature wine tastings at top cellars and an excellent lunch.

If your interest in wine is limited, you're better off taking a general-interest tour of the Winelands that throws in only a couple of wine tastings. In the Winelands, contact **Travelmark** (☎ 021/872–1994 or 021/872–1938) or **Vintage Cape Tours** (☎ 021/872–9252), both based in Paarl. Otherwise, call one of the big Cape Town operators like **Hylton Ross, Ideal Tours,** or **Mother City Tours** (☞ Cape Town A to Z in Chapter 4).

For about R500, **Cape Eco Safaris** (☎ 02211/63–8334) offers 30-minute flights over Paarl and the surrounding area for two to three adults. **Civair** (☎ 021/419–5182) offers 2½-hour helicopter tours of the Winelands and part of the peninsula for R1480 per person, including lunch at a winery.

VISITOR INFORMATION

Franschhoek Vallée Tourismé. ⊠ *Huguenot Rd., Franschhoek,* ☎ *021/876–3603,* FAX *021/876–2768.* ☉ *Mon.–Sat. 10–5, Sun. 10–1.*

Paarl Tourism Bureau. ⊠ *216 Main St., Paarl,* ☎ *021/872–3829 or 021/872–4842,* FAX *021/872–9376.* ☉ *Weekdays 9–5:30, Sat. 9–1, Sun. 10–1.*

Somerset West Tourist Information Bureau. ⊠ *11 Victoria St., Somerset West,* ☎ *021/851–4022,* FAX *021/851–1497.* ☉ *Weekdays 8:30–1 and 2–4:30, Sat. 9–noon.*

Stellenbosch Tourist Bureau. ⊠ *36 Market St., Stellenbosch,* ☎ *021/883–3584,* FAX *021/883–8017.* ☉ *Weekdays 8–5:30, Sat. 9–5, Sun. 9:30–4:30.*

THE BREEDE RIVER VALLEY

There are few areas in South Africa that have boundaries as fuzzy as the **Boland** (literally "Upper Land"). It is safe to say that the area is bounded more spiritually than geographically, but at its heart lies the **Breede River Valley.** Cape-Dutch homesteads and undulating vineyards typify what is essentially the immediate hinterland of the Western Cape, making the Boland the source of much of the Western Cape's traditional folklore. Most of the fabled Voortrekkers (often likened to America's pioneers) trekked northward from farms in this area, so that today, in the minds, but especially in the hearts of most non-indigenous South Africans, it is the source of much of the entire country's emotional heritage. As a result, the inhabitants of this area, not too distant from Cape Town, often see themselves as the proud guardians of this patriarchal heritage.

Especially relevant to the visitor with time constraints, a sojourn or even a day excursion into this undeniably atmospheric area is essential. A short drive over any one of the scenic mountain passes is sure to bring you into a secluded valley, resplendent with the greens of spring, the grape-laden vines of summer, the myriad colors of autumn, or the snowcapped peaks and crisp misty mornings of winter. Whatever the season, you have entered a region where hospitality is a proud way of life, where the country squire and roadside peasant will greet you with equally open arms.

A natural climatic combination of comparatively mild but wet winters, followed by long, warm summers, makes this area perfectly suited for the cultivation of deciduous fruit, especially viticulture. In the summer, the intense sunshine allows the rich ruby colors to develop on the wine and table grapes. Virtually devoid of rain in summer, the fungus-prone vines nurture their precious crop, irrigated from the meandering Breede River and her many tributaries like the Hex and the Nuy. Fed by mountain streams, the catchment area collects runoff from the melting snows, which fall only on the mountain peaks during winter, effectively creating a frozen water reservoir for the farms in the interleading valleys below.

While most vintners have made some effort to enhance the aesthetic qualities of their wineries, more often than not a faux–Cape Dutch structure forms scant facade to unlovely winery sheds, mercifully camouflaged somewhat by trees. But what these plentiful wineries that dot the area might lack in architectural beauty is made up for in the warmth of the farmers' hospitality (many wineries are staffed by extended families) and in the quality and variety of their wine, often available by the bottle and readily and reliably shipped to any destination abroad.

Apart from winery-hopping, the Breede River valley offers visitors a plethora of activities. Almost every town of significance has its own museum, often housed in a historic building. Outdoor-based pursuits also abound. If you are of the more laid-back bent, take time to cool off in the mineral-rich "cola water" at one of the camping-picnic resorts, or if you prefer more energetic pursuits, there are opportunities galore for hiking, horseback riding, or golfing.

A quaint, if outdated, local custom is for businesses and even museums to close for lunch between 1 and 2, often to the puzzlement and frustration of visitors, so wherever you find yourself at this time, your easiest option is to follow local custom and stop off for lunch.

Towns and sights are marked on the Western Cape map.

The Bain's Kloof

16 km (10 mi) north-northeast of Paarl.

The **Bain's Kloof Pass,** built by engineer Andrew Geddes Bain, was opened in 1853, linking Wellington to Ceres and Worcester. The road winds northward from Wellington, through the **Hawekwa Mountains,** revealing breathtaking views across the valley below. On a clear day, you can see as far as the coast. The road has a good tar surface, but unlike many Western Cape passes, the Bain's Kloof has not been widened much since it was built, so take your time and enjoy the views. From Paarl, take the R303 toward Wellington, about 16 km (10 mi) distant. Follow R303, which becomes the main road through Wellington, and this will soon pan out into a eucalyptus-lined avenue, which becomes Bain's Kloof Pass.

En Route As you approach the initial slopes of the Bain's Kloof, look out for the **Bovlei Winery** on the left. Built in 1987 in traditional style, the building itself is not particularly noteworthy, but it has a vast picture window offering a stupendous view of the undulating vineyards beyond. Be sure to try their light new-world-style reds and the rare fortified Red Hanepoot Muscat d'Alexandrie. ✉ *Box 82, Wellington, 7655,* ☎ *021/873–1567,* ℻ *021/873–1386.* ✉ *Free.* ☉ *Weekdays 8–5, Sat. 8:30–12:30.*

Tulbagh

50 km (32 mi) north of Paarl.

As the Bain's Kloof Pass ends, turn left onto the R46, which will lead you through Wolsely (not worth stopping at) and then directly to **Tulbagh** after about 15 minutes. Founded in 1743, the town of Tulbagh is nestled in a secluded valley bounded on three sides by the Witzenberg, Winterhoek, and Qbiqua mountains. A devastating earthquake in September 1969 shook the city and destroyed many of the original facades of the historic town.

The bulk of the town is unlovely, having simply been rebuilt, often prefab-style, on old foundations, but the real attraction of Tulbagh is **Church Street** parallel to the main Van Der Stel Street, where each of the 32 buildings was restored to its original form and subsequently declared a National Monument.

The **Oude Kerk** (Old Church) museum stands at the entrance to Church Street and is the logical departure point for a self-guided tour of the area, which is well signposted. The church has been extensively restored, and has an interesting collection of artifacts from the area including carvings made by Boer prisoners of war. A ticket includes admission to another three buildings on Church Street, which operate as annexes of the main museum. These show a practical history of events before, during, and after the quake. The buildings have been authentically reconstructed, and show painstakingly accurate period interiors. ☎ *023/230–1041.* ✉ *R5.* ☉ *Weekdays 9–5, Sat. 9–4, Sun. 11–4.*

Just 3 km (2 mi) out of town, built on high ground commensurate with its status, is the majestic **Oude Drostdy Museum.** Built by renowned Cape architect Louis Thibault in the mid-1700s. The building was badly damaged by fire around the turn of the 19th century, and later by the 1969 quake, but it has been painstakingly restored to its original glory, and is a fine example of Cape Dutch architecture. The building now houses a fine collection of antique furniture and artifacts. As the original magistrate's house, the Drostdy has a cellar, which served as the local jail. Now the cellar acts as a cool refuge from the heat of the day where you can sample one of the area's naturally sweet wines. ☎ *023/ 230–0203.* ☒ *Free.* ☺ *Mon.–Sat. 10–12:50 and 2–4:30, Sun. 2:30–4:50.*

If you have time, **Vera's Miniature Houses** museum is well worth a visit. Owner-curator Vera Humphris has created some 30 or more miniature houses, each with its own furniture. Each piece of furniture is a replica of an actual piece, so ask her to open the rolltop desk or the drawers of the amoire. ☒ *4 Witzenberg St., Tulbach,* ☎ *023/230–0651.* ☒ *R5.* ☺ *Daily 9:30–12:30 and 2:30–4:30, Sun. 9:30–12:30.*

Dining and Lodging

$$–$$$ ✕ **Paddagang.** Though originally built as a private residence in 1809, by 1821 Paddagang was already serving as one of South Africa's first tap houses (like a pub with wine on tap). Immaculately restored after the 1969 earthquake, it was turned into a wine-house restaurant, where you can enjoy traditional Cape fare like South Africa's national dish *bobotie,* a light Malay curry of minced meat and dried fruit topped with a thin baked béchamel crust. As a starter, be sure to try the pâté of smoked *snoek* (a local fish). All the decor is traditional, including *riempie* (thong-upholstered) chairs. In good weather you can opt to dine under an immense vine-covered pergola. ☒ *23 Church St.,* ☎ *023/230–0242. AE, DC, MC, V. No dinner.*

$$ ✕ **Readers.** Housed in what was once the residence of the church reader (hence the name) diagonally opposite the old church, the restaurant is run by Carol Collins, a graduate of one of South Africa's most respected culinary schools—and it shows in the superb cuisine. The decor mirrors Carol's love for felines, with cat pictures and statuettes as well as a friendly well-fed tomcat guarding the door. The menu changes daily, depending on available fresh ingredients, but is sure to abound with creations like pork fillet with pears and blue cheese, trout with smoked mussels and mushrooms, or medallions of beef fillet with asparagus and Pont l'Évêque (an uncooked, Brie-like cheese). ☒ *12 Church St., Tulbach 6820,* ☎ *023/230–0087. AE, DC, MC, V. Closed Tues.*

$$$ ☷ **Rijk's Ridge Country House.** This spot is located on the outskirts of the village, on a ridge overlooking a lake where you can enjoy sweeping views of the surrounding mountains. Each suite, decorated in a plush Cape cottage style, has a private terrace leading to the poolside garden. ☒ *Main Rd., Box 340, 6820,* ☎ *023/230–1006,* ☒ *023/230–1125. 12 suites, 3 cottages. Restaurant, pool, billiards. AE, DC, MC, V.*

Ceres

30 km (18½ mi) southeast of Tulbagh on the R46.

Named after the Roman fertility goddess, this town is at the center of one of South Africa's most important deciduous fruit- and fruit juice–producing areas in a scenic valley bounded by the Skurweberg, Witzenberg, and Hex River mountain ranges.

The town itself has few attractions but serves as a way station to scenic drives. The first, 42 km (26¼ mi) along the R46, leads to the **Theronsberg Pass,** with its panoramic views of the valley. About 6 km (4 mi) after the pass, turn onto the R356 onto a good gravel road to view **Karoopoort,** formerly the last stopping place for travelers and prospectors before embarking on the long trek through the arid Karoo.

Dining and Lodging

$$ ✕ **Oom Ben se Vat.** Meaning "Uncle Ben's Barrel," this old-style grill room offers silver-service fare in a *régime ancien,* with hefty portions, largely untouched by modern food fashion. For starters try the deep-fried Camembert, and go on to the pepper fillet steak or the gargantuan fried sole. ⊠ *Belmont Hotel, Porter St., Ceres 6835,* ☎ *023/312–1150. AE, DC, MC, V. Closed Sun.*

$$ 🏨 **Belmont Hotel.** Within walking distance from the town's center, this charming family-run hotel has a resort-like feel with facilities such as a heated indoor swimming pool and squash and tennis courts. The rooms are scrupulously clean, with quaint, if not opulent, decor. This is a great place to spend a day or two relaxing. ⊠ *Porter St., Ceres 6835,* ☎ *023/312–1150,* 𝗙𝗔𝗫 *023/312–1150. 31 rooms, 7 chalets. 2 restaurants, 1 indoor and 1 outdoor pool, beauty salon, hot tub. AE, DC, MC, V.*

Worcester

60 km (37½ mi) south of Ceres via R43 to N1.

Worcester is by far the largest town in the Breede River valley, often termed the region's capital by locals, and with good cause. Much of the town's burgeoning commerce and industry are connected to agriculture— viticulture in particular—and its brandy cellars produce the highest volume of the spirit in the country.

The **KWV Brandy Cellar** is the largest distillery of its kind in the world, with 120 pot stills under one roof. Informative guided tours, followed by a brandy tasting, will take you through the process of brandy making. The well-informed guide will give a layman's rundown of the various methods used, the pros and cons of pot still distillation as opposed to the continuous still method, as well as a description of the maturation process. ⊠ *Worcester Wine Route,* ☎ *023/342–0255,* 🎫 *R9.* ☉ *Tours Mon.–Sat. at 2.*

The **Karoo National Botanical Garden** lies on the opposite side of the N1 highway to the town of Worcester but is easy to find if you follow the signs eastward from the last set of traffic lights on High Street. Billed as one of the most important botanical gardens in the world, the collection here includes several hundred species of indigenous flora, succulents, aloes, and trees. Follow the road from the entrance to the main parking area from where you can take one of three clearly marked walks. A special Braille Garden allows the visually impaired to touch, feel, and smell. 🎫 *Free.* ☉ *Daily 8–6.*

The **Kleinplasie Living Open-Air Museum** is a a welcome change from dusty artifacts in glass cases. The fascinating museum is actually a collection of original buildings from the area which have been re-erected around a working farmyard. Following a narrated slide show, venture out into the farmyard and watch the museum staff intent on keeping traditional skills alive. They bake bread, twist tobacco, make horseshoes in a smithy, and distill *witblits* (moonshine). The museum also has a shop where you can buy produce from the farmyard. ⊠ *Kleinplasie Agricultural Showgrounds,* ☎ *023/342–0255.* 🎫 *R12.* ☉ *Mon.–Sat. 9–4:30, Sun. 10:30–4:30.*

Dining and Lodging

$$ ✕ **St. Geran.** In spite of the town's appeal to visitors, locals still form the bulk of the clientele, so don't expect a chichi presentation here. That said, the steak house–style decor in this converted house belies a cuisine with touches of unexpected subtlety, coupled with superb value for money. Try the mussel bisque or the grilled asparagus with cheddar cheese to start. Apart from the predictable selection of grilled steaks—all excellently prepared— there are also superb spareribs, and a panfried pepper steak with cream and sherry. ⊠ *48 Church St., 6850,* ☎ *023/342–2800. AE, DC, MC, V.*

$$–$$$ 🏨 **Cumberland Hotel.** Easily the best hotel in the area, the Cumberland is a destination on its own, in spite of being close to the center.

The reception area pans out into a secluded courtyard and the dining area and spa and gym facilities have been placed around a central landscaped swimming pool, a great spot to take a break from sightseeing. Rooms are all air-conditioned against the hot Karoo summer, scrupulously clean, and decorated in a modern style. Take time to look at the original watercolors which adorn the walls throughout the hotel. ⊠ *2 Stockenstrom St., 6850, ☎ 023/347–2641, ℻ 023/347–3613. 54 rooms, 1 suite. Pool, sauna, health club, squash. AE, DC, MC, V.*

Robertson

45 km (28 mi) southeast of Worcester.

Robertson was founded primarily to service the surrounding farms, and it retains its agricultural and industrial character. Some effort has been made to beautify the town with tree-lined roads, but there is little for visitors here, except as a stop-off for lunch on the way to McGregor or Montagu.

Take the R64 from the northern end of Worcester's High Street, and the road, lined with vineyards and farms, will take you straight into Robertson, but not before you have passed the **Rooiberg Winery** on the left. Try the red muscatel—reputedly one of the best in the world. ⊠ *Box 358, Robertson 6705, ☎ 023/626–1663, ℻ 023/626–3295.* ▨ *Free.* ☉ *Weekdays 8–5:30, Sat. 9–3.*

If you have time, take a detour to **Van Loveren Winery,** just 9 km (5 ½ mi) along the R317 from Robertson in the direction of Bonnievale. Apart from sampling the excellent charmat-style sparkling wines, an unusual Fernao Pires, and a very delicate shiraz blanc de noir—all of which are very inexpensive—make sure to visit the unique grounds. The owner's mother has planted a garden of indigenous and exotic plants and trees, surrounding a water fountain that supplies the entire farm. Instead of visiting the usual tasting room, you sit out under the trees and the various wines are brought to you—and, if you are lucky, you will be offered a snack from the farm kitchen. ⊠ *Off R317, Robertson, ☎ 023/615–1505, ℻ 023/615–1336.* ▨ *Free.* ☉ *Weekdays 8:30–5, Sat. 9:30–1.*

Dining

$$ ✕ **Brannewynsdraai.** You will see the sign to this restaurant as you enter Robertson; it is a superb place to have lunch. Try South African bobotie, or ostrich-neck stew, similar to oxtail but with a fraction of the fat content. ⊠ *1 Kromhout St., ☎ 023/626–3202. AE, DC, MC, V. Closed Sun.*

McGregor

20 km (12 mi) south of Robertson.

Saved from development as a result of a planned mountain pass that never materialized, McGregor is the epitome of the sleepy country hollow, tucked away between the mountains.

From the R64, which runs through Robertson, take the turnoff to McGregor, which is clearly marked on the right, just after the entrance to the town. The road snakes between vineyards and farms—a picture of bucolic charm. Slowly, the farmsteads become less frequent, and you will see small cottages with distinctive red-painted doors and window frames. The McGregor Winery on the left heralds your entry into the town, with its thatched cottages in vernacular architecture.

TAKE PICTURES. FURTHER.™

© Eastman Kodak Company, 1999. Kodak, Max and Take Pictures. Further. are trademarks.

Ever see someone

waiting for the sun to come out

while trying to photograph

a charging rhino?

New!
Kodak Max film:

Now with better color, Kodak's maximum versatility film gives you great pictures in sunlight, low light, action or still.

It's all you need to know about film.

www.kodak.com

Distinctive guides packed with up-to-date expert advice
and smart choices for every type of traveler.

Fodor's. For the world of ways you travel.

McGregor has gained popularity in recent years with artists who have settled here permanently and with busy executives from Cape Town intent on getting away from it all. Frankly, this is an ideal place to do absolutely nothing, but you can take a leisurely stroll through the fynbos, watch birds from one of several hides on the Heron Walk, or follow one of the hiking or mountain-bike trails if you are feeling more energetic.

The **McGregor Winery** is a popular attraction, with surprisingly inexpensive wines considering their quality. Try the unwooded chardonnay and the exceptional port. ⊠ *Main Rd.*, ☎ *023/625–1741*, FAX *023/625–1829.* ☐ *Free.* ⊙ *Weekdays 8:30–5, Sat. 9:30–1.*

Dining and Lodging

$$ ✕🖬 **The Old Mill Lodge.** You have to travel through the town toward the mountains to get to this country house, a remnant of the 19th century. Upon arrival you'll be shown to your room in a thatched cottage decorated with antique-style beds and wood beams and thatch. Before dinner take a walk through the olive grove or a dip in the swimming pool. The lodge prides itself on a good table, and the menu changes daily, depending on what's in season. The room rate includes dinner and breakfast, but you have to pay for your own wine and drinks. ⊠ *Box 25, McGregor 6708*, ☎ *023/625–1841*, FAX *023/625–1941. 8 rooms. Pool. MAP. AE, DC, MC, V.*

Montagu

36 km (22 mi) northeast of Robertson.

Montagu bills itself as "the Gateway to the Little Karoo," and its picturesque streets lined with Cape Victorian architecture lend this some credence. Today, the town's main attraction is the natural hot springs, and many of the Victorian houses have been transformed into bed-and-breakfast guest houses. Take the R64 from Robertson (you will have to return there from McGregor), and after 29 km (18 mi), you'll pass through the unlovely agricultural town of Ashton; keep left (don't turn off to Swellendam) and enter the short but spectacular Cogmans Kloof Pass. On either side of the pass, which runs in a river gorge, you can see the magnificent fold mountains, which are ultimately the source for the hot springs.

A three-hour ride on the popular **Langeberg Tractor Ride** will take you to the summit of the Langeberg (Long Mountain) and back. The tractor winds up some tortuously twisted paths revealing magnificent views of the area's peaks and valleys. After a short stop at the summit, a similarly harrowing descent follows, but you won't be disappointed by the views. Following your trip, you can enjoy a delicious lunch of *potjiekos* (traditional stew cooked over a fire in a single cast-iron pot). Reservations are essential. ⊠ *R318 Protea Farm, Montagu/Koo*, ☎ *023/614–2471.* ☐ *R25.* ⊙ *Wed. at 10, Sat. at 9:30 and 2.*

Dining and Lodging

$$ ✕ **Jessica's Restaurant.** This is a Victorian house that has been converted into a restaurant. Veteran restaurateurs Reiner and Shay Poewe (Jessica is actually a lovable Staffordshire Bull Terrier) create superb cuisine. Formerly the executive chef of one of Cape Town's most prestigious hotels, Reiner here offers panfried springbok steak, mussel risotto, and vineyard snails. Make sure to leave enough room for Reiner's legendary crème brûlée. ⊠ *47 Bath St.*, ☎ *032/614–1805. AE, DC, MC, V. Reservations essential. No lunch Mon.–Sat., no dinner Sun.*

$$ ✕ **Views Restaurant.** Perched on the top floor of the Avalon Springs Hotel (☞ *below*), this restaurant commands breathtaking views of the mountains and valley that contain the hot springs. Chef Eugene Marais

enlivens the daily-changing menu with his experience culled from his extensive travels; expect the unexpected. Look forward to options like Cantonese quail, Barbary duck and, yes, really, crocodile à la mode. ⊠ *Avalon Springs Hotel,* ☎ *023/614–1150. AE, DC, MC, V. Closed Mon. No lunch.*

$$–$$$ 🏨 **Avalon Springs Hotel.** This family-owned hotel presides over the main hot springs of Montagu, just 2 km (1¼ mi) outside the town. After leaving your bags in your air-conditioned room, don one of the bathrobes provided and take a short stroll to the baths. Five pools lead into each other; the hottest directly above the spring gushes forth healing waters at a constant 109°F. For lunch, treat yourself to a poolside barbecue of delicious Karoo lamb cutlets. Afterward, work it all off in the gym, spa, or sauna, or just let the warmth of the water wash away your cares. ⊠ *Box 110, 6720,* ☎ *023/614–1150,* 𝔽𝔸𝕏 *023/614–1906. 12 rooms, 2 suites, 30 chalets. Sauna, health club, recreation room, meeting rooms. AE, DC, MC, V.*

Breede River Valley A to Z

Arriving and Departing

BY BUS

Intercape Ferreira Coaches (☎ 021/386–4400) and **Translux Express Bus** (☎ 021/405–3333) offer regular services via the N1 to Worcester and the N2 as far as Swellendam. You will have to organize other transportation (like a rental car) from here, so it almost pays to take your rental car from Cape Town in the first place. The ticket agent for both bus lines in Swellendam is **Milestone Tours** (☎ 0291/42137).

BY CAR

The N1 highway from Cape Town will fist take you to Paarl after 50 km (30 mi) and then on to Worcester and into the heart of the area, but if you want to start your tour at Tulbach or Ceres, turn off the N1 onto the R303 at Paarl, and cross the Bain's Kloof Pass.

Getting Around

BY CAR

Public transportation is nearly non-existent in the Breede River valley, so unless you are on a guided tour, your best bet is to get a rental car in Cape Town from **Avis** (☎ 021/887–0492), or **Budget** (☎ 021/887–6935), or if you are in Paarl contact **Wine Route Rent-a-Car** (☎ 021/872–8513 or 083/225–7089).

Contacts and Resources

EMERGENCIES

Ambulance (☎ 10177). **Police/Fire** (☎ 10111).

GUIDED TOURS

Scheduled guided tours of the Breede River valley are run by **Hylton Ross Tours** (☎ 021/511–1784, 𝔽𝔸𝕏 021/511–2401), but departure days and itineraries vary widely according to season, so be sure to book in advance. Most other tour operators like **Classic Cape Tours** (☎ 021/686–6310, 𝔽𝔸𝕏 021/686–9216) will run a custom-designed tour, provided you have a group of at least five people.

VISITOR INFORMATION

Breede River Valley Tourism. ⊠ *Box 91, Worcester 6850,* ☎ *023/347–6411,* 𝔽𝔸𝕏 *023/347–1115.* ☉ *Weekdays 9–4:30.*

Montagu Tourism Bureau. ⊠ *24 Bath St., Montagu 6720,* ☎ 𝔽𝔸𝕏 *023/614–2471.* ☉ *Weekdays 9–4:30, Sat. 9–1.*

THE OVERBERG

Overberg means "over the mountains" in Afrikaans, an apt name for this remote region at the bottom of the continent, separated from the rest of the Cape by mountains. Before 19th-century engineers blasted a route through the Hottentots Holland range, the Overberg developed in comparative isolation. To this day, it possesses a wild emptiness far removed from the settled valleys of the Winelands.

It's a land of immense contrasts, and if you're planning a trip along the Garden Route (☞ Chapter 6), you would be well advised to add the Overberg to your itinerary. The coastal drive from Gordon's Bay to Hermanus is as beautiful as anything in the Cape—an unfolding panorama of deserted beaches, pounding surf, and fractured granite mountains. Once you pass Hermanus and head out onto the windswept plains leading to Cape Agulhas, you have to search harder for the Overberg's riches. Towns are few and far between, the countryside comprising an expanse of wheat fields and sheep pastures. The occasional reward of the drive is a coastline of sublime beauty. Enormous stretches of dunes and unspoiled beaches extend for miles. Unfortunately, no roads parallel the ocean, and you must constantly divert inland before heading to another part of the coast.

Hermanus is the best place in South Africa to watch the annual migration of southern right whales, but you can spot the great creatures all along the coast between July and November, when they sometimes come within 100 ft of shore. Spring is also the best time to see the Overberg's wildflowers, although the region's profusion of coastal and montane fynbos is beautiful year-round.

The upper part of the Overberg, north of the N2 highway, is more like the Winelands, with 18th- and 19th-century towns sheltered in the lee of rocky mountains. Here the draws are apple orchards, inns, and hiking trails that wind through the mountains. The historic towns of Swellendam and Greyton make the most logical touring bases.

To tour the whole area would take three to four days. For a shorter trip, focus on the splendors of the coastal route from Gordon's Bay to Hermanus, and then head north toward the Winelands.

Towns and sights are marked on the Western Cape map.

Gordon's Bay

70 km (44 mi) southeast of Cape Town.

Gordon's Bay is an attractive resort built on a steep mountain slope overlooking the vast expanse of False Bay. You can often see whales and their calves in False Bay in October and November.

From Gordon's Bay, the road hugs the mountainside, slipping between the craggy peaks of the Hottentots Holland Mountains and the sea far below. The coastal drive between Gordon's Bay and Hermanus is one of the country's best, particularly if you take the time to follow some of the dirt roads leading down to the sea from the highway.

The road passes tiny Rooielsbaai (pronounced "*roy*-els-buy") then cuts inland for a couple of miles. A turnoff leads to **Pringle Bay,** a collection of holiday homes sprinkled across the fynbos. The village has little to offer other than a beautiful wide beach (check out the sign warning of quicksand). If you continue through Pringle Bay, the tar road soon gives way to gravel. This road, badly corrugated in patches, runs around the looming pinnacle of **Hangklip** and along a deserted stretch of magnificent beach and dunes to Betty's Bay (☞ *below*).

If you don't fancy the gravel road, return to the R44 and continue 1½ km (1 mi) to the turnoff to Stony Point, on the edge of Betty's Bay. Follow Porter Drive for 3 km (2 mi) until you reach a sign marked MOOI HAWENS and a smaller sign picturing a penguin. Follow the penguin signs to a **colony of African penguins,** one of only two mainland colonies in southern Africa. The colony lies about 600 yards from the parking area along a rocky coastal path. Along the way, you pass the concrete remains of tank stands, reminders of the days when Betty's Bay was a big whaling station. The African penguin is endangered, so the colony has been fenced off as protection against man, dogs, and other predators. This particular colony was once savaged by a leopard.

Return to Porter Drive and turn right to rejoin the R44. Back on the main road, go another 2 km (1 mi) to the **Harold Porter National Botanical Garden,** a 440-acre nature reserve in the heart of the coastal fynbos, where the Cape Floral Kingdom is at its richest. The profusion of plants supports 78 species of birds and a wide range of small mammals, including large troops of baboons. You couldn't ask for a more fantastic setting, cradled between the Atlantic and the towering peaks of the 3,000-ft Kogelberg range. Walking trails wind through the reserve and into the mountains via Disa and Leopard's kloofs, which echo with the sound of waterfalls and running streams. Back at the main buildings, a pleasant restaurant serves light meals and teas. ⊠ Box 35, Betty's Bay 7141, ☎ 028/272–9311, ℻ 028/272–9333. 🖼 R2. ☉ Daily 8–6.

Kleinmond

25 km (15½ mi) southeast of Gordon's Bay.

The small town of Kleinmond ("small mouth") is nothing special—it has a couple of restaurants and guest houses—but it presides over a magnificent stretch of shoreline, backed by the mountains of the Palmietberg. Close to the town, and clearly marked with signs from the main street, is the **Kleinmond Coastal Nature Reserve,** a 990-acre area of fynbos that extends to the sea at the Palmiet River Estuary. The beach and small lagoon that front the reserve are also accessible from the Palmiet Caravan Park. Take one of the well-marked nature walks through the reserve, and you are sure to see some of the area's magnificent flora and bird life. ⊠ *Palmiet River Estuary,* ☎ 028/271–5138, ℻ 028/272–9333. 🖼 *Free.* ☉ *Daily 9–5.*

Even more impressive are the 10 km (6 mi) of sandy beach that fringe Sandown Bay, at the eastern edge of town. Much of the beach is nothing more than a sandbar, separating the Atlantic from the huge lagoon formed by the Bot River. Swift currents make bathing risky.

Dining and Lodging

$$$$ ✕🖼 **Beach House on Sandown Bay.** In quiet, seaside Kleinmond, this comfortable hotel overlooks a 10-km (6-mi) crescent of beach and a beautiful lagoon. It's a good base for whale-watching in October and November, as well as for walks in the surrounding nature reserves. The hotel itself is attractive, the rooms simply decorated with wicker furniture and floral draperies and bedspreads; in sea-facing rooms sliding doors open onto small balconies with tremendous views of Sandown Bay. The restaurant specializes in seafood fresh in the local harbor. ⊠ *Beach Rd., Kleinmond 7195,* ☎ 028/271–3130, ℻ 028/271–4022. *22 rooms, 1 suite. Restaurant, bar, pool. BP. AE, DC, MC, V.*

En Route   The R44 cuts inland to circumnavigate the Bot River lagoon. Ten kilometers (6 miles) past Kleinmond, the road comes to a junction; turn right onto the R43 toward Hermanus and cross the Bot River. The R43 swings eastward around the mountains, past the small artists' colony of Onrus.

Less than 2 km (1 mi) farther is the turnoff to the R320, which leads through the vineyards and orchards of the scenic Hemel-en-Aarde (Heaven on Earth) Valley and over Shaw's Pass to Caledon. **Hamilton Russell Vineyards** lies a short way down this rutted road, in an attractive thatched building overlooking a small dam. This winery produces some of the best wine in South Africa. The pinot noir won loud acclaim from Frank Prial of the *New York Times* and is one of the two best produced in the country. The chardonnay comes closer to the French style of chardonnay than any other Cape wine, with lovely fruit and a touch of lemon rind and toast. It will be at its best after one to two years. ⊠ *Off R320, Walker Bay,* ☎ *028/312–3595,* FAX *028/312–1797.* ✉ *Free.* ☉ *Weekdays 9–5, Sat. 9–1.*

★ Return to the R43 and drive 3 km (2 mi) to Hermanus. On the outskirts of town, keep watch on your left side for a pair of white gateposts set well back from the road, painted with the words ROTARY WAY—if you pass the turnoff to the New Harbour you've gone too far. The **Rotary Way** is a scenic drive that climbs along the spine of the mountains above Hermanus, affording incredible views of the town, Walker Bay, and Hemel-en-Aarde Valley, as well as some of the area's beautiful fynbos. It's a highlight of a trip to the Overberg and you shouldn't miss it. The Rotary Way turns to dirt after a few kilometers and becomes impassable to all but four-wheel-drive vehicles about 2 km (1 mi) after that. The entire mountainside is laced with wonderful walking trails, and many of the scenic lookouts have benches.

Hermanus

24 km (15 mi) southeast of Kleinmond on the R43.

Hermanus is a popular holiday resort and the major coastal town in the Overberg. If you're looking for a base from which to explore the region, Hermanus is your best bet. Restaurants and shops line the streets, and the town retains a pleasant holiday feel, having been spared the worst excesses of developers with more money than taste. The town is packed during the Whale Festival in September and October and Christmas school holidays, though, so head elsewhere if you want solitude.

Just a couple of miles away, pristine beaches extend as far as the eye can see, and the Kleinriviersberg provides a breathtaking backdrop to the town. Hermanus sits atop a long line of cliffs, which makes it the best place in South Africa to watch the annual whale migration from shore. An 11-km (7-mi) **cliff walk** allows watchers to follow the whales, which often come within 100 ft of the cliffs as they move along the coastline. In addition, a whale crier, complete with sandwich board and kelp horn, disseminates information on whale sightings.

Originally, Hermanus was a whaling center. The **Old Harbour Museum,** in a small building at the old stone fishing basin, displays some of the horrific harpoons used to lance the giants. There are also exhibits on fishing techniques, local marine life, and angling records. Photographs of old Hermanus and some of its legendary fishermen are also displayed at the PFV Old Harbour Museum Photographic Exhibition, in the white building next to the harbor parking lot. ⊠ *Old Harbour, Marine Dr.,* ☎ *028/312–1475.* ✉ *R2.* ☉ *Mon.–Sat. 9–1 and 2–5, Sun. noon–4.*

From Hermanus the R43 continues eastward, hugging the strip of land between the mountains and the **Klein River Lagoon.** The lagoon is popular with waterskiers, boaters, and anglers. You can hire a variety of boats down at Prawn Flats, including motorboats, canoes, and board sailers; expect to pay R20–R40 an hour depending on the type of boat. It's also possible to take a boat up the Klein River into the bird sanctuary to watch the birds roost at sunset. Contact the **Boathouse** (✉ Prawn Flats, off R43, ☎ 0283/770925).

Dining and Lodging

$$ ✕ **Burgundy.** This restaurant occupies a fisherman's cottage overlooking the old fishing harbor. Ask for a table on the veranda or the lawn, from where you can savor views of Walker Bay. The menu brings French flair to South African ingredients, with an emphasis on seafood. The grilled line fish is a good choice and will be well complemented by one of the superb wines of the region. There is always a traditional South African dish to try, and the grilled ostrich, perched on samp and teamed with a quince sauce, is popular with guests from abroad. Desserts are mostly ice cream–based, or you could indulge in the chocolate mousse cake. ✉ *Market Sq.,* ☎ *0283/22–800. AE, DC, MC, V. No dinner Sun.*

$$ ✕ **Trattoria-Ouzeri.** Step off the vacation track and into this colorful eatery, where you can order from a Greek or an Italian menu. Look for everything from a tasty bean salad with olive oil, lemon, and herbs to fish cakes or lamb stew—and from pizzas to pasta with mussels, tomatoes, and herbs. The Greek menu is unavailable Sunday, the Italian Monday. The restaurant is on a lane off the main road in the center of town. ✉ *60 St. Peter's La.,* ☎ *028/313–0532. AE, DC, MC, V. No lunch.*

$$$$ 🏨 **Marine.** In an incomparable cliff-top setting, this venerable hotel has undergone a major refurbishment, reopening with sumptuously decorated rooms and suites, under-floor heating, and luxurious facilities. The sea-facing rooms, some with private balcony, provide whale-watchers with grandstand views over Walker Bay. The revamped orangery invites guests to linger over tea or drinks, while the two restaurants tempt with sophisticated menus. The Pavilion restaurant has sea views; Seafood at the Marine has a menu cooked with Gallic passion by a young French chef. ✉ *Marine Dr., Box 9, Hermanus 7200,* ☎ *028/313–1000,* 𝖥𝖠𝖷 *028/313–0160. 47 rooms. 2 restaurants, bar, room service, 2 pools, billiards. AE, DC, MC, V.*

$$$ 🏨 **Windsor.** If you come to Hermanus in October or November, stay at this hotel in the heart of town. It's a family-run hostelry that offers comfort but little pretense of luxury; however, the hotel's position atop the cliffs makes it a great place to view the annual whale migration. Request one of the second-floor, sea-facing rooms, with their huge sliding-glass doors and unbeatable views. ✉ *Marine Dr., Box 3, Hermanus 7200,* ☎ *028/312–3727,* 𝖥𝖠𝖷 *028/312–2181. 60 rooms. Restaurant, 2 bars. BP. AE, DC, MC, V.*

Bredasdorp

60 km (37½ mi) east of Stanford.

Bredasdorp is a sleepy agricultural town that has a certain charm, as long as you don't catch it on a Sunday afternoon, when everything's closed and an air of ennui pervades the brassy, windswept streets.

Once a year, however, the usual lethargic atmosphere is abandoned, and a radical sense of purpose takes its place when Bredasdorp hosts the Foot of Africa Marathon each spring. Don't be lulled by the small-town, country setting into thinking that this race is a breeze and that you might give it a go. Word has it that the undulating landscape has the fittest athletes doubting their perseverance.

Housed in a converted church and rectory, the **Bredasdorp Museum** has an extensive collection of items salvaged from the hundreds of ships that have gone down in the stormy waters off the Cape. In addition to the usual cannons and figureheads, the museum displays a surprising array of undamaged household items rescued from the sea, including entire dining-room sets, sideboards, china, and phonographs. ⊠ *Independent St.*, ☎ *0284/424–1240.* ⊠ *R2.* ⊙ *Mon.–Thurs. 9–4:45, Fri. 9–3:45, Sat. 9–12:45; Sept.–Apr. also Sun. 11–12:30.*

OFF THE BEATEN PATH

ELIM – About 45 km (32 mi) west of Bredasdorp and accessible only by dirt road, Elim is a Moravian mission village founded in 1824. Little has changed in the last hundred years: Simple whitewashed cottages line the few streets, and the settlement's colored residents all belong to the Moravian Church. The whole village has been declared a national monument. The easiest access is via the R317, off the R319 between Cape Agulhas and Bredasdorp.

De Hoop Nature Reserve (☎ 02922/700) is a huge conservation area covering 88,900 acres of isolated coastal terrain as well as a marine reserve extending 5 km (3 mi) out to sea. Massive white-sand dunes, mountains, and rare lowland fynbos are home to eland, bontebok, and Cape mountain zebra, as well as more than 250 bird species. Visitors can rent self-catering cottages. Access is via the dirt road between Bredasdorp and Malgas.

Pont Malgas, past De Hoop Nature Reserve on the dirt road from Bredasdorp, is the last hand-drawn car ferry in the country. Two operators use brute strength to pull the ferry across the Breede River. The setting is beautiful, and the ride is unusual. ⊠ *R6 per vehicle.*

En Route From Bredasdorp it's just 37 km (23 mi) through rolling farmland to Cape Agulhas. Although it's the southernmost tip of the African continent, it's less exciting in reality than in concept, so unless reaching the bottom of the continent has some great personal meaning, give it a miss and skip down to Waenhuiskrans.

Waenhuiskrans

★ *24 km (15 mi) northeast of Struisbaai.*

Waenhuiskrans, an isolated holiday village, is set on another of South Africa's most awe-inspiring stretches of coastline. The village is known among English-speaking South Africans as Arniston, after a British ship of that name that was wrecked on the Agulhas reef in 1815. Beautiful beaches, water that assumes Caribbean shades of blue, and mile after mile of towering white dunes attract anglers and holiday makers alike. Only the frequent southeasters that blow off the sea are likely to put a damper on your enjoyment. For 200 years, a community of Cape Malay fishermen and their families has eked out a living here, setting sail each day in small fishing boats. Today, their village has been named a national monument, and it's a pleasure to wander around the thatched cottages of this still-vibrant community. The village has expanded enormously in the last 15 years, thanks to the construction of a host of holiday homes. Fortunately, much of the new architecture blends effectively with the whitewashed simplicity of the original cottages.

Waenhuiskrans means "wagon-house cliff" in Afrikaans, and the village takes its name from a **vast cave** 2 km (1 mi) south of town that is theoretically large enough to house several wagons and their spans of oxen. Signs point the way over the dunes to the cave, which is accessible only at low tide. You need shoes to protect your feet from the sharp rocks, but wear something you don't mind getting wet.

Again, retrace your way to Bredasdorp. This time, take the R319 toward Swellendam. The road runs through mile after mile of rolling farmland, populated by sheep, cattle, and an occasional ostrich. In the far distance loom the Langeberg. After 64 km (40 mi), turn right onto the N2 highway. Continue for another 15 km (9 mi) before turning right to the **Bontebok National Park.** Covering just 6,880 acres of coastal fynbos, this is one of the smallest of South Africa's national parks. Don't expect to see big game here—the park contains no elephants, lions, or rhinos. What you will see are bonteboks, graceful white-faced antelopes nearly exterminated by hunters earlier in the century, as well as red hartebeests, Cape grysboks, steenboks, duikers, and the endangered Cape mountain zebra. Two short walking trails start at the campsite next to the Breede River. ⊠ *Box 149, Swellendam 6740,* ☎ *028/514–2735,* ℻ *028/514–2626.* ☞ *R14 per vehicle.* ☉ *Oct.–Apr., daily 7–7; May–Sept., daily 8–6.*

Dining and Lodging

$$$ ✕🖭 **Arniston Hotel.** You could easily spend a week here and still need
★   to be dragged away. The setting, in a tiny fishing village on a crescent of white dunes, has a lot to do with its appeal, but the hotel has also struck a fine balance between elegance and beach-holiday comfort. Rooms have a true beach feel, thanks to the cheery use of wicker and fabrics in cool ocean colors. Request a room with a sea view where you can enjoy the ever-changing colors of the horizon and have a grandstand view of the large concentration of cow and calf pairs found here during the whaling season, between May and October. On request, the hotel takes guests by four-wheel-drive into the dune field for sunset cocktails—a not-to-be-missed experience. A four-course dinner menu changes daily, and the wine list has won more than one award. À la carte lunches on the patio feature light Mediterranean fare. ⊠ *Beach Rd., Waenhuiskrans (mailing address: Box 126, Bredasdorp 7280),* ☎ *0284/45–9000,* ℻ *0284/45–9633. 30 rooms. 2 restaurants, 2 bars, room service, pool. BP. No children under 12. AE, DC, MC, V.*

Swellendam

★   *72 km (45 mi) north of Waenhuiskrans.*

Return to the junction with the N2 and cross the highway into beautiful Swellendam, lying in the shadow of the imposing Langeberg. Founded in 1745, it is the third-oldest town in South Africa and many of its historic buildings have been elegantly restored. Even on a casual drive along the main street, you'll see a number of lovely Cape Dutch homes, with their traditional whitewashed walls, gables, and thatched roofs.

The centerpiece of the town's historical past is the **Drostdy Museum,** a collection of buildings dating back to the town's earliest days. The Drostdy was built in 1747 by the Dutch East India Company to serve as the residence of the Landdrost, the magistrate who presided over the district. The building is furnished in a style that was common in the mid-19th century. A path leads through the Drostdy kitchen gardens to Mayville, an 1855 middle-class home that blends elements of Cape Dutch and Cape Georgian architecture. Across Swellengrebel Street stand the old jail and the Ambagswerf (closed Sunday), an outdoor exhibit of tools used by the town's blacksmiths, wainwrights, coopers, and tanners. ⊠ *18 Swellengrebel St.,* ☎ *028/514–1138.* ☞ *R5.* ☉ *Weekdays 9–4:45, weekends 10–3:45.*

Swellendam's **Dutch Reformed Church** is an imposing white edifice, built in 1911 in an eclectic style. The gables are Baroque, the windows Gothic, the cupola vaguely Eastern, and the steeple copied from Belgium. Surprisingly, all the elements work together wonderfully. Inside is an interesting tiered amphitheater, with banks of curving wood pews facing the pulpit and organ. ✉ *7 Voortrek St.,* ☎ *028/514–1225.* ☉ *Services Feb.–Nov. at 10 and 6; Dec.–Jan. at 9 and 6.*

If you'd like to get your feet on the ground and breathe some clean local air, take a hike in the **Marloth Nature Reserve,** in the Langeberg above town. Five easy walks, ranging from one to four hours, explore some of the mountain gorges. An office at the entrance to the reserve has trail maps and hiking information.

Dining and Lodging

$$$$ ✕⌸ **Klippe Rivier Homestead.** Amid rolling farmland 3 km (2 mi) outside Swellendam, this guest house occupies one of the Overberg's most gracious and historic country homes. It was built around 1825 in traditional Cape style, with thick white walls, thatched roof, and a distinctive gable. Guests stay in enormous rooms in the converted stables. The three downstairs rooms are furnished with antiques in Cape Dutch, colonial, and Victorian styles. Upstairs, raw wood beams, cane ceilings, and bold prints set the tone for less-expensive, Provençal-style rooms, with air-conditioning and small balconies. Some public rooms cannot support the sheer volume of antique collectibles, taking on a museumlike quality. Delectable dinners are table d'hôte, prepared with fresh herbs, vegetables, fruit, and cream from surrounding farms. No children under 10. ✉ *On a dirt road off R60 to Ashton (mailing address: Box 483, Swellendam 6740),* ☎ *028/514–3341,* 🖷 *028/514– 3337. 7 rooms. Restaurant, saltwater pool. BP. AE, DC, MC, V.*

$$$ ✕⌸ **Adin's and Sharon's Hideaway.** The Victorian homestead and its three luxury cottages are set in a peaceful garden that displays some 400 rosebushes and is home to varied bird life. While the setting and beautifully appointed cottages are excellent reasons to stay at this establishment, the level of hospitality sets this place above the rest. Adin and Sharon Greaves (former owners of Mimosa Lodge in Montagu) have won awards for best bed-and-breakfast establishment for three years running. Their service dedication extends to providing lifts, planning routes, and presenting the best breakfast for many miles around. It's an affordable and well-situated base from which to explore historic Swellendam and environs. ✉ *10 Hermanus Steyn Rd.,* ☎ 🖷 *028/ 51–43316. 3 cottages, 1 room. BP. DC, MC, V.*

En Route   From Swellendam return to the N2 and turn right toward Cape Town. The road sweeps through rich, rolling cropland that extends to the base of the Langeberg. A few kilometers after the town of Riviersonderend (pronounced "riff-*ears*-onder-ent"), turn right onto the R406, a good gravel road that leads to the village of Greyton in the lee of the Riviersonderend Mountains.

Greyton

32 km (20 mi) west of Swellendam.

The charming village of Greyton, filled with white, thatched cottages and quiet lanes, is a popular weekend retreat for Capetonians as well as a permanent home for many retirees. The village offers almost nothing in the way of traditional sights, but it's a great base for walks into the surrounding mountains (☞ *below*) and a pleasant place to pause for lunch or tea (☞ Dining and Lodging, *below*).

After Greyton, the R406 becomes paved. Drive 5 km (3 mi) to the turnoff to **Genadendal,** a Moravian mission station founded in 1737 to educate the Khoikhoi and convert them to Christianity. Seeing this impoverished hamlet today, it's difficult to comprehend the major role this mission played in the early history of South Africa. In the late 18th century it was the second-largest settlement after Cape Town, and its Khoikhoi craftsmen produced the finest silver cutlery and woodwork in the country. Some of the first written works in Afrikaans were printed here, and the colored community greatly influenced the development of Afrikaans as it is heard today. None of this went over well with the white population. By 1909, new legislation prohibited colored ownership of land, and in 1926 the Department of Public Education closed the settlement's teacher's training college, arguing that coloreds were better employed on neighboring farms. Genadendal began a long slide into obscurity until 1994, when then President Nelson Mandela renamed his official residence Genadendal.

In town, you can walk the streets of the settlement and tour the historic buildings facing Church Square. Genadendal is still a mission station, and the German missionaries will often show interested visitors around. Of particular note is the **Genadendal Mission Museum,** spread through 15 rooms in three buildings. The museum collection, the only one in South Africa to be named a National Cultural Treasure, includes unique household implements, books, tools, al instruments, among them the country's oldest pipe organ. Wall displays examine mission life in the Cape in the 18th and 19th centuries, focusing on the early missionaries' work with the Khoikhoi. Unfortunately, many of the displays are in Afrikaans. ⊠ *Off R406,* ☎ *028/251–8582.* ▨ *R5.* ☉ *Mon.– Thurs. 9–1 and 2–5, Fri. 9–3:30, Sat. 9–noon.*

En Route   To head back toward Cape Town, follow the R406 to the N2. After the town of Bot River, the road leaves the wheat fields and climbs into the mountains. It's lovely country, full of rock and pine forest interspersed with orchards. **Sir Lowry's Pass** serves as the gateway to Cape Town and the Winelands, a magnificent breach in the mountains that opens to reveal the curving expanse of False Bay, the long ridge of the peninsula, and, in the distance, Table Mountain.

Dining and Lodging

$$$ ✕⛰ **Greyton Lodge.** Built in 1882 as a trading store, this comfortable guest house looks right at home amid the whitewashed Cape homes of historic Greyton. The focal point of the hotel is the tea garden, filled with roses and fruit trees and dominated by the sheer walls of the Riviersonderend Mountains behind. The standard rooms are small; you're better off taking the pricier deluxe rooms decorated in country style with light floral draperies and brass or antique bedsteads. Only some rooms have phones, and none have TVs. The lunch menu is inexpensive and features tried-and-true dishes like ploughman's lunch, steak and chips, salads, and quiche. ⊠ *46 Main St., Box 50, Greyton 7233,* ☎ *028/254–9876,* ⅁⅄ *028/254–9672. 19 rooms. Restaurant, bar, room service, pool. BP. AE, DC, MC, V.*

$$$ ✕⛰ **Post House.** Once the village post office and now a national monument, this 138-year-old country inn has loads of charm. The rooms, all named after Beatrix Potter characters, face onto a lovely lawn where guests can relax over drinks or tea. The rooms themselves, furnished in Edwardian country style, have been refurbished, and the public rooms will follow suit. Restoration is likely to be an ongoing affair, given the age of the rustic white-walled building. Dinner is a table d'hôte four-course menu that satisfies while not attempting any gastronomic heights. ⊠ *Main Rd., Greyton 7233,* ☎ *028/254–9995,* ⅁⅄ *028/254–9920. 18 rooms. Restaurant, bar, pool. BP. No children under 12. AE, DC, MC, V.*

Hiking

Walking is one of the major attractions of the Overberg, and almost every town and nature reserve offers a host of trails ranging in length from a few minutes to an entire day. For detailed information about these trails, contact the local visitor information offices (☞ Contacts and Resources *in* Overberg A to Z, *below*).

A fabulous one-day hike is the **Boesmanskloof Trail,** 32 km (20 mi) through the Riviersonderend Mountains from Greyton to the exquisite hamlet of McGregor. McGregor has several charming guest houses and cottages where you can spend the night, but you need to make transport arrangements to get back. Serious hikers should also consider the **Genadendal Hiking Trail,** a two-day hike that wends 24 km (15 mi) through the Riviersonderend Mountains, beginning at the Moravian Mission Church, with one night spent on a farm. Permits are required for both trails. Contact the manager, Vrolijkheid Nature Conservation Station (⊠ Private Bag X614, Robertson 6705, ☎ 02353/621).

Horseback Riding

Greyton Scenic Horse Trails and Riding Center (⊠ 21 Vine St., Greyton 7233, ☎ 028/254–9009) takes visitors, including novices, on 90-minute rides through the beautiful hills and mountains surrounding Greyton.

Overberg A to Z

Arriving and Departing

BY BUS

Intercape Ferreira Coaches (☎ 021/386–4400) and **Translux Express Bus** (☎ 021/449–3333) offer regular service from Cape Town along the N2, stopping at Swellendam before continuing on to the Garden Route. Once there, you're stuck unless you arrange for other transport. The ticket agent for both bus lines in Swellendam is **Milestone Tours** (☎ 028/514–2137).

BY CAR

Leave Cape Town via the N2 highway. If you're following the above tour, take the R44 turnoff to Gordon's Bay. Otherwise, stay on the N2 over Sir Lowry's Pass to reach Swellendam, 232 km (145 mi) distant.

Getting Around

BY CAR

Unless you're on a guided tour, you will need a car to explore the Overberg. Distances are long, towns are few, and public transportation is infrequent, if it exists at all.

Contacts and Resources

EMERGENCIES

Ambulance (☎ 10177). **Police/Fire** (☎ 10111).

GUIDED TOURS

In addition to the services listed below, all of the large tour operators in Cape Town offer whirlwind tours of the Overberg (☞ Guided Tours *in* Chapter 4).

VISITOR INFORMATION

Cape Town Tourism Association. ⊠ *The Pinnacle, Burg St., Box 1403, Cape Town 8000,* ☎ *021/426–4260,* FAX *021/426–4266.* ☉ *Weekdays 8–5, Sat. 8:30–1, Sun. 9–1.*

Hermanus Tourism Bureau. ⊠ *Main Rd., Hermanus 7200,* ☎ *0283/22–629,* FAX *0283/700–305.* ☉ *Weekdays 9–5, Sat. 9–2, Sun. 10:30–noon.*

Suidpunt Publicity Association. Information is available here for Bredasdorp, Elim, Cape Agulhas, Struisbaai, and Waenhuiskrans. ⊠ *Dirkie Uys St., Bredasdorp 7280,* ☎ FAX *02841/42584.* ☉ *Weekdays 8–1 and 2–4:30, Sat. 9–1.*

Swellendam Publicity Association. ⊠ *Oefeningshuis, Voortrek St.,* ☎ FAX *028/514–2770.* ☉ *Weekdays 8–1 and 2–5, Sat. 9–12:30.*

WEST COAST

During much of the year, the West Coast is a featureless expanse of fynbos scrub stretching from Cape Town to Vanrhynsdorp (pronounced "fan-*rainz*-dorp"), 288 km (180 mi) to the north. Lonely fishing villages dot a coastline of endless beaches fringing a cold, harsh Atlantic. It's a stark, empty land that you either love or hate. But every spring the West Coast explodes in a fiesta of wildflowers that transforms the entire region. Even the most hardened urbanites make the pilgrimage to witness this Cinderella miracle, driving up from Cape Town just for the day or basing themselves in coastal towns, such as Langebaan and Lambert's Bay.

As spring warms to its task, the flower show spreads inland to the Hantam, a high plateau where Afrikaner farmers raise merino sheep and hardscrabble laborers still shear wool by hand. The quality of the morning and evening light—a silky caress of reds, blues, and gold—has long drawn artists, and the delightful farming town of Calvinia is an obvious overnight choice. Spreading south from Calvinia, the high plains of the Hantam collapse into the Cedarberg, one of the great mountain wildernesses of South Africa. Bizarre rock formations hide delicate San (Bushmen) paintings and the last remnants of the enormous cedar forests that once blanketed the region. Hiking here is great, and you can disappear for days at a time into its remote recesses. The historic town of Clanwilliam, lying in the shadow of the Cedarberg, makes a great base for short walks and scenic drives.

It can be difficult to plan a holiday around the flowers in the West Coast, since it's impossible to tell exactly when they'll bloom. The season is notoriously fickle, dependent on wind, rain, and sun. The display begins on the coast around July, with cooler mountain areas coming to life as late as August and lasting into October. As you might expect, some years are not nearly as good as others.

Tourist offices in all the towns provide up-to-date sometimes hourly information on wildflower action in their areas. Day by day they'll tell you where the flowers are blooming and the best routes to follow. Call them before you head out, or your whole trip may be wasted.

The best time of day to see color is between 11 and 3, but flowers are unlikely to open if the weather is cold and windy. Plants move with the sun, so make an effort to drive with the sun at your back to get the full effect.

Traveling by car is the only way to tour the West Coast properly. A rental car can easily handle the tours mapped out below, despite the fact that much of the driving is along gravel roads. These roads are all in good condition, but stones can damage the underside of your car, particularly if you drive with a heavy foot. It's always a good idea to carry drinking water and a spare tire and to fill up with gas whenever you can since service stations can be few and far between.

Towns and sights in West Coast, Hantam, and Cedarberg are marked on the Western Cape map.

West Coast, Hantam, and Cedarberg

A loop around the West Coast, Hantam, and Cedarberg starting from Cape Town will take a minimum of three days. Allow more time if you plan to walk extensively or frolic in fields of flowers.

Darling

From Cape Town, take the N1 toward Paarl. After just under 2 km (1 mi), exit left onto the R27 (the sign reads Paarden Eiland and Milnerton), drive 80 km (50 mi) to the junction with the R315, and turn right.

Darling is a sleepy village in the heart of wildflower country, but in mid-September the village presents an annual **Wildflower and Orchid Show** (☎ 022/49–2422) that's famous throughout the Western Cape. This part of the coast usually flowers about two months after the first rains and fades out between mid-September and mid-October. Expect to see daisies, bluebells, arum lilies, vygies, and namesias.

Back on the R27, head north 11 km (7 mi) to **West Coast National Park.** Even if you don't spend time here, the road that runs through the park to Langebaan is far more scenic than the R27 and well worth taking. The park is a fabulous mix of lagoon wetlands, pounding surf, and coastal fynbos. For a beautiful detour, follow the rutted dirt track 16 km (10 mi) onto the narrow peninsula that separates the Atlantic from Langebaan Lagoon. On a sunny day, the lagoon assumes a magical color, made all the more impressive by blinding white beaches and the sheer emptiness of the place. Birders will have a field day identifying waterbirds, and the sandveld flowers are among the best along the West Coast. At the tip of the peninsula's Postberg Nature Reserve, you'll likely catch glimpses of zebras, wildebeests, and bat-eared foxes. ⌧ *Off the R27,* ☎ *022/772–2144.* ◪ *R25 per vehicle during high season (Easter, Christmas, and flower season); half price at other times.* ◷ *Daily 9–5.*

Langebaan

50 km (30 mi) northwest of Darling.

The paved road emerges from the park near Langebaan. Turn left out of the park, then right onto Oostewal Street and drive into town. Whereas many of the communities along the West Coast are bleak and uninviting, Langebaan is charming, and it makes a good base for exploring the surrounding area. The town sits at the mouth of Langebaan Lagoon, overlooking West Coast National Park and the vast expanse of Saldanha Bay. The beaches are excellent, and the lagoon water is warmer than the ocean—although that's not saying much. There are several restaurants, a yacht club, and even a shop renting sailboards and small boats.

Return to the R27 and continue north. After a couple of miles, turn left onto the R79, which ends at a T-junction. From here, you can turn left to Saldanha or right to Vredenburg.

DINING AND LODGING

$$ ✕ ⌂ **Farmhouse.** Less than 90 minutes by car from Cape Town, this lovely
★ guest house sits on a hillside overlooking the turquoise waters of Langebaan Lagoon. It's a great base for exploring West Coast National Park and a popular retreat for bird-watchers. The guest house, in a restored farmstead built in the 1860s, features thick white walls, tile floors, and timber beams. The rooms, decorated with rustic pine furniture and bright floral fabrics, have their own fireplaces and views of the lagoon. The hotel's à la carte menu features a good selection of Cape cuisine, prepared fresh and served in the attractive dining room, notable for its Oregon-pine furniture, fireplace, and high ceiling. ⌧ *5 Egret St., Box 160, Langebaan 7357,* ☎ *022/772–2062,* FAX *022/772–1980. 10 rooms. Restaurant, bar, pool. BP. No children under 12. MC, V.*

Paternoster
50 km (30 mi) northwest of Vredenburg.

Paternoster remains a truly unspoiled village of whitewashed fishermen's cottages perched on a deserted stretch of coastline. The population here consists mainly of fishermen and -women who for generations have eked out a living harvesting crayfish and other seafood. Despite the overt poverty, the village has a character and sense of identity often lacking in larger towns.

Along the coast just south of Paternoster is the **Columbine Nature Reserve,** a great spot for spring wildflowers, coastal fynbos, and succulents. Seagulls, cormorants, and sacred ibis are common here. ☎ 022/ 752–2718. 🎫 R4. ☾ Daily 7–7.

Stompneusbaai
1 km (½ mi) northeast of Paternoster.

Like Paternoster, Stompneusbaai is home to a community that relies on the sea for its livelihood. The stench of fish from the local fish-processing factory detracts from the charm of the village's whitewashed cottages and their brightly colored roofs. An unimpressive monument just outside of town marks the spot where Vasco da Gama landed in 1497, after a three-month voyage from Europe.

Velddrif
26 km (16 mi) east of Stompneusbaai.

Velddrif sits at the mouth of the Berg River. Forming a long estuary as it nears the sea, the Berg is a haven for waterbirds, including flamingos, pelicans, and the rare blue heron and redshank. Velddrif is a fishing community, and you can still see fishermen hanging bunches of *bokkems* (fish biltong) to dry in sheds along the estuary.

After the Berg River bridge, turn left on Voortrekker Street, which leads into **Laaiplek,** Velddrif's sister town and the site of the fishing harbor and beach. Turn right on Jameson Street and head out of town. After 11 km (7 mi), the tar road reverts to good-quality gravel.

Elands Bay
60 km (37½ mi) north of Velddrif.

Compared with the barren flats of the sandveld, Elands Bay enjoys an incredible setting, backed by a lagoon fringed with reeds and dotted with flamingos and waterfowl. A line of rocky cliffs runs down one side of the lagoon, ending at Baboon Point and a crayfish-processing factory. Drive out to Baboon Point (the sign says JETTIES) and look back toward the town. Fishing boats ride at anchor on startlingly blue water, and in the distance, a great field of white-sand dunes slopes down to the water's edge. The beach fronting the town is superb and draws crowds of Cape Town surfers on weekends and holidays. Birders, too, flock here to see the 200 species of birds that frequent the lagoon. Several San (Bushman) rock-art sites are also hidden away in the region, but they're almost impossible to find on your own; ask around for guides in Elands Bay. Unfortunately, the town itself is completely forgettable, with a characterless hotel and a couple of shops.

En Route Follow the gravel R366 out of town for 4 km (2½ mi), and then turn left at the sign to Lambert's Bay. After 13 km (8 mi), turn left again at a T-junction. This road passes high above the **Wadrif Salt Pan,** formed by the Langvlei River. After a rain, the pan fills with water and attracts thousands of flamingos and other waterbirds.

Lambert's Bay
30 km (18½ mi) north of Elands Bay.

Lambert's Bay isn't some spruced-up version of dock life like Cape Town's Victoria & Alfred Waterfront but a working fishing town—you can smell the fish-processing plants, and the boats in the harbor look like they spend their days battling Atlantic swells. If you don't expect anything cute, the innate charm of the town will seduce you. One of its major attractions is **Bird Island,** accessible along a stone breakwater from the harbor. The island is home to a colony of 14,000 Cape gannets, aggressive seabirds that live packed tightly together, fighting and screaming. The odor and the noise are incredible, but the colony must rate as one of the best bird-watching spectacles in South Africa. If you can see beyond the blur of gannets, you can also sometimes spot African penguins and seals.

OFF THE
BEATEN PATH

DORINGBAAI – From Lambert's Bay, take the R364 past the BP station toward Clanwilliam (to which you could proceed directly for a shorter tour; ☞ *below*). After 5 km (3 mi), turn left onto a dirt road leading to Doringbaai and Vredendal. The wildflowers along the coast usually bloom from mid-July to mid-August, and the ordinarily featureless sandveld explodes with violets, wild tulips, harpuis, and sporrie. After 32 km (20 mi), turn left again to reach Doringbaai, perched on a deserted coastline of rocky cliffs. It's a popular holiday retreat for farmers from the Karoo but of little interest to most other travelers. **Strandfontein,** a few miles farther north, is another isolated holiday resort, backed by steep hills but ruined by the unsightly brick houses so common in the region. The road becomes tar again at Strandfontein and runs north along the coast. After a couple of miles you descend into the Olifants River valley, an oasis of vineyards, fields, and orchards. Continue into Vredendal, a nondescript agricultural center, and then on to Vanrhynsdorp via the R27.

DINING AND LODGING

$$ ✕ **Muisbosskerm.** For the true flavor of West Coast life, come to this
★ open-air seafood restaurant on the beach south of town. It consists of nothing more than a circular *boma* (enclosure) of packed *muisbos* (mouse bush), with benches and tables haphazardly arranged in the sandy enclosure. Cooking fires blaze and you watch food being prepared before your eyes: Snoek is smoked in an old drum covered with burlap, bread bakes in a clay oven, and everywhere fish sizzles on grills and in giant pots. Bring your own drink, and prepare to eat as much as you can, using your hands or mussel shells as spoons. Be sure to try some of the Afrikaner specialties like *bokkoms* (dried fish) and *waterblommetjie* (water lily) stew. Unless you have an enormous appetite, don't order the half crayfish (it costs extra). The only drawback is high-season crowding: As many as 150 diners can overwhelm the experience. ⊠ *Elands Bay Rd., 5 km (3 mi) south of Lambert's Bay,* ☎ 027/432–1017. *Reservations essential. V.*

$ ▥ **Marine Protea.** Next to the harbor in the center of Lambert's Bay, this modern hotel offers conventional comfort but little charm. It's a good overnight choice, though, if you're dining at the nearby Muisbosskerm (☞ *above*). Rooms are large, decorated in blue tones, and feature a sitting area with TV and phone. ⊠ *Voortrekker St., Box 249, Lambert's Bay 8130,* ☎ 027/432–1126, FAX 027/432–1036. *46 rooms. Restaurant, 2 bars, room service, pool. AE, DC, MC, V.*

Vanrhynsdorp
64 km (40 mi) northeast of Lambert's Bay.

At Vanrhynsdorp you have a choice. You can strike north on the N7 into the empty vastness of Namaqualand (☞ Chapter 7) or cut eastward along the R27 toward the **Hantam,** a high plateau that marks the fringes of the Karoo Desert and the extreme range of the winter rainfall area. The wildflowers usually bloom here in mid-July and last through mid-September. Among the most common are vygies, daisies, katsterte, and pietsnotjies.

To reach the Hantam Plateau, you must first scale the looming wall of the Bokkeveld Escarpment, which rises almost vertically from the flat expanse of the sandveld. The road zigzags up Vanrhyns Pass, providing excellent views back over the Olifants River valley.

Nieuwoudtville
58 km (36 mi) northeast of Vanrhynsdorp.

On the cusp of the escarpment, Nieuwoudtville gets more rain than elsewhere in the Hantam, and its vegetation differs accordingly. The town is famous for its bulbs, including a mass display of more than half a million orange bulbinellas, which are endemic to the area.

Calvinia
72 km (45 mi) east of Nieuwoudtville.

Calvinia finds shelter under a looming mesa known as the Hantamsberg. Founded in 1851, it's a lovely farming town, with a relaxed feel and several beautifully restored historic homes. It makes a good base for exploring the **Akkerendam Nature Reserve** north of town. Two hiking trails of one and six hours traverse the slopes of the Hantamsberg and the plateau on top.

The **Calvinia Museum** is one of the best country museums in South Africa. Displays examine the fashions and furnishings that prevailed in this remote corner of South Africa over the past 150 years. Many of the exhibits reflect the town's agricultural focus, especially sheep farming. ✉ *44 Church St.,* ☎ *0273/411–043.* 🎫 *R1.* ☉ *Weekdays 8–1 and 2–5, Sat. 8–noon.*

NEED A BREAK?   **Die Hantam Huis,** a lovely 1853 Cape Dutch homestead, is the oldest surviving building in Calvinia. It's now a delightful lunchroom and coffee shop. ✉ *44 Hoop St.,* ☎ *0273/41–1606.* ☉ *Daily 24 hrs during the flower season; rest of year, weekdays 7:30–5, Sat. 7:30–2.*

En Route   Drive 37 km (21 mi) back along the R27 toward Nieuwoudtville, and then turn left onto the gravel R364 to Clanwilliam. This is a magical 112-km (70-mi) drive, especially in the two to three hours after sunrise or before sunset, when the desert colors take on a glowing richness that is almost mystical. Thirty-two kilometers (20 miles) before Clanwilliam you come to a farm called **Travellers Rest** (☎ 0274/82–1824). A host of San rock paintings lie within a two-hour walk of the farmhouse, but you must get permission before walking out to look for them. The gravel road descends to Clanwilliam through the beautiful **Cedarberg,** a mountain range known for its San paintings, bizarre rock formations, and, once upon a time, its cedars. Most of the ancient cedars have been cut down, but a few giant specimens still survive in the more remote regions. The Cedarberg is a hiking paradise for Capetonians—a wild, largely unspoiled area where you can disappear from civilization for days at a time. About 172,900 acres of this mountain range have been declared the Cedarberg Wilderness Area, and entry permits are required if you wish to hike or drive into this part of the range. It's advisable, if you intend to explore this protected area, to contact the **Nature Conservation offices** in Cape Town (☎ 021/483–4098) for permit details.

$$$$ ✕⊞ **Bushmans Kloof Wilderness Reserve.** The most attractive, sophisticated, and comfortable base from which to explore this area is Bushmans Kloof and its surrounding 10,600 acres of reserve. What makes the place so special? The stark beauty of the mountains, the prehistoric rock formations, the waterfalls, the 125 sites of ancient San (Bushman) rock paintings, five different botanical communities, the beasts—wildebeests, zebras, elands, mountain leopards, aardwolves, genets, mongoose, Cape clawless otters, to name but a few—and the birds—from waterbirds to raptors and everything in between. The freestanding, thatched double cottages have every possible modern convenience; the food is of a high standard and in abundance; the hospitality is sincere and sophisticated; and the game rangers are experts in their field. ⊠ *Box 53405, Kenilworth 7945,* ☎ *021/797–0990,* FAX *021/761–5551. 10 rooms, 4 suites. FAP.*

$ ⊞ **Die Dorphuis.** In a restored Victorian house that is now a national
★ monument, this lovely bed-and-breakfast offers warm Afrikaner hospitality amid elegant period furnishings. Rooms have antique brass bedsteads and elaborate ceilings and are hung with photos of old Calvinia. If you want something completely different, book the slave quarters: The room, lit only with candles and kerosene lanterns, features a reed floor and ceiling as well as bedcovers made from animal skins. ⊠ *Water St., Box 34, Calvinia 8190,* ☎ FAX *0273/411–606. 10 rooms. BP. No credit cards.*

Clanwilliam

120 km (75 mi) southwest of Calvinia.

Clanwilliam serves as the base for hiking trails and drives into the Cedarberg. It's better geared for tourism than Calvinia, and it's equally charming, with tree-shaded streets and several restored 19th-century buildings. The town was founded around 1800 and has blossomed into the center of the rooibos-tea industry. Rooibos is a bush that grows wild in the Cedarberg and forms the foundation of many herbal teas sold worldwide.

Wildflowers hit their peak in Clanwilliam in the second and third weeks in August. One of the best places to see them is the **Ramskop Wildflower Garden,** less than a mile out of town. ⊠ *Ou Kaapseweg, Clanwilliam,* ☎ *027/482–2133.* ⊞ *R7.70.* ☉ *Daily 7:30–sunset.*

Return to the N7 and head south to the turnoff to **Algeria.** A scenic dirt road winds into the Cedarberg to this Cape Conservation outpost and campsite, set in an idyllic valley amid towering eucalyptus trees. Algeria is the starting point for several excellent hikes into the Cedarberg. No permit is needed for the short, one-hour hike to a waterfall, or a longer hike to a copse of cedars atop the mountains.

Continue down the N7 to **Citrusdal,** a fruit-growing town in the Olifants River valley surrounded by the peaks of the Cedarberg. From here, it's just 90 minutes back to Cape Town through the **Swartland** (Black Land), which takes its name from the dark renoster bush that grows in the area. Today, the Swartland is a rolling landscape of wheat fields and vineyards. From July until the end of October, you can see plenty of flowers from the highway, including lovely arum lilies. There are a number of commercial protea farms here, too.

$ ✕⊞ **Strassberger's Hotel Clanwilliam.** Right on the main street, this friendly, family-run hotel makes an excellent base for exploring the Cedarberg. Rooms are large, decorated with rustic cane furniture and plaid country fabrics. The hotel can arrange hikes and tours into the surrounding mountains. Dinner in the hotel restaurant is a traditional four-course affair that is satisfactory but lacks inspiration. Reinholds, the à la carte restaurant, serves more innovative fare, like crumbed pork chops with sweet-and-sour sauce. ⊠ *Main Rd., Box 4, Clanwilliam 8135,* ☎ *027/482–1101,* ℻ *027/482–2678. 17 rooms. 2 restaurants, bar, pool, squash. BP. AE, DC, MC, V.*

West Coast A to Z

Arriving and Departing

BY BUS

Intercape Mainliner (⊠ Captour office, Adderley St., ☎ 021/386–4400) operates daily service up the West Coast to Springbok (⊠ R165), stopping at Citrusdal, Clanwilliam, and Vanrhynsdorp, and on to Garies and Kamieskroon in Northern Cape province.

BY CAR

The southernmost towns on the West Coast lie within 80 km (50 mi) of Cape Town.

Getting Around

BY CAR

With the great distances involved and the absence of any real public transport, the only way to get around is a car.

Contacts and Resources

EMERGENCIES

Ambulance (☎ 10177). **Police/Fire** (☎ 10111).

GUIDED TOURS

Lambert's Bay Travel and Exploration (⊠ Waterfront, Lambert's Bay, ☎ 027/432–1715) offers one-hour boat trips (R50) up the coast to see Benguela dolphins, seals, great white sharks, and African penguins. Evening trips head up the coast to a quiet bay, where guests feast on crayfish and wine. By advance arrangement, the company also conducts four-wheel-drive expeditions onto the Cedarberg, the Karoo Desert, and Botswana.

VISITOR INFORMATION

The **Flowerline** is a central hot line that offers details about where the flowers are best seen each day. ☎ *082/990–5395, 082/990–5394, or 021/418–3705.* ☾ *June–Oct., daily 8–4:30*

Calvinia Tourist Office. ⊠ *Calvinia Museum, 44 Church St., Calvinia,* ☎ *0273/411712,* ℻ *0273/411–2750.* ☾ *Weekdays 8–1 and 2–5, Sat. 8–noon.*

Clanwilliam Tourism Association. ⊠ *Main Rd., Clanwilliam,* ☎ *027/ 482–2024,* ℻ *027/482–2361.* ☾ *Daily in flower season 8:30–6; rest of year, weekdays 8:30–5, Sat. 8:30–12:30.*

Lambert's Bay Information Office. ⊠ *Strandveld Museum, D.F. Malan St., Lambert's Bay,* ☎ *027/432–1000,* ℻ *027/432–2335.* ☾ *Mon.–Sat. 9–1 and 2–5. Open Sun. during flower season.*

6 THE NORTHERN CAPE

A land of sand dunes and spectacular
vistas—the rugged desert panoramas
of the Kalahari, the old diamond mines
of Kimberley, the miraculous carpets of
Namaqualand wildflowers spread out in
spring—these are the lasting images of the
Northern Cape, South Africa's least-known,
yet in many ways most beautiful province.

By Tara
Turkington

THE NORTHERN CAPE IS South Africa's largest and least-populated province, covering almost a third of the country, yet most South Africans know very little about it. Its deserts and semi-deserts—the Karoo, the Kalahari, Namaqualand, and the Richtersveld—stretch from the Orange River down vistas of space to the Western Cape border, and from the small towns of Springbok and Port Nolloth on the Atlantic coast in the west 1,000 km (630 mi) across, via places with names like Pofadder and Hotazhel, to its diamond capital, Kimberley, in the east. It is a province of grand and rugged beauty—a far cry from the verdant greenness of Mpumalanga and the Western Cape. The Northern Cape's appeal is in its sense of loneliness and its lunar landscapes, which would make an episode of *Star Trek* look tame. All told, it covers an area of 363,389 square km (225,665 square mi), roughly a third bigger than the entire United Kingdom, but only has a population of about 840,000 people (a sparse 2.3 per square km). With its alien landscapes and endless horizons, it's the perfect place to reconnect with your soul. For the few travelers who do venture into the Northern Cape, its hidden treasures are all the richer for their isolation.

Many of the Northern Cape's attractions are linked to mining, which has been the province's economic backbone for more than a century. First, there was the copper mania of the 1840s in Namaqualand; the deepest copper mines in the world are still operating here, although they are now nearing the end of their productive lives. But the history of copper mining was eclipsed 30 years later by the frenzied scrabbling for diamonds on the other side of what is now the Northern Cape. Kimberley, known as the "City of Diamonds," is the provincial capital and was the site, in the 1870s, of one of the world's greatest diamond rushes. Thousands of hopeful diggers trekked to the hot, dusty diamond fields in more or less the geographical center of South Africa. In Kimberley, five diamond-bearing volcanic pipes were eventually discovered within a couple of miles of one another—a phenomenon unknown anywhere else in the world. Apart from diamonds, the province's mineral deposits range from manganese to copper, zinc, lime, granite, gypsum, gemstones, and even oil and gas fields off the Namaqualand coast.

While only a fraction of the province is regarded as arable due to low rainfall, the Orange River, known as the *!ariep* (the exclamation mark indicates a click of the tongue against the roof of the mouth) or "mighty river by the Nama," flows the breadth of the province, emptying into the Atlantic Ocean at Alexander Bay, on the Namibian border. South Africa's largest and longest river, the Orange supplies water to numerous irrigation schemes, which sustain various farming activities, most noticeable in the "Green Kalahari." Agriculture employs the most people in the province and ranges from the second-largest date plantation in the world at Klein Pella near Pofadder to thousands of acres of grapes under irrigation in the Orange River Basin around Upington. The province boasts the country's second-largest national park, the newly named Kgalagadi Transfrontier Park (formerly the Kalahari Gemsbok National Park). Together with an adjoining national park in Botswana, this park forms one of the largest conservation areas in the world. Ecotourism also includes the annual pilgrimage of thousands of visitors to see the spectacular Namaqualand flowers.

The Northern Cape is not for the fainthearted. It's a harsh province, not yet really catering to travelers, but therein lies its beauty. There's plenty to see if you're the type who's not afraid to ask questions and to go where your nose leads you. Don't expect luxurious accommodation, fine cuisine, or well-stocked gift shops. What you can expect, given a little time and patience, are sleepy villages still much like they were a century ago, charming locals who appreciate visitors tremendously, and an unusual and unique getaway that could well turn out to be the highlight of your trip to South Africa.

Pleasures and Pastimes

Arts and Crafts

Technology lags behind in the Northern Cape—most of the province has no cell-phone reception, and the full range of TV channels you would get elsewhere is a rarity anywhere outside Kimberley. Perhaps because of technology's tenuous reach, many of the old traditions and ways are still in place. All around the province it is possible to buy original and interesting crafts, from ostrich shells painted by San (Bushmen) to Nama reed matting and curios made out of tiger's eye—one of the many semiprecious stones abundant in the province.

Dining

The Northern Cape cannot be described as gastronomically exciting. In the larger towns of Kimberley, Upington, and Springbok there are one or two good restaurants, but they are the exception rather than the rule. Where you are likely to taste something memorable is out on a farm in the midst of the Karoo, where Karoo lamb—often roasted on a braai—is a delicacy. Fresh fruit, especially grapes, is delicious and abundant in the summer months in the Orange River valley, from Upington to Kakamas. In winter, look out for homemade preserves like peach chutney and apricot jam.

Lodging

Like good food, good hotels are hard to find in the Northern Cape. There are, though, guest houses in just about every little town, and the bigger centers like Kimberley and Upington are brimming with them— from basic self-catering units to luxurious bed-and-breakfasts. Many farms also offer overnight accommodation, which can be a savior late at night on the province's long and lonely roads.

Exploring the Northern Cape

The Northern Cape's vastness makes it a difficult place to travel, and you will probably decide to see only part of it on your first trip, such as Namaqualand in flower time, the Kalahari, or Kimberley. Namaqualand is most easily visited from Cape Town and the Western Cape, while Kimberley and the Kalahari are far more accessible from Johannesburg. If you are planning to drive from Johannesburg to Cape Town or vice versa, Kimberley makes an ideal stopover. The Kimberley route (along the N12) is less than 100 km (63 mi) longer than the sterile N1 route with its huge garages and stereotypical fast-food places. It's also more scenic and not as busy. While Upington and the Kgalagadi Transfrontier Park are about the same distance away from Cape Town as they are from Johannesburg, the roads from Johannesburg are far better.

Great Itineraries

IF YOU HAVE 3 DAYS

If you have three days, spend them in ⊡ **Kimberley,** soaking up its history and culture. Spend your first morning with a reasonably priced registered guide, seeing the town and its landmarks. Ask to see the **Honored Dead Memorial,** built to commemorate those who died defending Kimberley during the Siege, and the imposing and strange-looking Henry Oppenheimer house, where diamonds from all over South

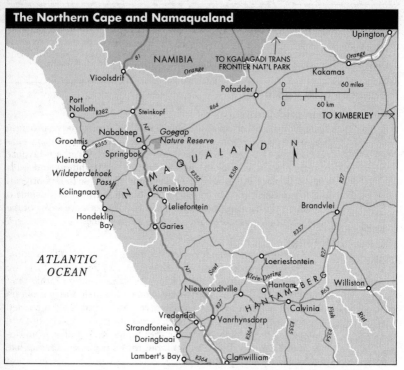

Africa are sorted for export (public access is prohibited for security reasons, but you can view it from the outside). Spend the afternoon at the **McGregor Museum,** or take a stroll through the **William Humphreys Art Gallery.** Finish off the day with dinner at Barnato's, in an old colonial house. On your second morning, book an underground tour offered by **De Beers** down a working diamond mine—Kimberley is the only place in the world where you can take such a trip. To get the fuller picture of what life in Kimberley was like at the time of the diamond rush, make your way to the **Open Mine Museum,** but first stop at the Star of the West for a pub lunch. Spend a good three hours at this unusual museum, and then rest your weary feet with a ride on an historic restored tram to the 100-year-old town hall and back. Devote most of your third day either to seeing the alluvial diggings with a guide, taking in the **Platfontein San Craft Centre** and the **Nooitgedacht rock engravings** on the way, or going out to the evocative Anglo-Boer War battlefield, **Magersfontein,** where the Boers beat the British marching to relieve Kimberley in December 1899. Take a picnic and have it under one of the ubiquitous thorn trees scattered across the battlefield.

IF YOU HAVE 5 DAYS

If it's spring, ⌧ **Namaqualand** is worth a five-day visit (☞ If You Have 7 or More Days, *below*), but if it's the middle of the year (wintertime in South Africa), head for the huge spaces of the **Kalahari,** via ⌧ **Upington** (by air or road), perhaps even squashing in the Augrabies Falls National Park as an extra. Spend three nights roughing it in the ruggedly beautiful **Kgalagadi Transfrontier Park** (previously the Kalahari Gemsbok National Park), cooking your own meals and driving your own vehicle in search of the black-maned Kalahari lions and the beautifully symmetrical gemsbok. Then head for the decadent luxury of two nights at ⌧ **Tswalu Desert Reserve,** where you'll appreciate the game drives, bush walks, and attention to detail all the more for having done it on your own.

If you enjoy huge, empty spaces, the drive from ▣ **Kimberley** to ▣ **Springbok**—perhaps taking in the **Kalahari** on the way—is a memorable one, with some excellent places to stop and stay along the way. But beware: This is a long and lonely trip and should only be considered if the flowers are going to be in bloom when you get to **Namaqualand** (August–September). This route showcases the best the province has to offer, from the diamond fields in the east to the desert in the north, the Green Kalahari in the northern center and the flowers along the western seaboard. Then drive to ▣ **Upington,** where you can spend a night in a guest house after taking a quick peek in the museum and a paddle in the Orange. Then head north for two nights in the vast **Kgalagadi Transfrontier Park,** and continue back down to **Augrabies Falls National Park** for another night. Next day, drive to ▣ **Springbok,** the heart of Namaqualand. Stay two nights here and perhaps another in **Okiep,** using this area as your base to explore the picturesque towns of **Leliefontein** (with the nearby Namaqua National Park) in the south and **Port Nolloth** in the north. Head south down the N7 to Cape Town, where the madding crowds will catch you by surprise after the loneliness of the beautiful Northern Cape.

When to Tour the Northern Cape

Between late November and the end of February it's exceptionally hot in Kimberley and just about intolerable in Upington and the Kalahari. Any other time is fine, although it can get very cold in the winter months—between the middle of May and early August. The best time to see the flowers in Namaqualand is usually between the middle of August and the end of September, depending on when and how much rain has fallen. The weather is generally milder in Namaqualand than the rest of the province. By South African standards, the Northern Cape's climate is exceptionally hot in summer, often rising to above 35°C (95°F), and bitterly cold in winter, commonly dropping below 0°C (32°F) at night, so come prepared to sweat or shiver. The province, coincidentally, has the dubious honor of being home to the hottest town in South Africa in summer (Upington) and the coldest in winter (Sutherland, in the Karoo).

KIMBERLEY

Kimberley was born in the dust, dreams, and disappointments of a rudimentary mining camp that grew into a city of grace and sophistication in some quarters, still evident in many of its early buildings. Today Kimberley is a city of about 170,000 people, spread out around its diamond mines—giant holes in the earth, like inverted koppies. Kimberley has a host of comfortable guest houses, one or two decent restaurants, and many historical attractions, making it a wonderful place to spend a few days. It's an easy trip of less than 500 km (313 mi) from Johannesburg and is about 970 km (606 mi) from Cape Town.

Kimberley's beginnings date back to 1869, when diamonds were first discovered in the area. Through the late 1860s, alluvial diamonds had been mined on the banks of the Vaal River near Barkly West, about 30 km (19 mi) away. These workings were all but forgotten after the finds in Kimberley of five pipes bearing the diamondiferous "Kimberlite," or "blue ground," so called because of its color. In 1871, the richest pipe of all, the Kimberley Mine (now known as the Big Hole), was discovered. Diggers from around the world flocked to stake claims in the mine, which produced more than 14½ million carats before its closure in 1914, making it one of the richest diamond mines in history. At times, there were as many as 30,000 people working in the hole, burrowing like a giant colony of termites. The history of the diamond fields is dominated by eccentric personalities, like Barney Barnato, who came to South Africa with so little he had to walk to the diamond fields yet died a magnificently wealthy man after mysteriously disappearing overboard on a trip to England. Then there was Cecil John Rhodes, the diamond magnate and colonizer who aspired to paint the map of Africa red for Britain and to build a railroad from Cape Town to Cairo.

Both Rhodes and Barnato were shrewd businessmen who watched the diggers toiling in Kimberley's five holes, excavating their individual claims. As the miners met what they perceived to be bedrock they would often give up and stop digging, but what they were actually hitting was the unweathered and hard blue ground, fabulously rich in diamonds. The two men then snapped up claims at bargain prices, all the time growing their shares in the mines. Eventually Barnato and Rhodes merged their companies into the De Beers Consolidated Mines Ltd, which is still headquartered in Kimberley.

In addition to the allure of diamonds, another central part of Kimberley's history was its attack by the Boers during the Anglo-Boer War (1899–1902). Kimberley's close proximity to the border of the then-Boer Republic of the Orange Free State, and its international fame as a diamond town occupied by prominent British citizens (including Rhodes), made it an ideal siege target. For four months in the summer of 1899, the town's citizens suffered dwindling rations, disease, Boer shell fire, and other hardships. British efforts to relieve the town were thwarted by the Boers at the famous Battle of Magersfontein, but eventually a sustained cavalry charge led by Major-General John French broke through to the beleaguered town. Kimberley's part in the Anglo-Boer War is brought to life everywhere through monuments, buildings, and statues.

★ **Kimberley Mine Museum and the Big Hole.** If there's one thing you do in Kimberley, visit the **Big Hole**, the largest hand-dug hole in the world. It is 800 yards deep, and while water now fills the majority of its depth, it's still an impressive sight. On the lip of the Big Hole is the extensive, open-air **Open Mine Museum,** comprising a host of authentic old buildings, many of which were moved here from the city center rather than being torn down. They include the first house erected in Kimberley, in 1877, which was brought piece by piece to the diamond fields from Britain by ship and ox wagon; a boxing academy; and a bar reminiscent of a Wild West saloon. Replicas of the world's most famous diamonds, including the Eureka, a 21-carat yellow diamond that was the first diamond discovered in South Africa in 1866, are also on view. Allow a few hours here, and wear comfortable shoes.

While at the Big Hole, take a ride on a restored **1914 tram** through Kimberley to City Hall (built in 1899) and back. Admission is R6 roundtrip or R3 one-way, with departures from the Big Hole on the hour, every hour daily from 9 to 4. Departures from City Hall are at a quarter past the hour, every hour daily from 9 to 4. ⊠ *Tucker St.,* ☎ *053/ 833–1557.* ▦ *R15.* ☉ *Daily 8–6.*

De Beers Tours. You can take an underground tour in Kimberley of a working diamond mine, the only place in the world you can experience such a trip. The tour entails quite a lot of walking and takes about 3½ hours. The tour is offered Monday, Wednesday, Thursday, and Friday at 7:45 and Tuesday at 9:15, with a fee of R60. The underground tour needs to be booked about two weeks in advance; in addition, no children under 16 are allowed, and you're advised not to wear contacts because of the air pressure. If you can't get on an underground tour, the surface tour is the next best thing (it's not necessary to do both). Surface tours are offered weekdays at 9 and 11. The tour lasts 1½ hours and costs R10. ⊠ *Visitors' Reception Centre, Bultfontein Mine Gate, Molyneux Rd.,* ☎ *053/842–1321.*

The **McGregor Museum** is housed in a graceful Kimberley landmark that was built at Rhodes's instigation. It was used first as a sanatorium, then an upscale hotel, and later as a girls' convent school. Rhodes stayed here himself during the siege. The museum houses quite a good (if a bit moth-eaten) display on the Anglo-Boer War. More impressive is the new Hall of Ancestors, the most up-to-date and extensive exhibition in South Africa on the history of humanity. It traces the evolution of prehistoric life up to the early 20th century, all with a focus on the Northern Cape but within a global context. The museum also runs tours of Dunluce and Rudd House (☞ *below*). ⊠ *Atlas St.,* ☎ *053/842–0099,* FAX *053/842–1433.* 🔳 *R5.* ⊙ *Mon.–Sat. 9–5, Sun. 2–5.*

The **Duggan Cronin Gallery** houses early photographs of Africa and its inhabitants taken by A. M. Duggan Cronin, an Irishman who arrived in 1897 to work as a night watchman for De Beers. A keen photographer, he traveled widely through southern Africa, capturing his impressions—mostly of African peoples—on film. ⊠ *Egerton Rd., adjacent to the McGregor Museum,* ☎ *053/842–0099.* 🔳 *R2.* ⊙ *Mon.–Sat. 9–1 and 2–5, Sun. 2–5.*

In the leafy suburb of Belgravia, **Rudd House** is the rambling home of early diamond magnate Cecil John Rhodes's first business partner, Charles Dunnell Rudd. The house has been restored in the Art Deco style of the 1920s, when the "Bungalow," as the house was known, was in its heyday. Look out for the croquet ground made out of Blue Ground and the massive snooker table surrounded by a multitude of animal heads from Rudd's trips north to Matabeleland. ⊠ *Lodge Rd., Belgravia,* ☎ *053/842–0099.* 🔳 *R10.* ⊙ *By appointment only.*

John Orr's **Dunluce** is a well-known Kimberley landmark, with its colonial wraparound veranda painted a distinctive green and white. A tour points out such details as the swimming pool (the first in Kimberley) and the memorable red dining room, which received a shell through its ceiling during the siege. ⊠ *Lodge Rd., Belgravia,* ☎ *053/842–0099.* 🔳 *R10.* ⊙ *By appointment only.*

The **William Humphreys Art Gallery** in Kimberley's Civic Centre is considered one of the finest art museums in the country and is an air-conditioned haven of tranquillity on a hot summer's day. The gallery has impressive collections of South African works as well as Dutch, Flemish, British, and French Masters. Free guided tours (book two weeks in advance) will cater to specific interests on request. ⊠ *Jan Smuts Blvd., Civic Centre,* ☎ *053/831–1724 or 053/831–1725.* 🔳 *R2.* ⊙ *Mon.–Sat. 10–1 and 2–5, Sun. 2–5.*

Worth a quick stop is **Sol Plaatje's House,** where the multitalented Plaatje (1876–1932) lived much of his life. In addition to being the first general secretary of the African National Congress, he was the first black South African to publish a novel in English. Plaatje was also an influential early African newspaper editor and was an energetic campaigner for human rights. As a young man he was besieged in the town of Mafeking during the Anglo-Boer War and wrote the only known war diary by a black South African. His house is now a small library and museum, with displays on his life and extracts from his diary. Call ahead for opening times; they tend to change daily. ⊠ *32 Angel St., Kimberley,* ☎ *082/804–3266,* ☎ FAX *053/833–2526.* 🔳 *R2.*

Magersfontein Battlefield, is an evocative, barren national monument where the Boers resoundingly defeated British forces marching to relieve besieged Kimberley in December 1899. There is an excellent site museum, upgraded in 1999, with an 11-minute multimedia display that recalls the battle in pictures and sound so well it will give you goose bumps. There are also several monuments dotted around the battlefield to visit and a pleasant tearoom. The battlefield is well signposted from Kimberley. ⊠ *31½ km/20 mi outside Kimberley on Magersfontein Rd.,* ☎ *no phone.* ⊠ *R8 per car with 1–5 passengers, R15 per car with 6 or more passengers.* ⊙ *Daily 8–5.*

Dining and Lodging

$$$ ✕ **Barnato's.** Set in a picturesque old colonial home dating to the turn of the 19th century, Barnato's offers plenty of atmosphere and well-presented, tasty food, although both at a price, comparatively speaking in Kimberley. The meat dishes here are especially good; try the pepper steak or fillet in red wine. Fish is also a tasty choice, in particular the sole, which is prepared in a variety of ways. ⊠ *6 Dalham Rd.,* ☎ *053/833–4110,* FAX *053/831–3520. Reservations essential. AE, DC, MC, V. Closed Sun. No lunch Sat.*

$$ ✕ **Mario's.** The relaxed atmosphere in this historic Kimberley house and cool outdoor seating in summer make this one of the town's most popular restaurants. The extensive menu includes excellent pizza and pasta. Steaks and fresh seafood flown up from Cape Town are recommended. ⊠ *159 Dutoitspan Rd.,* ☎ *053/831–1738. Reservations essential. AE, DC, MC, V. Closed Sun. No lunch Sat.*

$ ✕ **Star of the West.** The oldest continuously operating bar in Kimberley, the Star is a national monument and worth a visit even if just for a drink. Typical pub fare such as steaks, salads, toasted sandwiches, and burgers makes it a good lunch option. Its sleepy, nostalgic atmosphere during the day is traded at night for noise and smoke, when it's always well frequented by locals. ⊠ *North Circular and Barkly Rds.,* ☎ *053/832–6463. DC, MC, V. Closed Sun.*

$ ✕▣ **Langberg Guest Farm.** On the west side of the Magersfontein Bat-
★ tlefield, Langberg is far removed from the buzz of city life. Rooms here are all part of restored thick-walled, whitewashed farm buildings that date back to the days of the diamond rush. Since it's still an operating game and cattle farm, hunting for kudu, gemsbok, and other antelope can be arranged. The atmosphere is relaxed and the food is excellent: A three-course set meal is served every night except Sunday and typically includes hearty dishes such as homemade chicken pie. Meals aren't included in the lodging price—breakfast will cost you R28 extra and dinner another R59 per person. Langberg is inexpensive considering the luxurious service, though, and is highly recommended. ⊠ *21 km/13 mi from Kimberley on the N12, the main road to Cape Town, and 2½ km/1½ mi on a farm road (Box 10400, Beaconsfield 8315),* ☎ FAX *053/832–1001. 5 rooms. Bar, pool, tennis court. MC, V.*

$$$–$$$$ ▣ **Edgerton House.** In this gracious guest house, every room is dedicated to a different personality who had some relationship with early Kimberley, including prominent architect D. W. Greatbach and Princess Radziwill. There is much attention to detail, from claw-foot baths in almost every bathroom to the reading material on the Anglo-Boer War carefully laid out in the sitting room. Nelson Mandela and President Thabo Mbeki stay here when they come to Kimberley. There's also a pleasant tea garden in the courtyard, where you can have a light lunch or a luscious piece of cheesecake. ⊠ *5 Egerton Rd., 8300,* ☎ FAX *053/831–1150. 11 rooms. Pool. BP. AE, DC, MC, V.*

$ ⌂ **Lodge Guest House.** Set on beautiful Lodge Road, nicknamed Millionaire's Row for the wealthy diamond investors who lived here at the turn of the century, the Lodge offers an opportunity to stay in a historic home with a South African family (although in separate parts of the house). Jan and Lynn Botes are hospitable hosts and will make guests a traditional South African braai if asked. This is a far cheaper type of accommodation than the more formal hotels and guest houses and is more personal as well. ⊠ *9A Lodge Rd., 8300,* ☎ *083/261–5836,* ☎ ℻ *053/832–1520. 4 rooms. CP. No credit cards.*

Shopping

The **Jewel Box & Big Hole Diamond Cutting Factory** specializes in diamond jewelry and can custom-make a piece if you will be in town for a few days. Although it doesn't boast about its prices, they are among the most reasonable in the country and draw customers for things like engagement rings from as far afield as Johannesburg. There is also a factory on the premises where visitors can watch goldsmiths at work (weekdays only). ⊠ *18 West Circular Rd. (directly opposite Big Hole),* ☎ *053/832–1731. Closed Sun.*

If you're looking for an odd piece of authentic memorabilia like a 100-year-old ginger beer bottle manufactured in Kimberley or a pair of binoculars used in the Anglo-Boer War, head for **Granny's Antiques,** near the Diamantveld Information Centre. ⊠ *25 Angel St., Newpark,* ☎ ℻ *053/831–6886. No credit cards. Closed Sun.*

Kimberley A to Z

Arriving and Departing

BY AIR

The Kimberley to Johannesburg round-trip flight on **South African Express** (☎ 011/978–5569) or through the **Kimberley Airport** (☎ 053/838–3337) is approximately R1,750 (R877 one-way), but if you specifically ask for an "L-class" seat and book at least a month in advance, you should be able to get a 50% discount on this route. Kimberley to Cape Town is R2,164 round-trip (R1,082 one-way) on SA Airlink (contact through the Kimberley Airport; ☎ 053/838–3337). To book air tickets, contact **Rennies Travel** (⊠ Box 512, Kimberley 8300, ☎ 053/831–1825 or 053/831–1826, ℻ 053/833–5081).

BY BUS

Greyhound (☎ 053/831–4548) operates daily service between Johannesburg and Kimberley for R120 each way. **Translux** (☎ 051/408–4888) operates daily services between Jo'burg and Kimberley for R115 one-way, as well as buses between Cape Town and Kimberley for around R250 one-way, every night except Tuesday and Thursday.

BY CAR

Having a car in Kimberley is a good idea as it gives you more freedom, but it's not mandatory if you're only staying a day or two and you hire a good tour guide (☞ Guided Tours, *below*). **Avis** (⊠ Kimberley Airport, Box 222, Kimberley 8300, ☎ 053/851–1082, ℻ 053/851–1062). **Budget** (⊠ Kimberly Airport, Box 1409, Kimberley 8300, ☎ 053/851–1182 or 053/851–1183, ℻ 053/851–1154). **Imperial Car Rentals** (⊠ Kimberley Airport, Box 187, Kimberley 8300, ☎ 053/851–1131 or 053/851–1132, ℻ 053/851–1108).

BY RAIL

Train services between Kimberley and Johannesburg and Cape Town depart from all three cities at least once, sometimes twice, a day. Travel first class only and preferably with a companion. One way between Kimberley and Jo'burg currently costs R125 and between Kimberley and Cape Town R245. For inquiries, call **Spoornet** (☎ 053/838–2731 or 053/838–2631 in Kimberley; ☎ 011/773–2944 or 011/773–2131 in Johannesburg; ☎ 021/218–3871 or 021/218–3018 in Cape Town).

Emergencies

Ambulance (☎ 10177). **Police** (☎ 10111). **Curomed Hospital** (✉ 144 Dutoitspan Rd., ☎ 053/831–4730).

Contacts and Resources

GUIDED TOURS

A variety of one-day tours tramping the battlefields where Boers and Brits clashed in the Northern Cape is offered by well-known local historian Steve Lunderstedt of **Steve's Tours.** ✉ *Box 3017, Kimberley 8300,* ☎ *083/732–3189,* ℻ *053/831–4006.*

First-class Anglo-Boer War registered guide **Scotty Ross** concentrates on the Kimberley Battlefield Route or will hone in on particular battles, such as Magersfontein or Paardeberg. ✉ *115 Main Rd., Kimberley 8301,* ☎ ℻ *053/832–4083.*

For an in-depth and academic guide of battlefields without any fancy frills contact **Fiona Barbour,** who is something of a local legend for the depth of her knowledge about the Anglo-Boer War. ✉ *Box 316, Kimberley 8300,* ☎ *053/842–0099 (McGregor Museum) or* ☎ *053/842–1018.*

Janet Welsh offers specialized tours to sites relating to early nursing sister Henrietta Stockdale and another on human rights activist Sol Plaatje and is also registered to do Kimberley and battlefield tours. ✉ *4 Camelot, Francey St., Kimberley 8301,* ☎ *053/832–8343 or 082/856–2280.*

Jean Bothomley is an excellent person to show you around the Open Mine Museum, especially if you've got limited time. ✉ *Box 451, Kimberley 8300,* ☎ *053/833–5213 or 053/832–4712,* ℻ *053/831–2640.*

Yvonne Dreyer is very knowledgeable about Kimberley history and the history of diamond mining. ✉ *13 Nicole St., Lindene, Kimberley 8301,* ☎ *053/861–4765, 053/842–1321, or 082/469–0275.*

Dirk Potgieter of Diamond Tours Unlimited offers a good day tour to the alluvial diggings about 40 km (25 mi) from Kimberley as well as bird-watching, canoeing on the Vaal River, fly-fishing, and visiting the Kalahari. ✉ *Box 2775, Kimberley 8300,* ☎ *083/265–4795,* ☎ ℻ *053/843–0017.*

VISITOR INFORMATION

The **Diamantveld Visitors' Centre** has maps and brochures and can make tour and travel bookings. The center is also the starting point for extremely popular Kimberley ghost tours. ✉ *121 Bultfontein Rd. (Box 1976), Kimberley 8301,* ☎ *053/832–7298,* ℻ *053/832–7211.*

At the **Northern Cape Tourism Authority** you can pick up information on the province and make bookings for places owned by the provincial authority. ✉ *187 Dutoitspan Rd., Private Bag X5017, Kimberley 8300,* ☎ *053/832–2657,* ℻ *053/831–2937.*

UPINGTON, THE KALAHARI, AND THE ORANGE RIVER BASIN

Upington

411 km (257 mi) northwest of Kimberley.

Home to about 100,000 residents, Upington is a thriving agricultural center on the north bank of the Orange River. In the 1870s, a Koranna captain named Klaas Lucas invited missionary Christiaan Schroder to come to *Olyvenhoudtsdrift* ("ford at the olive wood trees"), as Upington was first known. Construction on the first mission buildings, now part of the Upington museum complex, was started in 1873. The town was renamed after Sir Thomas Upington, an attorney-general of the Cape who was responsible for ridding the area of its notorious bandits in the 1880s. While convention has it that the first person to irrigate crops from the Orange was Christiaan Schroder himself, recent historical research has revealed that this honor should go to Abraham September, a *baster* (person of mixed race) and a freed slave, who first led water from the Orange in about 1882. Upington, which is known for its heat, is the start of what is called paradoxically the "Green Kalahari"—a basin of irrigated lands, mostly vineyards, which stretches about 80 km (50 mi) to the west, to the town of Kakamas. Also to the west and 40 km (25 mi) north of Kakamas is the Augrabies Falls National Park, which is well worth a visit. Upington is also the gateway to the Kalahari proper, the arid dunelands that are home to the oryx and black-maned lion.

The **Kalahari-Oranje Museum Complex** comprises simple, whitewashed buildings that were erected by missionary Christiaan Schroder in the 1870s. There are displays on agriculture and local history, and collections of minerals and items used by the San (Bushmen) of the area. Just outside the complex is the unusual **Donkey Monument,** a bronze sculpture by Hennie Potgieter that is a testimony to the role played by the animal in developing the Lower Orange River valley. ⊠ *Schroder St., Upington,* ☎ *054/332–5911.* ⌦ *Free.* ☉ *Weekdays 9–12:30 and 2–5, Sat. 9–noon.*

The **SA Dried Fruit Cooperative** has a free 45-minute factory tour, focusing on how raisins—one of the area's most famous products—are sorted and packed for domestic consumption and export. ⊠ *5 km/3 mi outside Upington, on the Groblershoop Rd.,* ☎ *054/334–0006,* FAX *054/334–0185.* ⌦ *Free.* ☉ *Tours daily Mon.–Thurs. at 9:45 and 1:45, Fri. at 9:45.*

In Upington's industrial area is **Oranjerivier Cooperative Wines Cellars,** the second-largest wine cooperative in the world in terms of members (the largest is in South America). A variety of white wines, from the sweet and rich dessert wine, Hanepoort, to the lighter steins and sauvignon blancs as well as grape-juice tastings, are offered. During December and January you can also take a tour of the cellars (reserve in advance). ⊠ *Industrial Rd., Upington,* ☎ *054/332–4651.* ☉ *Weekdays 7:30–5, Sat. 8:30–noon.*

The unusual **Camel Statue,** about 2 km (1 mi) down Schroder Street away from the museum, is a bronze monument in front of the Upington Police Station. It commemorates the police who used camels as mounts when they patrolled the Kalahari in frontier days.

At the center of the small **Spitskop Nature Reserve** is an outlook of granite boulders. An easy climb to the top offers a good view of the reserve. There is a telescope to help you spot the ostrich, gemsbok, eland, Burchell's zebra, and odd camel that inhabit the park. There are three walking trails, ranging from a morning to a full-day hike, as well as braai and picnic facilities and pretty basic overnight accommodation. ⊠ *15 km/9 mi north of Upington on R360,* ☎ *054/332–1336.* 🖼 *Free.* ☉ *Daily sunrise–sunset.*

Dining and Lodging

$$$ ✕ **Le Must.** Easily the best restaurant in town, and probably the best in the province as well. Candlelight and starched linens set off the interior, and the atmosphere is intimate and welcoming. Meat dishes are especially good; try the rump with a Kalahari biltong and Gariep port sauce or a T-bone with a banana, sweet mustard, and bacon sauce. For dessert, finish off with a piece of delicious brandy and date tart. There is a good wine list of mostly Cape wines, but there are also one or two of the local vintages. Both Mandela and President Mbeki have eaten here; it would be hard to find higher recommendation. ⊠ *11 Schroder St., Upington,* ☎ *054/332–3971,* 𝖥𝖠𝖷 *054/332–7830. Reservations essential. AE, DC, MC, V. No lunch Sat.*

$$ ✕ **Collector's.** A pleasant little place with a lovely view of the Orange River, Collector's is on the museum grounds, behind the Donkey Monument. It's a good choice for a light meal such as Caesar salad or chicken curry, or just a drink. It also sells a small selection of local curios. ⊠ *4 Schroder St., Upington,* ☎ 𝖥𝖠𝖷 *054/331–2290. No credit cards.*

$$ 🏠 **Le Must Guesthouse.** This Cape Dutch house is elegant without being pretentious; original artwork hangs in every room and the beds are covered in French linens. There is a great view of the Orange from the guest house, and the garden—where you can sit and have a cup of tea or a gin-and-tonic—sweeps right down to the waterside. Guests can take a dip in the river or a lazy paddle in a canoe. There is also access to the neighboring pool. ⊠ *12 Murray Ave.,* ☎ *054/332–3971,* 𝖥𝖠𝖷 *054/332–7830. 5 rooms, 2 with shared bath. Air-conditioning. DC, MC, V.*

$ 🏠 **Nirvana Guesthouse.** A little way out of town, and favored by businesspeople, the guest house is custom-built around and above large koi ponds, and the constant sound of running water is soothing in sweltering Upington. Don't expect much personal attention or originality in the interior decoration, but it's a pleasant enough place to spend the night. ⊠ *5 km/3 mi out of town on the Olifantshoek Rd. (Box 193), Upington 8800,* ☎ *054/338–0384 or 082/820–2303,* 𝖥𝖠𝖷 *054/332–402. 5 rooms. AE, DC, MC, V.*

$ 🏠 **Riviera Garden Lodge.** In the middle of a row of guest houses, the Riviera is an oasis of personal attention, charm, and tasteful interiors. Hostess Anneke Malan loves to chat and tell people all there is to know about Upington and its environs, but she's sensitive enough to leave you alone if you want quiet. Breakfast, of scrambled ostrich eggs if you like, is included and is served on the veranda in summer. ⊠ *16 Budler St., Upington,* ☎ *054/332–6554. 2 rooms. BP. No credit cards.*

The Kalahari

In an odd little finger of South Africa that juts north and is surrounded by Botswana in the east and Namibia in the west lies the giant **Kgalagadi Transfrontier Park,** South Africa's second-largest park after Kruger National Park (☞ Chapter 3). Still better known as the Kalahari Gemsbok National Park, it is joined to an even larger park in Botswana (there are no fences between the two), forming one of the largest protected wilderness areas in the world—an area more than 3,6000 square km (2,236 square mi). The Twee Rivieren Gate lies about 250 km (156 mi) to the north of Upington, on the R360. Passing through the gate, you will encounter a vast desert under enormous, usually cloudless skies and a sense of space and openness that few other places can offer.

The Kgalagadi Transfrontier is less commercialized and developed than Kruger. None of its roads are tarred and you will come across far fewer people and cars. That said, you will also see less game on the whole than in Kruger, as the Kgalagadi Park cannot compete with Kruger's range of animal and bird species. Perhaps the key to really appreciating this barren place is understanding how its creatures have adapted to their harsh surroundings in order to survive. Take the gemsbok, for example, which keeps its body temperature hotter than the desert sun to avoid perspiring and losing precious liquid. Its blood is so warm it would short-circuit its brain if not cooled, so the white area around the gemsbok's nose is home to a sophisticated cooling system that lowers the blood temperature before it circulates to the head. There are insects in the park that only inhale every half hour or so in order to save the moisture that breathing expends.

The landscape—endless dunes punctuated with blond grass and the odd thorn tree—is dominated by two dry riverbeds: the Nossob (which forms the border between South Africa and Botswana) and its tributary, the Auob. The Nossob only flows about once a century, while the Auob flows only once every couple of decades or so. A single road runs beside each riverbed, along which windmills pump water into man-made water holes that help the animals to survive and provide good viewing stations for visitors. A third road traverses the park's interior to join the other two. The scenery and vegetation on this road change dramatically from the two river valleys dominated by sandy banks to a more grassy escarpment. From Nossob camp, a road leads to Union's End, the country's northernmost tip, where South Africa, Namibia, and Botswana join. Allow a full day for the long and dusty drive, which is 124 km (77½ mi) one-way.

The park is famous for its gemsbok and its large, black-maned lions. It also boasts leopard, buffalo, and rhino, but no elephant, along with a host of specialized desert species rarely seen elsewhere, such as the elusive aardvark and the tiny Cape fox. The busy antics of meerkats and mongeese are an added attraction. For birders, the raptors alone are worth a trip.

The park can be stinking hot in summer and freezing at night in winter, but the winter months of June and July are the best time to visit. It's best to make reservations as far in advance as possible, since accommodation can be booked up, particularly during school holidays.

★ The park's legendary **night drives** depart every evening at about 5:30 in summer, earlier in winter (check when you get to the camp), from Twee Rivieren Camp (☞ *below*). Reservations are essential and can be done at the same time as your accommodation booking. The drives go out just as the gate closes to everyone else, in an open truck high off the ground that seats about 30 people. A ranger gives a brief background on the history, animals, plants, and insects of the Kalahari before setting off. The night drives offer a rare chance to see nocturnal animals like the brown hyena and the bat-eared fox by spotlight and are highly recommended. The drive lasts a few hours and costs R60 per person.

Rest Camps

There are shops selling food and some basic equipment at all three camps, but Twee Rivieren has the best variety of fresh produce, milk, and meat. Gas is also available at all three camps. Electricity only runs for part of the day, and at different times in each camp, so inquire on arrival about availability. All accommodation in the park has its own self-catering kitchen and braai, and bathroom facilities, unless otherwise stated. For reservations, contact the **National Parks Board.** ⊠ *Pretoria: Box 787, Pretoria 0001,* ☎ *012/343–1991,* ℻ *012/343–0905. Cape Town: Box 7400, Roggebaai, 8012,* ☎ *021/222–810 or 021/222–816,* ℻ *021/ 246–211, www.parks-sa.co.za. AE, DC, MC, V.*

$$ ▦ **Twee Rivieren.** Situated on the park's southern boundary, the camp is home to the park's headquarters. It is the biggest of the camps and has the most modern facilities; all units have fully equipped kitchens, and the camp shop here is the best around, with a wide range of groceries and other necessities. Guests can choose between three types of bungalows, from a two-bedroom, six-bed family cottage to a bungalow with two single beds and a sleeper couch. There are educational exhibits on the Kalahari's animal and plant life. The recommended route from Upington to Twee Rivieren is 260 km (163 mi) on a relatively good road (only the last 52 km/32 mi is gravel). *1 6-person cottage; 2 3-person bungalows; 28 4-person bungalows. Restaurant, bar, air-conditioning, pool.*

$–$$ ▦ **Nossob.** This is northernmost camp, on the Botswana border 166 km (104 mi) from Twee Rivieren. Its facilities are basic, but for real bush atmosphere it can't be beat. There is no electricity in the camp, and the generators are turned off at 10 PM. *4 6-person cottages, 2 3-person bungalows, 4 3-person huts with shared bath.*

$ ▦ **Mata Mata.** This camp is 120 km (75 mi) from Twee Rivieren on the Namibian border with South Africa, which is a straight vertical line down the 20th meridian. The camp's facilities are not as modern as those at Twee Rivieren. There is no access to Namibia through Mata Mata. *2 6-person cottages, 3 3-person huts with shared bath.*

Lodge

Tswalu Private Desert Reserve

$$$$ Near the Kgalagadi Transfrontier Park is Tswalu, which at 1,100 square km (683 square mi) is the biggest privately owned game reserve in Africa, it is the perfect place to photograph a gemsbok against a red dune and an azure sky. It was initially started as a conservation project by the late multimillionaire Stephen Boler, primarily to protect and breed the endangered black rhino. Today it spreads over endless Kalahari dunes covered with tufts of blond veld and over much of the Northern Cape's Korannaberg mountain range. It is possibly the best place in Africa to see rhino—the reserve boasts 50 white and 10 black rhino now adapted to living in the desert. Other rare species include roan and sable antelope, black wildebeest, and mountain zebra. The only one animal out of the Big Five that's missing at the moment is elephant, although there are plans afoot to change that. There is not as much game as, say, in the private reserves of the Lowveld, because the land has a lower carrying capacity (the annual rainfall is only about 250 mm). But when you do see animals, the lack of vegetation makes sightings spectacular. And the fact that only three or so Land Rovers are traversing an area two-thirds the size of the entire Sabi Sands makes your escape from the rat race all the more complete.

Tswalu is made up of freestanding thatch and stone suites clustered around a large main building, with a heated, natural-color pool and a floodlit water hole in front of it. The rooms are beautifully and tastefully decorated in a pan-African style, with weapons from East Africa, fabrics and masks from West Africa, and baskets and paintings from southern Africa. As this is one of only 12 Relais & Châteaux lodges in South Africa, you can be sure that nothing is left wanting at Tswalu. The food almost

In case you want to be welcomed there.

We're here to see that you're always welcomed at establishments everywhere. That's why millions of people carry the American Express® Card – for peace of mind, confidence, and security, around the world or just around the corner.

do more